for Miriam

with best wishes

Renée Levine Me...

Heretics or Daughters of Israel?

Heretics or Daughters of Israel?

The Crypto-Jewish Women of Castile

Renée Levine Melammed

New York   Oxford

Oxford University Press

1999

Oxford University Press

Oxford   New York
Athens   Auckland   Bangkok   Bogotá   Buenos Aires   Calcutta
Cape Town   Chennai   Dar es Salaam   Delhi   Florence   Kong Kong   Istanbul
Karachi   Kuala Lumpur   Madrid   Melbourne   Mexico City   Mumbai
Nairobi   Paris   São Paulo   Singapore   Taipei   Tokyo   Toronto   Warsaw

and associated companies in
Berlin   Ibadan

Published by Oxford University Press, Inc.
198 Madison Avenue, New York, New York 10016

Oxford is a registered trademark of Oxford University Press

Library of Congress Cataloging-in-Publication Data
Melammed, Renée Levine.
Heretics or daughters of Israel? : the crypto-Jewish women of
Castile / Renée Levine Melammed.
p. cm.
Includes bibliographical references and index.
ISBN 0-19-509580-4
1. Jews—Spain—Castile—History. 2. Marranos—Spain—Castile—History.
3. Jewish Christians—Spain—Castile—History.
4. Inquisition—Spain—Castile—History. 5. Jewish women—Spain—
Castile—Religious life. 6. Castile (Spain)—Ethnic relations.
I. Title.
DS135.S75.C336 1998
305.48'8924—dc21   97-50630

1 3 5 7 9 8 6 4 2

Printed in the United States of America
on acid-free paper

Preface

THE WOMEN WHOSE lives are reconstructed in this book have been my constant companions for many years. Each Inquisition trial opens new worlds to the reader, for the lives of these conversas were multifaceted. One trial leads to entanglements with the Jewish community while a second reveals family tensions and complications. Others center on messianic hopes that were eventually dashed while yet another leads to an investigation into medieval Spanish midwifery.

There is never a dull moment when these conversas are involved, but one always must start from the beginning, which involves the painstaking encounter with the Spanish paleography that was used in order to record the proceedings. This entails deciphering the numerous scribal manuscripts now immortalized by fifteenth- and sixteenth-century notaries (who, in this particular period, often created their own abbreviations for the sake of expediency). Each file contains the scripts of a number of notaries; the easily decipherable ones became my friends while the tougher demanded more time, patience, and imagination on my part. Once the script is transcribed into legible medieval Spanish, one attempts to understand precisely what transpired; if and when a file contains hundreds of pages, this is by no means an easy task. Occasionally, one file is intricately related to another, as with the three trials of the López-Villarreal family or the two proceedings dealing with the Alcázar trials of the late sixteenth century. In these cases, one has to unravel relationships that are not always fully revealed at any given time. When one sets out to interpret and analyze these trials, the challenge is immense, and the possibilities are endless.

Needless to say, I am grateful to the Archivo Histórico Nacional in Madrid for enabling accessibility to these documents during my visits as well as from afar; its staff photocopied all the Inquisition documents that I needed, and efficiently mailed the dossiers to me at various locations. My colleagues Carlos Carrete Parrondo and Moisés Orfali graciously helped me gain access to this material. I also thank the staff of the Judaica Reading Room at the National Library in Jerusalem for its readiness to help in every way possible throughout the years.

I could not have begun this project without having received a year's postdoctoral grant from the Annenberg Research Institute (now Center for Judaic Studies) in Philadelphia during 1990–1991, and I thank the American Philosophical Society for a timely grant for the summer of 1991 as well. My two years as scholar-in-residence at Franklin and Marshall College from 1991 to 1993 enabled me to continue my research as well as to participate in many superb conferences commemorating the 500 years since the Expulsion; most of the papers from these meetings helped to shape this book, and I thank my colleagues Bernard Cooperman (University of Maryland), Jay Berkovitz (University of Massachusetts, Amherst), Ray Waddington (University of California, Davis), Esther Benbassa (CNRS, Paris), Aron Rodrigue (Stanford), and Mark Meyerson (University of Toronto, formerly of University of Notre Dame) for their gracious invitations.

Portions of this book have appeared in print in various forms. An earlier version of chapter 2 appeared in *Religion in the Age of Exploration*, ed. Menaham Mor and Brian Le Beau, pp. 15–37 (Omaha: Creighton University Press, 1996). An abbreviated version of chapter 4 can be found in *Women at Work in Spain from the Middle Ages to Early Modern Times*, ed. Marilyn Stone and Carmen Benito-Vessels, pp. 81–100 (New York: Peter Lang, 1998), and an extremely brief version will appear in Proceedings of the Twelfth World Congress of Jewish Studies, Jerusalem. The story of María López, which forms a part of chapter 5 and 6, can be found in *Women in the Inquisition: Spain and the New World*, ed. Mary Giles, pp. 53–72 (Baltimore: Johns Hopkins University Press, 1999). An earlier version of chapter 7 was published in *The Expulsion of the Jews: 1492 and After*, ed. Raymond B. Waddington and Arthur H. Williamson, pp. 53–72 (New York: Garland, 1994).

The Harvard Divinity School afforded me the opportunity to begin writing, and I thank Dean Constance Buchanan for inviting me to the Women's Studies in Religion Program (1993–1994) and for her enthusiastic support. My special thanks to two former teachers and dear friends who pushed me onward, Denah Lida (Brandeis University, Emeritus) and Irene Eber (Hebrew University, Emeritus), and to my counterpart in research of Muslim conversas, Mary Elizabeth Perry; their faith in me has been inspirational. The list of dear friends who lent me moral support over the years both in person and by electronic mail is overwhelming; my gratitude extends from Jerusalem to Saragossa, Salamanca, Paris, Hamilton, Boston, Amherst, Philadelphia, Albany, Morristown, Washington, D.C., Tennessee, and Palo Alto. I am grateful to Cynthia Read of Oxford University Press and her terrific staff of editors headed by Robert Milks, who paid such fine attention to every detail of the book. Lastly, I thank my family, my mother, my husband, and my two beautiful children, for sharing their love with me over the years and for having faith in me as I ploughed through numerous trials of the Spanish Inquisition. I pray the memories of these women and the tenacity they displayed will give us all strength and hope.

Jerusalem
July 1998   R. L. M.

Contents

Heretics or Daughters of Israel?

Introduction

The Judaizing Heresy, the Inquisition, and the Conversas

W HILE 1492 IS OSTENSIBLY the most significant date in the history of Spanish Jewry, the demise of this unique community actually began in 1391. The developments during that year resulted in unprecedented changes for all involved—for the Jews, for the Spanish masses, for the Church, and for the monarchy.

The story of the upheavals at the end of the fourteenth century has already been told as part of Jewish history. Yitzhak Baer was the first to detail the events in this context;[1] Haim Beinart continued to analyze the situation in terms of the experience of the Jewish community and its future.[2] A basic understanding of these developments is necessary if one is to confront the history of the Jews and crypto-Jews of Spain.

Ferrant Martínez, the archdean of Ecija,[3] conducted a vitriolic and successful anti-Semitic campaign, which began in 1378 and continued for thirteen years. His inflammatory sermons advocating the destruction of synagogues and the confinement of Jews to their quarters were effective;[4] his investment paid off with substantial interest, or so it seemed. A series of riots and attacks on Jewish communities ensued: the first was in Martínez's territory, Seville, on June 4, 1391. Synagogues were burned or converted into churches in this city in southwestern Andalusia. Many Jews were murdered; some were sold to Muslims; most, under duress, converted to Catholicism. The riots spread throughout the rest of Andalusia and then north to Castile; by July, Aragon, north and east of Castile and Andalusia, had become the center of activity while rioters from Castile moved on to Valencia on the east coast. Neither the more remote communities of Catalonia in the northeast nor the island of Majorca, east of Valencia, was spared.[5]

The motives of the rioters of 1391 were not as clear-cut as one might think; they have been accused of having pure religious motivations, economic and socioeconomic motives, and anti-Semitic tendencies, as well as class resentment.[6] Accounts often blame the *pueblo menudo* or the "little people" for the looting and lawless behavior.[7] Whatever the reason and whoever the participant, the results were similar:

tremendous loss of Jewish life, perhaps as much as a third of Spanish Jewry, major destruction of property, and also forced conversion and baptism of tens of thousands of Jews, perhaps another third of the community.[8]

One must emphasize the fact that this wave of conversions was by no means part of a planned campaign. I daresay Martínez himself never imagined that his followers would be so thorough or effective in their spontaneity. The irony was that neither the Church nor the Crown had any official part in these occurrences, and the latter rather pathetically attempted to deter such activities from afar; nonetheless, both would have to cope with the consequences of these events. While in certain areas, local clergy led or encouraged the anti-Semitic masses, in others, municipal leaders, noblemen, or adventure seekers such as sailors stationed in harbor were incited to join or even lead the rabble-rousers. In other words, as the riots spread, no clear-cut leadership seemed consistently to emerge; oddly enough, certain types of individuals or social classes that were aggressively on the offense in one locale could be found taking the opposite stance elsewhere and perhaps even tried to come to the defense of the Jews.

The consequences were overwhelming for both the Jews and the non-Jews of Spain. This was the largest mass forced conversion of Jews in history; never had there been so many converts nor had they represented so many walks of life. Precisely because this was not a planned campaign, no one had seriously considered what the next steps should or would be. Because the Church was caught completely off guard, and particularly because the number of converts was so great, no flexibility could be offered to the victims who had survived the riots by means of succumbing to conversion. Baptism was an irrevocable act, and even conversions by force were binding; the possibility of permitting so many newly baptized individuals to revert to their former religion was unthinkable, for it would make a mockery of the Catholic Church and its dogma. Spain was going to have to deal directly with this unexpected development; the converts would have no choice but to accept their newly imposed religion.

This, needless to say, was easier said than done. While the "problem" of a Jewish presence was partially solved, a new and more complex problem arose. No one was really at ease with the new situation—not the Jews who survived, not the Catholics who witnessed this metamorphosis, and not the *conversos,* or converts. The Jewish leaders who survived essentially directed their energies to attempting to rebuild their communities;[9] however, the majority of those who did convert continued to reside alongside their former Jewish brethren since no arrangements had been made for their relocation. The resulting situation was embarrassing for the Church. How to deal with these new converts? Some of the influential leaders favored educating the conversos in order to help them assimilate; others argued that such an attempt would be futile and deemed all the converts to be nothing but Jews in Catholic guise.

The conversos themselves were in a quandary. Should they attempt to resume

Jewish lives elsewhere in Spain or perhaps even relocate to communities outside the Peninsula? Should they accept the fait accompli and make a concerted attempt to take advantage of their newly acquired status? Or should they "compromise" and lead an outwardly Catholic life while actually adhering to the religion of their ancestors? If these decisions were not difficult enough for any given individual to make, there were often families that disagreed on the appropriate path to take.

There could be no single, set response on the part of the recently converted. Some sought to relocate on familiar soil and return to their former Jewish lifestyle in an attempt to salvage rather than abandon Spain; others simply left their homeland.[10] Some preferred to adapt to their new reality and explore those options now open to them; among these were men who entered monasteries and the clergy or who sought to attain public office and entrance into the university or into military orders. Yet others, both male and female, were unable to break with either their heritage or their birthplace. The fact that Jews, whether former friends, neighbors, or family members, were still quite accessible to them provided an ideal source of inspiration for those desiring to continue observance of Jewish traditions. While contacts between these groups were obviously frowned upon by the Church, the reality is that at first, little to no concerted attempt was made to separate them or to prevent the fostering of any influence. However, as early as 1393 an itinerant Dominican preacher named Vicente Ferrer suggested the creation of separate quarters for each group as well as the implementation of additional restrictions. In 1412 a set of laws was passed in Castile that aimed to segregate Jews from Christians;[11] however, it would be another eighty years before a true separation of all the Jews and Christians would be accomplished.

No one had imagined that the conversos would form a group of their own, but the fact is that they were not part of either the Jewish or Christian communities. As was already emphasized, this "group" of converts was by no means monolithic. Aside from the fact that each Jewish community had quite different experiences during the riots, the results and aftermath of 1391 varied. While entire communities were either murdered or converted in some locales, in others they were essentially torn asunder. Circumstances revealed the unexpected: a rabbi who converted whereas his flock did not, only to find itself leaderless after 1391; the father out of town on business who returned to find that all of his family was now Catholic; a grandmother who did not reside in the same village as her grandchildren discovering that she and they were no longer of the same faith.[12] This damage was not easy to repair.

At the same time, the reactions of the converts themselves were as varied as they could possibly be, and any given converso might alter his or her path more than once. A convert might make a serious attempt to live as a devout Catholic, genuinely hoping to assimilate; as society became less tolerant of the converso presence, this same individual was apt to encounter discrimination and decide that all efforts to gain acceptance had been in vain. Many of the conversos fluctuated during their lifetimes, uncertain which religious group was more appropriate, expedient, or comfortable for them; often the reality was that neither would ever provide a perfect fit.

In addition, even when a choice was made, it was rarely a simple matter. For example, the converso who left the mainland in order to return to Judaism had to face rabbinic judgment as to his or her status within Jewish law. There were numerous cases of married *conversas* (female converts) who wanted to leave Spain and return to Judaism and whose converso husbands were not of the same mind. Once she left, did she need to obtain a *get*, the Jewish divorce, or not? And if so, how could she possibly obtain it from her spouse still in Spain without undue risk, once she left Iberia? The crux of the problem was that without the prospects of a divorce, she could never remarry.[13] If she remained in Spain, her faithfulness to Judaism could imperil her life, especially if her partner objected to her judaizing. While New Christian women married Old Christian men with far less frequency than they married men of converso extraction, her options were inherently limited by the choice of spouse. These conversas feared judaizing while living with Old Christian men, who certainly would have no sympathy for their religious inclinations and loyalties.

At the same time, Christian Spain had a series of new issues to confront. The converts had become fully privileged members of their society, but most members of this society were not comfortable with this notion. The *conversos* were as identifiable to them as were the Jews, but now there were no limits on their activities and aspirations. The idea of too many former Jews unabashedly assimilating into their midst was simply intolerable to many Spanish Christians. The way was now paved for the rise of a new and intense hatred, this time aimed at the conversos; an ethnic anti-Semitism was developing that would express itself quite poignantly by the middle of the fifteenth century in Toledo.

Once again, events took both the Church and Crown by surprise, and once more they were not in keeping with policies advocated by either body. Riots took place in Toledo in 1449, but this time the victims were not the Jews. Now the conversos and their descendants, or *nuevos cristianos,* bore the brunt of the local anger; society was divided again, but this new division separated the Old Christians from the New Christians. The latter included those who had been baptized at birth as Christian and experienced their entire lives as Christians, but whose ancestors had converted some time earlier. A new basis of exclusion had been created: one's origin was now the essential factor. Following the violence there, the municipality of Toledo in 1449 established the *Sentencia-Estatuto,* excluding Jews and conversos of Jewish origin from public office; purity of blood (*limpieza de sangre*) was to become the essential requirement for one to hold civil or ecclesiastical office, to bear witness, to serve as a notary, or to display authority over an Old Christian. Later these limitations would be expanded to exclude the converts from military orders, from attending university, and from various titles, offices, and honors.[14]

These laws contradicted the teachings of faith and universality advocated by the Church; baptism of a neophyte should not evince ethnic discrimination but rather should create a sense of equality and brotherhood. However, the Church did not have the strength to defy the municipality or the growing belief that the conversos constituted a threat that was actually more unnerving than that presented by the Jews. At least the Jews could be clearly identified as nonbelievers; many members of Spanish society believed that the conversos, however, were no more than false Christians, mostly atheists or judaizers, neither of which was an acceptable alternative. The passing of these laws only helped emphasize the origins of each Spaniard, while adding tension and suspicion to the hostile environment.[15]

The next step in this process was the establishment of an inquisition, and it was only a matter of time until its advocates achieved their goals. Whereas previous papal inquisitions, namely intensive inquiries conducted outside the realm of legal procedure, had been concerned with Christian heretics, the fear here was of the judaizer, who ostensibly was a Christian.[16] Every converso and conversa was a potential judaizer, or believer in the Law of Moses. While observance of Judaism (by a Jew) is not heresy in the eyes of the Catholic Church, observance of Jewish traditions, rites, or beliefs is heretical if practiced by the baptized. The New Christian would be most apt to judaize and apostasize, for the mere presence of Jewish blood in that individual was seen as creating a proclivity to undermine the Church and its dogma. This deep-rooted fear and ethnic hostility were combined with political considerations, for an inquisition would help the newly established Crown strengthen its authority.

There is no doubt that the Crown had its own agenda in 1478 in requesting a papal bull to establish an inquisition on the reconquered lands of Spain. Traditionally, the kingdom of Aragon had been on close terms with Rome; because of these ties and pressures from Rome in the thirteenth century, a papal inquisition had already been established in that realm.[17] While most papal tribunals elsewhere were only temporary, since they were established specifically to deal with a particular outbreak of heresy, the Aragonese tribunal was still extant and functioning. As a matter of fact, it is surprising to discover that as late as 1460–1467, fifteen cases appear in inquisitorial records in Valencia.[18] The defendants were all conversos, two-thirds of them women. Yet if the Valencian inquisition was already dealing, albeit fairly leniently, with the judaizing problem, why were Ferdinand and Isabel so adamant about creating their own?

The Crown's concern here was with unifying the kingdoms and thus, it was precisely because the kingdoms of Valencia, Catalonia, and Navarre had conducted inquiries on their own that a royal institution seemed so urgent to the Crown. The local laws, or *fueros,* which carried great weight in these parts, provided the basis for legal resistance to many aspects of the new royal policy, which clearly emanated from Castile; for example, when the National Inquisition was established, there was strong opposition to the confiscation of the defendant's property as well as to the policy of maintaining secrecy concerning the identity of prosecution witnesses. The pope, too, objected strenuously to withholding the names of these witnesses. The Crown, however, ignored all these objections in its quest to increase its own authority and to control lands outside of the more heavily populated Castile.

Consequently, a national inquisition would serve to help the kingdom of Castile influence the inner workings of the kingdom of Aragon,[19] and of the other kingdoms as well. Religious uniformity, although far from a reality, was an ideal to be pursued; ensuring the loyalty and purity of the baptized was necessary and could be executed only with the aid of an inquisition directed from within Spain. The Jewishness that remained in the New Christian minority had to be dealt with and extirpated as heretical.

The precarious situation of the Jews in this scenario becomes clear. Those conversos who were unfaithful to Christianity were apparently receiving instruction and inspiration from the Jews. The Jews living alongside them were responsible for leading these baptized souls astray. However, the Inquisition, ostensibly of a penitential rather than punitive character, was anxious to save the souls of the baptized and rarely prosecuted the nonbaptized such as the Jew. As a result, while the Inquisition could prosecute conversos galore, its access to the Jewish community was limited. Inquisitorial handbooks ascertained which categories of Jews were subject to their jurisdiction; these included blasphemers against Christianity or Christian beliefs, usurers, sorcerers and magicians, proselytizers among Christians, and those receiving relapsed Jewish converts to Christianity. But unbaptized Jews could not be convicted of practicing Judaism and were technically forbidden to bear witness against a Christian. While Jewish testimonies do occasionally appear in Inquisition dossiers, most of the statements contained in them were made by Christians, both Old and New.[20]

Yet the Jews were clearly influencing the New Christians negatively, and the very existence of convicted judaizers proved the power of their influence. The Crown was simply providing the logical solution to this intolerable predicament, which eventually also provided a convenient explanation for the final scenes in the history of the Jews in Spain. Thus the expulsion edict itself stated that the Jews must be evicted because of their pernicious influence upon the conversos; without a doubt, the same anti-Judaism that pervaded the motivation for the inquisitorial trials is at work here. The distinct and proud sense of Spanish Christianity was at the zenith of self-expression both when they established a national inquisition and when they expelled the Jews. The Jews would be removed from Spain by means of an edict, and the Jewishness of the judaizers would be removed by means of the Inquisition.

Thus one can see the direct path that exists from the events of 1391 to the establishment of the Inquisition to the expulsion of the Jews from Spain. The papal bull authorizing an inquisition in Spain was signed in 1478; the first tribunal was set up in Seville in 1481, followed by the establishment of numerous other central courts in the next decade. By 1483, the National *Suprema,* or Council of the Supreme and

General Inquisition, was established with Tomás de Torquemada as the inquisitor general; this body and its leader would centralize all activities by making each of the twenty-one tribunals regularly submit reports on its activities.[21] Because the Jews were supposedly the prime movers behind the judaizing heresy and apostasy, their departure should have seriously lessened the educating of the judaizers and, ultimately, the perpetuation of crypto-Judaism. Yet the activities of the Spanish Inquisition continued long after the demise of the Jewish community in 1492; judaizers were prosecuted well into the middle of the sixteenth century and were sent to the stake more than any other group categorized as heretical.

Judaizing was the rationale for the establishment of an inquisition, which rapidly transformed itself into the Spanish Inquisition. Recent historians of the Inquisition classify the first years—from 1481 to 1550—as the period devoted basically to dealing with judaizers.[22] Although the Inquisition was more active during these years in the kingdom of Castile, scholars such as William Monter cite the execution of more than 500 conversos in Aragon from the time the Castilian inquisition established itself in its adjoining kingdom in 1484 until the 1530s. Interestingly enough, by this time, the institution that was originally resented in Aragon not only had become an integral part of life there but became more active than its counterpart in Castile in the pursuit of heretics for the century to follow (1530–1630). The various tribunals in Aragon were creative in maintaining an ongoing supply of heretics; only a fifth of the defendants during this period were accused of judaizing. Other victims were categorized as Protestants and Lutherans, Erasmian humanists, pietists or *alumbrados, Moriscos* (Christianized Moors), sodomists, witches, sorcerers, bigamists, and the like. The Protestants, most of whom were of French origin, and the Moriscos were perceived as outsiders, identifiable as foreigners and therefore vulnerable; one can see how they easily joined or replaced the conversos in the prisons of the tribunals. The sixteenth century was also a period when the tribunal initiated censorship along with the supervision of the clergy and a preoccupation lest incorrect beliefs or scandalous and blasphemous expressions rage rampant among the Catholic masses. In other words, the Old Christians, particularly in Castile but also in Aragon, were eventually subjected to the scrutiny of the Inquisition.

Not until the seventeenth century did judaizing arise again as a major heresy to be actively prosecuted; Monter maintains that in Aragon, the surviving conversos had finally assimilated by the mid-sixteenth century, thus precluding further trials. While trials concerning judaizing most definitely existed during the intermediary period, 1530–1630, their numbers fell off significantly. However, as the result of the union of Spain and Portugal in 1580, numerous Portuguese conversos, descendants of the Jews forcibly converted in 1497, chose to cross the border and seek opportunities in neighboring Castile. The year 1632 is cited as the date for the first trial of a Portuguese converso in Spain;[23] the century to follow was full of trials of similar defendants of Portuguese descent, mostly in Castile. Consequently, the judaizing heresy again preoccupied the Holy Tribunal.

The Inquisition was established as a means to control and protect Spanish society and culture; its strength stemmed from the psychological power of fear and the belief that one could inherit a proclivity to engage in heresy. The notion that blood determined one's faith or caused an inability to assimilate the values of Christianity helped to undermine converso society. The means for dealing with this intolerable situation would justify the persecution involved. The Holy Tribunal followed a long-established set of rules and guidelines of previous inquisitors; legal precedent would ensure a sense of continuity and uniformity among the various courts. By encouraging the masses to identify or denounce judaizers, the Inquisition was effectively promoting anti-Semitism. At the same time, when the Jews of Spain were faced with the choice of exile or conversion in 1492, a large number of them did choose the latter; ironically, the state thereby substantially enlarged the despised group of converts and thus of potential judaizers in its midst. These conversos were qualitatively different from the descendants of the converts of the late fourteenth and early fifteenth centuries, for these latest had personally experienced Judaism, and those who ultimately judaized could bring direction and inspiration to the already existing converso community.

Consequently, the Holy Tribunal prosecuted the "veteran" conversos, those whose ancestors had converted in or since 1391, for scarcely more than a decade, from 1481 to 1492. Some of these suspected judaizers could trace their ancestry to the forced converts of 1391; others were descendants of Jews who had converted voluntarily over the course of the century, possibly because of disillusionment with the deteriorating situation of the Jews or as the result of major psychological blows to the community, such as the aftermath of the rigged debates that took place in Tortosa from 1412 to 1414.[24] Again, there were those among them who seriously hoped to be accepted into Christian society and leave their Jewish ancestry behind. But the *limpieza de sangre*, which was eventually accepted by Iberian society as the appropriate way to determine one's societal merit, succeeded in curtailing any such hopes. And the Inquisition, instilling fear and suspicion into homes and communities, would effectively stifle any lingering illusions of the convert desiring to submerge his or her past into a newly acquired identity.

The standard techniques of the Inquisition need to be mentioned, if only briefly, for the shadow of the Black Legend and its horrors hovers over the entire history of Spain during this era.[25] When the decision was made to set up a tribunal in a particular location, certain procedures were carefully followed. A series of sermons were presented to the residents of that locale; the seriousness of heresy and heretical tendencies was emphasized, accompanied by explanations describing judaizing and telling how to identify characteristics of this particular heresy or apostasy. For example, in a trial that took place in 1531, the key witness, who provided detailed information about a family with whom he had lived and worked for a number of years, was asked why he had waited so many years before coming forth with his testimony. He replied that only recently had he heard an edict read at the time of the inquisitor's visit to the village of Villafranca; prior to this, he simply had no inkling that it was his duty to unburden his conscience in this manner.[26] The masses needed guidance, and the Inquisition was prepared to provide it both for the witnesses and for the potential heretics.

Once the preconditions were established, a grace period was declared during which anyone with anything to declare was welcomed to the tribunal. This period could last from two weeks to as many months as were deemed necessary. In other words, both informers and confessants were encouraged to present themselves and testify. The informers did not always have useful information, nor were they always well intentioned; the prosecution needed to sort through the depositions and determine what, if anything, in these statements was of potential value for a trial. The confessants were forewarned: absolution and reconciliation, perhaps accompanied by some penance, would be offered to all who professed their sins, but the confessant must seriously repent and abide by the teachings of the Church, henceforth living the life of an exemplary Catholic. If he or she should deviate in the future, no mercy would be shown; the reconciliation would be offered only once. If there were to be a second encounter, the now relapsed heretic would be turned over to the secular arm to be burned at the stake.

This procedure was quite effective; numerous depositions were always made during the grace period, and the prosecutors were kept busy sorting through the information. Everything was scrupulously recorded, for data that might not seem relevant at first might later prove to be useful. Testimonies had to be examined, for various pitfalls existed concerning the reliability and accuracy of the depositions. The witness was often inexpert in identifying judaizing rituals, and unwittingly might include some idiosyncracy or oddity noted in the suspect's home. The most common danger was the attempt by someone with a grudge to even a score by informing on a converso. Sometimes that converso might in fact have been a judaizer, but if it could be proven that the information was provided with malicious and harmful intent, it was to be disqualified automatically. The inquisitors were quite serious about this point and made every attempt to exclude testimony that could be unreliable because of personal vendettas. Unfortunately, it was not always possible to prove the existence of malice, even if the suspicion existed, so this system was far from flawless.[27]

Thus two books were compiled during the first stages of setting up any inquisitorial court: a book of testimonies and a book of confessions. The former contained statements by both Old and New Christians and, as will be seen, had particularly abundant testimonies of servants. This fact is not surprising, since household help was common in most lower-middle-class homes as well as among higher social strata; these servants were precisely the individuals most apt to witness judaizing activities taking place in the home. These testimonies were predominant in the women's trials, and understandably so. The average household had more than one servant, at least one of whom was assigned to the kitchen. The very

nature of Jewish observance leaves the judaizing women vulnerable precisely because their activities were at home, and often kitchen centered. Not having servants
would only raise or confirm any suspicions. A crypto-Jewish woman would have to
rely upon her wile and ingenuity in covering up her judaizing. Unfortunately, as
will become clear, these servant–mistress relationships were very volatile and often
short lived. A servant who might remain silent about the activities in the mistress's
home would reconsider his or her options after being dismissed from a post. Rarely
did the employees leave with a sense of loyalty to their former employers; on the
contrary, the disgruntled former servant seems to be the rule.

The other book of records contained statements and confessions made by New
Christians; the descriptions ranged from succinct and rather limited in scope to all-
encompassing descriptions of crypto-Jewish life. No matter what the length of the
confession, once the statement was made, the confessant's activities were apt to be
monitored; reconciliation and the fate of a soul reunited with the Church was not a
matter to be taken lightly.

Once the evidence was assessed by the appropriate theological consultants, the
decision could be made as to whether or not the court had a case. If there were at
least two witnesses who seemed credible, the prosecutor began to formulate his
charges.[28] The list began with whatever transgression was considered to be the
most serious, and it continued in descending order of importance. There was a
qualitative difference in wording in the accusation lists of women and men. Time
after time, there was a sense of passivity on the part of many of the men, who were
often accused of "allowing" or "permitting" their wives to perform Jewish rites. The
wives, on the other had, were more likely accused of actively judaizing. These differences will be noted in numerous cases that come under discussion. It is important to note here that even the prosecution was aware of the strong and unusual
role of the women in crypto-Judaism.

One cannot assume that all defendants were present during the course of their
trials, for many were not. Some were tried in absentia, presumably because they
had fled, and others were tried posthumously.[29] If the defendant was accessible, he
or she was arrested once the charges were made, his or her goods were sequestered,
and an inventory was made of all property, which was held at least until the end of
the trial, often a matter of years.[30] The confiscation of goods and the means of dating the period of seizure were matters of controversy and conflict between the Pope
and the Spanish Crown; it could be extremely significant for the economic fate of
an individual or family if a confiscation began at the time of the arrest or the beginning of the trial or if it was considered to begin retroactively to the time when the
defendant transgressed—in these cases, began to judaize.[31]

The defendant or the defendant's family was responsible for his or her upkeep
while on trial and incarcerated; once the charges were made, they could provide a
defense attorney, who was obviously at a disadvantage since the prosecutor had
prepared his case in advance. Yet there were many attempts to seriously defend the

accused. At first, the defense tactics were two-pronged: to prove the sincerity of the defendant as a devout Catholic, and to prove that the witnesses for the prosecution were unreliable. The first approach entailed compiling lists of *abonos,* or character witnesses, who could vouch for the Christian lifestyle of the accused, and *indirectas,* or questions to be posed to them. These lists were often lengthy, with at least two witnesses named for the verification of each claim; frequently names of sextons and parish priests appeared on these lists. There was only one drawback to this line of defense: a truly successful judaizer would have managed to create a façade whereby the outside world would be convinced of his or her devotion to the Church. An integral part of this lifestyle was to deceive the Christians while participating secretly as a crypto-Jew. The court realized the futility of this tactic, and by the turn of the century, abonos rarely appear in dossiers.

The second defense tactic offered more hopeful prospects for the accused. Again, lists were provided by the defendant and defense lawyer, but these were *tachas* or attempts to discredit witnesses.[32] These lists were often quite lengthy as well, due to the fact that the defense was desperately groping in the dark. It was trying to nullify the testimony of witnesses for the prosecution with no information as to who these individuals were. The policy of withholding these names was another bone of contention between the Roman and the Spanish Inquisition. The latter arranged for two lists of witnesses to appear in each trial; names and identities were included in the account for the prosecution and the rest of the inquisitorial court, but they (and any identifiable comments) were omitted in a special copy prepared for the defense. However, if the defense did list the name of an actual witness for the prosecution (in the tacha list) and a reason why that witness might have cause to provide false testimony, along with the names of two people who verified this contention, then the testimony of that witness would be unacceptable. It is not surprising to discover long tacha lists, for the defendant, sitting for long periods of time in a cell, would reconstruct his or her life and think of numerous incidents and tensions during his or her lifetime that might have influenced someone to provide incriminating testimony. There were even cases in which the defendant named all the witnesses for the prosecution, provided reasons for each one's malice, and supplied the names of others who then verified this claim; the court had no choice but to dismiss such cases. Ironically, this dismissal did not mean that the defendant was not guilty as charged, but simply indicated that the prosecution had chosen "unreliable" witnesses; should more reliable providers of information be located at a later date, a second trial would be convened. While the use of tachas was trying and often exasperating, it occasionally was successful, probably the only successful technique utilized by the defense.

Obviously, these methods were applied only when a confession was not made in the course of the trial. Surprisingly, most confessions were not obtained by torture; technically, any information provided during torture had to be repeated and confirmed the following day.[33] The decision to apply torture would be made by the inquisitorial committee at the *consulta-de-fé*, or conference toward the end of the trial following the presentation of all relevant information. The members of this committee included the inquisitor, local theological advisers, and a representative of the bishop. They might opt to interrogate the defendant further, with or without the use of torture, or simply to determine a sentence on the basis of the information at hand.[34]

The sentences varied, and some, such as total absolution and reconciliation, usually accompanied by a penance such as a fine or a short prison term, were not so onerous. More serious sentences included exile and service in the galleys of a ship; the latter, instituted in the sixteenth century, was dreaded and rarely if ever the fate of a judaizer.[35] Life imprisonment was also an option; this was the first time that prison was utilized as a penitential discipline. Last, there was the condemned heretic; since the Church had no right to impose the death sentence, the accused was turned over to the secular authorities, who provided two alternatives. If the heretic repented at the last minute and was reconciled to the Church, he or she would be shown mercy and hanged before being burned; if not, the individual would be burned alive at a public *auto-de-fé*. These demonstrations would be planned so that numerous transgressors would be paraded in public simultaneously. William Monter wrote that "most secular legal systems punished their prisoners more severely than the Inquisition, but none pronounced its judgments more theatrically or perpetuated the memory of its condemnations more assiduously."[36] The latter part of this statement refers to the *sanbenito*, the infamous outer clothing assigned to the sinner, worn by those repenting and bombastically hung in the parish churches after the expiration of sentence or the death of the heretic; because one's name appeared on the *sanbenito* along with a set of flames, shame would be associated with certain families for generations to come.

In truth, the severity of the Inquisition in its dealing with the judaizers varied according to the time, the location, the inquisitors themselves, and the makeup of the tribunal.[37] One can discover very different sentences for the identical "crimes" either at different times or in different jurisdictions. During the two main periods when the Inquisition concentrated on the judaizing heresy, 95 percent of the defendants were judaizers. However, between 1481 and 1530, the first stage of the Holy Tribunal, some 1,500 judaizers were condemned to death, whereas during the second wave of antijudaizing activity, from 1630 to 1730, only about 250 of the defendants faced the death sentence.

Ironically, both those conversos who judaized and those who did not faced lives of fear and insecurity, for they were all suspect in a society unwilling to absorb them. Those who faced the Holy Tribunal often paid with their lives and property. Yet the inquisitors believed that they were saving souls; a baptized Christian must remain within the fold of the Church, and it was their responsibility to bring back those who went astray. As a result, the judaizer who was faithful to Judaism was unfaithful in the eyes of the Church and would be burned at the stake, for his or her Jewish soul was eternally lost to the Church.

The stories of numerous conversas tried for judaizing in Castile will unfold in the pages to come; the Inquisition was well aware of their active and central role in perpetuating these acts of apostasy and heresy. The inquisitors realized the unusual importance of the home in crypto-Judaism and understood that the women willy-nilly became the carriers of the tradition that they viewed as inimical. The interactions between these women and their adversaries in court will reveal more than a mere list of judaizing activities; the determination of these women emerges and often triumphs over the "superior" power of the feared Holy Tribunal. As they themselves explained, although the mother might be burned at the stake, she would leave behind her children to carry on her teachings. Thus the technical completion of any given trial did not necessarily guarantee the end of the prosecutor's travails in combatting the judaizing heresy.

Jews and Conversas

The First Century of Crypto-Judaism

On MARCH 31, 1492, King Ferdinand and Queen Isabel signed the infamous edict declaring the expulsion of the "Jews and Jewesses" of all of their kingdoms;[1] this event would take place in July of that year. The edict itself states:

[W]e were informed that in these our kingdoms there were some bad Christians who Judaized and apostatized from our holy Christian faith, this being chiefly caused by the communication of the Jews with the Christians . . . it is evident and apparent that the great damage to the Christians has resulted from and does result from the participation, conversation, and communication that they have had with the Jews, who try to always achieve by whatever ways and means possible to subvert and draw away faithful Christians from our holy Catholic faith and to separate them from it, and to attract and pervert them to their injurious belief and opinion, instructing them in their ceremonies and observances of the Law, holding gatherings where they read unto them and teach them what they ought to believe and observe according to their Law, trying to circumcise them and their children, giving them books from which to read their prayers, and declaring the fasts that they ought to fast, and joining with them to read and teach them the histories of their Law; notifying them of Passover before it comes, advising them what they should observe and do for it, giving them and taking unto them the unleavened bread and the [ritually] slaughtered meats with their ceremonies, instructing them on the things that they should stay away from, thus in the foods as in the other matters, for observance of their Law and persuading them as much as they can there is no other law nor truth besides it.[2]

Thus did the monarchs blame the Jewish community for the corruption of the New Christians, and rationalize their drastic measure of eviction.[3] The Crown claimed that its knowledge of this pernicious contact between Jew and Christian, the description of which is impressive in its detail, was based on information pro-

cured by inquisitorial proceedings. Since the Inquisition already had been functioning for eleven years, this contention certainly seems plausible. Nevertheless, a
closer look at the nature of the contact between the Jews and their former brethren
is essential, for one still tends to suspect the motives of the king and queen and
question whether they were using the Jews and Jewesses of their kingdoms as
scapegoats. While there is no doubt that the two communities had contact with one
another, it is hard to imagine that this was the sole motive for expelling the Jews. Yet
in light of the ethnic anti-Semitism pervading Spain, and Castile in particular, such
a reason would not be difficult to accept.[4] We need to know just how extensive the
relations were between the two groups, and just how active the conversas were in
this type of interaction that transpired prior to the Expulsion.

It is difficult to substantiate theories concerning the nature of the Jews' influence
on conversos following the forced conversions of 1391. There are documents that
specifically refer to the Crown's concern about contact between the two groups, and
various attempts to separate the living quarters of Jews from those of Christians
confirm the fact that the government was unhappy about the situation.[5] However,
with the establishment of the Inquisition, a great deal of information of a different
nature became available to both the prosecutor and the researcher. There were numerous grace periods declared between 1483 and 1486; many of the conversos and
conversas who chose to confess at this time revealed essential information that a
confession after 1492 might not contain, namely, information about contact they
had had with the Jewish community.

The Edict of Expulsion emphasized the belief that instruction was provided by
the Jews to the conversos, especially at gatherings. These Jews supposedly induced
the New Christians to circumcise their sons, gave them books, told them when to
fast, and instructed them in their law. They taught them about Passover, provided
them with unleavened bread and ritually slaughtered meat, and taught them what
was forbidden in their law. Analysis of the trials reveals that many of these accusations were indeed true, although by no means for all of the conversas who were under scrutiny in the chambers of the Holy Tribunal. Yet when one or a few crypto-
Jewish women admitted to some degree of contact with the Jewish community, we
can assume that there were probably others who had similar relations but chose not
to mention that particular "transgression" in the list provided in the grace period
confession. It is logical to assume that these women did not always offer comprehensive confessions but were often selective about which judaizing activities they
included. They must have been concerned that they appear to offer ample information to substantiate the fact that they had been crypto-Jewesses, yet at the same
time needed to seem capable of repenting and reverting to the Church. Offering
too much information might have created the impression that a smooth reconciliation would be problematic. Yet some conversas apparently did not abide by this
theory and provided rather lengthy and detailed confessions. Attuned as it was to
the inner workings of the human mind, the Inquisition did not ignore the possi-

bility that full confessions had not been offered, particularly during grace periods. Thus when the path of a particular conversa led her back to its domain at a later point in her life, a concerted attempt would be made to expand upon that first confession via interrogation, and to discover if other past activities had been ignored or intentionally omitted.

At any rate, both the crypto-Jews and crypto-Jewesses often relied upon their Jewish brethren for support, be it moral, spiritual, or culinary; sometimes these crypto-Jews even provided economic support for the devastated communities of their ancestors, and it seems that the Jews did not hesitate to turn to them for help.[6] The Crown emphasized what it termed "subversion" and "perversion" on the part of the Jews who were instructing the Christians in observance of their Law. If one could examine the trials upon which the above declaration was based or if one knew how the inquisitor had composed his list, then the accuracy or inaccuracy of this list could be determined. Since doing this is not possible, we can examine the confessions or trials of conversas that occurred prior to the Expulsion and compare that information with the picture presented by the edict. Perhaps the king and queen had received a distorted image of the role of the Jews, or perhaps that image had been accurate. Another possibility is that these data will only partially coincide with the information available in the trials.

There is no doubt that some of the New Christians communicated with Jews. A conversa witness named Catalina Martínez testified in 1484 that two years prior, she had seen a Jewish woman, apparently from Córdoba, present in the house of María Alonso, a defendant accused of judaizing, and talking to her; "later this witness found the same Jewish woman in the home of a niece of this witness and asked her in order to fully certify if she was a Jewess, and (that) she answered her that she indeed was a Jewess." The same witness also recounted having come to María's house to order a garment from her, for she was a cloth-weaver; a Jew arrived at the house then as well.[7] In other words, Jews and Jewesses were freely going in and out of this conversa's home. Although the witness did not know why they were present or what they were doing there, this account attests to an open relationship between Jews and conversos; there was no attempt to hide the fact that these individuals were frequenting María's home or that they were Jews. In the same trial, a different witness expanded upon the details of the situation. Catalina González testified that she "saw a Jew enter her [María's] home some three times, and she saw that he read inside the room where she had a loom and she listened to the said Jew."[8] No specific book is mentioned, but presumably the Jew was reading to the neighbor of this witness, namely María; an attempt at seclusion had been made, since the conversa's spinning room rather than a central room was chosen for this exchange, but obviously the Jew and the conversa had not successfully avoided notice.

More than once, Jews were identified by witnesses as having visited converso homes; sometimes the witness simply recognized the visitor's clothes as being Jewish. The prosecutor in the trial of Rodrigo Marín and his wife, Catalina López, accused them of having listened to readings by Jews who were dressed like rabbis.[9] This charge was based on the testimony provided by Lope Franco in 1484. He described prayer sessions in this couple's home which their relatives attended, and "many times he saw another Jew [who was] wearing white linen there, delivering a sermon and reading to them."[10] The prosecutor apparently associated such dress with that of the rabbis. Again, it sounds as though the gatherings referred to by the Crown truly took place, highlighted by reading and teaching. "Subversive" activities such as joint participation, conversation, and communication that were on the royal agenda are documented here.

Information about María Alfonso of Herrera and various Jews is provided by the conversa herself. She mentions having heard readings from Jewish books from her brother and from a Jew. She specifically confesses to having enjoyed a visit from a Jew who came to her house.[11]

Teresa Acre of Toledo related an interesting incident in her confession in 1485. Some ten years prior, she had wanted to learn how to read and approached a Jewish woman to come to her home and teach her. She obviously had no compunctions about inviting the Jewess to her home, nor in approaching her for lessons. Teresa apparently paid this teacher to show her how to read; it turns out that five years prior, she had begged a sister-in-law to teach her a prayer she knew. According to Teresa's testimony, neither of these classes was successful: in the former, she supposedly discovered that she had no ability to read, and in the latter case, she claimed to have stopped the lessons as she realized that the prayers were not proper for a good Catholic.[12] While it is uncertain if the sister-in-law was a conversa or a Jewess, the first female teacher was indeed Jewish, and willing to educate her conversa sister.[13]

Following the royal edict point by point, one can perceive that there are quite a few allegations that simply do not appear in any of the trials of the conversas under discussion. This does not mean that the allegations are false, although it does seem odd not to find any indications of what one would expect to be a common occurrence. The one activity that obviously would not appear in the files of the conversas is the attempt to circumcise them.[14] At the same time, a good portion of the allegations are general, as the Jews "try to always achieve by whatever ways and means possible to subvert and draw away faithful Christians." We do not know what transpired when the Jews and Christians met; we do not know if the Jews were attracting the conversos and perverting them "to their injurious belief and opinion." However, at times, they were indeed "instructing them in their ceremonies and observances of their Law" or reading to them.

It is difficult to know if the Crown made certain assumptions or based all of its notions upon information provided by the Inquisition. For example, how did the conversos know when particular holidays occurred? The edict states, for example, that the Jews declared "the fasts that they ought to fast." The only incident of this nature (in the trials under discussion) alludes to one conversa sending her daughter to the house of another conversa, namely María Alonso, "to ask her if this was the day of the fast or [if it was] the other yet to come; she answered and said: `Today is not the day of fasting, but rather tomorrow.'"[15] María had been seen receiving Jews and Jewesses in her home; however, there is no indication of a connection between the two incidents and no means of proving that the Jews who visited her had done so for the purpose of alerting her that a Jewish fast day was near. Presumably, María Alonso the conversa was considered to be a reliable source for the other crypto-Jewesses; thus, even in the case of this conversa, there is no evidence to prove that the Jews declared that she should fast on Yom Kippur.

Likewise the Crown assumed that the Jews notified the Christians in advance of the advent of Passover, "advising them what they should observe and do for it, giving them and taking unto them the unleavened bread." Analysis of the trials under scrutiny presents a somewhat different picture: the conversas seemed to know when Passover was coming and how to observe this holiday. Nevertheless, when they could not bake the unleavened bread, they frequently turned to the Jewish community as a source of supply. For example, Elvira López of Toledo ate the *matsah* that had been given to her by Jews in exchange for fruit.[16] Here the Jews and the conversa utilized a barter system; one would have expected the zealous, subversive Jews to have showered the conversa with gifts of their baked goods, but they did not. When the conversa María González of Casarrubios del Monte did not bake matsah, her husband sent flour to a Jew and paid him to prepare the unleavened bread in his oven.[17] Here is a second example of purchasing the matsah rather than receiving it gratis. This same conversa would also send a servant in search of matsah if she did not have enough or if her husband did not procure it from the Jewish baker. In addition, she would have the servant go in search of other holiday foods she might need; if she had been making a seder, there were many unusual items that would have been difficult to procure in the open market.[18] The Jewish community did supply these conversas with the necessary goods, but not in the proselytizing manner which would be expected from the description of Jewish behavior contained in the edict. While the Jews clearly were not refusing the requests of their converso brethren, they were frequently providing the desired goods on a commercial basis.

Catalina Sanchez of Madrid "requested and demanded unleavened bread from the Jews and ate it on that festival of Passover to honor and observe it";[19] there is no mention of payment or barter here. Oddly enough, the image created by the prosecutor in this trial depicts the conversa as more aggressive than the Jews, whereas the Crown presents an image of the Jewish community as the aggressor. The trial of Blanca Rodríguez of Guadalajara leaves a similar impresssion. She was accused of eating unleavened bread and of having "requested it from the Jewish women during the Passover festival in order to observe it."[20] Beatriz González of Toledo admitted that sometimes she bought it and sometimes it was given to her;[21] thus payment was considered appropriate at times and not at others. The accusation in the trial of Beatriz Xarada of Chinchón does not concern itself with the issue of payment. "In order to observe the said Passover, she ate unleavened bread of the said festival of the Jews, and she brought it from the house of Jews and she ate it."[22] This conversa might have paid for it or might have received it as a gift; the crux of the issue is the source of her supply.

In the trial of Aldonza de Herrera, there is a record of the interrogation of her brother, who said that the Jews gave matsah to his family. When questioned as to whether his wife or mother had ever baked it, he said no. However, he asserted that all the members of the household ate unleavened bread at Passover time and that his mother was the one who distributed it at the table, giving each individual a small piece of matsah.[23]

The final example of conversos receiving matsah from Jews is a clear case of largesse, although it occurred within the context of a business relationship. Elvira López of San Gil explained that she and her husband had some houses "and in some of them lived Jews, from those Jews we received some gifts; among those gifts they sometimes sent me cakes of unleavened bread, which we ate, I and my husband and the girls who were in my house."[24] While the Jews did initiate the act of gift-giving in this case, with the recipients being their landlord and landlady, even this instance does not approach the conditions described in the edict; the relationship seemed to be rather casual, and the converso family welcomed the gift of unleavened bread but did not appear to be under the influence of any pernicious Jews bearing gifts.

According to the edict, the Jews brought not only matsah, but ritually slaughtered meats to the conversos. Again, the distinction needs to be made: were the Jews bringing the goods to the conversos, or were the conversos coming to the Jews to get supplies of foodstuff? Apparently, the traffic was two-way: Jews came to the homes of conversos, but more often, as will be shown, conversos obtained kosher meat on their own, frequently purchasing it directly from Jewish butcher shops. For example, Teresa Acre confessed in 1493 that she had eaten a hen beheaded by a Jew who was her neighbor.[25] Here the Jew is merely serving as the slaughterer, providing the conversa with kosher fowl and, to the dismay of the Crown, living side by side with her.

A witness in the trial of Catalina López claimed that she had seen that "sometimes Jews from out of town came to her [Catalina's] home and slaughtered meat in her house, [and] the aforesaid Ruy López [Marín] and his wife ate it."[26] Here the Jews are clearly providing a professional service, coming to the home to prepare the meat for consumption; this was the equivalent of the ritual slaughterer making house calls, a service provided to the Jewish community as well.[27] In the trial of Leonor González, it was said that she and her husband had a Jewish butcher who slaughtered their meat for them, and if it came out *trefa* (nonkosher), they would not eat it.[28] What is not clear here is whether the butcher came to their home to surreptitiously slaughter animals for them, or if they patronized his shop, although it seems the former was the case. Since there is no mention of his shop, there is certainly room for speculation as to whether or not he also came privately to carry out his work within the confines of their property. Yet there is no doubt that this conversa was concerned with the dietary laws, as exemplified by a different witness's statement that "he knew that they did not eat any meat other than that slaughtered by Jewish hand and with the Jewish ceremony."[29]

Many of the descriptions of conversos who procured kosher meat do not include details that enable us to determine whether they bought it in Jewish shops. Inés de Belmonte confessed in 1484 that she ate meat slaughtered by Jewish hand; she used the fact that she was pregnant as an excuse for what she hoped to pass off as an aberrational "indulgence." Yet in the same confession, mention is made of an interesting transaction that did not seem to preoccupy the Crown. Inés had also received meat from the Moors of Almagro.[30] Traditionally, Muslims buy and eat meat slaughtered by Jews, but the reverse situation is a rarity, occurring only under extenuating circumstances. Perhaps an exception was made because buying this meat seemed to be less incriminating than buying kosher meat. We find other conversas who conducted themselves similarly. Elvira Martínez of Toledo ate meat slaughtered by Jew and Moor, and Elvira López of San Gil had eaten meat from the butcher shops of both Jews and Muslims.[31] Apparently, they felt that the Muslim *halal* was preferable to the Christian slaughtering techniques, and they were satisfied as long as they had non-Christian meat for consumption.

A different distinction was made in the case of María González. Although her trial was initiated in 1511, evidence against her had been collected as early as 1475; María would offer a confession some eight years later during the grace period of 1483. The witness against her specified which of the various animals and meats María did not eat; she also pointed out that the conversa and her husband would not eat any birds or beasts except those that were "beheaded ceremonially by Jew or by converso."[32] The distinction here is the grouping together of the converso and the Jew, both groups maintaining a distance from the Old Christian; as in the previous case, the Christian hand was not to touch meat destined for converso palates.

The whole notion of who had (or had not) come in contact with the meat appears frequently in these trials. Constanza Núñez confessed in 1486 that "I sinned that sometimes I ate meat slaughtered by the hands of Jews and I ate their victuals." The latter portion of her statement seems to imply that she either ate in the homes of the Jews or received prepared foods from them which she consumed. Her daughter, Mari Núñez, also confessed that she sinned by eating "meat beheaded by Jewish hand," and a third member of the same family, Juana Martínez, confessed that she "ate meat slaughtered by Jewish hand."[33] Here two daughters and their mother all used the identical term to describe their activities. Because of the wording chosen, one cannot ascertain the actual source of this kosher meat and whether these conversas were unabashedly patronizing Jewish butcher shops or were receiving their supply secretly.

On the other hand, some of the other trials of conversas during this period contain precisely this detail. The accusation presented to Aldonza de Herrera in 1530 included the charge that "the said Aldonza and other persons ate meat slaughtered ceremonially, and at other times they brought it from the butcher shop of the Jews in honor and observance of the Law of Moses."[34] Others unabashedly frequented Jewish shops or sent their servants to purchase for them. María González of Casarrubios del Monte bought meat from the Jewish butchery because she would not consume *trefa* meat; she also sent her servants to look for it there.[35] While one would assume that she preferred not to go in order to avoid being noticed, there is no doubt that those who were in her employ were identified as such; an observer would assume that it was the conversa mistress and not the servant, most likely of Old Christian heritage, who was interested in purchasing meat from Jews.

Conversas used their servants to procure numerous goods for them; the same María sent her servants in search of matsah and other Passover food, and if she had not prepared a Sabbath stew, she would send them to a Jewish home seeking stew.[36] In other words, if she herself had not made the Sabbath day meal in advance, rather than abrogating the day of rest and engaging in forbidden work, namely, cooking, she would depend on the mercy of Jews in her community to send some of their prepared meals to her. It seems that she completely relied upon this community, which is not surprising in light of the fact that she had relatives there. Sometimes she obtained kosher wine from them by sending a messenger, in this case a Jewish relative of hers.[37] She was not alone in attempting to obtain kosher wine, for María Alfonso also mentioned that a Jew provided her and her husband with kosher wine.[38]

It appears that the conversa of Casarrubios went still a step further. She brought a Jew into her home to make the wine on the premises. Samuel Abenjamín testified that he had tread upon grapes in the winepress that belonged to this family and closed the wineskins so that the wine would be kosher.[39] María would borrow from them, send servants to their homes, and receive Jews in her home as well. For example, before María gave birth, the local rabbi, who lived across the street from her, came to visit her and prayed by her bed in the company of another Jew.[40] Another conversa, in a moment of distress when she had to flee her home because of the plague, found refuge with Jews;[41] again, the conversa felt more comfortable turning to the Jew rather than to the fellow Christian.

Once again, the movement between the two communities was not one-way, contrary to what is implied by the king and queen. Conversos sought out Jews at the same time that Jews sought them out. Sometimes these relationships were based on friendship and sometimes on kinship. In the 1460s, a neighbor saw two identifiably Jewish men coming to the home of Marina González in Ciudad Real. She recognized them as cousins of Marina and noted that they joined the conversa and her husband at the table for a meal.[42] Needless to say, if Marina did not abide by the Jewish dietary laws, these Jewish cousins would never have eaten in her home. While the relatives might have visited her nonetheless, here is clear proof that Marina observed in a manner that was acceptable to her Jewish brethren. The witness intimates that this meal took place on the Sabbath, an even more significant fact. If Marina did not observe the Sabbath precisely as a Jew would, the Jewish members of her family would have just cause not to dine with her.[43]

The conversa landlady from San Gil who received matsah from her tenants and bought meat from Jews and Muslims had a unique relationship with the Jews. She seems to have been considered kin at times and a non-Jew at others. In her confession in 1486, she mentioned that a Jewish neighbor who had no servants of his own begged her to light a fire for him on the Sabbath; she decided that doing so was not a sin and acceded to the request. In the same statement, Elvira explained that she also loaned her maidservant to various Jewish neighbors to serve as a *goy shel shabbat* and light their lights (fires).[44] This is fascinating because in the first instance, when under duress, she herself served this function for the Jew who lived under the same roof; as a baptized Catholic, she could light fire on the Sabbath. Yet her other neighbors did not ask her to engage in this menial task but rather requested the use of her non-Jewish help.

The Edict of Expulsion does not mention other Jewish holidays or even standard social events such as celebrations of birth or marriage. This omission is rather surprising, since these occasions provided predictable opportunities for the establishment of contact between Jews and conversos. In fact, the edict mentions only fast days and Passover by name; other events are not even alluded to, but, as will be shown, clearly should have been included.

Some conversas mentioned joining their Jewish brethren on various occasions in addition to Passover and the Sabbath. Blanca Rodríguez of Guadalajara spent all of the holy day of Yom Kippur with Jews.[45] Elvira López of Talamanca invited Jews to attend *hadas* at her home. One witness said:

> [W]hen the wife of Alonso López cloth-shearer, resident of the said locale, gave birth and within six or seven days after she gave birth, the said Alonso López invited this witness and her husband and others, some Jews, and gave them a collation and fruit in the fashion in which the Jews practice for their sons and daughters that is called *hadas*, which was seen twice when the said wife of Alonso López gave birth.[46]

A second testimony, given by a Jew himself, corroborates this social mingling of Jews and conversos: "[t]wice when his wife [Elvira López] gave birth, the said Alonso López invited this witness and his wife, both times the night before baptism."[47] It is likely that both witnesses attended the same festivities, although they might not have known one another.

A less common celebration among the conversos was the Jewish wedding. For example, María Díaz of Ciudad Real assisted in the enactment of a Jewish wedding ceremony with the help of her daughter, two fellow conversos, and a Jew named

Fernando de Trujillo. Catalina de Zamora, the witness for the prosecution who later would stand trial, described the events of 1482. Constanza de Bonilla had been veiled in the church ceremony with Pero Franco.[48] While supping after returning from church, the newlywed converso couple was confronted by two fellow conversos, who insisted that Constanza had to be veiled by Jewish hand and that she had to be given a ritual bath as well. The defendant and her daughter took the bride, covered her with a sheet, and bathed her in a stream near the village of Palma, where they all resided. The Jew Trujillo appeared with a cup of wine, recited certain words, and instructed both of the betrothed to drink from the cup. At that point, María's son-in-law, a devout Christian, appeared on the scene, extremely agitated and infuriated; he struck the Jew, declared loudly that he was a Christian and not a Jew, and effectively broke up the gathering.[49] The son-in-law seems to have been a converso, but obviously one who adamantly objected to judaizing and to any contact between his conversa wife and mother-in-law and the Jewish community. He had caught the women of his family in the "act" and was less than pleased to witness such events.

The Festival of the Booths, or Sukkot, was another occasion for contact between Jew and converso. Most conversos could not find a suitable place to build a booth (*sukkah*) that would not be noticed, and they were often content with frequenting those erected by others, in this case, by Jews. Elvira Martínez of Toledo went to a booth by herself "not on account of the ceremony but rather in order to see the said booth and when I was there, they distributed refreshment and [that] I believe that they gave me toasted chickpeas and this confessant received the said refreshment."[50] There is a discrepancy in the trial of Beatriz González, also of Toledo, who was accused of making booths in her home. Interestingly, her confession contains no mention of her erecting any booths, but rather a declaration that "sometimes I went into the booths of Jews and ate their fruit in them."[51] Similarly did her neighbor Catalina Gómez confess that she sometimes went to the booths.[52] Teresa of Acre admitted to comparable activities in the second confession she offered the Holy Tribunal. In 1493, she referred to going to some of the Jews' booths, entering them, and eating their fruit.[53] Once again, the conversa was dependent upon the Jewish community to provide what she could not make or obtain at this time of the year.

At the same time, the Jewish community was not always able to provide for all of its communal needs, nor were many of its members able to meet their own personal needs. As a result, the conversos either responded to requests from the Jews or offered aid on their own initiative. In light of the rather depleted state of the Jewish communities after the riots of 1391, a state that did not improve significantly during the subsequent generations, this situation is not surprising. The damage was so great that the Jewish leaders could never fully rebuild their communities or even compensate for their losses. Consequently, we find conversos providing material and financial aid of various types. For instance, a prosecutor charged that a conversa had "lent Jews clothing for the booths, essentially in order to honor and celebrate the Festival of the Booths of the Jews." The defendant, Elvira López of Toledo, admitted that she had in fact lent cloth(ing) for the booths of the Jews.[54] The term *ropas* was used here, not in its common use referring to personal clothing, but rather meaning cloth or other material suitable for making or adorning a *sukkah*.

Juana Rodríguez also had contact with Jews on Sukkot; she specified that "she remembered well how she had lent a rug and a bordered sheet to a Jew so that he could make his booth, all of which I did in honor of and in keeping with the Law of the Jews, thinking that I would be saved by it."[55] The sheet was probably used for one of the sides of the booth, or possibly the entrance, and the rug was probably placed on the floor inside the booth. María González of Casarrubios del Monte also confessed that "I lent them cloth(ing) for their festivals and for their booths and I entered them and ate of their fruits and their foods."[56] Here the term *ropas* has both meanings: the cloth needed for covering or adorning the booth as well as clothing lent to the Jews who did not have an adequate wardrobe for the festival. It seems that the wealthier conversas were lending various items to their Jewish brethren at holiday time, ranging from rugs and sheets to festival clothing and jewelry. In 1485, Inés González confessed that she had lent some jewels for some of the festivals of the Jews.[57] This implies a great deal of trust, for loaning sheets is far easier than loaning one's personal jewelry. The conversa was helping her Jewish sister(s) celebrate in the style that she would have done herself, had she been able to do so.

Contact between Jews and conversos was even more extensive at times. Considering the relative impoverishment of the Jewish community at the end of the fifteenth century, it is not surprising that some conversos were involved in charity work. One interesting testimony concerns Leonor González, who had a special room in which she and her husband prayed. In about 1475, she was seen using this room to distribute charity to both Jews and conversos.[58] The grouping together of Jews and conversos is significant; perhaps the beggars arrived separately, perhaps in tandem, but there seems to be little distinction made as to who is the recipient of such goodwill and generosity.

The conversos often confessed to having given donations to Jews. One conversa recalled encountering a Jewish beggar in the 1460s who held out a silver cup; she opened her purse and gave him a silver coin. She explained to the inquisitors that she did not think this act would offend God.[59] In 1486, Constanza Núñez stated that she sinned by giving alms to Jews and others and oil for the synagogue.[60] One donation went to individuals, while the other's recipient was an institution. Constanza's daughter, Mari Núñez, also said that she sinned by giving charity to Jews;[61] this obviously reflected a family value that had been successfully transmitted.

The practice of supplying such oil requires some clarification here. In medieval Spain, a society called *Ma'or* had been organized to supply oil and light the synagogues, the study houses, and the perpetual light in the synagogue.[62] It was obviously one of many charitable institutions that sought donations from its Jewish constituents and, as we shall see, from the conversos, who were also in their potential donor pool.

In this light, we find Inés González admitting in 1485 that she sinned by giving alms to Jews for the purchase of oil.[63] Mencia Rodríguez of Cadahalso gave money and wine as donations so that there would be oil in the synagogue.[64] When her son was ill, a conversa from Guadalajara sent oil to the churches and to the synagogue; the latter received the donation in a bowl.[65] Catalina Sánchez gave alms to Jews who asked her to do so; she explained that the Jews had been sent by the *aljama* (religious community) to obtain oil or money for purchasing oil for the synagogue, as well as for repairs for the synagogue and for shrouds and proper burials for poor Jews.[66] When asked, Blanca Rodríguez gave *zedaka* (charity) for the funding of the Jewish community and also gave donations for the purchase of oil for the synagogue.[67] In an interesting interplay between the prosecutor and the defendant, we discover that the day before Yom Kippur, a Jew entered the house of María Alvarez of Guadalajara and asked for oil (or money to purchase oil) for the synagogue. The conversa supposedly told him that if he would return at a later date, she would grant his request. Thus was she accused of intending to make the donation, since the intention was often as serious a crime as the actual deed in the eyes of the Inquisition. When interrogated, María pointed out that although she was intending to give him the money, he did not return; but apparently this was not the central issue.[68] The Jew obviously had no compunctions about approaching the conversa; the Inquisition considered this near act to be as serious as a fulfilled act.[69] Regardless of the outcome, the inquisitors were concerned with the tangible contact between the two groups.

In another case of a conversa involved in donations, it appears that there had been a group of conversas supervising the almsgiving. According to the confession of Leonor Alvarez in 1495, "once I gave a measure of oil to one of those conversa women, because she told me that it [this quantity] had been promised on my behalf, and I paid her in cash, and I was told that it had been promised to the synagogue, and I gave her the monies so that she could fulfill that pledge."[70] The conversas of Ciudad Real seem to have organized the equivalent of a *Ma'or* society and were pressuring their cohorts in order to increase the donation level from the conversa constituency.

Elvira Ruíz of Escalona confessed that her mother had taught her to give donations; among other things, she had been told to give money to the synagogue for oil, and she specified that her mother was quite strict about this.[71] María Alfonso had given alms to poor relatives and other Jews in need as well as money for oil for the synagogue lamp; in addition she stated that she had given the synagogue linen towels for drying hands (which were washed prior to prayer).[72] Mencia Rodríguez of Guadalajara was accused of having a great deal of contact with the Jews and their synagogues. In 1493, the prosecutor claimed that Mencia had sent contributions of oil to the synagogue in order to save her soul and that she had actually gone to the synagogue "to clean and adorn the synagogue's lamps, placing wicks in them and pouring oil inside them."[73]

Many of the synagogue-related activities of the conversas revolved around Yom Kippur. The *Ayuno Mayor* (Great Fast) was a day of special significance for the conversos: it was the day of forgiveness, and the judaizers had, wittingly or unwittingly, committed many transgressions of Jewish law. Accordingly, a conversa like Beatriz González of Toledo was accused of engaging in numerous activities on Yom Kippur such as bathing, cutting her nails, wearing clean clothes, going barefoot, asking for forgiveness of others, "and some nights before the Great Fast, she went to the synagogue to see how the candles burned and how the Jews prayed and she heard them." She was also accused of getting up "many nights before Yom Kippur approximately at midnite in order to pray Jewish prayers, and sometimes going to synagogue to pray, that which only the most devoted of the Jews do."[74] This judaizing conversa was able to observe part of the fast day on her own but felt the need to join or at least witness her Jewish brethren in action. Thus she went to the synagogue, sometimes as a passive observer, sometimes as an active participant, especially during the pre-Yom Kippur period when the prayers of forgiveness (*Selihot*) are recited in the wee hours of the night. One can be certain that the Jews in the synagogue were well aware that she was a conversa, but they apparently did not object to her presence.

Prior to 1492, the temptation to listen to the once-familiar Hebrew liturgy or to attend services at the synagogue was obviously overwhelming for some conversas. Passing by a synagogue and hearing one's childhood melodies flooding out into the street would have had a strong pull on some individuals, whether because of nostalgia or deep-rooted ties to the past. By the late fifteenth century, most of these women were descendants of the descendants of the converts of 1391, and in actuality at least fourth-generation conversas.

Considering the fact that so much time had passed since their ancestors were practicing Jews, it is remarkable that the synagogue still held an attraction for them. But it did attract them, and clearly was more than the object of mere curiosity, whether or not they admitted it. When her father was dying, Mencia Rodríguez de Medina went into a synagogue with her niece, and on another occasion she entered one with the niece's daughters. When she was worried about her son, who was away at war, she begged a Jew to pray to God in the synagogue so that the soldier would return home safely.[75]

In her confession of 1486, Elvira López stated that once, on Yom Kippur eve, she went inside the synagogue to witness the Kol Nidre service on the eve of this holy day. She claimed that she just "wanted to see a synagogue."[76] María Alfonso left her home town and went to the city of Toledo in order to see a Jewish synagogue; she confessed to taking this journey, entering the establishment, and seeing some Jewish children there.[77] The charge presented to Inés Rodríguez of San Pedro is very clear about the intentions of this conversa. She was said to have celebrated the Day of Atonement as being a major holiday and one of great devotion among the Jews; on the eve of the fast, she would go and went to the synagogue to hear the prayers that were prayed there by the Jews, believing that on this day they would be forgiven their sins, and that all that they requested of the Lord would be granted them as the Jews believe.[78]

Again, the traditional and symbolic service of Kol Nidre was attended on the eve of the fast; Inés was joining the Jewish community in prayer, in fasting, and in the quest for repentance as determined by Jewish standards.

When preparing the edict of 1492, the Crown would have done well to examine the confessions of the women in the de la Higuera family. Although some of the information about their interactions with the Jewish community did not become known until after the Expulsion, the testimonies offered by two sisters in 1486 in Alcázar de Consuegra are quite telling and could have been useful for proving the case of the monarchy. The data offered later, in 1493 as well as in 1521, simply offer more details and expand upon the impression created beforehand.

The confessions of two of the sisters in this family can be found in the trial of Inés de la Higuera, who was being tried posthumously in 1521. In 1486, Isabel, who was to face trial along with Inés thirty-five years later, described a lifestyle of sharing and interaction with the local Jewish community that would have delighted the king and queen. She admitted to observing Passover and to eating unleavened bread: "The said unleavened bread was sometimes baked at home, and other times was given to me by some Jews, and likewise sometimes I went to help them bake the said bread in the house of the Jews, my neighbors."[79] The government had claimed that by living in close proximity to the converted population, the Jews would corrupt the New Christians. Here was the living proof.

In addition, Isabel confessed to eating the meat of the Jews, as well as fruits and other foods. Further elaborating upon her transgressions, she confessed that she also "entered the homes of the Jews to celebrate [with them] and to see them, and they entered [her home] to see her, especially a Jewish doctor from the prior of San Juan." Note the informality that existed between the two groups, freely entering one another's home and caring for one another in time of need. Isabel further confessed, "And I gave charity to the Jews." Lastly, she confessed to sometimes eating fowl that was beheaded by the Jews ceremonially.[80]

The confession of Isabel's younger sister, María, also appears in their deceased sister's trial. This testimony is almost identical to that of her older sister. The family had probably prepared the various testimonies beforehand, and the similarity of the wording is almost uncanny. In 1486, María told of eating matsah and baking it at home as well as with her Jewish neighbors; of eating Jewish foods including meat, fruit, and ritually slaughtered birds; of entering Jewish homes; of celebrating with the Jews; of receiving medical care from a Jewish doctor; and of giving alms to Jews.[81] During the interrogation of María in 1521, she clearly said that all of the sisters and their mother observed everything together.[82] The conformity of their confessions certainly leaves this impression.

Had the Crown read these confessions, all its fears and suspicions could have been quickly confirmed. There indeed had been participation, conversation and communication between the two groups. Just as they suspected, the Jews supplied matsah as well as kosher meat to the conversos. A witness, in testimony presented in 1493 from this same file, describes a gathering in which a Jew read to these conversas. María Alfonso, a neighbor of this converso family, said that in the 1480s, "a Jew was reading to them from a book and they [the mother and her daughters of the la Higuera clan] were sitting around the said Jew."[83] A second witness confirmed this report, for she had repeatedly seen the women of the family engaging in such activities. "And she saw Felipe, who was a Jew, who is now a Christian, a resident of this village, who was reading to them at that time in a book, and they were listening to him and were sitting around him, and he was with them sometimes from mealtime until nightfall on the Sabbath."[84] Once again, the pernicious influence of the Jews on the Christians is well documented.

To complete the picture of this family with whom the Jewish community was so intertwined, one must include María's replies to the inquisitor's questions in 1521. The fact that she emphasized total family unity in observance has already been pointed out. The de la Higuera women also entered the booths of Jews "only in order to see them" during the holiday of Sukkot. Last, but by no means least, they observed the festivals of the Jews "when they saw that they were observing them."[85] An admission like this would seal the fate of the Jews in 1492: their very existence was indubitably deleterious to the purity of the Christian way of life. Even if the Jews were not proselytizing, even if they were not instructing the Christians or declaring when the fasts were, their very presence spoke for itself.

These conversas had lived their sinful lives based on the example provided by the nearby Jewish community. Nothing needed to be communicated, no public announcements needed to be made; one had merely to see with one's own eyes when the Jews celebrated a festival and to follow their lead. As will be seen in the upcoming discussion of conversas at work, it was difficult to conceal preparations for most of the Jewish holidays, for each required intensive labor and extensive activity. María de la Higuera had provided the Crown with an ideal justification for the Expulsion Edict: rid Spain of the Jews, and there would no longer be an example to follow. These women who had depended upon the Jewish community and had interacted with them would be bereft of the center of their world; judaizing would certainly die out once the Jews could not inspire them. Perhaps the plan would succeed; despite the passage of time, it is worthwhile trying to determine the validity of this contention. What would happen to the crypto-Jewish community after 1492? Could it survive on its own, and for how long?

The Lives of Judaizing Women after 1492

THE EXPULSION OF THE Spanish Jews had major repercussions for the Jewish exiles as well as for all of their converso brethren interested in judaizing on Spanish soil. During most of the first century following the riots of 1391, those conversos and conversas who desired to maintain contact with Jews were apparently able to do so.[1] As has been demonstrated, the presence of a Jewish community was significant in providing moral as well as instructional support. Goods could be provided through their auspices, and deficiencies in the everyday life of a converso could be compensated. As has been emphasized, this presence was equally significant in the eyes of the Crown, in light of its decision to expel the Jews because of their pernicious influence upon the converts to Christianity and their descendants.

Once the Jewish community was banished, life for the remaining converso community would be affected in numerous ways. In addition to losing their sole source of certain supplies, be they food, wine, or books, the conversos no longer had the benefit of the living example of their forefathers' Judaism. Crypto-Judaism could not be the same as normative Judaism. There are various examples from judaizing life before 1492 that illustrate this fact, for a religion observed clandestinely, by its nature, is destined to change. The fact that it is transmitted by word of mouth and relies upon the fallible human memory is extemely pertinent; such a religion will suffer from inadvertent omissions, additions, and distortions.

How even more difficult would it be to continue a traditional observance of Judaism once the community had been exiled? One need only take a look at the nature of normative Judaism in order to begin to fathom the changes that presented themselves to the crypto-Jewish community after 1492. Judaism is a male-oriented religion. The men are required to fulfill all of the commandments, including those that are time bound; women are exempt from the latter. One of these time-bound duties is to engage in prayer three times daily, preferably in the presence of a quorum of ten; prayer sessions usually take place in a synagogue. The Jewish male trains his son by means of example; the son accompanies him to the synagogue or *beit midrash* (house of study). There additional activities also take place, such as the ongoing study of the Torah, the Commentaries, the Prophets, Midrash, Talmud, and other sacred writings. The center of the Jewish male's world is outside the home; he is tied to the various communal institutions and bound to be present in some of them at very specific times.

As a result, the demise of Jewish institutional life in 1492 left the male Jew without the framework within which he had functioned. Without the synagogue, the house of study, and the communal organizations, he was destined to be at a loss. At the same time, the functionaries, again male, disappeared along with the community. In other words, there were no more ordained rabbis, teachers, judges, ritual slaughterers, circumcisers, butcher shop owners, and the like. These central roles had been held by men, and now, at best, those who remained could hope to organize prayer or study groups clandestinely or to slaughter animals surreptitiously. Lastly, the books of the "People of the Book" accompanied them into exile (or destruction). While a few conversos had precious copies of prayerbooks or Hebrew texts, the converso community was essentially to become a people without a book. The prayerbooks, Bibles, copies of the Talmud, and other texts from the vast literature that is integral to male Jewish life had suffered a fate identical to that of Spanish Jewry itself.

By contrast, the women had never been dependent upon a center outside of the home, nor were they overly dependent upon books.[2] While they often attended synagogue, usually on the Sabbath and on holidays and festivals, and they donated money or oil to this institution and sometimes even cleaned the oil lamps, the women were never more than peripheral in the functioning of the community. The center of their lives was always the home, and when all the other institutions disappeared, they did not have to undergo a major transition.[3] Thus, whereas the men lost their center of Jewish life, the women continued, albeit under extenuating circumstances. The activities that were in the domain of the women were now the focus of attention for the Inquisition and its prosecutors. Traditionally the women had kindled lights on Friday evening, prepared Sabbath meals, baked matsah, observed the dietary laws, and the like; now these observances were to become the major symbols of crypto-Judaism. The new thrust of crypto-Jewish life was no secret to any of the parties involved, including the Holy Tribunal.

Assessing the life of crypto-Jewish women after 1492 is not as simple a task as might be imagined. One would assume that this fateful year would be the natural cutoff date, for the Jewish community was no longer present, and changes ensued. Those conversas who faced trial prior to 1492 had either experienced conversion themselves or, more likely, were descendants of converts, possibly even dating to the riots of 1391. After the Expulsion, those conversas accused by the Inquisition of judaizing might have, but did not necessarily, come from similar stock. This was so because many Jews opted to remain in Spain, having no choice then but to convert in 1492, thus swelling the numbers of New Christians residing on Spanish soil.

These conversos, if they chose to judaize, had the potential to revitalize and sustain the crypto-Jewish community, for they had a rich life experience from which to draw.

At the same time, a problem of periodization arises; one would naturally categorize available Inquisition documents according to the date of the trials that were recorded. However, the fact that a trial was held after 1492 does not necessarily mean that the defendant's judaizing occurred after that year. For example, information might have reached the Holy Tribunal years after the actual practice of heretical acts occurred. The judaizer was still held responsible for these actions, although if he or she could prove that such practices had desisted in the interim, the tribunal would probably take this into account. Likewise, the court could try defendants posthumously for activities carried out prior to the Expulsion. Obviously, neither type of case would help to illuminate crypto-Jewish life after 1492.

Furthermore, the role played by the grace period, when many confessions were recorded and frequently stored for possible future use, must be taken into consideration. Many conversas offered confessions and received absolution along with a severe warning that no mercy would be displayed in case of a relapse. There is no doubt that numerous conversas in Castile presented themselves to the court, particularly between 1483 and 1486, in order to confess. Having done so, these confessants considered themselves to have cleared their names and consciences and to be out of danger. Yet it is amazing to see how often the Inquisition later returned to investigate and probe the sincerity of some of these conversas. If the slightest doubt existed in the mind of the prosecutor, that reconciled conversa found herself on trial. At the outset of a trial of this type, an earlier confession from the 1480s was cited. Then either new information would be amassed to prove that the defendant had relapsed, or interrogations would be arranged to ascertain if information had been withheld at the time of the confession. This type of trial was extremely common during the first decades following the Expulsion and can even be identified in records dating to the 1530s. In these "post-Expulsion" cases, one again uncovers aspects of judaizing prior to 1492, yet sometimes references to late judaizing appear as well.

Those conversas who obviously would not be in the category of supplying information from before 1492 were either those who had been too young to come forth and make a statement during a grace period, or those who converted or whose whose forebears converted rather than leave. It should also be pointed out that the converts of 1492, that last wave of bona fide Jews to be baptized on Spanish soil, stand apart because they formed a distinct group of converts with knowledge and experience of Judaism. The earlier group had the disadvantage of never having seen a practicing Jew and having no personal memory from which to draw, thus relying solely on the memories of those who had taught them about their heritage. This group as well as the converts of 1492 present no complications in terms of periodization, for all of their judaizing experiences occurred either before or after 1492.

This analysis will attempt to differentiate between those conversas whose judaizing began prior to 1492 and those who were initiated or chose to observe after that time. Nonetheless, the majority of conversas on trial during the first decades after the Expulsion were accused of having judaized beforehand. While attempting to deal with these trials chronologically, a parallel attempt will be made to first present those trials that included pre-1492 judaizing without turning the chronological order topsy-turvy.

In a trial that lasted from 1492 to 1493, a conversa from Guadalajara was condemned for judaizing. She was convicted of fasting on Yom Kippur and breaking her fast by eating Jewish cuisine; of observing the Sabbath by lighting clean wicks at an earlier than usual time, by preparing her food beforehand, and by wearing clean clothes; of abstaining from eating or cooking with pork and pork products; and of giving the synagogue oil in the belief that this act would save her soul.[4] It is this final charge that clearly emphasizes the fact that her judaizing was pre-Expulsion and had involved contact with the Jewish community as well.

The trial of María Alvarez, wife of Pedro Alvarez, transpired concurrently with the previous one; the defendant was condemned as well, but since she had died prior to the proceedings, her bones were to be exhumed and burned. In this case, there is no doubt that her judaizing activities can be dated to pre-1492, since she had already passed away by this time. A brief look at the prosecutor's accusation corroborates this fact. This conversa was charged with observing the Sabbath by adorning herself and her home and lighting clean wicks, and with fasting on Yom Kippur, the day she claimed that the heavens opened. Observance of a second fast was attributed to her, namely Tisha B'Av, the Ninth of Av, commemorating the fall of the Temple in Jerusalem. In addition, she had not eaten or cooked with pork, had kashered her meat (salted it in accordance with kosher requirements) had eaten matsah, and had partaken of postburial meals served at low tables while she was seated on the floor. Lastly, she was accused of donating money for oil or of sending oil to the synagogue in the belief that, as a Jewess, she would be saved and forgiven her sins.[5]

Another María Alvarez from the same locale was tried at this same time and was condemned to life imprisonment on the basis of her pre-1492 activities. This defendant was somewhat unusual, for she had converted to Catholicism in 1482, leaving behind a Jewish husband and children. Apparently, she left them for a Christian man, who subsquently proved to be a violent and abusive husband; her life was understandably miserable as a conversa. She related details of her life in her confession of 1492, including having insulted the Church and its symbols. She remembered having given a silver piece to a Jew or Jewess who came to her home seeking alms, and she admitted that she had eaten Jewish foods including matsah when she had been pregnant. María explained that, without her Christian husband's knowledge, she had sent money and other things to her Jewish children and even to some siblings, relatives, and former servants.[6]

The judaizing activities in this case are almost nonexistent, or at best, extremely weak in terms of procuring a successful prosecution. Giving alms to Jews or sending oil to the synagogue are not among the high-priority transgressions on the prosecutor's list; thus the verdict. Yet the torment experienced by this conversa was perhaps more severe than that of facing the Inquisition. She readily admitted the error she had made by converting; her connection to her Jewish children had not been severed, and the beatings she received at the hand of her second husband did not endear her new religion to her at all. Before 1492, she had lived as both a Jew and a Catholic while straddling the two worlds. After 1492, her fate paralleled that of her Jewish family. Her imprisonment exiled her from all of her worlds; it is not known if her Jewish family left Spain or converted, but this María Alvarez was destined to be deprived of any further contact with either family, Jewish or Christian.[7]

The trial of Elvira López of San Gil took place from 1492 to 1494. The incriminating evidence here seems to be based upon the confession she offered years earlier, in 1486; it revealed a great deal of contact with the Jewish community. This is the conversa previously mentioned who ate meat from Jewish and Muslim butcheries; with her husband, owned houses and received gifts such as unleavened bread from the Jewish tenants; went to synagogue one Kol Nidre eve; and served as a Sabbath gentile for a Jewish boarder and sent her handmaiden to light fires for Jewish neighbors. In addition, she fasted on Yom Kippur and ate fish, eggs, and olives while seated on the floor at the *cohuerzo* (postburial meal) of her brother-in-law.[8] All of these activities took place prior to the Expulsion of the Jews.

The 1493 trial of Blanca Rodríguez also contains information about pre-1492 judaizing, for, like María Alvarez, Blanca was deceased at the time of the proceedings. She was found guilty of fasting on Yom Kippur in the company of others; observing the Sabbath by resting and dressing up on that day; giving *zedaka* (charity) to the treasury of the Jewish community as well as oil for the synagogue; eating matsah and requesting it of Jews; and asking Jews how to kasher her meat in order to fulfill the commandments of the Law of Moses.[9] Again, most of the charges against this conversa entailed life that was possible only pre-1492.

Another trial that clearly deals with judaizing long before the Expulsion is that of Mencía Rodríguez; as the defense attorney pointed out, the defendant had died over thirty years prior to 1493, the year in which the charges were made. Mencía frequently had sent oil to the synagogue in honor of the Sabbath as well as Yom Kippur; on the latter fast day, she even went to the synagogue to clean and decorate the lamps there, placing wicks and oil in them.[10] For these sins, her bones were exhumed, she was excommunicated, and her goods were confiscated.

The trials of two conversas from the village of Fuente de Encima demonstrate the same pattern: prosecuting the deceased whose activities clearly took place prior to the Expulsion. Both trials are dated 1493–94. The wives of Alvaro Gil and Juan Alvarez were accused of lighting clean lamps with many wicks which they placed in a special inner cabinet, as Jewish women were said to have done.[11] The former,

María, was also charged with fasting on Yom Kippur, with praying Jewish prayers on that day and on the Sabbath when her face was turned to the wall; during prayer, she was reported to have rocked back and forth as did the Jews.[12] She ate Sabbath stews on this day and never ate pork or anything cooked with it. The latter conversa, also named María, was charged with lighting Sabbath lamps and preparing food in advance for the Jewish day of rest, which she observed while wearing her best clothes.[13]

In 1494, Marina González of Ciudad Real was tried as a relapsed judaizer. Ten years before, she had confessed to numerous observances including the Sabbath, some festivals, Yom Kippur, kashering meat, abstaining from eating pork, celebrating *hadas,* eating at postburial meals, and eating foods forbidden by the Church on certain days (i.e., meat on Fridays or during Lent).[14] The prosecutor accused her of having falsely reconciled herself to the Church and of observing the Sabbath as a day of rest during the past decade. He also accused her of kashering her meat, refraining from eating pork, and not having images of male or female saints in her house.[15] Among the witness testimonies were accounts that while pork was served in her home, she would never partake of such dishes; one witness said that he had never seen her eat such foods or even use the same cup as did her husband, who did eat pork and other nonkosher foods. This witness was a friend of her husband's who frequented the house regularly; he never saw her working or spinning on the Sabbath, although sometimes she pretended to be engaged in some light work so as not to be thought idle.[16] This trial contains information about judaizing that could have occurred before as well as after 1492.

Since Beatriz González of Almagro is classified as having been an insincere penitent, the counts in the accusation presented to her in 1497 concentrate on judaizing that took place after her reconciliation. She was said to have observed the Sabbath by dressing up in clean blouses and donning fancy clothes and hairdos. On this day she celebrated with others whom she visited; thus, by leaving the premises, she cleverly avoided engaging in housework. Beatriz also kashered meat after her reconciliation just as she had done before. Lastly, she did not eat pork or anything cooked with pork products or use utensils that had come in contact with pork.[17] While the nature of these observances was not limited to either before or after the Expulsion, the prosecutor specifically charged that her reconciliation was insincere and that she had continued judaizing for about a decade, thus spanning the two periods.

Mencía Rodríguez of Cadahalso was apparently a relapsed penitent as well, for the accusation presented to her in 1497 began: "she is a heretic and an apostate of our holy Catholic faith by continuing observing the Law of Moses and its rites and ceremonies." The prosecutor accused her of observing the Sabbath and wearing holiday clothes, fasting on Yom Kippur, and contributing money and wine to the synagogue to ensure that oil would be available.[18] Needless to say, the final charge refers to the pre-1492 days, but the other observances could easily have been upheld until the time she was apprehended.

Evidence of relapsing is again found in a trial that took place from 1497 to 1499. Isabel Alvarez of Toledo confessed to three judaizing activities during her trial, more than sufficient to warrant her condemnation. The Church had forgiven her once and had warned her, as it did all penitents, that no mercy would be shown if she appeared before them a second time. Isabel confessed that she fasted on Yom Kippur at least five or six times including the previous year, that she removed the fat from meat she ate, and that on the Sabbath eve, she did not work but rather recited a prayer.[19] Obviously, the crypto-Jewish education that had been received prior to the Expulsion was not easy to eradicate; the Inquisition realized that while the Jews might be gone, the judaizing was not.

The case of Inés Rodríguez does not include a confession from any grace period, although the accusation clearly refers to observances that could have occurred only prior to the Expulsion. Perhaps the witnesses in her trial, for whatever reasons, did not offer testimony until 1498; however, because they had seen her judaizing six or more years earlier, the information offered pertained to the earlier period. Inés was accused of observing the Sabbath by wearing clean clothes, of fasting on Yom Kippur, of attending services at synagogue on that day, and of using Jewish prayer-books in order to pray and be forgiven her sins. She had also been seen throwing a cross on the ground and saying that she had bought it as a toy for the children.[20] This conversa had probably been judaizing all along and had never presented herself to be reconciled; this fact, in the long run, proved to be to her advantage. She was treated as a first-time offender rather than a relapsed heretic, and in this case she had only to gain from her status. As can be seen, when the Jewish community was present in Spain, she made use of some of their institutions and printed matter.[21]

The trial of Catalina Sánchez of Madrid is similar to that of Inés in that while it took place from 1502 to 1503, many of the charges pertain to pre-1492 activities. Catalina has already been cited as the conversa who gave alms to Jewish representatives to help their community, which needed oil and repairs for the synagogue as well as money for shrouds and proper burials for its poorer Jews. In addition, she was accused of fasting on Yom Kippur, a day on which she walked around barefoot and waited for the stars to emerge before breaking her fast with a meat meal. The prosecutor also claimed that she had asked Jews for unleavened bread at the appropriate time of year.[22] Her fate is unknown, but her unacceptable activities spanned the pre- and post-Expulsion years.

In 1507, the inquisitors once again began to investigate a conversa who had been seen having contact with Jews or observing Jewish precepts prior to 1492. A Jew had been seen coming to the home of a conversa in Toledo on Fridays, asking for financial aid; the witness specified that the mistress of the house gave the Jew coins to help pay for his son's studies. The Sabbath had been observed in this household when the mother and all her children, both small and grown, wore clean shirts. In addition, a Jew would come on this day and join the family in a room for two or three hours; the witness did not know in what they were engaged. Then the mother and her eldest daughter would go off to visit relatives, dressed in their best clothes.[23] Although this file is also incomplete, and there is no confession or formal accusation, the witnesses specifically referred to pre-1492 activities during proceedings that took place fifteen years after the Expulsion.

Cases of trials tied to the pre-Expulsion years continue to appear for the second and third decades following this traumatic event. The following three proceedings concern reconciled conversas and thus qualify as trials that include information from the earlier period, since almost all the reconciliations of grace periods that appear in these trials took place in the 1480s. Elvira Martínez of Toledo had confessed to fasting on Yom Kippur, to removing the fat from meat,[24] to lending clothes to Jews, and to eating meat slaughtered by Jews and Moors. She pointed out that because she and her husband lived in very close proximity to a Jewish home, they were recipients of unleavened bread, fruit, and other foods from their neighbors. Elvira had eaten meat, eggs, and cheese on forbidden days of Lent. Lastly, she confessed that she had employed a Jewess as a wetnurse for her son, explaining that she could find no other woman.[25]

During the actual trial from 1509 to 1512, Elvira was questioned about the eating of Jewish foods to which she had referred in her more than twenty-year-old confession. She explained that during a plague she had to abandon her residence; she found shelter in a Jewish home, where she partook of these foods. During this interrogation, she categorically denied ever having lit candles, on the grounds that she had no knowledge of Jewish law. Thus when she visited the Jewish booth, it was merely out of curiosity, and when she ate the toasted chickpeas served there, she was, in fact, functioning as nothing more than a polite guest.[26]

The prosecutor tried to prove, nonetheless, that this conversa was still judaizing; he accused her of continuing to kasher her meat and of preparing herself and her home for the Jewish Sabbath. He claimed that she would simulate spinning on this day of rest and refrain from performing any work. Lastly, he charged her with continuing to fast in honor of Yom Kippur, when she would break the fast by attending a communal meal where fowl was served.[27] Elvira, sixty-five years of age by this time, did not admit to any of the above, and apparently the prosecutor was unable to prove that the defendant was involved in any serious judaizing; the conversa was absolved in 1512.

The second defendant in this group was also absolved at the conclusion of her trial in 1512. Constanza Díaz had confessed in 1484; at this time she admitted to observing the Sabbath by wearing clean clothes, lighting lamps, and preparing her meals before sundown on Fridays. She also baked matsah in her home, cleansed her meat of blood, ate ritually slaughtered meat, and fasted on Yom Kippur. Sometimes, during Jewish holidays, she went to hear Jewish prayers and even entered the synagogue; she had donated oil to the house of worship as well. She referred to attending a Jewish wedding, and attending Jewish postburial *cohuerzos*. In her statement, Constanza very clearly asserted that she had hidden all of her judaizing activities from her husband. She then added that when her father died, she observed various rites; lastly, the conversa admitted to having taken a piece of dough from the *hallah* when she baked it.[28] Needless to say, this conversa was reconciled by the Church.

Twenty-seven years later, Constanza confronted a rather unusual accusation which included mention of a combination of activities from her original confession, other Jewish practices, and an emphasis on her attitudes toward the Inquisition and Old Christians. Normally the charges were listed in the order of their priority or severity; in this case, the first count deals with the conversa's attitudes. The defendant supposedly said that those who were burned as heretics had died as martyrs and were going to paradise, that they had been burned not because of heresy, but rather so that their estates could be sequestered. The second count claimed that during the previous year she had made a similar statement, including the contention that those burned had been good Christians, whose souls were destined for glory. Only in the third count does an allusion to judaizing appear: the accusation is that Constanza beheaded fowl, particularly young pigeons, and would not partake of drowned birds, even if they were already cooked and served to her. The fourth charge states that when a Christian would come to her house asking for alms, she refused, sending the unlucky beggar out the door "with the devil." However, she was charitable and generous to converso beggars. Lastly, she was accused of not eating pork or other food prohibited to Jews.[29] Once again, the prosecutor did not succeed in convicting the defendant; perhaps his failure was due to the emphasis upon her unorthodox and unacceptable sayings but no sufficient proof of her judaizing. This woman clearly did not conceal her feelings toward the Old Christians and the Inquisition, or her sense of solidarity with the converso-Jewish group. Yet by Church law, such attitudes did not suffice by themselves as proof of heresy or judaizing.

The third conversa in this trio faced a lengthy trial, from 1512 to 1522, and unlike the two previous cases, she was condemned. Her confession of 1486 was extremely detailed; perhaps it was this extensive detail that whet the appetite of the prosecutor, who seemed convinced that she had continued her fallen ways. María López of La Membrilla began her list of transgressions by admitting to lighting candles on Friday evenings and doing Sabbath cooking in advance for herself and her family. She admitted that she observed the Sabbath by wearing clean clothes of wool and flax and preparing similar clothes for the members of her family. María fasted on fast days such as Yom Kippur, asking forgiveness of others on that day; at that time, she also listened to others read from books. She celebrated other holidays such as Passover, when she and her household would secretly eat matsah. This conversa gave alms to Jews and removed the fat from meat.

María confessed to having observed *hadas* after births and to eating fish and eggs at low tables following burials. She blessed her children by placing her hand upon their heads and they would kiss her hand.[30] Some of the Christian holidays and Sundays had been abrogated; meat, milk, and eggs were sometimes eaten on forbidden days. The conversa had eaten meat of animals and fowl that were ceremonially slaughtered, and had refrained from eating rabbit, drowned birds and animals, pork, and fish without scales. Sometimes, when she was baking bread, she took out a piece of dough and tossed it in the fire. When her children were ill, she permitted drops of oil to be applied to them.[31] Lastly, María said that when she menstruated, she slept in a separate bed from her husband, and she bathed ceremonially after completion of her cycle.[32]

The accusation that this conversa faced twenty-six years later was not based entirely upon the earlier confession. First María was accused of continuing in her erroneous path of heresy by observing the Sabbath and abstaining from doing housework, dressing in her best clothes, and refusing to sell the merchandise that she normally sold during the week. In addition, she was charged with lighting clean lamps with new wicks on Fridays, at an earlier time than she lit them during the week. The prosecutor claimed that she cleansed meat, removing the fat carefully just as she did before her reconciliation. This conversa was also said to have offered a piece of dough to be burned when she was baking *hala* [sic], reciting certain words at that time.

The prosecutor was convinced that María was meeting with others in order to judaize, and the last two counts emphasize this belief. She was charged with joining other heretics on Friday nights and Sabbath days, when they ate cold food that had been prepared beforehand; she was also suspected of bathing on Friday afternoons. Lastly, when these judaizers gathered together, they spoke of the honor they had for the Law of the Jews, how it is the good and true law, and at the same time, they belittled the Catholic faith and those who observed it.[33] This time, the prosecutor had a stronger case against the defendant, who was ultimately condemned to the stake in 1522.

While almost all of the aforementioned conversas had offered confessions on their own volition during grace periods, and all of the others made references to judaizing that had clearly occurred before 1492, this was not necessarily the case for all of the conversas on trial. Sometimes it is difficult to discern when the judaizing had taken place, for when the trial transpired in the 1490s, the likelihood that there had been observance during the pre-Expulsion period was great.

For example, Mencía Díaz of Illescas was tried from 1498 to 1499. According to the relatively short accusation, in honor of the Law of Moses she observed the Sabbath when she dressed up festively as did the Jews. In addition, she cleansed the meat she was to eat, splitting open legs in order to remove the nerve, in compliance with the "dead" Law of Moses. She believed that by observing this law, she would achieve the salvation of her soul.[34] These particular charges could pertain to any judaizing at any time; the time could have been before or after the Expulsion or cover both periods.

The trial of María Franca took place from 1511 to 1512; five main charges were presented by the prosecutor to this resident of Moral del Campo de Calatrava. First, the defendant was accused of observing the Sabbath by abstaining from house-work, sweeping and cleaning the house beforehand, and wearing clean and festive clothes such as a French skirt; sometimes she feigned illness in order to retire early without arousing suspicion; prior to doing so, she would light new wicks in the lamps that she had cleaned and prepared, letting them burn out by themselves only on Friday nights.

This conversa, whose mother, Mayor González of Ciudad Real, had faced the In-quisition as well, was also accused of taking a piece of dough and tossing it in the fire. Third, María supposedly removed the fat from meat, opening legs of meat and extracting the vein or nerve, in other words, preparing her meat according to Jew-ish law. Also, she was said to have eaten meat on days prohibited by the Church. Fi-nally, the prosecutor claimed that in the company of others while seated at festive tables covered with clean tablecloths, she would dine on hens, capons, and other birds and meats in honor of holidays such as Passover; in addition, Passover fell during Lent when partaking of such foods was forbidden. María did not succumb to torment, however, nor did the prosecutor manage to convict her at that time.[35]

A few years later, Francisca Alvarez of Puente de Arzobispo was not as successful with her defense, for she was convicted of judaizing. There is no mention of a grace period confession; it seems that her observances occurred in the decade or two af-ter the Expulsion. In 1514, the prosecutor accused the defendant of abrogating the Christian holidays and Sabbaths by working on those days precisely as she would on normal workdays. Next, she was charged with neither eating pork nor cooking with it; instead she cooked with olive oil and chickpeas as do the Jews. She was also said to have removed the fat from meat and to have washed it thoroughly, draining the blood as do the Jews. The conversa did not cross herself or make appropriate signs or pray as a true Christian would, either inside or outside of her home. She observed the Jewish Sabbath by dressing up, resting, preparing stews and other food on Fridays that would be eaten cold on that day, and lighting clean lamps with new wicks on Friday nights. Part of her judaizing included refraining from eating hare, rabbit, or other meats forbidden to Jews. Finally, a rather unusual statement appeared: Francisca was perceived by others, including her husband, to be a Jewess in precisely the same manner as before her baptism.[36] This assertion also explains the court's emphasis on her poor performance as a Christian, a point emphasized only slightly less than her performance as a crypto-Jew. As was mentioned earlier, the defendant was convicted and relaxed by the secular arm; the ecclesiastical judge had to hand over the prisoner to the secular arm so that capital punishment could be carried out.

Mayor Meléndez was, like Francisca, a first-generation conversa; before her bap-tism in 1493, her name had been Reyna. Yet like María Franca, she offered no con-fession, even after facing torture; she too offered many tachas and was ultimately absolved. The accusation in the file of this sixty-year-old woman was relatively short. She was accused of lighting many new wicks in clean lamps on Friday evenings at an earlier hour than usual; it seems that she then did not place the lamps in their usual spot. In addition, she was charged with removing the fat and nerves from meat and the legs of meat, cleansing it all thoroughly, and removing the blood before she cooked, eating it as would a Jew. Lastly, she was accused of not eating meat containing blood, pork, or lard. The prosecutor continued most descriptively: if the conversa saw that pork was being roasted or lard dissolved, she removed herself to a room which she closed tightly, covering up any holes so that the odor of the pork would not enter.[37] While this might well have been an accurate report, Mayor did not suffer the ancitipated fate for a judaizer, because she had built an effective defense.

Two final trials of women from Hita will be cited in this discussion of conversas; neither could have judaized prior to the Expulsion, since both converted after that time. Both trials began in 1520 and both defendants were absolved. The trial of Beatriz López née Bellida lasted a year, while her neighbor, Isabel García née Clara, remained imprisoned until 1523. As will be seen, both faced truly formidable lists of charges.[38]

The prosecutor began the first trial by accusing the eighty-year-old defendant, Beatriz, of Sabbath observance, emphasizing the fact that she dressed in clean, festive clothes in honor of the Law of Moses. He added that in honor of this day, the defendant refrained from working, retiring to her bed earlier on Fridays than on other nights. Third, at an earlier hour than during the rest of the week, she lit clean lamps with a greater number of wicks. She also removed the fat from meat and then ate the meat ceremonially.

Beatriz was accused of preparing Sabbath stews and Jewish cuisine such as a combination of meat, onions, chickpeas, and crushed spices all cooked together for a long time; this entree was eaten with great enthusiasm. Next, this conversa was charged with eating unleavened bread. In addition, the birds she consumed were beheaded in secret sites; once this task was done, she covered the blood of the dead birds with earth and ashes. The defendant was said to have cut open the leg of mutton lengthwise in the Jewish way and to take out certain things, then to have washed the meat with a good deal of water until the meat was white and bloodless; she ate it in this manner as do the Jews.

The ninth charge stated that Beatriz did not eat spotted dogfish or conger-eel or octopus or hare or rabbit, although these animals were brought to her home; she also did not eat pork or anything made with pork. Only toward the end of the trial did the prosecutor invoke her laxity as a Christian. She supposedly did not pray or cross herself or do outwardly Christian acts. Lastly, she belittled the saints of the Church, never swearing by them, and she covered up the heretical activities of other apostates.[39]

When confronted with these counts of judaizing, and warned that she should provide a full confession, Beatriz denied the validity of the denunciation; she claimed never to have apostasized or engaged in any Jewish ceremony after she was baptized in Lisbon in 1496. On the contrary, she stated, she had lived as a good, faithful Catholic Christian, attending mass and sermons and other divine offices; she observed the (Sunday) Sabbath and all of the holidays mandated by the Church. The defendant made a lengthy plea for herself, attesting to her innocence and requesting that justice be fulfilled.[40]

The court ordered torment in order to procure a confession, but after a short while decided to desist because of the age of the defendant. In her defense, the conversa and her son provided thirty-four witnesses to attest to her upright life as a Christian. Beatriz herself insisted that she was not a heretic. True, when she fell ill, she had refrained from eating pork and eel, but she ate the broth of the eel; she had never even seen an octopus. Besides, she protested, one who cuts open the leg of meat lengthwise or refrains from eating certain foods or washes meat or lights candles at night does not qualify as a heretic.

This particular proceeding was sent to Valladolid to be evaluated in order to determine how to proceed with sentencing; the octogenarian was ultimately absolved, and given some penances, such as six pilgrimages to be made on Saturdays, certain prayers to recite, and a modest fine to be paid. The conversa's mettle had served her well, yet there is no doubt that her age played a factor in the court's display of mercy, because, in actuality, the defense had not disproved the many claims of the prosecutor.

The accusation presented to Isabel García was even lengthier and more descriptive than that of her neighbor, Beatriz. The younger, fifty-year old defendant was similarly charged first with Sabbath observance and dressing in clean clothes and festive attire in its honor. In addition, she was said to have cooked or arranged to have food cooked on Fridays for the Sabbath; in honor of the Law of Moses, she and others would eat these victuals without warming them up. Third, Isabel was said to have adorned her home and swept it on Friday afternoons as do the Jews. As in Beatriz's second count, she was accused of retiring to bed earlier on this night and refraining from everyday housework. According to the prosecutor, on Friday nights, both conversas of Hita lit many more clean wicks in clean lamps at an earlier hour than was habitual during the week.

The sixth charge paralleled the previous case: the defendant had eaten unleavened bread. Next, Isabel was accused of joining others to drink wine from the wine cellar, which they blessed by Jewish rite precisely as done by the Jews. The eighth count was similar but by no means identical to the seventh presented to Beatriz. Before Isabel beheaded any bird, she would examine the knife and pass it by her nail in the Jewish way, and then slaughter the bird, watching over the blood per the Jewish rite. Moreover, the defendant cut the birds' claws above the wings and then dealt with them according to the rite of the Jews.[41]

The next four charges dealt with death and mourning rites and were compiled on the basis of various graphic witness testimonies. The first of them, the tenth count, stated that Isabel and others were behind a closed door for nine days following a certain person's [her husband's] death, sitting with a bandage, grieving and singing and crying and clapping their hands as do the Jews.[42] Next, the defendant was accused of going to console certain persons who were mourning the death of a deceased individual and of lamenting with them, behind the door, in the Jewish way. The twelfth charge claimed that Isabel and others lamented the death of a certain person by walking around the bed of the deceased, climbing on top of the bed at times, and at other times climbing underneath it, praying in the Jewish way by raising and lowering their heads. In addition, the defendant bathed the body of a deceased person according to Jewish ceremony.

The list of charges seems endless as the prosecutor named other activities such as the observance of dietary laws. Like Beatriz, Isabel was accused of opening the leg of mutton lengthwise and removing certain things like fat and the nerve as the Jews would do. Also like her neighbor, she was accused of washing the meat with large quantities of water and then applying salt; she would place the meat in a certain place until it was entirely cleansed of the blood, according to Jewish rite. The sixteenth charge concerned the eating of Sabbath stews and meatballs and other Jewish foods; also she ate food that was prepared in advance. Isabel supposedly joined others in entering a secret location in order to carry out Jewish ceremonies in honor of the Law of Moses.

The final two charges were the weakest in terms of attaining conviction. Isabel was charged with speaking badly of Christianity and with committing many more crimes of heresy and apostasy than were listed by the prosecutor.[43] She tried to counter these last two accusations by presenting thirty-five witnesses testifying to the fact that she had been a good Christian since converting in Badajoz in 1493; she took communion frequently and even went on pilgrimages. She and her son also rejected the witnesses for the prosecution on the grounds that they were their mortal enemies and infamous individuals. After unsuccessfully submitting Isabel to torture, the court decided to declare her innocence. However, it seems more likely that because she and her son had succeeded in casting serious aspersions on their prosecution witnesses, there was no means of convicting her without procuring a confession; this judaizer had beaten the system.

In retrospect, the types of observances that appeared in these accusations are fairly comprehensive. The inquisitors realized that the last wave of conversas created by the Expulsion was still a real challenge to confront; some Jews had even left Spain, only to convert and return later. The Jewish memory of these individuals was neither distorted nor faded; they knew the details of Jewish observance. While the loss of the Jewish community was significant after 1492, it was not totally devastating for the judaizer; as has been seen, a woman who had converted in her own lifetime had personal experience from which to draw and could then create a clandestine life that was well grounded in her not-so-distant past.

3

Messianic Turmoil circa 1500

In 1500, an unexpected turn of events created a new set of challenges for the Inquisition and the Castilian converso community. A number of visionaries of Jewish ancestry appeared on the scene, all claiming to be prophets bearing a message of salvation that was specifically directed at the conversos.[1] Needless to say, this group of converts and their descendants provided fertile ground for such tidings. Almost every family had had an encounter of some sort with the Inquisition; those who seemed to have been spared still contended with constant fear that would not dissipate as long as they remained on the Peninsula. Although the judaizers were in the most precarious position of all, no one with converso or Jewish blood could live a secure life in sixteenth-century Castile.

Three different messianic sets of tidings were proclaimed at the turn of the sixteenth century, all emanating from the region of Extremadura.[2] These reports of halcyon days were extremely appealing to the converso community, and many conversas in Castile jumped on the messianic bandwagon. Two of the messengers themselves were conversas: the most eminent and charismatic was Inés of Herrera, although the second, Mari Gómez of Chillón also had a significant following.[3] At the same time, a converso butcher named Luis Alonso made promises of better days and imminent redemption, approaching some of the same conversos who would be influenced by Inés; the earliest accounts of contact with these individuals dates to 1495.

The Inquisition realized that a movement of this nature was extremely dangerous as well as disruptive; it had the potential to spread quickly throughout Spain and to awaken dormant Jewish proclivities in conversos who had never before judaized. Clearly, it needed to be nipped in the bud; expedient and drastic measures had to be taken to round up all of its followers as quickly as possible. Since such tidings had wide appeal, followers ranged from extremely young conversas to older women who had been reconciled in the 1480s. In the eyes of the Inquisition, the involvement of the latter group demonstrated the reality of the ever-present danger of relapsing. This phenomenon thus substantiated the claims of those who contended that even after seemingly honest acts of reconciliation, the Jewishness of these converts could never be uprooted. There seemed to be a potential judaizer in each and every converso; as a result, the messianic fervor was sometimes an initiation into Judaism and sometimes a reintroduction to a lifestyle that had once been experienced.

The cases under discussion are divided into two categories: those who relapsed and returned to their Jewish ways, and those whose first involvement with Judaism derived directly from this messianic fervor. Naturally, one would assume that among conversas in the former category, the level of observance would be much higher than that of the neophytes, for they had a storehouse of experience from which to draw (see chapter 4).

The first two women under discussion were both from Herrera and had similar experiences. Each had confessed during a grace period in 1486 and was later tried in 1500. There is no doubt that the first conversa, María Alonso, had been a serious judaizer; her confession is extremely detailed and lengthy, containing forty-one items.[4] She began by referring to Sabbath observances and preparations such as sweeping, adorning her house, preparing food in advance, removing a piece from the hallah, lighting candles, and wearing clean shirts. In honor of Yom Kippur, María first pared her nails and bathed, then fasted and remained barefoot throughout the day. She would light candles and dress festively in honor of other holidays; before Passover, the confessant would clean her house thoroughly. She also observed various mourning rites, bathed the deceased, and ate at *cohuerzos;* she likewise observed purity rituals when she menstruated.

Her list included observance of dietary laws, kashering meat, and refraining from eating forbidden animal meat. María threw drops of oil on her children when they were ill. She ate forbidden foods during Lent and did not cross herself at the appropriate times; her attendance at mass was irregular, and various Sundays and holy days of the Church were not observed. This conversa had a great deal of contact with Jews and even admitted to having spoken ill of the Holy Inquisition. There is little that seems to be missing in this confession; María appears to have lived close to a full Jewish life and had attempted, to the best of her ability, to ignore the fact that she was Catholic.

As a result, not surprisingly, in 1500, the Holy Tribunal was by no means lenient with María after she again confessed to judaizing. The defendant stated that about two years prior, she had been in the house of Luis Alonso when she heard him preach.[5] He was telling all the conversos to fast and observe the Sabbath and to believe in the Law of Moses; in this manner, he assured them, their present state of captivity would be terminated, for they would be transported to the Promised Land. María was convinced by his declarations and began to observe fasts which lasted until the stars emerged at night; once or twice she managed to keep the fast of Yom Kippur, and on this day she would refrain from work.

Because María knew how to observe the Sabbath, reenactment was not difficult, and again she made it her day of rest, lighting candles on Friday evenings and and decorating her home. She also reverted to kashering meat and abstained from pork and other forbidden meats and fish. Someone had even tried to teach her a Jewish prayer but met with no success in this venture. María believed that the Law of Moses was given through Elijah and the Messiah. At the end of her statement to the inquisitors, she pointed out that these ideas were the teachings of the daughter of Juan Estevan, who had implanted in her these beliefs and hopes, which were so offensive to the Holy Catholic Faith.

This conversa had indeed offended the Church by heeding the bearers of these false prophecies, and even more so by returning to the Jewish faith. Both she and her neighbor Mayor González were relaxed by the secular arm in 1500, since there was no need to tarry when dealing with such blatant and dangerous heresy.

Mayor, like María, had a rich crypto-Jewish heritage from which to draw.[6] In 1486, she confessed to observing the Sabbath by lighting candles, taking out a piece of dough when she baked hallah, sweeping and decorating the house, preparing food in advance, refraining from work, wearing clean clothes, setting the table with a clean tablecloth, sleeping on clean sheets, and so on. She fasted, especially on Yom Kippur, on which day she also rested, went barefoot, and asked forgiveness of others; on the day before this fast, she secretly bathed.

Mayor observed other festivals when she could do so without impediment. She baked matsah and ate it. In addition, she gave alms to poor Jews and donated money for oil for the synagogue. She ate at postburial meals while seated on the floor, and she blessed her children in the Jewish manner. Mayor kashered her meat, ate meat slaughtered by Jews, and refrained from eating forbidden meat and fish. She had occasionally been in the company of Jews when she heard them read from books. This crypto-Jewess also separated herself from her husband when she was unclean.

Some Sundays and holy days were abrogated, and at times this judaizer had spoken irreverently of the Church. She admitted that her heart was not in the Church services she attended; despite these frank statements, she was permitted to be reconciled to the Church in 1486. Yet her life was to be drastically changed scarcely a decade later, for she said in her trial that in about 1496, she came into contact with Luis Alonso, the prophet. He revealed to her a dream that he had had in Chillón in which his deceased father-in-law appeared and told him about many marvelous things that were awaiting the conversos in the Promised Land. However, in order to merit this reward, the conversos had to believe in the Law of Moses, keep Jewish fasts, observe the Sabbath, and perform other deeds commanded by Jewish law.

Consequently, Mayor began to fast on Mondays and Thursdays from dawn until after the evening stars appeared. She also attempted to observe the Sabbath properly, cleaning her lamps as well as her home, wearing clean blouses, and sometimes preparing meat and fish dishes in advance. In addition, she reverted to kashering her meat and to not eating pork and pork products as well as other forbidden meat and fish. While under the influence of these prophecies, she believed that Elijah and the Messiah were en route and that when they arrived, she would be carried off, together with all the other conversos, to the Promised Land; there they would enjoy the riches and good life that awaited them.

Mayor was exposed to more than one contemporary prophet;[7] she had also been to the home of Inés, the daughter of Juan Esteban, and heard her tidings. There she had been taught a prayer which was to be recited at the time of fasts; she was also instructed to say "Holy, Holy" on fast days.[8] Once, when she was told that it was Yom Kippur, she donned a clean blouse and fasted all that day.

While recounting her sins in 1500, Mayor realized that this time she was in grave trouble with the Church. Thus in her confession, she cast aspersions on these prophets and attempted to denigrate herself and even portray herself as disturbed. This ploy did not convince the prosecution, which accused her of having anxiously awaited the Messiah and rejecting Church beliefs and practices for those of the Law of Moses.

Other relapsed conversas were discovered in the hometown of Inés; both Beatriz González and María García faced trials, accused of having fallen prey to the bearers of false messianic hopes. Like their neighbors María and Mayor, these two women presented the Holy Tribunal with two different confessions during their lives, one during a grace period in the 1480s and the other in 1500 during the trial proceedings. It is clear that all four of these women had been serious judaizers before the establishment of the Inquisition. All had relapsed and were subsequently condemned by the tribunal.

Beatriz said in 1486 that she observed the Sabbath by lighting clean wicks, preparing food beforehand, and wearing a clean blouse.[9] She observed various fasts, in particular that of Yom Kippur, when she asked forgiveness of her relatives. She celebrated Passover, especially by eating matsah. In addition, when a family member died, the conversa ate meals of fish served at low tables. Beatriz gave alms to Jews and charity to synagogues. She ate meat on days forbidden by the Church, meat that she had prepared according to Jewish law.

After she menstruated, she bathed according to *halakha* (Jewish law). This conversa explained that she did not eat the various kinds of meat or fish forbidden to Jews. Also she and her father read from a Jewish book, and she and her mother had once entered a synagogue. She further declared that her uncle would bless her in the Jewish manner, and when she kneaded dough, she removed a piece which she tossed into the fire. This was all she claimed to remember at that time.

Her confession of 1500 was even longer. Beatriz estimated that she encountered Luis Alonso in 1495 or 1496, the earliest date reported by any of these conversas. The prophet came to Herrera and told of amazing things that he had seen in a vision in which his father-in-law appeared to him. Because a full report would have been too long, the conversa streamlined her account. The vision dealt with the pain the conversos suffered as Christians, made an appeal to those of them with children who were "lost" (presumably to Judaism), and cajoled them to return to certain practices. These practices included fasting, giving alms, and observing the Sabbath, especially by lighting candles in its honor. Only in this manner would God take them out of captivity and transport them to the Holy Land.

Beatriz had also been in the presence of the maiden from Chillón, who told her that she could leave her sins behind; the defendant told the inquisitors that she (temporarily) left her senses when she believed this prophetess.[10] This conversa had also encountered Inés, something that is by no means surprising, for they were neighbors. She admitted to believing everything she had heard and to trying secretly to observe again. Thus Beatriz engaged in frequent fasting and in adorning her house on Friday evenings, when she lit candles earlier than on other nights of the week. She observed the Sabbath, wearing clean shirts, preparing food in advance, and eating these meals with her entire family.

In addition, Beatriz explained that she and her husband instructed their children to observe with them on the Sabbath as well as on fast days. This couple also prepared their meat according to Jewish law; Beatriz stopped eating pork products, drowned animals, and fish without scales, and she gave alms. She mentioned reciting two Jewish prayers, which she claimed she could no longer recall.

The conversa admitted that she had believed Elijah would come to predict the future; the Messiah would subsequently appear, for he was destined to transport all of the conversos to the promised Holy Land. The conversos had to observe many days as holidays in order to be totally prepared for the journey to this desirable destination. She also believed what Inés told her about the resurrection of the dead and how they would join forces with the living to journey together to those lands. Apparently a conversa named Elvira García sang some Jewish songs in honor of the coming messianic days. Thus Beatriz observed the Jewish laws mentioned, in preparation for the salvation of the oppressed conversos.

The judaizing experience of María García, also of Herrera, was comparable to that of Beatriz. In 1496, this conversa confessed to a multitude of crypto-Jewish activities.[11] She lit her lamps earlier on Friday evenings, allowing the wicks to burn out on their own. María had swept and adorned her home, prepared food in advance for her household, attempted to refrain from work when she could, wore clean clothes of cloth and linen and clean headpieces, and set the table with clean tablecloths.

On Yom Kippur she secretly bathed, rested, asked forgiveness of others, went barefoot, fasted and spent most of the day standing.[12] She observed holidays to the best of her ability, that is, when she felt fairly certain that she would not be noticed; on Passover she baked and ate matsah. When some relatives passed away, she ate fish and eggs at postburial meals.

María admitted that she went to confession so as not to be reprimanded, hoping to appear to be a good Christian. When she heard mass, she did not really adore the savior. She gave alms to Jews and donated oil for their synagogues. In addition, when her children kissed her hand, she placed it on their heads and blessed them in the Jewish manner.

This conversa kashered her meat after it was first slaughtered by Jews; sometimes they slaughtered fowl within the confines of her home. She abstained from consuming forbidden fish and meat; if and when she did succumb to eating either, she did so not by choice or any desire to abrogate the Law of Moses. Some celebrations were held with Jews, and sometimes she said hateful and crazy words that were scornful of our Lord. She ate meat, eggs, cheese, and milk on forbidden days and during Lent.

When María baked, she removed a piece of dough and threw it in the fire. She did not observe some of the Christian Sabbaths and holidays. When this conversa gave birth or menstruated, she separated herself from her husband and did not return to him until after bathing. On the seventh night after giving birth, an evening of celebration (*hadas*) took place in her home. The confessant also read from Jewish books and said she washed her hands ceremonially prior to retiring at night.[13] An additional statement included details of washing and salting meat as well as of how she cut her nails before taking ritual baths. Again, a rather full picture of crypto-Jewish life was presented by this conversa, ever so penitently in 1486.

In 1500, María told the court that two or two and a half years before, she had heard about Luis Alonso, the butcher. He had recounted that when the Inquisition came to Herrera, his deceased father-in-law appeared before him and revealed to Luis that he was in pain because the Law of Moses—in particular, the Sabbath and fast days—were not being observed. It was important that all who desired salvation observe the rites and ceremonies, he warned. María received her information from Isabel Alonso of Chillón and her niece, who added that many more things were being prepared for the conversos in that Holy Promised Land.[14]

Thus this conversa observed some Jewish fasts until nightfall whenever she could; these included the weekly Monday and Thursday fasts as well as that of Yom Kippur. She tried to refrain from working on the Sabbath. In 1500, she heard Inés, the daughter of Juan Estevan, who reinforced her beliefs and convinced her of the correctness of her actions. Consequently in September, she told her husband that they should fast and ask forgiveness of certain persons. Eventually her daughters were convinced as well, and they all observed the Sabbath together, donning clean blouses, lighting lamps, and preparing food in advance. She excused herself from eating pork and other unkosher meat, drowned birds, and fish without scales. She kashered meat ceremonially.

María explained that she believed Elijah would come to carry all the conversos to the Promised Land. She looked for signs to behold in the sky, since Inés had presented a detailed description of what to expect, including the color of the ship that would transport them. As part of her practices, she gave alms to poor conversos. A look at the accusation reveals that the prosecutor was very concerned that the defendant had convinced others to join this movement; she had even told them that they were born at a good time, for the Lord's law had returned and, although it had come late, they would not be left behind in the doorway with the nonbelievers. María was far too involved in the movement to be forgiven and was relaxed by the secular arm in 1501.

Mencía Alvarez, another local of Herrera, suffered a fate similar to her neighbor's. The file of the wife of Diego Alvarez does not contain her confession of reconciliation; the extant information, namely, the accusation and the confession of 1500, do detail the messianic activities of this judaizer. The prosecutor began by describing her observance of the dead Law of Moses by celebrating the Sabbath and dressing up in her finest clothes and clean blouses as on festival days. In addition, as the Jews did, she fasted on Mondays and Thursdays until the stars emerged.

The defendant was awaiting the Messiah, believing that he would appear and carry her and her converso relatives to the Promised Land according to Jewish credence. Moreover, in order to be prepared for him, she celebrated many days as festival days, taking pleasure in them with great mirth and making new clothes; she also believed that she would be transported in the outfit she was wearing at the time of the Coming. Furthermore, she strove to certify the arrival of the Messiah by looking to the sky; she said that she saw signs indicating to her whence he would come. The defendant also conversed and collaborated with other heretics about this and went to hear the one assumed to be a prophetess. She then obeyed her and believed what she said and instructed. She voluntarily engaged in the aforesaid ceremonies and gave alms to those heretics who were believing and observing Jewish ceremonies of the Law of Moses.

In her confession, Mencía dated her relapse to 1497. In that year, Leonor Martínez, the sister of Luis Alfonso, told her how Luis's long-deceased father-in-law appeared to him while he was out on a walk one day; the information this relative relayed was simply amazing. This gentleman was none other than Mencía's own grandfather, so the power of the related experience was even greater for her than for the two previous conversas. In the long run, he insisted that the Law of Moses and its ceremonies be observed; otherwise no one would be saved! The conversa was extremely confused by this news. A few days later, she married and subsequently she moved with her husband to Herrera.

Ironically, it was her young spouse who espoused the Law of Moses and believed that one should fast on Yom Kippur and observe the Sabbath by dressing in clean and festive clothes. Whenever she could, she lit candles on Friday afternoons before sundown in honor of the Sabbath and cleaned her house and decorated it to the best of her ability. She also prepared Sabbath meals on Fridays which were later eaten cold. She tried to avoid consumption of bacon, hare, rabbit, and drowned birds or animals, and she drained red meat of blood, washing it with water numerous times, removing the vein of the leg either with a knife or by hand. All these activities were done in honor of the dead Law of Moses, willingly and with the full consent of her husband. They also asked one another for forgiveness on Yom Kippur day.

In addition, in about 1499, the confessant's mother came to Herrera to visit her and her sister and brought tidings from Luís Alonso and Mari Gómez of Chillón. She believed these messianic advocates and received instruction and encouragement to observe Jewish law. She then began to fast on Mondays and Thursdays, especially after hearing about what happened to Inés, the daughter of Juan Estevan; she and her mother were convinced by the message of the prophetess and did whatever they could. The instruction she received included recitation of a blessing when she washed her hands. Sometimes she gave alms with intentions of helping conversos.

Lastly, the confessant explained that when Inés and the woman from Chillón told her that all the *confesos* would depart for those holy and rich lands, she refrained from doing housework in light of the expectations she had,[15] Here is the first time that abstaining from daily chores is connected not to the Sabbath or a holiday, but rather to messianic expectations, complementing the reports of others who were wearing their best clothes daily. Mencía added the fact that she was consorting with fellow messianic followers who espoused identical hopes and beliefs to hers. The accusation and confession contain similar information, but this confessant's style is far more expressive and provides greater insight as to the mindset of the conversos at the time.

Isabel Rodríguez of Agudo is the sixth relapsed judaizer who succumbed to this messianism; her file contains two sets of confessions.[16] Confessions are not available for all seven of the remaining relapsed conversas to be discussed; as a matter of fact, four have no confession available. Both of Isabel's confessions were shorter in length than those of her cohorts, but her devotion to Judaism at both junctures in her life is no less obvious.

This conversa also began by admitting to Sabbath observance, when she lit or ordered lamps to be lit, when she prepared food on Friday and celebrated to the best of her ability, wearing clean clothes on that day. When she was aware of the date of holidays, she would observe them; in particular, she celebrated Passover, baking and consuming matsah. The conversa fasted often, especially on Yom Kippur, at which time she asked forgiveness of her relatives. Isabel often prayed by herself and heard her husband pray from a book of Jewish prayers. Sometimes she bathed and would perform the ceremonial *tibila*.[17] Fish and eggs were eaten at postburial meals, and alms were given to both Jews and Muslims.

Isabel ate meat slaughtered by Jews and did not eat those things forbidden by the Law of Moses. When she kneaded bread, she removed a piece of dough and threw it into the fire. Seven nights after she gave birth, relatives came to eat fruit and sing and dance and celebrate the *hadas*. This conversa had abrogated some of the Church holy days and had also eaten meat, eggs, milk, and cheese during Lent. Lastly, she confessed that her children had kissed her hands when she placed them on their heads in order to bless them Jewishly. At this time, Isabel was reconciled to the Church.

Like the women from Herrera, this resident of Agudo confronted the Holy Tribunal later in her life, in 1501. Her confession is very powerful as a first-hand attestation of the influence of the *moza* (young unmarried maiden) of Herrera. Isabel had heard that the daughter of Juan Estevan had ascended to heaven and was approached there by an angel; this maiden had told of the marvelous things she had seen and how Elijah was due to come and prophesy before the Messiah came to take the conversos to the Promised Land. Having heard all this, she decided to go and see for herself; Isabel paid a visit to Inés's home in Herrera.

In the home of Juan Estevan, she heard about a journey to these lands and was assured that "we should not fear the Inquisition, because it is God's will"; according to the defendant, all her fears were allayed by this visit. "Convinced of these false words and deceptive accounts of our adversary, the devil, she willfully, yet under deception," believed all she had heard from the maiden. Isabel was then convinced that the Law of Moses would provide her salvation and did what the maiden said, such as fasting on some Mondays and Thursdays until the evening stars appeared.

Likewise, under the influence of the maiden, she observed the Sabbath, at times excusing herself from doing housework, and lighting candles on Friday evenings at the appointed time. In addition, this conversa removed the fat from meat and refrained from eating pork products or dead or drowned animals, rabbit or hare, and fish without scales. The false hope that she had of going to the Promised Land inspired her to make a special blouse for herself to wear for the occasion. Lastly, she often looked to the sky in the hope of seeing one of the various signs described by the maiden. Isabel maintained this belief until she learned that the inquisitors had ordered the moza to be seized in Herrera and that she was indeed taken prisoner.

The penultimate of the relapsed conversas' files that contains any confession at all is that of Elvira Núñez of Toledo. The file is incomplete, lacking the accusation, although there are numerous witnesses attesting to the defendant's messianic beliefs.[18] The confession therein is from 1486, when Elvira referred to observing some Jewish fasts, especially on Yom Kippur, when she sometimes bathed on the previous day. On this holiday, she went barefoot, asked forgiveness of certain individuals, prayed Jewish prayers all day and night, and at times joined with others. Some Sabbath days and festivals were celebrated at which time she wore clean clothes.

Matsah was eaten a few times, and birds were slaughtered ceremonially; all was done as secretly as possible. The fat was removed from meat, and alms were given to those Jews who petitioned her. Sometimes Elvira spoke highly of the Law of Moses and even told some people that observing it would bring about salvation. At times she did not eat certain foods because they were forbidden by Jewish law. This conversa abrogated some Sundays and Christian holy days; she occasionally ate foods that the Church forbade. While this confession underemphasizes Sabbath observance, Elvira was aware of this day as well as of many other holidays and appears to have judaized with devotion.

In 1501, the prosecutor managed to find witnesses who provided a good deal of information about this Toledana's activities. Many of them testified that she had believed the maiden of Herrera's claims to have ascended to heaven and met with angels, and that she was certain that the journey to the Promised Land was imminent. Another witness even specified that the Messiah was due to pass through the countryside of Toledo. Elvira supposedly attended messianic gatherings of conversos and spoke against the Inquisition. According to one witness, she had said that the Inquisition was essentially interested in confiscating the conversos' property. On the basis of these witness reports, this conversa was sentenced, but not to death. Without specific judaizing activities on the list and without a confession, the case was not as strong as it might have been; thus Elvira was condemned to prison.

This confessant, like many other prisoners, made an attempt to denigrate the messianic movement once she actually faced trial. Yet despite attempts at denial, it is obvious that the moza of Herrera had a tremendous influence upon the conversas of the region. Those who would not ordinarily have come into contact with her learned of her reputation and traveled to seek her out. Inés was obviously a charismatic young woman, and those who met her did not easily escape her charms. Her message appealed precisely to the conversos, and for that very reason was so successful. Unfortunately, however, once she was apprehended, her followers did have good cause to fear the Inquisition. On the other hand, as will be shown, when confessions were not extracted, the prosecutor's case was clearly much weaker, making it more difficult to obtain a condemnation. It appears that simply believing in any of these prophets was not heretical enough; convictions were more easily procured when actual judaizing activities were undertaken. Again, the previously reconciled conversas were in the most precarious position; thus it is all the more amazing to find that some of them succeeded in eluding punishment and were granted absolution.

For example, Elvira González was a reconciled conversa from Almadén, a village alongside Chillón.[19] The prosecutor's accusation is extremely descriptive and worth examining. Elvira was charged with observing the Sabbath after her reconciliation to the Church; on this day she was said to have dressed in her best clothes and chatted with other heretics about the maiden of Herrera, whom they considered to be a prophetess. The shift from the Sabbath to the messianic belief is quite swift; one gets the impression that her observance consisted of wearing good clothes. The remainder of the statement deals with this messianic movement, alluding to Inés's claims that she ascended to heaven and saw angels and those burned as heretics all seated on seats of gold. Included as well is the belief that Elijah will come to earth to prophesize to the conversos and that the Messiah will come to transport them to a wonderful Promised Land where many goods are available; in order to achieve these things, one has to believe in the Law of Moses and to observe the Jewish fasts that last until nightfall. Those who did not believe would remain lost by the doorpost; those who believed and yearned to go to the Promised Land would proceed to celebrate while dressed in their finest.[20]

To further this cause, Elvira spoke with Mari Gómez of Chillón and other heretics who were taken to be prophetesses and wise women in the ways of the Lord. Signs supposedly appeared in the sky which helped direct those preparing for the departure to the Promised Land. Elvira was accused of believing that soon she would be delivered by the Messiah in the very outfit and state in which she would be found, a belief that proved she did not accept the Lord Jesus Christ as redeemer.

Here is a case of a conversa who had come into contact with two prophetesses and was convinced that she should be awaiting redemption. However, rather than giving her a death sentence, the Holy Tribunal absolved her, presumably because it was easier to convict a heretic on the basis of his or her actions; without a confession, these notions, while contrary to those of a true believer, did not suffice to condemn the defendant.

The fate of a resident of Chillón, who had indubitably encountered Marí Gómez, was remarkably similar. This was the same Isabel Alonso who had informed María García of Herrera about the messianic movement.[21] While the latter was sentenced to death, the case against the former was not as strong, and she too was absolved. There are no confessions, but the prosecutor states that she had been reconciled, and afterwards, in honor of the dead Law of Moses, she fasted as did the Jews, not eating all day until the evening star appeared.

In addition, she anticipated the imminent arrival of the Messiah, believing that he would come to transport her to the Promised Land along with the other conversos. As a heretic, she taught others (such as María García) and advised them to believe in the Law of Moses so that they would go to the Promised Land. Isabel told them that this fact was certain. She consorted with many other heretics about the prophecies of the moza of Herrera and of Marí Gómez of Chillón, and she told how she had gone to Heaven and seen there "the burned ones" in golden chairs.[22]

The prosecution further accused Isabel of informing the heretics that in order to be truly ready for their journey to the Promised Land, they needed to celebrate for many days while dressed in their finest clothes, since they would be carried off by the long-awaited Messiah in the very clothing in which they would be found. He concluded here as well that she obviously did not believe in our Lord Jesus Christ as redeemer. Again, her actual judaizing activities were minimal, no confession was obtained, and the defendant was absolved although she had been extremely active as a follower of these prophetesses.

María González of Almadén was not as fortunate, for she was condemned by the tribunal. No confessions appear in the proceedings but, again, it is the prosecutor who informs the court of what she is accused of having done after her reconciliation to the Church.[23] María reverted to observing the Sabbath, excusing herself from menial work that she would do during the rest of the week, and going to visit relatives on those days. In addition, she dressed in her best clothes and clean blouses. Already, the reference to María's judaizing is far more detailed than that of the previous two women.

The prosecutor also charged this conversa with cleaning meat, removing the fat with a knife, and washing the meat with salt in order to remove all the blood; she would eat only that meat that she had prepared herself. María also excused herself from eating partridges, drowned birds, hare, rabbit and eels, all forbidden to the Jews by their "blind" law.[24] Thus, in addition to having information about her Sabbath observance, the prosecutor wanted to prove that she observed the dietary laws.

Only at this point do details of the messianic movement enter the accusation. The defendant had heard and spoken with other heretics about the things said by the maiden of Herrera, who is accepted as a prophetess, and the one from Chillón: how she had ascended to the heavens, where she saw the angels and the relaxed heretics seated in golden chairs. Likewise, she heard that Elijah was coming to earth to prophesy to the conversos and that the Messiah would carry them to the Promised Land. However, in order to go, one had to believe in the Law of Moses and observe its fasts. The defendant took pleasure in hearing these things and believed them; she made unleavened bread and ate it at Passover in order to properly observe it. She also spent many days attired in her best clothes as if they were holidays, believing that the clothes in which she was found would be the ones worn when carried off by the awaited Messiah.

Again, the prosecution was convinced that María had not believed in the Lord Jesus Christ as redeemer and savior of the world or that he was the true messiah. She had belittled the oath she had taken, and she was silent and had withheld what she knew of other heretics and their sins. In this particular case, the witness testimonies enabled the prosecution to point to specific judaizing observances such as those relating to the Sabbath, the dietary laws, and Passover; these were enough to indict María in 1503.[25]

The trial of Elvira Alonso is similar to those of Elvira González and Isabel Alfonso, for they were all reconciled conversas who were miraculously absolved. Elvira lived in this same region, in the town of Almodovar del Campo, southeast of Chillón. Again, no confessions appear in the proceedings, and the prosecutor relied on witness accounts while the defense provided lists of tachas in an attempt to disqualify these witnesses.

Again, the prosecutor informed the court that the defendant was reconciled yet had consorted with other heretics and spoken with them of those things said by the maiden of Herrera, whom they accepted as a prophetess.[26] This maiden said that the law of the Jews was the true one and that Elijah would come through the countryside of Toledo;[27] all the conversos would be carried to the Promised Land, where they would find everything they needed. In order to achieve this end, they had to observe and believe in the law of the Jews and their ceremonies and to keep their fasts, observe their Sabbaths, cease eating pork and drowned birds and fish without scales, and discontinue other things forbidden by that law.

According to the prosecutor, Elvira affirmed that all that was said there was true and that she believed and was indeed waiting; thus it appeared that she could not be taken as a Christian and that she did not believe in our Redeemer. Yet the belief in these ideas is by no means identical to acting upon them; unlike María González of Almadén, who observed many commandments, Elvira had thus far only verbalized her agreement with the ideas of the prophetesses. If she had acted upon these Jewish injunctions, she had not been witnessed in action as a judaizer and thus her life was spared.

Beatriz Ramírez is the final example of a woman who successfully reconciled herself to the Catholic Church in 1486 and, fourteen years later, would reverse her fate because of her attraction to messianic tidings. This conversa was not as fortunate. In 1486, Beatriz lived in Alcázar while married to Alonso de Barca. Her lengthy confession at that time included details of Sabbath observances such as lighting candles on Friday evenings, wearing clean clothes, occasionally tossing a ball of dough in the fire when baking, and preparing food in advance of the Sabbath. She had observed other holidays, including Passover, when she ate unleavened bread. Her dietary habits included eating meat that had been ceremonially beheaded by Jews, removing the fat from meat, and refraining from eating pork, rabbit, hares, and other forbidden animals as well as seafood.

Beatriz had given alms to Jews for oil in the synagogue and had bathed in preparation of the great fast of Yom Kippur, a day on which she remained barefoot. She had observed the enshrouding and bathing of deceased individuals, and after the deaths of some relatives, she had eaten fish and eggs at low tables. When her nephews and other children were ill, she had placed drops of oil on them in order to avoid the evil eye.[28] In addition, she had abrogated some holy days of the Church. At the conclusion of her statement, this conversa pointed out that her mother, and possibly her father as well, had taught her all of the above; she had observed these practices for about nine years but had discontinued as of Easter past.

This file reveals a great deal more. In 1500, the prosecutor accused Beatriz of observing Jewish fasts, usually on Mondays and Thursdays. In addition, she was accused of observing the Sabbath, at which time she dressed up in clean blouses and special headdresses. This woman also had listened to the one presumed to be a prophetess and believed what she preached about observance and belief in the Law of Moses and messianic hope; she was convinced that the Messiah was about to appear and transport her with other *confesos* (converted Jews) to the Promised Land. Because Beatriz believed this news of salvation and hope that had been delivered by the so-called prophetess, she had been instructed to give her (Inés) pleasure by dancing and singing in her presence and observing many days as if they were festivals while dressed accordingly. Apparently, the defendant believed that she would be saved and transported by the awaited Messiah in the very attire and state in which she was found (waiting).[29] Thus it appeared to the prosecutor that this baptized woman had no genuine belief in the tenets of the Catholic Church.

In fact, there was extremely good cause to suspect Beatriz of having totally devoted herself to the messianic movement, for by 1500 she had remarried. Her third husband, Juan Estevan, was none other than the father of the moza of Herrera. In other words, the defendant, now herself a resident of that rural hotbed of heresy, had become the stepmother of the prophetess Inés. If guilt by association did not suffice for the purposes of the court, the confession provided by Beatriz in 1500 surely sealed her fate.

The confessant stated that Christmas past, her husband Juan Estevan told her how his daughter Inés had ascended to the sky, where she saw the deceased and the living, how the conversos were very well prepared for the Messiah, and many other wonderful things which, she said, would have taken too long to recount. In effect, her husband told her that their salvation was in believing and serving the Law of Moses and its rites and ceremonies. Convinced of the aforesaid, which had been repeated to her numerous times, she began to observe the Sabbath willingly. Sometimes she excused herself from engaging in work when she could; she dressed in clean blouses whenever possible and lit candles early on Friday evening in honor of the Sabbath. In addition, she decorated her home, sometimes managed to prepare the Sabbath meals on Fridays, and once prepared a clean shirt for her husband to wear.

While renewal of Sabbath observance was the major activity to which she returned, she also fasted on Mondays and Thursdays when her husband told her to do so. Beatriz pointed out that she was judaizing because she believed doing so would be advantageous for the salvation of her soul; this is what she had been told by her husband and his daughter, Inés. She then related that she refrained from eating pork and that all of these things were done because of her belief in the Law of Moses and the coming of Elijah and the Messiah; she hoped to go with the other conversos to the Promised Land as had been described to her by the aforementioned. She knew she was a sinner for having offended our Savior and Redeemer Jesus Christ and our Holy Catholic Church.

Lastly, the defendant asked for mercy because she had removed the fat from meat and sometimes drained it of blood, and refrained from eating dead animals, drowned birds, rabbit, hare, and fish without scales as per Jewish law.[30] Except for the biweekly fasts, which were among the classic observances advocated during messianic periods, Beatriz had observed the remainder of the above observances while still married to her first husband. Her childhood training, although publicly abandoned in 1486, was easily reactivated in adult life. Needless to say, the fact that she lived with the maiden and her father intensified the quality of her experience, especially on the level of anticipation of salvation. The prosecutor was acutely aware of this fact, for although he began his accusation by referring to fasting and Sabbath observance, he then shifted the emphasis to the defendant's fervent belief that salvation was imminent. Rather than referring to her adherence to the dietary laws, he preferred to emphasize her loyalty to the prophetess and to emphasize witnesses' description concerning her state of readiness for the journey to the

Promised Land. Whether judged on the basis of her judaizing or on the basis of her messianic anticipation, Beatriz could not be spared by the prosecution. She represented one of the central figures to be destroyed by the Castilian Inquisition in its attack on what was perceived to be a menacing messianic converso movement.[31]

While these tidings had stirred the hearts and memories of many "older" conversas, they also succeeded in attracting first-time offenders. With a youthful representative like Inés so actively advocating judaizing, it is no surprise that many young women and girls flocked to her side. The first trial of this genre took place in 1500; the defendant was María González, wife of Lorenzo Martín, a resident of Halia. While her file is incomplete and her fate was not recorded, the accusation as well as confession that remain are quite telling.

This conversa was accused of honoring the Law of Moses by observing Jewish fasts, not eating until the evening star appeared, and then supping as do the Jews. She was charged with celebrating the Sabbath as if it were a festival, dressing in her finest clothes and headdresses and clean blouses. She heard and conversed with other heretics about what the one they accepted as prophetess had said; María believed her and kept the Law of Moses and awaited the Messiah, believing that he was due to arrive and transport her with the other confeso heretics to the Promised Land. Inés had said that all the conversos would be carried off, and those who believed in the Law of Moses would pass through the entranceway while those who did not would remain in the portal.

María's confession was ordered precisely in the opposite manner, for she began with accounts of the prophetess and ended with judaizing activities. She recalled that a month or two after the most recent Christmas, a neighbor who had been to Herrera and spoken to Inés proceeded to enlighten her. She heard how an angel had carried the maiden to the sky and had revealed himself to her there; the message conveyed was that Elijah was due to come and prophesy and the Messiah would come to transport all the conversos to the Promised Land. As a result, this conversa stopped eating pork, kept Jewish fasts, and began Sabbath observance.[32]

The trial of Beatriz, referred to as the servant of the secretary Luis de Toledo, is, unfortunately, also incomplete, so the fate of the defendant remains unknown. The accusation from these proceedings is not extant; there is only a long confession of this conversa, who, unlike María, had personally encountered the maiden. Beatriz was a resident of Herrera and apparently a cousin of Inés. While she does not state her age, she is clearly a young unmarried maiden.

According to Beatriz, her cousin's tidings were especially appealing in light of the prospect of seeing her deceased mother. The confessant explained that about a year prior to her court appearance in 1500, she was in the home of Juan Estevan when Inés approached her. The prophetess said:

Come here, cousin, would you like to see your mother who is long deceased? and to save your soul? and to go to the holy lands? There you will find many young men and your sisters and you will have good luck and good fortune there. I ascended to the sky and the angel carried me there with him and I saw there such thrones of gold and the deceased as well as the living as they were in their glory! You will see your mother and will go to the sacred Promised Land. Fast, for all these things can be attained through the Jewish fasts, not eating or drinking the whole day until nightfall when the stars appear.

Beatriz claimed that she replied that she could not do this; her cousin told her to do it when she was alone in her home, especially on Thursdays. She should say that she had eaten and then should not eat until nightfall. At this point, Beatriz was convinced by this and other things she was told; she explained that especially in light of the prospects of seeing her mother, who had passed away when she was a very young child, she was enchanted by the prophetess's lies and falsehoods. Thus she fasted on those Thursdays and Mondays when she could safely do so.

Similarly this conversa observed the Sabbath and sometimes even looked for a way to leave the house so that she might observe as best she could. Beatriz was also told by Inés that it was her obligation to bring meat and cook it whenever she could after she had removed the fat, and to refrain from eating bacon and pork. In addition, she was told to wear a clean blouse on the Sabbath, but she did not dare to do so; however, although unable to act upon her inclination, she was ready and willing. Lastly, Beatriz admitted to having believed in the Law of Moses and anticipated the coming of Elijah as well as the journey to that land with all of the other conversos.[33] The prospect of seeing her dear and long-departed mother was overwhelming. Although in the home of her employer, Luis de Toledo, where it was clearly dangerous to judaize, Beatriz did manage to do so at times; she was motivated by her belief in her cousin's message and in the coming of the Messiah.

By contrast, the accusation in the trial of María Alvarez, wife of Fernán García, the tax farmer, reveals more than the confession. In the latter statement, the defendant explained that her mother had conveyed the predictions of Luis Alonso and Mari Gómez of Chillón to both of her daughters. Because María believed these reports, she began to fast until nightfall in the Jewish way as often as she could. Since this conversa had resided in La Puebla as well as in Herrera, one would assume that news of Inés would have come her way, and eventually she does refer to this third prophetic figure as well. At the end of her confession, she describes how she was waiting to go to the Promised Land and how Inés had told the conversos that there would be certain signs in the sky; because of this promise, she often looked up to the sky in the hope of noticing an omen.

The accusation reiterates part of the confession yet contains more interesting details. The prosecutor began by charging that in honor of the Law of Moses, the defendant observed the Sabbath, when she would dress up and wear clean blouses, an attire appropriate for festivals. She observed Jewish fasts on Mondays and Thursdays, not eating until the stars appeared. Above all, she awaited the Messiah, who she believed would come to whisk her off with the other heretics, her relatives, to the Land of Promise. Because she avidly believed this, she affirmed that the deceased as well as the one whom she considered to be prophet told her that she was about to depart for the Promised Land together with the conversos and those who had taken part in this enterprise. She believed in the Law of Moses and gave alms to those she thought believed in this law, and above all, she looked toward the sky, saying that signs were appearing to herald salvation. María associated with other heretics, with whom she discussed these matters, as well as with the one they accepted as prophetess. The defendant carried her jewels on her person and wore them, believing that one would be lifted to the sky in one's state of readiness; there she (presumably, the prophetess) would already be betrothed to the son of the king of Judea and he would obey her in adoration.[34]

Again, the theme of readiness is emphasized, and these women were often wearing the clothes or, in this case, the jewelry, in which they expected to be transported to the Holy Land at any given moment. The charges end with a reference to the dead leviathan fish; now that it was dead, the conversos could be saved. This final image refers to a concept in the Talmud, in a discussion of the end of days, when there will be a banquet for the righteous made from the flesh of the leviathan.[35] The impression created by the accusation and the confession sufficed to justify a condemnation.

The charges presented to María Díaz, the wife of Francisco de la Torre, bear a striking resemblance to the above accusation, excluding the betrothal clause. This resident of Herrera presented a very brief confession, acknowleding that she observed the Sabbath, according to the Law of Moses, not engaging in her housework as she did during the week. The prosecutor claimed that in addition to this admission, she had kept Jewish fasts until nightfall. After her baptism, she anticipated the Messiah just as she had done while a Jewess; she believed that he would come to transport her and her relatives to the Promised Land.[36] In order to be better prepared, she observed many days as festivals and major holidays, wearing new blouses and other festive attire. Convinced that one should depart as honorably as possible, she adorned herself with jewels and other accessories, and she joined other heretics and discussed the coming of the Messiah. She believed what she was told and taught by the one whom they claimed was a prophetess.

After hearing the charges, the defendant begged forgiveness for not including the fact that she had observed the Sabbath and also observed Jewish fasts until nightfall, especially on Mondays and Thursdays; in the evening she broke her fasts with a meal of meat. She also confessed that she was waiting to go to the Promised Land in accordance with what was being said in Herrera; she pointed out that the fasts in which she engaged since the previous Christmas were few, perhaps only one. María named María García as her teacher and stressed the claim that neither her mother nor her husband judaized.[37] The court, nonetheless, condemned her as a judaizer.

The file of Beatriz González of Halia, while incomplete, nevertheless contains the prosecutor's accusation as well as a lengthy confession. The former points to a devoted messianic follower, who, in honor and observance of the Law of Moses, celebrated the Sabbath when she dressed in her finest clothes and clean blouses and headdresses as if these were festival days in which she took pleasure. The defendant also refrained from eating pork products or anything cooked with them. In addition, she listened and discussed those things related by the so-called prophetess and believed what she heard regarding observance of Jewish law and the Messiah. According to this view, when he arrived, he would carry her off along with the other heretical conversos to the Promised Land. Consequently, Beatriz fasted observed fasts, as did her cohorts, and it became clear that she did not believe in Our Lord Jesus Christ as redeemer.

The more detailed confession began with an explanation of how the messianic tidings arrived in Halia. A brother of the defendant had visited Herrera just before the previous Christmas; there he had encountered the daughter of Juan Estevan, who told him about ascending to the heavens, conversing with the angels, and other marvelous things such as how all the conversos would be going to the Promised Land. Because Beatriz did not want to be left behind, she began to keep fasts and observe the Sabbath and other ceremonies associated with the Law of Moses.

Her sibling had gone to great lengths to explain the details of this newly acquired information to the defendant and other conversos in the vicinity; in order to go the the Promised Land, one must avidly believe the message and execute the commands of the Law of Moses. Thus, Beatriz confessed, she fasted, sometimes on Mondays or Thursdays, without eating or drinking until nightfall when the stars appeared; she did so by choice, even adding fast days to the traditional ones. Likewise, she observed the Sabbath by choice rather than ritual, carrying out certain rites when she could do so.

In addition, she occasionally wore a clean blouse in honor of the Sabbath and sometimes prepared fish dishes on Friday for consumption on Saturday.[38] She lit Friday evening candles in honor of the Sabbath, and every so often, left them lit or did not extinguish them as she did during the rest of the week. Every Friday evening, she would dress up and sometimes celebrate at that time. Also, she removed the fat from meat and refrained from eating pork or pork products, the meat of dead animals (not ritually slaughtered), drowned birds, fish without scales, and meat procured from rabbit and hare.

Beatriz then explained that she admitted to believing in the Law of Moses, she was living in anticipation of the coming of Elijah, and she believed the prediction that all the conversos would be transported to the Promised Land. She had expected to be saved by these beliefs and hopes, and she would join the other conversos in their journey to the said land. But she realized her sins in having offended the Holy Evangelical Faith and begged for forgiveness from our Redeemer and Savior Jesus Christ.[39]

While the majority of these conversas were married women, a number of them were, like Inés, mozas. It is surprising to see precisely how young some of these defendants were. Beatriz de Villanueva, the daughter of Rodrigo de Villanueva, was only twelve years old in 1500, when her trial began. In her confession, one learns that Inés was her cousin, and since her family resided in Herrera, exposure to the moza's tidings would be a matter of course, most likely for all of the members of her family.

The confessant related that after she heard Inés's account of ascending to heaven and seeing the angels, she was told to fast without eating or drinking the entire day until the stars emerged. In this way, she would be able to go to those good lands with those young men; she did as she was told. Once when she was fasting, she went to sleep at her grandmother's home and was asked by the wife of Juan de Villanueva if she was fasting. Beatriz replied in the affirmative and was told to stay this second night as well, because her father would be going to the port. She followed her grandmother's advice and did not sup that night; another time she could not manage the fast when, at midday, her mother told her that she was suffering too much and should end that fast by eating. Her cousin Inés had also told her not to eat pork and to observe the Sabbath; she succeeded in abstaining from pork but did not manage to keep the Sabbath.[40] In this case, the family was involved on various levels, for the prophetess taught her own cousin and apparently convinced her cousins' mother, who was her aunt, as well as grandmother, who was her greataunt. The family network clearly played a significant role in this account.

The family played a crucial role in many conversas' lives, and, not surprisingly, particularly in those of the younger ones. Inesita García Jiménez of Pueblo de Alcocer was even younger than Beatriz when approached and advised to fast. Because she was only nine or ten years old, she found abstaining from food and drink for a full day to be far too strenuous. In her brief confession, she related how her mother, Leonor Jiménez, and her sister Juana told her to fast and said that if she did not, she would not be able to go to those lands. Thus, out of respect for her mother, she did as she was told, but in the late afternoons, she experienced a severe stomachache and felt quite bad. Consequently, her mother and sister told her to break her fast and she did.

This brief file includes one witness account: that of a neighbor of the Jiménez family. The wife of a cobbler said she knew that the widow Leonor and her four children—Juana, Israel, Inés (Inesita), and Sancho—observed Jewish fasts. She knew this because as their neighbor, she had seen them and heard them talk of awaiting the coming of Elijah and the journey to the Promised Land; she knew that they believed in the Law of Moses.[41] It is not surprising to discover that Inesita was absolved, for at a such a young age she was simply attempting to follow her mother's orders; as was noted, she was physically unable to execute the command to fast an entire day. She did not seem to observe anything else and was basically joining the family in whatever they did and allowed her to do.

Another young girl from Herrera followed her family's instructions and found fasting to be as difficult as did Beatriz and Inesita. Isabel Bichancho y González was, like Beatriz, a cousin of Inés who was encouraged to judaize by the prophetess as well as by her own parents, Diego Bichanco and Catalina González. In 1501, when Isabel was eleven or twelve years old, she confessed that she had been told by all three relatives to fast, not eating or drinking until the stars emerged. The rationale was to be able to join the other conversos in that good land.

Isabel fasted two or three days, as did her instructors, without eating or drinking the entire day.[42] However, after such fasting she was ill and had a severe headache, so she discontinued fasting. In addition, she was told not to eat bacon or pork products.[43] Interestingly, there was no formal sentence pronounced in this case; a light penance was demanded. Presumably, this judgment was made in light of her youth and the minimal experience she had in judaizing; these girls were most often following the exhortations of their elders and not necessarily making or capable of making a decision on their own.

Beatriz Alfonso from Herrera was also a young girl, age thirteen, when she faced the tribunal in 1500. The daughter of Luis Alfonso, the cobbler, explained that her mother had heard Inés in the first days that the moza was prophesying. As a result, Beatriz was ordered to keep Jewish fasts by not eating or drinking the entire day until nightfall. She followed these orders, fasting on Mondays and Thursdays as best she could. This conversa also was ordered to observe the Sabbath and wear a clean blouse. She and her mother had hoped to light Sabbath candles at the appropriate time but often did not dare to do so because, as she explained, Luis had customers in their house at all hours of the evening.[44] When her mother could prepare food for the Sabbath in advance without being noticed, she did so.

The defendant's mother had told Beatriz to do these things for the salvation of her soul and in order to encounter good fortune in those lands. Once or twice this girl thought she had seen what were interpreted by Inés to be signs that Elijah would come to prophesy. Her mother had told her how the Messiah would come to transport them to the Holy Land. Again the mother had a formative role in determining the fate of her daughter, whom she hoped to save along with her fellow conversos; the inquisitors, on the other hand, decreed a different fate, and Beatriz was condemned as a judaizer.[45]

The last two trials that began in 1500 pertain to two different conversas named Elvira, each married to a potter and each absolved by the court. Elvira Rodríguez was a resident of Talarrubias; her file contains no confession, only an accusation. The prosecutor charged this conversa with observing the Law of Moses by observing Jewish fasts. She was also charged with going to see those regarded as prophets and believing what was said to her concerning the belief in the Law of Moses. In addition, she was said to have eaten unleavened bread at Passover and to believe in and await the Messiah, who would come to take her and the other confesos to the Promised Land. In order to be truly prepared, she observed many days as though they were Jewish holidays and major festivals, because she believed that she would be carried off by the Messiah in the very clothes in which she would be found when he came. Thus she dressed up in her finest clothes on the Sabbath; it seems that she did not believe in the true messiah and in our Lord Jesus Christ as redeemer of the world.[46] Yet despite the seriousness of the counts presented by the prosecutor, this conversa was absolved of the charges, perhaps because a confession was lacking to corroborate the prosecution's evidence.

The rationale for absolution in the coterminous trial of Elvira Ruíz of Herrera is somewhat less elusive. Elvira had a successful defense that managed to cast doubt on the reliability of the witnesses. Nevertheless, she did provide a confession which elaborated upon the long process of convincing her to believe in the prophecies of the daughter of Juan Estevan. Once convinced, the widow of Luis Fernández engaged in many judaizing activities. After being exposed to the moza and eventually accepting the necessity of observing the Law of Moses in order to attain salvation, she engaged in many ritual observances. On Yom Kippur, Elvira fasted and remained barefoot; she fasted on Mondays and Thursdays as well. In addition, she was assured that the path to the Promised Land necessitated Sabbath observance. As a result, she wore clean blouses, lit clean candles on Friday evenings, cleaned her home on Fridays, and prepared food in advance for the Sabbath day. Lastly, she removed the fat from meat she cooked, and she refrained from eating bacon. A witness contended that she did not open her store until late in the day on Saturdays; this observation might point to judaizing, but since she eventually opened it on Saturdays, her observance of the day of rest was partial at best.

In contrast is the agenda presented by the prosecutor. He charged her with keeping Jewish fasts, when she would not eat all day, and awaiting the Messiah who would come and transport her and the other confesos to the Promised Land. He also mentioned her spending many days as if they were festivals: attired in her best clothes and anticipating the arrival of the Messiah. In order to be certain that she would be included and because she believed and obeyed all she had been told, she observed the Law of Moses, the Sabbath, and various Jewish ceremonies. She also gave alms to poor heretics. Lastly, she looked to the sky for signs and said that they had been sighted. She went to view the star of Joseph, proving that she was awaiting the Messiah as did Jewish believers.[47] Therefore, she did not believe in Jesus Christ as redeemer of the world and as being the true messiah.[48]

This trial was by far the lengthiest of those under discussion; it lasted seventeen years, yet in the end the defendant prevailed and was released by the court. Although there is no reference to a judaizing past on the part of Elvira, one wonders how she knew so many Jewish rituals. On the other hand, by virtue of living in the town of Herrera, one could easily learn and absorb a great deal at the turn of the century, even if there had been no prior introduction to one's heritage.

Although the majority of the trials pertaining to messianism were initiated in 1500, the tribunal continued tracking down troublemakers for the next two years.

Two young girls from Herrera were accused in 1501. The younger one was Isabel Ortolano y López, the daughter of Alvaro Ortolón and Catalina López. The interesting aspect of this case lies in the nature of the maternal role. Catalina López was an Old Christian and apparently unaware that her converso husband was a judaizer or was inspired by Inés to judaize. Isabel was taught by both her aunt and her father when she was a mere ten years of age. While visiting her aunt María García, the wife of Juan Alonso, the cobbler, she was instructed to fast, not to eat or drink the entire day until the stars emerged.[49] This fasting would enable her to join all the other conversos in their journey to that good land. Likewise her father, on two occasions, told Isabel to fast as did he and her aunt. Lastly, she was told not to eat bacon and pork products.[50] The Inquisition did not deal harshly with Isabel, probably in light of the fact that she had done minimal judaizing and at such a young age; she was required to do penance and was reconciled to the Church.

The second girl from Herrera, Inés Rodríguez y Rodríguez, was about twelve years old and her sister Juana was even younger when she was instructed in Jewish ways. This conversa's file is incomplete, although her confession is extant, and her sentence, condemnation by the court, was recorded. While Isabel's mother was not a factor in her judaizing experience because of her descent, Inés's mother was not present either, but in this case, because she was deceased. As in the previous family, the father was an active figure and initiated his daughter with the aid of a female relative, here the maternal grandmother. In other words, the daughter of the conversos Diego Rodríguez, the woolcarder, and Isabel Rodríguez was exposed to Judaism by her grandmother, Isabel García, wife of Fernán Sanchéz. She was instructed to fast as do the Jews, not eating or drinking the entire day until the stars were visible. Both relatives told her not to eat bacon so that she could go with all the other conversos to that good land; these instructions had been received from none other than the maiden, daughter of Juan Estevan.

Inés explained that she did as she was told and believed what she was told, fasting one entire day until the stars emerged. At the end of the fast, she ate with her father and grandmother and with her younger sister Juana. The defendant, because of this belief, strayed from her faith in Jesus Christ and requested pardon and penitence; she had also refrained from eating bacon per instructions by her father.[51] We do not know the fate of this young woman; the prosecution succeeded in mustering up one witness to testify against her, but it is unclear how severe they considered her heresy to be.

The trial of Mencía López from Pueblo de Alcocer, which also began in 1501, represented an effort on the part of the prosecution to convict a more mature woman; however, it did not meet with success, for she was ultimately absolved. There was no confession by the wife of Alvaro Rico, and the records contain many attempts by the prosecution to provide testimony, as well as defense tactics aiming to invalidate this testimony. As a result, the record is rather messy, with numerous cross-outs. It appears that, in the long run, the tribunal was unable to support the prosecutor's contentions on the basis of the accusation alone.

Nevertheless, a look at the list of charges is revealing. Mencía was accused of observing Jewish fasts in the Jewish way. According to this statement, she believed in and awaited the Messiah, whom she believed was coming to transport her with the other confesos to the Promised Land. This conversa supposedly asserted that Elijah was due to come to prophesy to them and that those who did not believe would not be able to go to that land but would have to remain in the portal full of fear. The prosecutor believed that the defendant not only believed the above, but was inducing and attracting others to these beliefs as well; she listened and discussed these heretical things, which were affirmed by the one she accepted as prophetess. In order to be in a state of readiness, she celebrated many days, walking about dressed in holiday or festival clothes, believing that in the clothes in which she would be found, she would be carried off by the awaited Messiah, and thus it seems that she did not believe in our Redeemer.[52]

The following accusation, presented to Juana de Córdova of Siruela, was similar but by no means identical to that of Mencia. Juana, the wife of Juan de Córdova, swordmaker, was also arraigned in 1501 and absolved by 1503. The prosecutor accused her of keeping Jewish fasts in observance of the dead Law of Moses, waiting until the stars appeared before breaking her fast. She also was charged with conversing with other heretics about the teachings of the one they accepted as prophetess, listening to her, and waiting to be taken by the Messiah to the Land of Promise along with the other conversos. She also engaged in dancing and singing and celebrating these tidings brought by the moza.

In addition, she celebrated for many days dressed appropriately for a festive occasion, believing that she would be transported by the Messiah in the clothes she was wearing at the time of his arrival. Thus it appears that she did not believe in Our Lord Jesus Christ as redemptor and savior of the world as the true messiah, and in this way, it appears that she negated the tenets of the Holy Mother Church. On the contrary, she maintained her heretical views and was silent, covering up her knowledge of other heretics and of their heresies, including her relatives; for this reason, she is an abettor of heretics and has concealed heretical activity in blatant violation of the censures of the Church.[53] No statements by the defendant are extant.

Despite the fact that her file is incomplete, the outcome is recorded in addition to the fact that she was tormented. In other words, the tribunal suspected that the defendant might be withholding evidence and voted to attempt to procure information through torture. Yet no confession is recorded, and the fact that she was absolved leads one to assume that she did not break under duress. If Juana had indeed judaized, she never volunteered any information of the sort; it is also possible that the defense managed to question the credibility of the prosecution witnesses.

By contrast, the file of María Flores of Chillón, while also incomplete, has no accusation and only an undated confession. The wife of Fernando Sánchez was tried in 1502 and confessed to having heard about the moza of Herrera from her mother-in-law, Leonor González. She had learned how Inés ascended to the heavens, how Elijah was due to come in a cloud, and how all the conversos were to be carried off to the abundant and rich Promised Land. In order to merit these rewards, it was better to fast, and because she gave credit to this bad advice, she fasted one day in the Jewish way, not eating until nightfall.

María also gave credibility to a woman named Isabel Alonso, the aunt of Mari Gómez, both residents of the village of Chillón. Again, she had heard how a young woman, Isabel's niece, had ascended to the sky and seen many things. From this source, she had also been informed that Elijah would arrive in a cloud, that the conversos were to be transported to the Promised Land, and that those who did not believe would remain in the doorway yelling at the top of their lungs. The advice given was, again, that it was necessary to fast Jewishly and to believe in God. The confessant explained that because of fear of her husband, she fasted only one day.

One evening, her mother-in-law and Isabel Alonso told her that Elijah was coming to transport them, so she stayed up all night while wearing a clean blouse and holding her three-month-old daughter. She gave credence to all these things while her husband was not at home. Presumably, the tribunal voted to condemn María because she was older, had been influenced by two prophetesses, and had confessed.[54]

While Chillón was a second potential hotbed of messianism, Almadén was a neighboring community affected as well. Leonor Díaz, the wife of Arias Díaz, was tried from 1502 to 1503; her file contains the accusation without any confession, similar to that of Juana de Cordova and others. The prosecutor claimed that in honor and observance of the dead Law of Moses, Leonor observed the fasts of Jews, not eating the entire day until the stars appeared. She also conversed with and listened to other heretical persons about topics related to the moza of Herrera, who was accepted as a prophetess. These included accounts of how she ascended to heaven and saw the angels and those burned as heretics there and how the Messiah was coming to carry them off to the Promised Land.

In order to attain these benefits, she had to believe in the Law of Moses and observe its ceremonies, excusing herself from eating bacon. She enjoyed hearing these teachings and prophecies and believing that the conversos would soon be departing for the Promised Land. Consequently, she spent many days dressed festively, believing that she would be carried off in the clothes in which she was attired when the awaited Messiah came. Clearly, this woman did not believe in our Lord Jesus Christ as redeemer of the world and as the true messiah. The evidence was apparently not strong enough to convict Leonor as a heretic who possessed no redeeming virtues; on the contrary, although she was instructed to do penitence and was presented with severe warnings by the Church, the defendant was ultimately absolved.[55]

The dossier of Elvira González from Agudo likewise contains the accusation without any confession. The prosecutor at length described her judaizing under the influence of the messianic movement. He charged that she awaited the Messiah, certain that he would come to carry her and the other conversos to the Holy Land of Promise. For this purpose, she dressed up, attired in her best clothes and blouses and clean headdresses. The notion that one would be saved in the very clothes worn at the moment the Messiah arrived was stressed. On this basis, her credence in Jesus Christ was sorely questioned.

In addition, it was charged that the defendant had fraternized with other heretics and discussed the things said by the supposed prophetess of Herrera. For instance, they related how she had ascended to heaven and seen the angels and the deceased as well as those burned at the stake by the Inquisition, all seated there in thrones of gold. Elijah was prophesying there and would arrive in a cloud to continue his work on land. The Law of Moses was supreme in their eyes, the Sabbath had to be observed, and Jewish fasts had to be practiced on Mondays and Thursdays from sunrise to sunset. The list continued with abstaining from eating bacon and other foods forbidden by the Jews and believing that those who had no faith would be abandoned at a gate. The defendant, it was charged, did believe, and observed and took pleasure in conversing about these issues with other heretics. She even instructed and induced others to believe, meeting with additional potential heretics and letting them understand that Jewish law was superior to that of the Christians. Since she believed, without any doubt, that the Messiah was coming, she met with relatives to communicate this message to them. Regarding all of the above, she had remained quiet and obviously had neglected her duties as a baptized Christian.[56] Once again, the defendant was absolved, either because no confession was forthcoming, or possibly because of the lack of strong corroborating evidence.

The last two conversas, both from Almadén, were also tried in 1502. One provided a confession, while the other did not, yet both were convicted and condemned as judaizers. Isabel González was unmarried and living at home with her father and stepmother. At the time of her confession, she did not state her age but did mention that her father, Fernando González, a cobbler, was not in the vicinity. Her statement was rather lengthy and, as will be revealed, contained a few unusual comments.

The defendant's acquaintance with messianic tidings began after a visit by her father to Herrera, where he met the moza. Upon his return, he told her, her stepmother, and a few other conversos from Chillón about his encounter. Fernán related how the moza had ascended to the heavens and seen angels and Elijah, and how he was told that the conversos would be going to the Promised Land. There, where food was abundant, they would see their deceased (loved ones) alive. They were not to believe in Jesus Christ, but rather in Moses, and all nonbelievers would be left behind.

The observances that Isabel was instructed to follow included fasting on Yom Kippur; if she did as told, her actions would be perceived as good in the eyes of the

Lord and she would see her mother, and if she did not, her mother would remain a lost soul. She was also told to clean the candle wicks and lamps on Friday evenings and to light them in honor of the Law of Moses. Likewise she saw that her stepmother did not spin on the Sabbath and was told that it was a sin to spin on this day. Two of the other conversas who had been present when her father brought the news told her to fast so that she would not be lost like her mother; she also should not believe in Jesus Christ.

Because Isabel believed all this, she moved away from the holy Catholic faith and fasted three or four days, not eating until nightfall; the fast was broken with eggs and sometimes fish. Isabel's sister joined her in fasting. The confessant also admitted to lighting clean candles on Friday evenings and apparently dreamed up an innovation to create a camouflage for her activities. She threw dirt on the candles so as to cover up their clean state! Isabel believed she would indeed be going to the Promised Land, where she would find her mother. She was under the impression that all the conversos would go and find abundant food there; lastly, she believed that once there, no one would have to do anything but celebrate. All of the above she believed and observed.

In his accusation, the prosecutor included some but not all of the above. The claim was that in honor and observance of the said dead law, the defendant awaited the Messiah, believing that he would come to transport her to the Promised Land with the other conversos. She had listened to and chatted with other heretics from Herrera, who spoke of what was said by the one taken to be a prophetess. This included how she had gone up to the sky and seen angels together with those burned as heretics all seated in chairs of gold.[57] Elijah was due to come to prognosticate to the conversos before the Messiah transported them. In order for this to occur, one had to believe in the Law of Moses and to observe Jewish fasts, which last until nightfall. In addition, one had to observe other ceremonies of the said law, and those who did not believe would remain lost at the entrance. The defendant heard and believed all this, and when her father brought the news that the departure for the Promised Land was imminent, she observed many days as holidays or festivals, believing that she would be carried off by the Messiah in the clothes she was wearing.[58] This orphaned conversa was perceived as having taken the messianic news seriously and was condemned by the tribunal in 1503.

A neighbor, Isabel Sánchez, the daughter of Fernando Sánchez Gordillo, was on trial at the same time. This Isabel was probably a bit older than the previous one; although the father–daughter relationship is recorded, Isabel was married to Gonzalo del Campo and therefore not living with her parents. No confession is available, but the court took the accusation quite seriously. Portions of these charges almost seem to be standardized. While many confessions contain similarities, the individual language of the confessant clearly differentiates them. Yet this particular list approaches what might be termed a classic compository accusation of a messianic believer.

The prosecutor began by stating that in honor and observance of the said dead Law of Moses, Isabel observed the Sabbath as holidays, excusing herself from doing work or any household chores that would normally be done during the course of the week. In order to better sanctify these days, she dressed in festive clothing and laundered blouses and headdresses. On Friday evenings, she decorated her home and observed these nights while desecrating Sundays and Church holidays.

The fact that she listened to and conversed about the things said by the moza of Herrera, who was accepted as a prophetess, only exacerbated her erroneous and heretical state. Isabel had also heard about the ascent to heaven by María Goméz of Chillón, who saw there the angels and those burned as heretics sitting in chairs of gold. She had been told that Elijah would come and prophesy to the conversos and the Messiah would follow and carry them off to the Promised Land. In order to attain such benefits, one needed to believe in the Law of Moses, and those who did not believe would be lost souls left behind.

The defendant took pleasure in hearing these tidings and believed the other heretics, it was charged, and thus it appeared that she was awaiting the Messiah. Consequently, many days she went about dressed up, waiting for amelioration, believing that she would be transported by the Messiah in the outfit she was wearing when he arrived. Clearly, it could be said that she did not believe in our Lord Jesus Christ as redeemer of the world, the true messiah, and she has withheld knowledge about other heretics and about her mother and other relatives.[59] As the result of this severe list of charges, the court found Isabel guilty of judaizing, and she was systematically turned over to the secular authorities so that her punishment could be executed.

The individuals blatantly missing from this group of women are Inés of Herrera and Mari Gómez of Chillón. The fact that the moza had been arrested and subsequently executed was mentioned by some of the defendants, but her file is not extant. In 1500, she was arrested in April, interrogated in May, condemned, and burned at the stake by the beginning of August! As for Mari, the only available information leads us to believe that she fled to Portugal.[60] There is no doubt that the presence of either of these prophetesses in the inquisitorial prisons of Toledo was extremely problematic, for their cells might be in proximity to any of the above-mentioned conversas, and their powers of persuasion had been attested to. Interestingly, two letters written by the monarchs of Spain dealt with the arrest of Inés, for it seems that there was reluctance on the part of the arresting officer to turn her over to the Holy Tribunal.[61] Nevertheless, it is most unfortunate that their proceedings are not available in these archives, for their accounts, no doubt, would have enrichened and rounded out the story of the development of this movement.

This analysis will have to be based on what actually is available in the records of the trials of conversas affected by the three coterminous sets of messianic tidings spreading throughout Extremadura. As has been demonstrated, the Inquisition acted swiftly, beginning the majority of the thirty-two trials under discussion in

1500, and initiating the rest no later than 1502. The duration of these trials averaged one to two years; only one of them continued until 1517. The intensity of this campaign had a twofold goal: to nip the movement in the bud, and to discourage potential followers because of the obvious danger involved in light of such an efficient system.

Twelve of the women were relapsed judaizers. One would expect to find a high percentage of condemnations in this group, for their previous judaizing would negate the option of leniency on the part of the court. Yet three of these conversas were miraculously absolved. A fourth was destined for prison, a recent and innovative, yet harsh enough punishment. The other eight were condemned and relaxed, presumably burned at the stake. All these women were proving the claim of those who insisted that the converted Jews were always potential Jews at heart and could never be a trusted or loyal element of Spanish society.

Nevertheless, the majority of the conversa followers in this movement were first-time offenders. As has been demonstrated, there were quite a few young girls among this group of twenty conversas. Four of the trials are incomplete and do not contain a record of the fate of the defendant.[62] Six defendants were completely absolved by the Church; they either did not provide confessions or had engaged in relatively little judaizing activity per se. Three others were given light sentences and allowed to be reconciled to the Church; since they were first-time offenders, the tribunal could allow itself more leniency. The youth of some of these conversas must have had an effect on the proclivities of the court. Only seven first-time defendants were blatantly condemned; together with the eight of the previous group, they make a total of fifteen, just about half of the cases that were tried.[63]

All the women were from Extremadura, and fourteen, were, not surprisingly, from Herrera. Five were from Almadén, two from Chillón, two from Agudo, and the rest from various neighboring towns and villages. These thirty-two women represent a very concentrated group, in terms of both geography and the dates of their trials. The determination on the part of the Inquisition to deal quickly and efficiently with this localized movement is unquestionable. Messianic tidings like these could and did spread like wildfire, and the tribunal devoted tremendous energies to dousing the flames before they spread to other regions. Apparently, it did its job well, for after 1502, no additional arrests were made that involved conversos affected by this movement. In addition, the reconciled apparently had been sufficiently frightened by this experience to discontinue their recently discovered religion. The inquisitors could then turn their attention to prosecuting other judaizers who would come to their attention under different circumstances.

4

Castilian Conversas at Work

Had the judaizing conversas been idle women, crypto-Judaism would not have survived. It is precisely their work, which on the whole was what is categorized as domestic work, that provided the only Jewish-style framework for the women and their families. The time and energy that was spent on keeping some semblance of Jewishness within the household had more significance than ever for these daughters of Israel.

While some of the conversas were employed professionally outside of the home, most of the women whose activities are presented here did not. Ironically, the midwife whose trial is analyzed in a later chapter and whose very profession and activities were those that brought about the wrath of the Church, was probably not a serious judaizer at all. Other women, as will be seen, worked with their husbands in their shops or sold the products of their handiwork; the majority, however, were busy running the household. Since there were always a number of household servants to be supervised, being the director of domestic activities was usually a formidable enough task. However, maintaining a crypto-Jewish home required a great deal more expertise, craftiness, and ingenuity.

We learn of this work precisely because the judaizing woman did not conduct herself in the same manner as her Old Christian neighbor; thus the Inquisition could discern acts of defiance, or observance of the Law of Moses, by identifying this conduct. Consequently the records are replete with information concerning the domestic activities of the judaizing conversa. As a matter of fact, many of the myths of the *marranos* concerned their mode of adapting domestic work to suit their lives; the most popular example was the way in which the judaizer was imagined to secretly clean the house for the Sabbath. Normally, after the house was swept, the front door was opened so the accumulated dirt could be swept outside. Marranos supposedly swept their dirt under the rugs so that no one (at least outside of the house) could witness this act.[1] Again, it is housework that might expose the crypto-Jew to the outside world.

Jewish law entailed a great deal of work for the judaizing woman; it is both logical and convenient to divide it according to legal or halachic categories. Observance of the Sabbath, one of the Ten Commandments, requires extensive labor every week. Most of the other holidays and festivals involved work, often by virtue of preparing for them; the preparation necessary for Passover is probably the finest example of intensive domestic labor that is not only thorough but thoroughly exhausting. The dietary laws demand serious work such as ritual slaughtering, kashering of meat, and, of course, the separation of milk and meat in cooking. Other aspects of Jewish life involve work as well; death rituals include the bathing of the deceased, a function most often performed by women; preparing special meals after the burial; and professional keening. Life for the crypto-Jewish woman thus entailed a great deal of work; more energy, creativity and cleverness were demanded of her than of her Jewish sister.

THE SABBATH

Preparation of food for the Sabbath was a common charge in the lists compiled by the prosecution. Some descriptions were quite brief and to the point, while others were far more detailed. In the 1490s, according to the trial records, the wife of Diego Rodríguez of Guadalajara "cooked food to eat on Friday for the Sabbath and ate it on the Sabbath," while Inés López "prepared food on those Fridays for the Sabbath" and María Alvarez, also of Guadalajara, on Fridays "prepared food for the Sabbaths and ate it on them."[2]

Variations of this charge abound, often including with whom the defendant ate the prepared food or what she had prepared. For example, María González was said to have "cooked for herself on Friday for the Sabbath and also had cooked [for] the Sabbath for her husband and for those of her household."[3] Isabel García of Hita was said to have "cooked food and had food cooked to eat on Friday for the Sabbath, and on the Sabbath, she and others ate cold from that which was prepared on Friday without warming it, in observance of the Law of Moses."[4] Cooking for an evening meal was, of course, the norm, but when the cooking was intentionally completed before sundown and did not resume again until the following sundown, something was awry. A house without fire was an eyesore and could lead to detection of judaizing from without as well as from within. The abstinence from work that was essential to observing the Sabbath was integral to crypto-Judaism, as to all Judaism. By eating cold food or food that had been left to simmer throughout the previous night on the Sabbath day, the conversa was arranging her work schedule to suit the demands of Jewish law. However, by doing so, she was often implicating herself as a heretic, for a Catholic would have no cause to refrain from cooking on Saturdays.

It was precisely this cooking in advance that was on the minds of the prosecutors. The second count in the accusation of Leonor Alvarez was that

. . . the said Leonor cooked food to eat for the Sabbath, and [on] the days of the Sabbath, she ate the said victuals cooked on Fridays with other persons; and she and other persons met in certain locations where they observed the Sabbath [in order] to have a light meal and snacked and ate the said victuals and made a large feast, being, as it has been said, dressed up, and there they sometimes ate meat and vegetables cooked in a pot prepared on the previous day and at other times other victuals.[5]

A similar accusation was presented to Juana Núñez that she, "in honor of the said Sabbath days and in order to celebrate them, cooked food on Fridays for the Sabbath day in this way, Sabbath stews as well as other foods, and she and other people ate them cold on the Sabbath as did the Jews in that time."[6] A neighbor of hers had joined with other judaizers where they ate fruit and also the *cazuela* "prepared on Friday for the Sabbath and they ate it cold on account of the faith, observance and credence that they hold in the law of the Jews, considering it to be a superior law to that of the Christians."[7] These Sabbath stews or *cazuelas* were usually made of meat and vegetables cooked in a crock, often prepared for the Sabbath lunch; the other common meal was the *adafina*, also a Sabbath stew comparable to the *chulent* or *hamin* prepared by the Ashkenazi women.

Whether the women were preparing the food for themselves and their own families or for a larger communal meal, there was clearly work involved. Three women in the González family were witnessed jointly celebrating the Sabbath after completing their preparatory work:

[O]n those said Sabbaths they ate what they had cooked the Friday before, because the said wife of Juan de la Sierra and her daughter Leonor de la Sierra, the maiden, and the said Isabel González were always accustomed to cooking on the said Fridays for the Sabbath, stews of fish and sardines and sometimes [made] with eggplant and with onions and coriander and spices, and they ate them on the following Sabbath day.[8]

Note that this was a fish stew, rather unusual, since meat is generally the central component of this dish.

As the witnesses and prosecutors provide the details of the culinary art, we get a more realistic picture of the work carried out in the kitchens of the conversas. For example, Beatriz López of Hita was charged with cooking (either by herself or by a servant under her supervision) "*adafinas* and Jewish cuisine with meat, onions, chickpeas, spices all crushed and cooked. After cooking for a long time, the broth was extracted and the meat was awaited; thus she ate it with the great devotion that she had for the Law of Moses."[9]

Yet another example can be found of a stew being prepared without meat; this time, the conversa seems to have cooked a vegetarian-dairy dish for the judaizers who congregated in her home. The confession of María González describes the product of her Sabbath preparation to be what she terms a light meal or *merienda*. In some locales, the *merienda* was a midday meal; elsewhere it was akin to a snack taken in the late afternoon or evening before supper. At any rate, the wife of Pedro de Villarreal explained that various judaizers had congregated in the home of Diego Alvarez and Gracia de Teva on the Sabbath:

> . . . and on those Sabbath days they ate some stews, prepared on the previous Friday, made of eggs and cheese and parsley and hot dishes and spices, and . . . sometimes they made them of eggplant and other times of carrots depending upon the season, and . . . they ate the said stews cold and they celebrated and enjoyed themselves all those said Sabbath days, until nightfall when they went to their homes.[10]

At the same time, some of the conversas managed to prepare the traditional Sabbath bread, the hallah. While relatively little is known about Beatriz Alonso, the wife of Fernando de Merida, she was accused of baking bread or burning a piece of dough before baking bread.[11] Jewish law requires the baker to toss a small piece of dough into the fire, separating it from the rest of the dough and allowing it to burn. In the trial of María González of Casarrubios del Monte, she was said to have separated pieces of hallah and to have burned these pieces in the fire.[12] Similar labor was engaged in by Juana de los Olivos as she prepared for the Sabbath; according to the prosecutor, she neglected to confess and "maliciously maintained silence that when she kneaded, she threw [a piece] of dough in the fire, and [of] the bread that she kneaded that the Jews called 'hala,' [this] being Jewish ceremony."[13]

Some of the women's work was based on law and some on custom; cooking in advance is the means by which the Jewish woman adheres to the injunction not to work on the Sabbath. As was pointed out, baking hallah is not simply bread-baking but requires expertise in Jewish law as well. However, other traditional preparatory activities are simply customs that are associated with the Jewish Sabbath. For example, while it is not necessary to clean or adorn one's house or to bathe or dress up in anticipation of the day of rest, these actions are interpreted to be important as a means of giving the Sabbath respect, and they are observed in a Jewish home as religiously as are the legal injunctions.

Thus, Isabel García was accused of joining others in wearing clean shirts and holiday garb in honor of the Law of Moses, of preparing meals, and "likewise that the said Isabel adorned and had adorned and swept and had swept the house on Friday afternoons in honor and observance of the Sabbath as the Jews did in honor of their law."[14] Three conversas, all named María González, were involved in Sabbath preparations in sixteenth century Ciudad Real. The first, the wife of Rodrigo de Chillón, was said to have "adorned and cleaned her house and had it decorated on those Friday nights in order to observe the Law of Moses."[15] In 1511, the second of them the wife of Pedro Díaz of Villarrubia, was accused of having donned clean clothes, lighting Sabbath candles, preparing meals in advance "and [having] cleaned and adorned their whole house on that day [Sabbath] and washed and cleansed and had washed and cleansed on the said Fridays and observed, as the saying goes, on the days of the Sabbath in honor of the said deadly law."[16] In addition, the wife of Pedro de Villarreal, the third María González, confessed that she had "ordered Catalina, her black servant, to sweep and wash the said house in order to better honor the said Sabbaths, and that the said Catalina did so as per her order and at other times, the confessant did so."[17] Here is an example of work that at times was executed by the household servant under the direction of the conversa and at other times was done by the mistress of the house herself.

The fact that judaizers wore clean clothes, or at least clean shirts, in honor of the Sabbath has been mentioned. Clothes were not changed daily, and consistently changing one's attire and wearing clean or new clothes on Fridays or Saturdays rather than on Sundays would be noticeable.[18] Having these clothes clean on time for the day of rest would also entail work, although the labor involved in preparation of the clothes is rarely mentioned. For example, a classic accusation in this regard is that of Juana Núñez:

> . . . through the affection that she had for the deadly law of the Jews and believing in it, [she] has observed and observed [*sic*] the days of the Sabbath in this way: that in good time on Friday night, she relinquished household activities and adorned her house as for a holiday and observed Sabbath days, not performing any household duties on them, as she was accustomed to do the other days of the week, and dressing herself and adorning herself with good clothes and clean blouses in honor of the Sabbath.[19]

Likewise, it was said of the González women that "on those said Sabbaths, they wore clean shirts and holiday clothes and dressed up and beautified themselves as for Sunday or holy days."[20] Another witness confirmed this statement and said that on Saturdays, the three would "wear good clothes, the very same clothes that this witness saw them wear on Sundays, and by-and-by on the following Monday, they would wear other non-holiday garb such as that which they wore all week until Saturday."[21]

One of the most interesting testimonies related to the wearing of clean clothes on the Sabbath clearly does involve work, although not quite what one would expect. In 1539, Juan García informed the inquisitors about the time that he was living in the household of Alfonso de Solis, a converso resident of Villafranca. He clearly remembered how his master's daughter would bring her father and her stepmother clean shirts every Saturday morning. The witness pointed out that sometimes he saw this girl heating up the clean but apparently wet shirts so that her parents could wear them that very morning. Although the shirts had been washed before the Sabbath, they had not dried in time. Drying them is indeed a form of work, obviously forbidden on the Sabbath, but the wearing of a clean shirt was seen as taking priority in this instance. Juan actually asked the girl why she was taking the trouble to dry that particular blouse for her stepmother; he was told that the conversa was ill-disposed and wanted to refresh herself, and for this reason desired a clean blouse. At other times, when witnessing the same activity, he was told that since his master had just returned from working outside, his shirt had been soiled, and therefore a clean one was required. The informant was certain he had witnessed this particular custom at least twenty-five times during his four-year stay with de Solis family. As a matter of fact, he believed that he had seen them wearing those very shirts on Sundays and couldn't understand why they were wearing clean shirts on these Saturdays that were not festival days. At the end of his testimony, this Old Christian recalled that one Saturday morning, he had also seen a young girl who worked for the family warming up the wet, clean shirts for the master and mistress to don.[22]

The Sabbath traditionally is ushered in by the lighting of candles, or rather lamps with wicks, as was common during this period. The actual lighting would not be considered work, but frequently, work was involved in the preparation of the lamps. In honor of the Sabbath, wicks were replaced or cleaned or the ends cut off in order to obtain a cleaner wick; also the external portion of the lamp itself would frequently be cleaned. Often the oil in the lamp was replaced by clean, unused oil.

For example, one conversa confessed that "on the said Friday nights, soon after sunset, this confessant lit two clean lamps with new cotton wicks, and at other times the said slave Catalina lit them as commanded by this confessant . . . most often this confessant cleaned them and lit them, putting in new wicks so that the said maidservants and slave would not notice."[23] Herein lay the danger: if the servants always replaced the wicks when they had burned out naturally, it would be perceived as odd that on Fridays, the old wicks were discarded before they burned down. At the same time, if this was a chore normally encumbant upon the servants, it would be equally suspicious when only on Fridays, the mistress would insist upon doing what was considered to be the servants' work.

Surprisingly, the González women made no attempt to hide their activities from their servants. A witness testified:

> . . . on Friday nights, the aforesaid ordered Francisca, the black woman, to clean three lamps they had, and after cleaning, when the sun was setting, the said wife of Juan de la Sierra said to the said slave: "See if the sun has set, light these lamps." And (that) the said slave cleaned the said lamps and put new wicks in them and lit them; and (that) they burned throughout the night and (that) they were not extinguished; and (that) when they wanted to retire, they filled them with oil; and (that) the other nights they were not lit early nor with new wicks nor did they burn all through the night.[24]

The lighting of candles signified the onset of the Sabbath, and once the day of rest began, it was the refraining from work that became an eyesore. If cooking was normal in every household and the judaizer didn't cook, if the middle-class woman sewed or spinned during the course of a typical workday and the judaizer didn't, if smoke emerged from the hearth of every home on every day but not from the abode of the judaizer because a fire was not lit on the Sabbath, then the act of not working clearly could implicate the suspected crypto-Jew. Consequently, the arraignment of Leonor Alvarez emphasized what she did as well as what she did not do:

> First of all, that the said Leonor Alvarez, through the blind affection that she had for the deadly law of the Jews, observed and has observed the days of the Sabbath, not performing the household duties on these days that she was accustomed to do on the other days of the week, adorning herself on these days with good holiday clothes and dressing herself in a clean blouse and other holiday finery and relinquishing household activities on Friday night in good time [sufficiently early] in honor of the Sabbath, going to visit other houses and other persons on these Sabbath days, [houses] where everyone was observing the Sabbath.[25]

The González women of Ciudad Real attempted to limit the work done in their house to a minimum. A witness testified "that on those Sabbath days, they did not prepare anything at all to cook, nor did they allow the witness or a black woman who was there to light a fire in the said house; . . . at most, they allowed a small fire to be made to heat the water for scrubbing."[26] Although according to Jewish law, it would have been permissible for the non-Jewish maid to light a fire by prearranging this chore prior to the Sabbath, these conversas preferred not to take advantage of this option and did their utmost to avoid any semblance of work on their holy day of rest.

Not all the judaizers were as strict or as knowledgeable as the González women, but they as well as others tried not to work. Juana de los Olivos was accused of observing the Sabbath and "excusing herself from doing menial work on these days that she did on the other days of the week."[27] María González, the wife of Pedro Díaz de Villarrubia, who was not from the González clan, was accused of having observed the Sabbath, especially by not spinning; interestingly enough, a witness pointed out that on this day, she did no purchasing, no selling, exchanging or business with anyone.[28] A servant who had lived with the Villarreal family for two years claimed that her masters would not work on Friday nights, for after their evening meal they retired early, whereas on other evenings her mistress would spin and smooth out the wool. Sometimes on Saturdays, this judaizer would take wool to her mother's house and return with it, apparently untouched.[29] Later María confessed that she had sometimes gone to observe the Sabbath at the home of Mayor Alvarez and took a slave girl and a maid with her; the latter would carry her spinning wheel or a wicker basket of spun portions on a spindle to spool and wool from the border to smooth out, but would return in the evening with all of it yet remaining to be worked on, because since it was the Sabbath, nothing was done.[30] This custom was confirmed by another conversa, Beatriz Alonso, who saw María go to her mother's home on the Sabbath with her spinning wheel and bunches of linen and sometimes wool to weave; she then put these items on a wall or on the floor and did not spin or do anything else. At nightfall, she took her things home so that she could spin.[31] Others apparently had similar habits, for a former servant of Juana Núñez said that her masters engaged in no labor on Friday nights "and that the other nights of the week, that they smoothed the wool and wrapped it around the spindle." She also pointed out that while they usually got up early in the morning and set to work, on Saturdays they got up late and did not work.[32] In addition, Juana made excuses to her servants to explain her inactivity; she would either complain of a headache and rest her head on two pillows or just say she felt poorly and lie down to rest on her pillows.[33]

When domestic activities were commonplace on every day but Sunday, the judaizing woman often had to be creative in explaining her stance, which often was to maintain a pretense of activity. Sometimes the women were hiding their judaizing from their servants or neighbors, and sometimes even from other family members. For example, "in order to show that she did not observe the said Sabbaths, she did some light things, laying hold of cloths and other items which entailed very little work, and if it had not been in order not to be perceived by her husband and by the other persons in her house, she would have entirely observed the said Sabbaths."[34]

Similarly, Leonor Alvarez confessed that "sometimes she did some light things, in order to insinuate that she did not observe the said Sabbaths, when some persons entered her home, and other times, she took her spinning wheel in her hand in order to insinuate that she was spinning."[35] One of the many witnesses in the trial of María González claimed that the defendant would never let her maidservants work on Saturdays but that they would do the housework on Sundays. This mistress of the house sought a day of rest for the entire household.[36]

Menial work was often done for the sake of appearances. A witness testified that Marina González was observed unknowingly; the conversa never spun on Saturday, "although she did some light things in the house; in the presence of the neighbor who witnessed her, it was as though she was pretending to be doing something."[37] The woman who denounced Leonor de la Higuera had lived in her home for half a year; she reported a different method used by her mistress to avoid work on the Sabbath. María López said that she "saw that she [Leonor] did nothing on the Sabbaths, except to observe them and to go to her mother's home; and she said that due to pain in her arms, she was permitted to do nothing on the Sabbath; and some Sundays I saw her sew and do some light work."[38] When Juana Rodríguez was asked why she was so dressed up and not engaging in any work, this conversa replied that it was only fifteen days since she had given birth and she was unable to work, but the witness told the inquisitors that she was not convinced by this ploy.[39]

One can see that even the most elaborate excuses were never failsafe. If one did not work, one was a judaizer; if one chose to perform light work, one was still remiss; if one concocted an excuse, it was perceived to be precisely that. In the case of María López, mentioned above, the very fact that this conversa engaged in some light work on Sundays, on the "true" day of rest, revealed the woman's proclivities to the witness. There were other women as well who were condemned for doing work on Sundays, obviously not respecting the Sabbath of their new religion. María González had been seen tossing the soapy water from her laundry into the canal that led to the street outside.[40] Catalina Gómez, a seamstress, was accused of spending some of her Sundays sewing until dinnertime, scrubbing her veils, and washing her children's shirts.[41] Here is a mixture of professional work, that of a seamstress, and domestic work, both which were forbidden on the day of rest.

Leonor Alvarez, who had feigned spinning on the Sabbath, was the daughter of a shopkeeper who ran a business with his wife. A converso tailor provided information about the Sabbath observance of this couple, because they did not work as they did during the rest of the week.

> He said that on the other days, they tended to a store which they had in the plaza, where they sold many things like oil and fish and oranges and other fruits that were in season; and that likewise there was another store in their home where they sold the same items, and that on the said Saturdays, this witness saw how, to the best of their abilities, they excused themselves from selling, in this manner in one store as in the other. And that this witness saw some people come to the house of the said Diego Rodríguez to purchase fish on the said Sabbath days, and this witness saw how Diego Rodríguez and his wife said that they had no fish.[42]

The witness, Francisco de Mesa, pointed out that when he saw that they did indeed have fish available, he asked why they had refused to sell it; he was told it was the Sabbath. Francisco said he saw them turn away potential customers at least thirty times on the Sabbath.

Lastly, we can sometimes find judaizers with a prepared excuse for indulging in work on Sunday. The same Marina González whose neighbor commented on the fact that she barely engaged in work on Saturdays was also observed by some guests staying in her home on that day. Juana de la Cadena and her husband Diego Falcón of Caracuel came to Almagro to visit Marina, who was Diego's cousin. Juana reported that her hostess rested on Saturdays, but on Sundays she sewed, apparently professionally, and engaged in light chores. The conversa justified her actions on the basis of economic need, claiming: "If it weren't for my work, because Francisco [her husband] is frail and does not know how to earn a living, I wouldn't be worth a thing and would have nothing with which to marry my daughter."[43] Since a six-day work week was the norm during this time, the judaizing working woman would lose two days' work, the Jewish Sabbath as well as the Christian Sunday. Here two seamstresses (the other the aforementioned Catalina Gómez) chose to abrogate the Christian Sabbath and proceed with their work.

YOM KIPPUR

Yom Kippur is similar to the Sabbath in that it is a day of rest, but unlike the Sabbath, it occurs only once a year. In addition, because it is a major fast day, preparation for this day is less physical and more spiritual. Nevertheless, the Inquisition files of judaizing women contain information on work-related activities that pertain to this holy of holy days.

For example, the fact that judaizers did not work on this day would be obvious to the observer. The first charge in the arraignment of Beatriz Jarada of Chinchón claimed:

> . . . the said Beatriz Jarada, believing that by the observance of the rites and ceremonies of the said deadly law of the Jews she would be saved, fasted the "Great Fast" of the Jews, not eating the entire day until the stars came out at night and observing on that day all the other things that the Jews were accustomed to observe or hold in honor and solemnity of this said fast. Also the said Beatriz, in order to further celebrate the said day of the Jewish fast, observed it and honored it by refraining from doing work on those said days and celebrating it as a holiday in which she demonstrated having great devotion in honor of the said law and rites of the Jews.[44]

Mayor González of Herrera twice confessed to Yom Kippur observance. In her first confession during the grace period of 1486, she said, "I fasted some fasts of the Jews, especially the one called the Great Fast, and on that day I was barefoot and shoeless; this day I observed and did not do any housework whatsoever as per ceremony, and the day before, I bathed as secretly as I could and I did not eat anything cooked on that day."[45] A neighbor of Mayor's, María Alfonso, had likewise confessed to judaizing in the fifteenth century and was subsequently tried at the beginning of the sixteenth century. María returned to her fallen ways after being convinced by Luis Alonso, the *carnicero* with messianic tidings. She said that he told her to keep the fasts of the Jews, not eating or drinking all day until the stars emerged; a few times he also informed her when it was the *Ayuno Mayor* (Great Fast) of the Jews and "likewise I fasted and observed it as best as I could, refraining from spinning and from doing other things, not eating or drinking the entire day until the evening star had emerged."[46]

Once the fast was over, the traditional break-fast was eaten, a meal obviously prepared by the judaizing women. Leonor Alvarez recalled having gone to her cousin's home in order to observe Yom Kippur; there they broke the fast with a meal of stew (*cazuelas*) and a hen.[47] Elvira Martínez of Toledo confessed to fasting on Yom Kippur; the prosecutor in her trial charged that she "observed and celebrated the day of the Great Fast of the Jews and on that said day, she had made and made with other persons great preparation for a dinner of fowl and other things and she and the other persons together dined on it on that said day."[48]

Passover (and Festivals)

All of the major holidays such as Yom Kippur and the three (pilgrimage) festivals of Passover, Sukkot, and Shavuot are days when it is forbidden to work. While Passover was extremely difficult to observe without being noticed, the festival of freedom was not overlooked by the judaizers. Again, the fact that a converso was not working was significant in the trial. For example, Catalina López of Almagro confessed that she ate matsah and that on this festival, "I refrained from working as much as I could, as I had been advised to do."[49]

The best-known symbol of this holiday, unleavened bread, had to be baked. Before the Expulsion, Jews could provide judaizers with this essential, but after 1492, there was no alternative but to bake it oneself. This activity was not easily hid from the kitchen servants. At any rate, a number of conversas confessed to kneading the dough for the matsah, preparation that was obviously work. Leonor Núñez y López of Alcazár said, "I observed some Jewish festivals, especially the festival of unleavened bread with the ceremonies that I knew, and I kneaded it and ate it."[50] María García of Herrera admitted to observing the festivals; if she had not observed any, it was because of some obstacle or fear of being seen by others rather than a desire not to observe; she kneaded the *pan cenceño* (unleavened bread), and she and her family ate it.[51]

Another conversa from Herrera began her explanation similarly; if she had been remiss or negligent in observing the holidays, she was so not by desire but rather in order to avoid being detected. However, she had kneaded the dough for unleavened bread, and she and her husband ate it ceremoniously. In addition, she had even kneaded and baked together with fellow conversas, obviously in an attempt to centralize the production process.[52]

Yet another conversa from Herrera referred to baking matsah; María Alfonso confessed to observing Passover by lighting candles before nightfall, dressing in her best clothes, and eating unleavened bread that she had made in her own home.[53] Marina González of Ciudad Real confessed that she had made and eaten unleavened bread, and her neighbor, Constanza Díaz, said that she baked the bread at home and ate it in order to observe as best as she knew.[54] Likewise Beatriz González admitted that she made matsah at home and that she and her husband ate it in celebration of Passover.[55] Isabel Rodríguez of Agudo confessed in 1501 that she observed many festivals, especially that of the unleavened bread, and she made and ate it ceremonially.[56] A witness in the house of Isabel García saw her making some very thin white tortillas without leavening, and the prosecutor charged her with eating the baked goods.[57]

The list of judaizing women concerned with making matsah in order to abide by Jewish law is lengthy, and the work involved was part and parcel of the acceptance of the law. As María González of Almadén said, "I made the unleavened bread and ate it at Passover in order to celebrate and observe it."[58] In her confession, María

López emphasized her attempt to maintain secrecy while carrying out the baking: "I confess my guilt that I observed some holidays, especially the festival of the unleavened bread in which I made it and ate it as did those in my house as secretly as I possibly could."[59]

The judaizers were working to observe Passover as best they could; some even prepared a festive meal and managed to prepare their homes for the holiday as well. A good example can be found in the trial of María Franca, who was accused of joining with others at Passover time; she ate various types of fowl, which, among other foods, were prohibited to Christians during Lent. Her house was said to have been festively decorated at this time; "everything was arranged as if for a holiday with clean tablecloths in honor of the Law of Moses."[60] Again, the work of cleaning and decorating the house, cleaning the linens for the table, and preparing a very special and essentially forbidden meal were seen as essential to the believer in Jewish law.

DIETARY LAWS

Observance of the Jewish dietary laws often involves work, in particular the proper slaughtering of those animals categorized as permitted for consumption and the ritual preparation of meat or the kashering process. The laws of ritual slaughter require examination of the animal in order to verify that no defects exist. In normative Judaism, a trained slaughterer both slaughters and then examines animals and poultry to be sure they are acceptable. After slaughtering, the kashering process serves to remove the blood, since consumption of blood, the symbol of life, is prohibited in the Bible.[61] The meat is salted or, if it is liver, roasted over an open flame, in order to drain it and generally remove nonveinal blood prior to cooking.

Certain organs must be cut or cleaned: the heart must be cut, the gizzard cut and cleaned, and a certain vein in the neck cut or removed. The sciatic nerve of animals other than fowl must be removed, and the fat portions attached to the stomach and intestines (*heilev*) cannot be eaten.[62] In addition, animals that died in a manner other than by ritual slaughter cannot be eaten; thus an animal that died a natural death, drowned, or might have been torn by a wild beast is not fit for consumption.[63]

Although the converso community could and did purchase meat from the Jewish slaughterhouses or butchers prior to 1492, they had to fend for themselves after the Expulsion. While slaughtering is a ritual that was and is most often performed by males, women are halakhically permitted to do so.[64] Thus we find women actually performing the slaughter, usually of fowl such as chickens and pigeons, which were the most commonly bred animals in many courtyards.

María González was seen beheading pigeons; when she herself did not personally execute this work, she preferred to give the dogs the unclean meat rather than to risk eating it.[65] Beatriz López worked hard both preparing fowl and attempting to hide her activities. The prosecutor in her trial claimed that "the said Beatriz slaughtered the birds that she was to eat in secret sites in order to kill them according to Jewish ceremony, and she ate them slaughtered in this way and would throw and have thrown dirt and ashes upon the blood of the birds in accordance with Jewish ceremony and rite."[66] Beatriz was not the only conversa in the village of Hita who ritually slaughtered birds at that time. Isabel García's accusation states:

> . . . the said Isabel, when she was about to slaughter some bird, prior to slaughtering it, would examine and pass the knife by her nail in the Jewish way and then slaughter the bird, watching over the blood as per Jewish rite and ceremony. And moreover, the said Isabel cut the claws above the wings and after cutting them, she dealt with them as according to rite and ceremony of the Jews and as a true Jewess that she appeared to be.[67]

Isabel examined the sharpness of the knife by passing it along her nail; the knife used for slaughtering must be regularly examined before and after use, to be sure that it is perfectly smooth, without a notch that might tear the flesh.[68]

The ritual slaughterer's work became the work of the fowl and livestock owners. Most households had chicken and other fowl, and those of greater means owned sheep; the wealthy also owned cows and flocks. While some of the conversos were wealthy, most of them had to procure meat other than chicken from outside the home and cleaned and cleansed it themselves. For example, Juana de los Olivos had neglected to confess "how she cleansed the meat very meticulously, in order to fulfill the commandment and Jewish ceremony, and how she refused to eat meat from the Christian slaughterhouse, and how she ate meat slaughtered by some heretic, believing that it had been killed by Jewish ceremony since it was prohibited to the Jews."[69] Juana was either unable or unwilling to slaughter herself and made an effort to obtain kosher meat; others innovated by buying meat from Christian slaughterhouses and proceeding with the kashering process within their homes.

The work of kashering meat had been undertaken by many of the conversas on trial. Beinart pointed out that removal of the nerves from the rear portion of the animal was a task performed by the women as well as by the men.[70] Women would remove the fat portions from the meat, kasher the meat with salt, and rinse it afterwards. Some of the trials only refer in passing to this work, while others go into considerable detail. The aforementioned Juana de los Olivos also "cleansed the meat very meticulously";[71] Marina González ate ritually slaughtered meat and "cleansed the meat she was going to eat in order to comply with and observe Jewish ceremony."[72] Sometimes the fact that fat was removed was mentioned: Juana de Chinchilla confessed that she "cleansed the meat, removing the fat from it," while Juana Núñez was accused of following Jewish law by "removing the fat from the meat that she was to eat and made others cleanse it."[73]

One cannot but be struck by the centrality of these particular dietary laws in the life of the judaizers, for so many conversas were charged with or confessed to engaging in work related to these laws. María Alvarez "cleansed the meat that she was to eat and removed the nerve from the leg [of the animal] in order to fulfill the command and ceremony of the Law of Moses."[74] Mayor Meléndez, also from Guadalajara, was accused of removing the fat and cleansing the meat as well as removing the sciatic nerve; Inés López confessed to removing the fat and then to frequently cleansing the meat and removing the nerve from the leg of the mutton.[75] Another conversa removed the sciatic nerve and the fat, salted the meat, and proceeded as required by law.[76]

The prosecutor in the trial of Beatriz López was convinced that the defendant was seriously involved in work that upheld the dietary laws. She was said to have eaten meat from which she had removed the fat, to have slaughtered poultry, and to have "opened the leg of mutton lengthwise in the Jewish way, and extracted certain things and washed the meat with large quantities of water until the meat was white and devoid of blood and thus she ate in the way that the Jews did."[77] Her neighbor was said to have

. . . cut the leg of mutton lengthwise and removed and washed certain things in it which would be fat and the nerve as do the Jews in observance of the Law of Moses. Similarly the said Isabel washed the meat with much water and after much washing she threw salt on it and put it in a certain place until she cleansed it and removed the blood in the Jewish way and according to the rites of the law of the Jews.[78]

As was mentioned earlier, it was difficult to engage in such activities and avoid the notice of one's servants. It is not surprising to discover that they were often the ones who provided details regarding this work as testimony for the prosecution. For example, a maidservant who had been employed by the González family explained:

. . . every time that they had meat from the slaughterhouse, this witness saw how the aforementioned, sometimes one, at other times another, cut up the meat, removing all the fat and suet so that none remained, and after removing the fat portions, they threw a bit of salt on it, and within a short while, they washed it with a lot of water and threw it in the pot.[79]

A neighbor's former servant recalled:

. . . that in the said time in which she lived with the said employers, that every time that they brought meat, the said mistress of this witness would remove the fat with her nails very meticulously. And she remembers that sometimes this witness saw the meat that was removed from the pot which was lean, devoid of all fat and suet, and how astonished she was that [this meat] that had been brought to the house fatty and soft was without a sign of fat.[80]

The mistress herself, María González, confessed to such actions and was aware that some of her servants had seen her, although they might not have comprehended the significance of the process. As a matter of fact, when the above witness asked how this meat had become so incredibly lean, María deftly explained that the cats had absconded with the fat. This conversa admitted that she had

> . . . removed the fat of the meat many times when they brought it from the slaughterhouse, prior to throwing it in the pot, and removing the suet and the fat; and that when leg was brought, this confessant split it open length-wise and removed the nerve; and that before placing the meat in the pot, she salted it and then removed the salt, washing it many times in different water, and that sometimes the said Catalina, black, and Catalina, daughter of the said Marcos Amarillo, and Isabel saw her removing the fat from the said meat, and washing it with a lot of water, and that it is possible that the said girls had seen her remove the nerve from the said leg, but she does not re-member well if they had seen it because this confessant hid from them when she could.[81]

The women preferred to hide their work in the kitchen from others, but they did not always succeed. Thus a relative of of Marina González reported that Marina had avoided her while she was dealing with meat, but she noticed that a piece had been removed and discarded, immediately gobbled up by a hen; presumably this was the gland from the leg.[82]

Just as the judaizing women were busy with their work of kashering the meat, they were similarly busy trying to hide their actions from their servants or some-times from their own family. Leonor Alvarez confessed to occasionally cleansing meat and removing its fat, but witness reports attest to family arguments in this re-gard. Her brother-in-law saw her "washing a piece of meat in a cauldron and she was washing it thoroughly and removing the fat and cleaning it until it remained free of suet and fat that it had." He then asked her about her actions, informing her that she was engaging in heresy.[83] Juana Rodríguez, Leonor's sister, tried to cover up her work with an excuse; she confessed "that sometimes she removed the fat from the meat as according to the ceremony of the Jews, and that in order not to be perceived, she said that the fat was not needed and that she removed it for some medicine."[84]

Other women did not encounter objections from their family members, but in-stead support and instruction. While Isabel de los Olivos y López was still living with her parents, she observed her mother judaizing and removing fat from meat. Isabel was then taught by her mother and continued this practice with her. Later, as a married woman, Isabel was instructed, or actually reinstructed, by her brother-in-law and "cleansed the meat, removing the fat and washing it, and she cleaned it and washed it thoroughly and arranged it for cooking."[85]

After preparing the meat, some of the conversas wanted to prevent their servants from cooking their food or partaking of their kosher meals. The González women separated their meat, not from the milk, as would be expected in a kosher kitchen, but from the meat of their servants. This action, needless to say, did not pass unnoticed. One of the servants explained how she and a slave in the household were given their meat to wash and cook; her mistress took the meat for the masters of the house, washed and cooked it herself, specifically preventing her servants from touching it. "And they did not want this witness or the said Francisca to scrub the plates and bowl in which the said masters ate with the [same] dishcloth with which this witness and the said slave scrubbed the platters and bowls in which they ate."[86] This is a marvelous innovation on the part of the judaizer; anything touched by the nonjudaizer was unclean and kept separate. As a result, however, the mistress of the house had extra work in the kitchen.

Others cooked separately for themselves; Marina González would serve pork products but not eat them herself. A visiting neighbor reported that she served bacon and pancakes made with lard but did not want to eat either dish, nor did she cook with pork in the stewpot from which she was to eat.[87] Mencia Rodríguez de Medina of Guadalajara was said to have cooked pork only so that the servants should notice;[88] as a result, she added more work to her daily chores in the hope of not standing out as a nonpork eater. Thus some hoped to hide their activities, some made excuses for them, and others clearly separated their food and food preparation from those of the nonobservers; the work involved was, as one can see, neverending.

DEATH AND MOURNING RITUALS

Death in a Jewish family is marked by numerous rites, based on both *halakha* (Jewish law) and ritual. While the mourner is expressly forbidden to work or engage in any activity other than eating, sleeping, praying, and mourning, there are still a great many things to be done after a death in caring for the deceased as well as for the mourners. However, this work must be undertaken by those not in mourning, and it is not surprising to discover that much of this work was carried out by women.

Beinart has pointed out that the Jews of Spain as well as the conversos traditionally had family members bathe the dead; in fact, "the washing of the dead was done by women."[89] It was the women from the family of the deceased who were usually the ones engaged in this onerous task. Verification of this practice is available in the trials of judaizing conversas such as María Alfonso of Herrera; she confessed that when some relative or person of her lineage died, including her own father, she bathed the deceased or supervised the bathing process.[90] Beatriz González of Toledo admitted that she had aided in the bathing of some deceased persons; she did not specify family members but rather a female neighbor.[91] Women in Spain and elsewhere might occasionally bathe males who were family members, as well as any Jewish women. However, men are permitted to shroud and gird the corpse of men but not of women.[92] An example in which both men and women were bathed can be found in the confession of the widow of Juan de Torres. This Toledan conversa explained: "I gave orders and aided in bathing my father when he died and bathed Gonzalo of Olmo and similarly my mother as well when they died, and I made preparations in the Jewish way that was required to prepare them in order that they could be buried."[93] While Elvira did not mention bathing her deceased husband, she specifically alluded to caring for each of her parents and for a third converso as well.

These conversas were fulfilling the role of the burial society, which, among other functions, traditionally organizes a vigil over the dead until the time of burial and cares for the body by bathing and cleaning it according to Jewish law. Inés López was accused of not admitting to bathing the dead and helping to bathe them.[94] Once the body is ritually clean, it should be clothed in a shroud. Evidence that the conversas continued this rite exists, as is illustrated in the trial of Isabel García, a document unusually rich in details about dealing with the dead. A witness testified that she

. . . saw in the house of Isabel, wife of Rodrigo García who is a widow, a certain deceased person whom she wanted to shroud, and who was covered up as if recently washed, and this witness marveled to see the corpse but recently washed and I believed that it was washed in the Jewish way and that when this witness entered the said house, there was no one present except for the said Isabel, [both of them] Jewish renegades.[95]

In the accusation at her trial, the prosecutor added that Isabel and others had bathed dead bodies according to Jewish ceremony.

The shroud is a very simple garb of muslin, linen, or cotton, usually white and without pockets; it is made by hand, and women obviously sewed the shrouds in addition to placing them on the bodies of the deceased. The judaizers were concerned with having proper shrouds made for them and occasionally left instructions to that effect on their deathbeds. Marina Gentil, ill and bedridden, instructed her husband regarding the quantity of linen to be used in her shroud; the prosecutor was certain that she died as a Jewess and was buried in a shroud as she had planned.[96] He obviously did not know who made the shroud per se, but a female had obviously bathed and enshrouded her.

Once the body was buried (and the conversos did not have the luxury of burying their dead in a Jewish cemetery), the mourners returned home, accompanied by friends and family, and partook of the traditional postburial meal, known as the *cohuerzo*. Again, work was entailed, as the preparers of this repast were usually women. Most of the confessions and accusations referred to the eating of this meal rather than to the preparation, perhaps because many more people were involved in eating than in preparing. However, Constanza Díaz admitted not only to sitting *shiva* (observing the seven days of mourning) and to eating the traditional meatless meal when she was in mourning, but to sending food to the home of other mourners at appropriate times.[97] The mourner, forbidden to work, cannot even prepare his or her meals; other members of the family or community must provide the food. Additional work was involved for the nonmourner seeking to comfort the mourner; since cooking was women's work, it is obviously the conversas who did this.

Another traditionally female occupation was that of the professional keener; women would sing dirges and lamentations and proclaim grief at the time of the funeral. There are various reports of women engaged in such activities, not at the gravesite but in private, during the mourning period; this is perfectly logical since they did not dare lead public displays and sing or chant traditional Sephardi dirges. There is no proof as to whether or not they were "professionals," as were their Jewish predecessors, who had received payment. Nevertheless, it is worthwhile to view the continuation of an effort to keen despite the fact that it might have been gratis; this type of work became as secret as the observance of the religion.

Isabel García was accused of lamenting, singing, crying and clapping her hands in mourning in the Jewish tradition. In a separate charge, the prosecutor added that she lamented and sang dirges with others. This charge was probably based on the witness account of a maidservant who explained:

> . . . she saw the wife of Rodrigo García, whom she believes is named Isabel, a New Christian of Jew[ish] origin, resident of Hita, and certain other persons who went to the home of a certain deceased person, climbed on top of the bed of the said deceased and sang and cried and wailed, praying, raising and lowering their heads, clapping their hands, and a certain person called out the songs and then the said Isabel and the others continued the singing and cried and prayed and walked around the deceased.[98]

Isabel was not the leader of the responsively recited dirges but was clearly part of the process. Presumably, the professional keeners would chant the solo lines and the others responded in unison.

Isabel was apparently active as a keener, both when she was in mourning and when she went to the homes of others in mourning. A different witness spoke of the time when the conversa was widowed, and "certain other persons came and all of them were there together in grief crying and lamenting and consoling themselves." She pointed out that after the burial, the entire group returned to the house, "closed the front doors of the house and threw down their cloaks and began to cry and lament and sing and clap their hands, crying for a while and singing for a while."[99] Catalina de Zamora was a keener as well; three different individuals testified to this fact in her trial.[100] As can be seen, the tradition of keening was continued in judaizing society.

It has already been emphasized that not working at a certain time could implicate a judaizer because Christian society would expect work at precisely that time. Whether the judaizer abstained from work because of observance of the Sabbath,

Yom Kippur, or other holidays, or during a mourning period, the outside witness who perceived this inactivity had incriminating evidence. The conversas in mourning certainly belong in this category; a servant noticed that the Isabel García mentioned above visited a mourner every day for an entire week, providing consolation for the woman who was sitting in mourning during the required *shiva* period (literally seven) "without engaging in any labor"; this witness emphasized that "all of those who gathered there were New Christians."[101]

The final example of a mourning judaizer who was seen observing Jewish rites was María Alvarez. This woman was mourning the death of her husband, also a converso, and the local clergyman passed by her home and remarked on his observations.

> When the novenas of the said deceased were made, this witness saw María Alvarez, wife of the said Diego de Sosa, behind [closed] door [for] some days and that one door was closed and the other open; behind the door that was closed, he saw her seated without doing any labor . . . and in the mornings the said María Alvarez went to the said church and that likewise after attending novenas some days he saw her in the said state, and that this seemed wrong to this witness, and that he had heard his father say that the Jews used to be behind the door like this when a Jew would die.[102]

Again, María was working hard to keep up the pretense of being a good Christian by attending church and offering prayers for the dead. This appropriate behavior was noted by the clergyman, as was her judaizing, since she remained seated within the confines of her home without engaging in any work during the mourning period.

OTHER WORK

If one prefers to revert to the traditional notion of work, then consideration of professions held by these women deserves some attention. Some have emerged in the context of religious observances; two professional seamstresses either sewed or refrained from sewing on the alternate days of rest.[103] Another was a professional teacher of sewing and embroidering who did not let her conversa pupils work on the Sabbath.[104]

Professional keeners had existed in medieval Spain, and this traditional activity was perpetuated. In addition, while most of these women had considerable households to run and were occupied as domestic managers, some engaged in outside work. Thus, a few more salaried workers can be noted.

The midwife Beatriz Rodríguez continued in her profession for most of her life until her incarceration by the Inquisition.[105] The first we hear of her activity is in 1511, when she was preparing spices which she ground before applying them to the stomach of a patient, a fellow conversa who was suffering from menstrual cramps.

Twenty-five years later, Beatriz was still the local midwife, serving the community in various capacities. At this time, she was involved with a couple and their new-born; presumably, she had delivered the child and provided postpartum care, but there is a great deal of confusion as to whether or not she also applied the baptismal waters to this infant. The priest and local sextons were clearly not pleased to discover this uncertainty, and the incident was reported to the Holy Tribunal. In this context, the fact that she was released and returned to her midwifery that same year, 1536, is significant. The Inquisition did not detain her again until 1550; this arrest seems to have curtailed her professional activities. Here was a conversa midwife who had been in the profession for at least forty years and possibly more. Her activities first came to the fore because of statements made when she was in her late twenties; she might even have become active in her profession as much as a decade earlier and, in all likelihood, was slowing down in 1550 as she neared the venerable age of seventy. There is no doubt that for Beatriz, midwifery was a lifetime profession, and the fact that she was a conversa working in this field indubitably complicated her life, since the Church did not look kindly upon New Christian midwives.

Women also owned property, which usually provided them with their own income and financial independence. Some owned land and houses; those that rented the houses collected the rent, as would any conscientious landlady.[106] Teresa de Villarreal is referred to as the owner of an olive grove.[107] Other women were known to have leased booths for the sale of tobacco.[108] María López of Cogolludo sold fabric, among other things. We learn about her activities because of the report of an altercation she had; she refused to refer business to certain tailors, who responded by boycotting her business and not sending their clients to purchase cloth from her.[109]

María Alonso was a cloth weaver; one of the witnesses in her trial claimed to have seen her working on her loom one Sunday afternoon, and another said she was weaving on All Saints' Day and making lye on San Sebastian's Day.[110] The making of lye soap by women was apparently common; a witness at the trial of Marina González commented that on Sundays, the defendant swept her house and made lye.[111] It is not clear, however, if these women sold the lye to others or made it solely for their own consumption. María Díaz was referred to throughout her trial as *la cerera,* a maker or seller of wax.[112]

Other women were workers from the lower class. The daughter of Marina González seemed to have had her own business dealings. We learn of this indirectly; her parents suspected that the woman who was supposed to sell their daughter's handiwork but had refused to do so was actively testifying against them.[113] Some paid others for piecemeal work; the husband of Leonor Alvarez complained that Luzia de Cuenca took a certain quantity of thread from her to weave and returned with less than she had taken.[114] In an explanation as to why the inquisitor should discredit a particular witness, a woman was accused of having stolen what she had been given to spin.[115] The defendant Beatriz of Ciudad Real was one of the few conversas categorized as poor. Because of her economic status, she earned her living by carrying water to people's homes.[116] Pasculina was a twelve-year-old maidservant in the home of Mayor González; here, one conversa was employing another.[117] Another conversa apparently sold flour at home, for she was reported to have cheated one of her customers.[118]

The life of the judaizing conversa carried risks whether she was working or resting. By observing the Jewish Sabbath, she was blatantly abstaining from either her domestic duties or the work she did outside the home, such as sewing, tending to a store, or serving as a midwife. By not observing the Christian day of rest, she was likewise declaring her loyalty to the religion of her ancestors. The preparation for the Jewish Sabbath was extensive and entailed substantial labor in the kitchen and the laundry room as well as in the rest of the home. Preparations by the crypto-Jewish woman for the various Jewish holidays was similar. On these days, and especially on Yom Kippur, the absence of labor and, in the case of the latter, the act of not partaking of food, were telltale.

While the Sabbath and the holidays are central to the Jewish calendar, the dietary laws were integral to the everyday life of the judaizer. As has been seen, these laws are demanding, and the woman took over tasks such as slaughtering that had traditionally been in the male domain. It was extremely difficult to hide such unusual observances as the kashering of meat, or not cooking with pork products, especially in light of the fact that almost all of these woman had kitchen servants afoot. Nevertheless, they continued to work in their kitchens, observing the laws to the best of their ability, preparing meat and foods for the Sabbath, for the holidays, for daily consumption, and for postburial meals. The work did not subside when families sustained losses; the women worked from the time of death until the end of the mourning period by bathing the dead, preparing shrouds, keening, and preparing food. At the same time, the mourner herself would stand out because of the absence of work on her part. Whether working or not working, the judaizer was apt unintentionally to reveal her true proclivities. The Inquisition was, needless to say, anxious to discover all these activities as well as the inactivity. Both were incriminating, for the intent behind the deed was clear; by virtue of their work or abstinence from work, these women were heretics in the eyes of the Church. Their fate was sealed.

5

The López-Villarreal Family

Three Convicted Judaizers (1516–1521)

THUS FAR, EXCERPTS from Inquisition dossiers have been used to develop patterns of behavior and to analyze particular tendencies. By analyzing a specific trial or group of related trials, however, one can procure a more focused picture. While examining the life of one or a few conversos cannot be used to draw conclusions about all of them, a very different result is achieved. One can delve into details of a particular trial in depth and begin to appreciate the complexity of the legal system as well as of the society of both New and Old Christians. Consequently, the remaining chapters will be devoted to narrower, yet more detailed and intense subjects: three trials dealing with one family, the trial of a midwife; and two trials from the village of Alcázar.

The pursuit of messianic enthusiasts in the converso community was concentrated in Extremadura, the region where the prophetic figures and their followers were located, and was expedited rather quickly. Needless to say, the Inquisition did not desist in its search of heretics and heretical activity once that mission was completed.[1] On the contrary, suspected judaizers from various locales throughout Castile were continually facing the tribunal either in Toledo or in one of its temporary courts.

An analysis of judaizers in the postmessianic period will serve to exemplify the continuing activities of the Inquisition in Castile. The files of three family members, all residents of the village of Cogolludo, represent a very intensive series of trials that took place between 1516 and 1521; they also reflected the determination of the inquisitors to quash any judaizing proclivities, even in one unimposing town.

Cogolludo was a modest agricultural village located approximately 33 kilometers north of the city of Guadalajara. It is included in a list of thirty-one Jewish communities that existed in the province of Guadalajara prior to the Expulsion. Its post-Expulsion population during the first half of the sixteenth century is estimated to have been between 350 and 400.[2] Because such a small village was under scrutiny and because of the comprehensive nature of the defense tactics utilized in these trials, a very large percentage of the population was involved, willy-nilly, in one family's trials and tribulations.

A number of issues need to be addressed in regard to these three court records. First, two women and one man from the same family were tried simultaneously; obviously a family network was under scrutiny, and the interactions between the family members will prove to be extremely significant. In addition, because of the nature and abundance of tachas, or lists attempting to discredit witnesses for the prosecution, more than 150 inhabitants of Cogolludo were involved or mentioned in these proceedings.[3] Third, there is the question of the level of judaizing in which the defendants actually engaged, and the validity of the charges leveled at them; even if one assumes that the charges were justified, the punishments meted out seemed rather harsh.

To begin with the third issue, the judaizing activities of this family, all three defendants were condemned by the tribunal; they all perished within a year. The trials of María López and her daughter Isabel López both began on September 9, 1516, and were conducted simultaneously. Exactly two years later, the trial of Pedro de Villarreal, María's husband and Isabel's father, began. The women's trials ended, for all intents and purposes, on November 30, 1518, at the auto-de-fé in which both women were relaxed; Pedro was relaxed on October 4, 1519, less than eleven months later. Both parents' trials officially concluded on April 15, 1521, when the court made a declaration determining the date on which judaizing began, so that condemnation of property and goods could be calculated.[4] By this time, neither of the two was alive, but the court could legally confiscate what it deemed appropriate from the surviving children.

The trials of mother and daughter are similar on many accounts and differ significantly from Pedro's. The fact that the first two were coterminous seriously affected the third trial, in particular the nature of the defense tactics as well as the psychological state of Pedro, who, after only two months of imprisonment, became a bereaved husband and father. It is not surprising to discover very similar lines of defense in the women's trials; Pedro actually took a very active role in the organization of their defense and was aided by one of his sons. Both women refused to confess to any heretical activities and withstood the torture meted out to them. On the other hand, the fact that on March 19, 1519, during the sixth month of his trial, Pedro confessed, comes as no surprise; he "weakened" less than four months after losing two of his loved ones.

In order to attempt to determine if the López women were judaizing, one must first examine the accusations as well as the witness testimonies upon which these charges were based. Each trial contains a list of witness testimonies: María's had six, Isabel's had five, and Pedro's had eight. In each trial, the prosecutor chose the information from these accounts that he decided was incriminating and listed them as charges in the accusation; details could be culled from more than one testimony as long as they belonged to the same category. Note that the order of the charges is not related to the order the witnesses' statements were recorded, but rather to the importance of judaizing activities in the eyes of the court. María's accusation listed nine counts, but only six of them related to judaizing. The other three are generic heretical charges, such as withholding the fact that she participated in heresies, perjuring herself by covering up her own as well as others' activities, and not confessing with regard to what she had done or the knowledge she had of others.[5]

The more specific charges began with observing Jewish law by not eating pork or anything cooked with it because it is prohibited in the Law of Moses; she also knew of and had seen others who did likewise. In order to determine from where this presumption arose, one must examine the witness accounts. There were six testimonies in the case against María, and, as will be shown, all of them were also used by the prosecutor in her daughter's and/or her husband's proceedings as well. Two of the accounts mention abstinence from pork in varying degrees. The second witness, Mayor, had lived with Pedro and María in 1507 for about half a year, during which time, she claimed, neither of them ate pork or anything cooked with pork.[6] Another maidservant, Madalena, the wife of Martín, the *cabronero* (goatherd), was the third witness cited; she testified that she had worked for this couple about four years earlier. During the year of her service, "she saw that her said employers did not eat pork or throw any in their pots," that is, cook with it.[7] These two declarations clearly provided the prosecutor with the grounds for his first claim.

The second charge was that the defendant had removed the fat of the meat or had it removed together with the suet and the like, cleaning the meat thoroughly, washing it many times in order to remove the blood; this was often done together with others. Once again, information provided by the second witness, Mayor, proved useful to the prosecution, for she told how she had seen her masters, Pedro and María, remove the fat and the suet from meat prior to cooking it; sometimes they would order a different maidservant to do this chore.[8] The latter statement clarifies the claim that at times they had the fat removed by others rather than doing it themselves. Madalena, too, alluded to removing fat with a knife when her masters noticed that their meat was not sufficiently lean.[9] The fourth witness, a former servant of Isabel's named María, provided a great deal of information concerning her past employers and had also had contact with Isabel's parents in 1513. She specified that she had seen her mistress's mother and her sister Catalina cleaning and removing the fat and washing the meat.[10] The sixth witness in this trial, Francisco Yague, had worked for Pedro and María as a youth, from the ages of eleven to fourteen (1511–14). "This witness saw how the said María López washed the meat that was brought from the slaughterhouse a great deal prior to cooking, far more than Old Christians were accustomed to washing." He did not know if she or one of her kitchen maids had removed fat or something else by hand, but he was certain that the meat-cleaning process in his mistress's household was quite different from that in other homes.[11]

The third charge accused her of continuing in her false beliefs, transgressing and making matters worse. For example, when a leg of meat was brought to her house, she opened it or had it opened lengthwise so that the sciatic nerve could be removed; again this was done in the company of others. This was the main contention of the first witness, Juan Ropero, a smith who had apparently visited the defendant's home. In 1504, he recalled entering María's kitchen, where he saw a leg of meat cut open and then consumed by Pedro, his wife, their son-in-law Francisco de Murcia, and two sons Francisco and Pedro.[12] Since he had seen so many family members involved, the identical account appears in all three trials.

Madalena's testimony, which was cited in both counts above, contains details pertaining to this activity as well. Her employers, Pedro and María, would slit open a leg of lamb lengthwise with a knife after cleaning it thoroughly.[13] Francisco Yague noted some activity in the kitchen when there was leg of lamb or other meat, but his description was not precise enough to stand by itself as an indictment of kashering meat. He referred to seeing the leg cut up into many large pieces about the size of a fingertip.[14] However, the two prior references were specific enough to enable the prosecutor to include the charge of opening the leg of an animal and removing the nerve.

The fourth charge maintained that María prepared Sabbath stews or gave instructions to have them or other Jewish cuisine prepared; these had been eaten together with other persons in a Jewish way. The only reference that seems to pertain to preparing stews is in the above description by Yague; after cutting the meat up, it was thrown into a stew pot to cook with spices for a very long time. While there is no reference to the Sabbath or a Sabbath meal per se, it was clearly a communal meal, for in addition to his employers, their sons Francisco and Pedro as well as their daughter Catalina shared in this meal; the assumption was that communal meals took place on the Sabbath and holidays.[15]

The fifth charge contends that conger eel, eel, octopus, spotted dogfish, or other fish without scales, or rabbit or hare, were not consumed because the Jews do not eat them. The same Madalena (third witness) said that during the time she worked for Pedro and María, she never saw them eat rabbit, hare, conger eel, eel, octopus, or spotted dogfish.[16] The fourth witness, María, claimed that during Lent, she had seen conger eel cooked in their house but had never seen her employers eat it; on the contrary, they gave it to their servants.[17]

The sixth charge in this accusation was that meat had been eaten on Fridays and on other days forbidden by the Church, despite the fact that María had no health problems that might justify her actions;[18] again, she was in the company of others. Judaizers who ate traditional Sabbath meals that included meat would have transgressed in this manner, but there are no direct claims made concerning María and Sabbath observance. However, in Madalena's description of processing meat, she mentioned being told to keep an eye on certain meat, sometimes raw and sometimes cooked; this task was usually performed on Thursdays or on Friday mornings. Subsequently, she would be sent out of the house on errands to places out of ear shot such as to the vineyards; upon her return, the meat was invariably gone, presumably having been cooked and eaten or cooked and saved for Sabbath meals.[19]

There are no direct references to Sabbath observance in María's accusation. However, one witness account is quite explicit about Sabbath activities of both the defendant and her husband. Closer examination reveals that this account was copied from the list of charges in the trial of Pedro, and thus dated May 20, 1518,[20] well after the presentation of the charges in María's trial. This is the most likely explanation for the fact that Pedro was accused of observing the Sabbath while his wife, with whom he had observed, was not. On the whole, the judaizing activities attributed to María concerned the dietary laws, in particular which foods are forbidden, the kashering of meat, and the leg of permitted animals. Both her daughter Isabel and her husband Pedro would be confronted with charges of observing the Sabbath as well as the dietary laws.

Isabel also faced six charges of judaizing, followed by the standard accusation that the defendant had committed perjury by claiming no knowledge of other heretical acts and had not confessed to what she knew about other judaizers. While there is some overlap in the lists presented to mother and daughter, they are by no means identical nor is the order of activities the same.

Isabel was first and foremost accused of observing the Sabbath by dressing in holiday garb and joining others in this celebration. The prosecutor culled his information from two sources: a testimony that was used only in Isabel's trial, and one that appeared in all three trials. The former belonged to Catalina de Cervantes, a fellow resident of Cogolludo whose employee had previously worked for Isabel and her husband, Francisco de Murcia, sometime prior to 1508. This data, obviously secondhand or hearsay, was of the weakest sort but was nevertheless included as the first witness testimony in Isabel's trial. The maidservant, Mari, who referred to her employers as *tornadizos* or turncoats, told Catalina that "on the Sabbath day, they dressed up and wore holiday garb, the said Francisco de Murcia and his wife . . . and that being so dressed up on the said Sabbaths, they did not exit the door to the street." Presumably, they stayed inside their home so as not to be noticed while wearing their best clothes.[21]

The next witness to mention Sabbath observance was Madalena, the wife of Martín Simón, who used to live with Isabel's parents from about 1513 to 1515; she was the fifth witness in all three lists. Her statement appears in all three trials but, as was mentioned above, does not seem to have been used by the prosecution against María; if it had been, María would have been charged with Sabbath observance, baking hallah, praying, dressing festively, and the like. While this was the testimony that was presented rather late in both women's trials, it was used as the basis of two Sabbath charges in Isabel's trial as well as in her father's case. Perhaps the prosecutor felt he had a strong enough case to indict the mother but wanted to strengthen his position against Isabel. At any rate, there is no doubt that he felt that the information provided by this resident of Sant Andre was useful; the first two counts in both Pedro's and Isabel's accusation are linked to Madalena's testimony instead.

Essentially, Madalena, their former employee presented a detailed account of the meetings of a group of Sabbath observers including Isabel, her husband, and her parents as well as another New Christian couple. This group of judaizers would dress up in holiday clothes from Friday afternoon at sunset through Saturday morning. "All of them were dressed festively and remained that way all evening and all Saturday morning until the said lamp went out. Not on Saturday night or on Sunday or on any of the other days of the week were they dressed up as they were on the said Friday nights and Saturday mornings." Their obvious change of garments clearly made an impression upon this maidservant.[22]

The second count against Isabel referred to praying; it was claimed that on the Sabbath as well as on other days, Isabel joined others in Jewish prayer.[23] The two witnesses above also referred to prayer, usually occurring on the Sabbath. Catalina, again on the basis of her employee's report, included an account of Isabel and her husband entering a room in which they prayed, raising and lowering their heads, and making *la baraha* (the blessing).[24] This testimony inevitably led to the charge of *sabadeando* (praying). Confirmation of such activities came from Madalena, who while working for Isabel's parents, saw the family remain behind a closed door for two or three hours at a time. Isabel had ordered Madalena to clean the candles on Friday afternoons and to place new wicks in the lamps; in addition, Isabel had joined her mother in baking hallah, from which she removed a piece of dough.[25] This testimony contains many more details that deal with Sabbath activities in which Isabel participated, but the prosecutor chose not to integrate them into his judaizing list. While this Madalena's testimony seems to have been overlooked by the prosecutor in his arraignment of María, it was utilized, albeit partially, in compiling the charges against her daughter, and in Pedro's trial it would be used to its fullest.

The third charge in Isabel's accusation was that she opened the leg of meat brought to her house and removed the sciatic nerve. In the fourth count, she was accused of having meticulously removed the fat from meat, cleaning the meat thoroughly, and removing the blood. Although these two activities are listed separately, they will be analyzed together in terms of witness testimonies, since they almost always appeared in tandem.

For example, there is the testimony of Juan Ropero, the first witness in María's trial and the second in Isabel's. He recalled having entered the kitchen in the Villarreal home in 1504

. . . and he saw the wife of the said Francisco de Murçia, daughter of the said Villarreal, who had a leg of lamb or beef in her hands and this witness saw how she cut it open lengthwise with a knife and cleaned the inside of the said leg with her nails and what this witness believes to have been the fat that she removed from the said leg and that later he saw the aforesaid throw the said leg into the pot to cook.[26]

A more detailed account appears in the testimony given by María, the fourth witness in both trials. This twenty-year-old had worked for Isabel.

. . . [at times] this witness observed the said Isabel, her mistress, when meat was brought from the slaughterhouse, she removed all the fat and took out every trace of fat, sometimes with a knife and at other times, with her nails without leaving any suet or fat at all. She washed it over and over with a lot of water until the said meat was bloodless and very white. When leg of lamb was brought into the house, the aforesaid opened it lengthwise from the gambrel or hone until the bottom and this witness saw that the aforesaid removed certain things which she does not know what they were. In addition, she is certain that the fat was removed from all around and that it was washed with a lot of water as [already] said.[27]

The fifth charge claimed that she did not eat pork, conger eel, octopus, eel, or other fish that had no scales, or hare or rabbit, because the Jews do not eat these things; she also knew of and had seen other persons who did not eat these for the same reason. A different Madalena, wife of Martín, the cabronero, who had been employed in Isabel's parents' house, referred to communal meals in which her employers and Isabel and her husband had been present. While most of her statement concerned María and Pedro, this third witness to testify in all the trials made some general statements about food. During the year with this family, she said, she never saw them eat rabbit, hare, conger eel, octopus, or spotted dogfish.[28] It is uncertain if "them" refers to the older generation or includes the defendant and family as well.

The fourth witness, María, made more specific references; the fact that she spent three years living with Isabel and family also strengthened her testimony. She mentioned that cooking was done without pork and that she had seen that the couple with whom she resided did not eat pork or cook with it; neither had she seen them eat conger eel during Lent.[29] The prosecutor had obviously combined these two testimonies to make his charge.

The sixth count stated that Isabel cooked stews and other Jewish cuisine, which she ate in the company of others. These family meals have already been alluded to. María, after describing the way in which meat was treated, referred to the porkless dish being cooked with chickpeas, spices, and onions.[30] The assumption here was that this was an *adafina* (a special Sabbath stew), presumably to be eaten on the Sabbath, although there is no specific mention of either the day or time in which the dish was eaten.

The López women vehemently denied being judaizers throughout their trials. After the prosecutor's list was read to each of them, the defendants offered their initial response to the charges.[31] María denied the charge of not eating pork, insisting that she had eaten pork and the meat of male pigs; she pointed out that she could tolerate neither fatty meat nor fatty pork, but there was no connection between these personal habits and judaizing.

In response to the second charge of kashering her meat, she said that the meat that went in her pots was lean but had not been purged or cleaned ceremonially. She denied removing the sciatic nerve of leg of lamb and the like. The fourth charge referred to Jewish foods and stews, which the defendant said she had not made or eaten since her conversion to Catholicism. As for the fifth count, she claimed she did eat rabbit, spotted dogfish, hare, and fish without scales. In response to the sixth charge of eating meat on days forbidden by the Church, she explained that she had done so with the permission of her physician and her priest. As for the last three counts concerning general heretical activities and affiliation with heretics, she denied and negated them.[32]

Her daughter Isabel was more terse in her first rebuttal, which also was an immediate response to the accusation presented on January 12, 1517. She said she had never observed the Sabbath and that she did not know to what the second (praying and *sabadeando*) or third (removing the sciatic nerve) charges were referring. She categorically denied the fourth (kashering meat), fifth (not eating nonkosher meat and fish), and sixth (adafinas) counts. Likewise she denied engaging in or hiding the activities of heretics and the like.[33] As a matter of fact, the only statement made by either of these women that was classified as a confession was totally unrelated to judaizing. Isabel said that in 1507, she took a sick infant daughter to an employee of the la Torres woman for healing; this woman did cure the child, but the defendant must have considered this action to have been unconventional and problematic for the Church.[34]

In the course of the trial, each conversa had additional time to prepare a response to the prosecutor's claims. On February 9, 1517, María again negated the first count, explaining that, on the contrary, she did eat pork and cooked with it, although perhaps she had once stopped eating it because of illness rather than any Jewish rite and ceremony. She also negated the second and third charges, claiming she had never removed anything from meat in compliance with any ceremony; if she cleaned her meat or removed the fat, there was no heretical motivation behind this act. Besides, men, and not women, traditionally remove the sciatic nerve.[35]

The fourth charge, preparing stews, was denied, as were the fifth, sixth, and seventh. The defendant emphasized that she ate all the nonkosher fish mentioned as well as hare, rabbit, drowned birds, and other foods not permitted to the Jews. In addition, she never ate meat on forbidden days, something that, had she done so without the permission of her priest and her doctor, would have been a sin rather than a heretical crime. On the contrary, she had lived her life as a good, loyal Catholic Christian and could not comprehend the reason for her denunciation.[36] Later in the trial, on August 6, 1518, when the actual testimonies were read to María, she asserted that they were false and that she had never done any such thing.[37] As was the custom, the defendant was given six days in which to prepare a detailed response to these claims.

Thus, on August 12, she presented a statement attesting to her innocence, claiming that she was being wrongly detained and that the witnesses' statements were based on hearsay and idle beliefs, which were all without any basis whatsoever. After this rather long statement of her innocence, she once again dealt with each charge individually. Most of her claims were identical to those already presented. She insisted that she had not kept the dietary laws of the Jews and that often the meat from the slaughterhouse was disgustingly dirty, which was why she had to clean it properly. On the whole, these witnesses were committing perjury. At the same time, it was by no means an act of heresy not to eat pork at times or to cook lean meat in a pot with chickpeas and spices. The witnesses were simply attempting to damage the defendant's reputation, they were unreliable, and her defense would prove her innocence by means of the *abonos* (character witnesses) and tachas to follow.[38]

Like her mother, Isabel presented a rebuttal to the accusation of the prosecution; both women made their presentations on the same day, although Isabel's was lengthier. Thus, on February 9, 1517, she reiterated the charges against her and then responded:

> I say that I negate the contents of the first and second clauses of the said denunciation and accusation, because I did not observe Sabbaths that were not holy days [that] we were instructed to observe by the Holy Mother Church and I never used to wear or wore the clothes mentioned unless I went out to a [Saturday] mass or a baptism or a wedding ceremony that happened to be on that day or to mass after childbirth and not per rite or ceremony or in honor of the Law of Moses. The prayers I recited as a Christian were the Ave Maria, the Pater Noster, the Creed, and the Salve Regina. And the raising and lowering of one's head during prayers is neither an act of judaizing nor a rite or ceremony of the Jews.[39]

Regarding preparation of kosher meat, Isabel claimed not to know what the sciatic nerve was, and insisted, as did her mother, that in general, the men dealt with the meat. However, she pointed out that cleaning meat prior to cooking was by no means a ceremony but rather an act of cleanliness. Then the defendant negated the fifth and sixth charges, emphasizing that she indeed ate all of the fish and animals listed and that she had not prepared the so-called stews or Jewish food; in fact she did not even know to what these witnesses were referring. Lastly, she denied having participated in heretical activities or committing crimes.

> I request of Your Paternal Reverends to order it [the accusation] declared null and to free [me] as innocent and not guilty of that which I have been denounced and accused, restoring to me my honor and good reputation and

sending me out of this prison I am in and remove whatever embargo and se-questering of my goods that has been done, imposing eternal silence upon the said prosecution attorney. For this and for what is necessary I implore the holy and noble office of your Reverend Fathers and negate the prejudicial in-novation henceforth, I conclude and request the fulfillment of justice.[40]

The witness testimonies were read anonymously to Isabel in two segments. After hearing the first four, the defendant briefly negated each one, asserting that she in-deed ate hare, rabbit, and pork. Likewise, her response to the fifth testimony was negative.[41] On August 12, the day on which her mother was responding to the charges against her, Isabel was given the standard six days in which to prepare her response. As did her mother, the defendant began with a rebuttal of the testimonies she had heard, followed by various tactics chosen by the defense.

On August 18, 1518, Isabel made her detailed statement, certain that she should be freed and that the evidence of the prosecutor was invalid, confused, false, and impossible to prove. She was a good Christian, and the depositions of the witnesses were absurd, since she had never engaged in any of the activities described. She did not observe the Sabbath or recite blessings.

> . . . no one can truthfully say what I did or did not do. The witnesses cannot testify and besides, raising and lowering one's head during prayer can be done without being a custom or Jewish ceremony, for Christians reciting Catholic prayers when they name the name of Our Father Jesus Christ and his glorious mother Mary and even some other saints tend to lower their heads.[42]

This was essentially a rebuttal to the testimony of Catalina de Cervantes.

As for the second testimony, Isabel explained that opening the leg of meat is not a heretical act and that the witness was not sure what was being done except that he thought fat was being removed, which, again, is no act of heresy. The third witness testimony was also inconclusive regarding heresy. It is no crime not to eat pork or cook with it or to clean one's meat; in addition, the mistaken impression was given that meat was cleaned after cooking as well. At any rate, no one in the household had cooked meat on Thursdays for consumption on Fridays. Mention was made of eating meat on prohibited days, something that was by no means a crime or a sign of heresy, and sometimes it was simply necessary to do so. As for which meats were eaten, she insisted that she had consumed all the fish and animals forbidden to the Jews.

As for the fifth witness account, she again emphasized:

> . . . having washed and cleaned meat before throwing it in the pot and adding spices and chickpeas is by no means a conclusive crime or proof of heresy, especially since I have been a meticulous and delicate woman and make efforts to have all my things very clean without thinking [that I was] doing or that I had committed a crime or a sin or a heretical act.[43]

Like other testimonies, this was little more than a bundle of lies and falsehoods, stated Isabel.

The defendant denied dressing up in holiday clothes on Fridays and Saturdays. On the contrary, Isabel considered herself to be a well-dressed and honorable woman who often wore very nice clothing daily. She had never seen a special lamp except at church, and God never wanted her to have her lamps cleaned or new wicks put on Friday afternoons rather than on other days of the week; there most definitely had not been any Jewish ceremony involved here. Again, cleaning the meat is no sign of heresy, but rather of diligence, because the meat was always filthy when brought from the slaughterhouse. As for the claim that she had thrown a piece of dough in the fire, perhaps she had. A piece might have fallen inside or been removed when she was checking to see if the dough had risen; sometimes one of the children would ask her to make separate little round rolls or balls of dough for them, and this activity might have been observed by the witness and misinterpreted. The defendant had no idea why such a person would hate and despise her, for only a mortal enemy would contradict the truth so blatantly.[44]

On August 25, 1518, María made two detailed objections to the fifth and sixth witness testimonies; these were synopses of the descriptions given by Madalena, the wife of Martín Simón, and by Francisco Yague. In her first clause, María contended that God never intended for lamps to be lit specially on Friday nights, Saturdays, or any other days. If she entered the underground cellar referred to in the testimony, the reason related to the functioning of her household or to getting wine, not to performing Jewish rites or ceremonies. At the same time, God never wanted her to dress up or wear different clothes on Friday nights or Saturdays; she did not change her mode of dress on one day or another unless it was a holiday. Besides, wearing a clean blouse on Fridays was never a ceremony. If she attended anything on Saturday mornings, it was mass. Finally, "God never intended for there to be lamps in my house on Fridays or on Saturdays or on any other day," or to throw some dough in the fire, and washing one's meat well is no Jewish rite but rather a sign of cleanliness and diligence.

In the second clause, María claimed that this last witness did her no damage because, as she already pointed out, cleaning and cooking meat is not a rite. When he said that she removed mounds (of fat) from the meat, it was done for the sake of cleanliness, and this activity is not prohibited by any of the laws. Therefore, it is obvious that these perjurers were her mortal enemies who spread falsehoods when she should be absolved by the Holy Tribunal.[45]

On the following day, the defense began in earnest with lists of abonos and *indirectas*, or questions to be asked of various witnesses whose names were also supplied by the defense. After the fact was established that the witnesses on the stand indeed knew the defendant personally, they were asked if she lived as a good Christian after her baptism, if she had gone to hear masses and sermons and other divine offices, and if she observed Sundays, Easters, and other holidays as would a good

Christian. Next they were questioned as to whether she confessed and received the sacraments annually as required by the Church, and if she was a clean and neat woman who took pride in her actions such as in preparing food, in wearing clothes, and in cleaning and decorating her home. The question that followed dealt with her eating habits: whether she ate the various animals and fishes that were prohibited by Jewish law. Was she someone who gave proper doctrines and good advice to her servants and made certain they were properly instructed in Catholicism? Could they verify the fact that when Don Alonso de la Cerda, the lord of the manor, had been ill, the defendant cared for him in her home and cooked meat daily for him as well as for his hawks and hunting dogs?[46] Two more questions pertained to her cooking of entire legs of meat and quarters of veal and lamb that were roasted with their kidneys and everything else inside them.

On October 16, 1517, four more questions were added to the list for the character witnesses. They dealt with times when either the defendant, the daughter, the husband, or the grandchild of the defendant were ill. In each instance, permission was granted to go for medical help, to a parish priest, or on a pilgrimage to seek a cure, after which special masses were recited.[47]

As one might imagine, the various witnesses' replies to the above questions were diverse; the list of names provided by the defense usually specified which questions were to be posed to which witness. The first list contained thirteen names, including clerics, chaplains, sextons, servants from Don Alonso's estate, and even one of the prosecution witnesses, Juan Ropero.[48] Some testified that María and her daughter had requested special masses or had confessed and taken the sacraments regularly and did the works of good Christians. One recalled seeing in the defendant's home pork, which was roasted and then eaten by her and her family. Juan Ropero, the Old Christian who had known the defendant for thirty years, responded to two questions. First, he ascertained that María was a very meticulous person who prepared food well; however, the rest of his answer, he pointed out, had already been submitted to the court. Then he said that sometimes when he entered the house, he saw the defendant roasting a partridge or hen; once she seemed to be tending very diligently to some sick person in her home.

Another witness, María Gaytan, revealed that the defendant' s son-in-law, Francisco de Villarreal, "told her that if the inquisitors should call upon her, that they beg of her to reveal whatever she knows and that she should say no more [than that]." She verified the claim that María's household and person were very clean and well kept; for more than seven years, the two women lived next to one another, and the witness came and went freely, often eating at her home, feeling very much at home there.[49] The final witness in this group was the wife of a sexton who had once accompanied the defendant on a pilgrimage to Santa María de Caritas.

The defense did not rest but continued to compose new lists of abonos and indirectas. This time they asked witnesses if they knew that the defendant entered her cellar in order to give wine to the wine butlers and that she never went there for other purposes. In addition, could they confirm that there was no lamp as described in her home and that there was often a great deal of activity and talk in her home that would be distracting? Next, did they know that María went to Saturday morning mass religiously and that on that day as well as on Fridays, she dressed no differently than any other? Last, did they know that her cellar had no doors or closures but was always open?

The defense then nominated fourteen people who could verify some or all of the above statements. This list included Don Alonso himself and a number of his servants, two former wine butlers, and assorted others, some of whom were New Christians but were, nonetheless, allowed to testify.[50] As it turned out, most of these people were unable to respond to the questions. One of Don Alonso's valets mentioned that some of María's household help would wash meat before cooking, but he knew no more than that. On September 23, an Old Christian named Catalina who had been a neighbor of María's from 1508 to 1515 testified. She was often in the defendant's home and had seen her and her maidservants bake and cook on Fridays as well as on Saturdays; she saw María boil the bread in preparing it for the kneading board. She recalled being there one Saturday night when a pair of suckling pigs were slaughtered because guests were due to arrive; Catalina herself had suggested waiting until Sunday morning. This was not the only time this family had dined on such animals. Also, on numerous occasions, this neighbor saw no difference whatsoever between Fridays, Saturdays, and other days of the week. In addition, Catalina never saw special cleaning of meat or preparations or opening of legs of lamb. "Once, by-and-bye, as she began to enter the house, she saw the said María López and Isabel, her daughter, wife of Francisco de Murcia, opening the leg of beef in half in preparation for cooking, but she did not see anything whatsoever removed from the middle." Lastly, she never saw the defendant wear a clean blouse on the Sabbath.[51]

A household servant named Juana had worked in the defendant's household for six years and prepared food for her employers. According to her, there was no noticeable difference between the way in which she or her mistress washed, prepared, or cooked meat. Juana had never seen a leg of lamb cut open or a clean blouse donned on Saturdays; on the contrary, the defendant often asked Juana to prepare a clean blouse for Sunday mornings.[52]

The defense continued in its attempt to prove that María was a good Christian and had not engaged in the activities of which she was accused. Additional questions to defense witnesses referred to the defendant's having eaten and cooked suckling pigs, especially on Sundays, and people coming to her house on the Sabbath eve or day in order to conduct business. Witnesses were also asked about her servants, who knew nothing of preparing meat in any special ways or dressing up on the Sabbath.

On September 19, none other than María's son-in-law, Sancho de Horozco, an *hijodalgo* (of noble descent), obviously an Old Christian, testified. He said he had seen his mother-in-law enter her cellar frequently, especially when she removed wine from it in order to make a sale. He himself had entered the home and wine cellar of the defendant and had never seen a lamp lit or unlit. In Sancho's opinion, "she was nothing but a stingy woman who did not trust anyone." In addition, he never saw her differ in her mode of dress on any day but Sundays, when she dressed up appropriately. He contended that there indeed was a door and a key to the cellar, which was necessary in order to protect the household goods, for this was the norm in houses in which there was a wine cellar.

Other defense witnesses had less information to offer. Two attested to the fact that María attended mass on Saturday mornings. Two others independently spoke about having entered the cellar often and never seeing any lamps, which would have been easily perceived. They had also seen the defendant enter the cellar to see what, if anything, was transpiring there. One commented on the lively conversation and level of activity often present in this household. Don Alonso's page appeared before the tribunal again and ascertained the fact that his master had often been in the home of María. A steward employed by Don Alonso stated that the defendant did not dress differently on any particular days of the week and that there was both a cellar and a wine cellar in her home. He was of the opinion that the cellar had no door or lock but the wine cellar had doors in front of it, which he had seen María open and close.

The parish priest Pedro Sánchez provided an amazingly detailed description of the Villarreal homes, and of the size, shape, and condition of the cellar as well as of the wine cellar. First he examined the residence of Francisco de Villarreal; presumably this had been the parents' residence at one time. The priest explained that opposite the street entrance of the house was most likely the cellar to which everyone was referring; it had an arch above it and an ancient wall. Measurements were in terms of palms, and the arch was fourteen palms high; obviously a small area was under discussion. There was another room that appeared to be at the entrance to the house which had a small round window that led out to the cellar.

Then the priest went to the houses (*sic*) where Pedro and his wife lived just prior to their arrest. There he entered a wine cellar to the left of the entrance. The entrance essentially divided an area that contained a wine cellar about 11 feet (the priest's feet) wide, 3 feet long, and 9 feet high. From there one could enter a cellar alongside the wine cellar that was about ten paces deep, constructed like descending stairs. There were many earthen jars at the top of the cellar which was just a little higher than a man's stature; this cellar was very humid and cold.

Pedro and his wife had indeed lived in various residences, a fact that explains not only the description of two houses' entrances, but other testimonies as well. Pedro had bought various houses, some of which clearly had no cellars but rather a corral and a cowshed, as attested to by one witness.[53] Undoubtedly this would explain the confusion as well as the conflicting testimonies. One would have to determine in which house they lived when a particular witness visited or worked for them. The fact that María denied having a door and key while one witness specified that there was a door and lock is baffling, unless each account refers to a different place of residence. It was not difficult to determine the size and condition of physical structures; certainly it was easier than determining if one was judaizing or not!

The same defense lawyer, de Bonillo, was assigned to both mother and daughter and later to Pedro de Villarreal. Until the time of his own arrest, Pedro was busy aiding de Bonillo in an attempt to build a defense for his wife and daughter. The abonos and indirectas were intended to convince the court that the defendant was a good Catholic and that there were many fallacies in the testimonies provided by the prosecution. Once this approach, which would never be successful in the case of a resourceful crypto-Jew, was exhausted, the defense continued with tachas. Since the defense was working simultaneously on parallel cases, an analysis of the indirectas and abonos supplied in Isabel's case and a comparison with those in her mother's should be edifying.

Isabel's lists were submitted, on August 18, 1517, a week prior to those of her mother. The first three questions were standard: did the witness know the defendant, had she been a good Catholic since her conversion, and had she attended masses, sermons, and other divine offices, observed Sundays and holidays, made confession, taken the sacraments, and done good works? Then the queries became more specific. Had she continued household duties such as washing, laundering, kneading, and the like on the Sabbath just as she did during the rest of the week? Was Isabel a meticulous and scrupulous woman who took great care with food preparation as she did with her dress and in decorating and cleaning her home? Did they know if Isabel ate all of the various kinds of pork, sausage, rabbit, hare, drowned partridges and birds, octopus, eel, and the like? Did Isabel clean meat before cooking it because it was dirty and unsuitable; if she removed its fat, did she do so in plain view while chatting with people; could they verify the fact that an entire leg of meat was never brought to her house?[54]

Eighteen names were suggested as defense witnesses, each to reply to some or all of the above questions. Fifteen were interrogated, thirteen of whom appeared on the list on May 18 and 20 and July 30 and 31 of 1518. Two clergymen said that Isabel appeared to have been a good Catholic since her conversion. Quite a few testified that she attended mass regularly, was indeed a clean and well-dressed woman, observed the holidays mandated by the Church, and went to confession. One had seen her eat rabbit and eel on two occasions.[55]

On August 3, 1518, Mari Díaz, who was the godmother of five of Isabel's children, testified. This thirty-five-year-old woman knew that Isabel was a good Christian, especially since she had lived in the house next to her for more than ten years. Mari had observed that when the local priest came to require confession and communion, Isabel and her children did as required. In all those years, she never noticed any difference in the defendant's household activities on Saturdays unless they were holidays. Isabel was indeed a meticulous woman who brought hares and rabbits into her home in which pigs were slaughtered. "This witness had smelled the aroma of roast pork cooking in her neighbor's home from her own home, and this witness had seen her purchase eel and cook stew pots of conger eel and eat them." Mari did not say if she was a New or Old Christian; the assumption is that she was the former. No matter which, her testimony provides a strong rebuttal of the prosecutor's claims.[56]

More witnesses testified in August and September. Isabel's brother-in-law, who had been so critical of her mother, attested that Isabel went to mass and sermons and observed Christian holidays. He had also frequently seen her eating rabbits, hares, eels, and pork. Don de la Cerda also testified that she had attended mass and behaved as would a faithful Christian; his only other comment was that she was fastidiously dressed when he saw her.[57]

More witnesses, including Don's wife, María, testified that they had never seen a difference between Isabel's clothing on any given day of the week and that she was without a doubt very neat and clean and well dressed.[58] While the aim of the defense was to disprove the charges, this technique was far from effective. Many of the witnesses openly attested to the Christian lifestyle of the defendants; however, even a successful crypto-Jew would attend mass, take communion, take the sacraments, and so on. The fact that Isabel was seen to have eaten unkosher foods would ordinarily lead one to assume that she had not been judaizing. Yet many crypto-Jews had no choice but to break Jewish law at times in order not to arouse suspicion. Since no confession was made, one can still conjecture as to the accuracy of the accusation and the stance of the defense. Certain inconsistencies appear as the result of the numerous statements made by both the defendants and those who testified on their behalf. As a result, one must try to view the proceedings through the eyes of the inquisitor. When are the testimonies absolutely convincing? When is there an element of doubt? How can one trust a potential judaizer who, if crafty enough, could deceive those living alongside him or her or even in the same dwelling?

The trials of mother and daughter are quite similar in structure despite the fact that each was accused of different heretical activities. Since no confessions of any substance were offered by either woman, the decisions would be based on the witness testimonies and on the efficaciousness of the defense. As has been demonstrated, the responses to the accusations ranged from outrage and direct denials to explanations of their actual activities as not being judaizing in any way. The truth of the matter is that some of these objections are convincing while others are less so; the problematic ones make it difficult to determine if the reply is nothing more than a cover-up rather than an honest objection by an innocent victim.

The extant trial of Pedro de Villarreal contains a confession, and the information that became available will inevitably color the above analysis. After seeing how unsuccessful the methods of the women were, he ultimately chose to respond differently. He seems to have hoped for a lesser penalty as he confessed to having done some, but not all, of the activities described by the eight witnesses for the prosecution. Pedro was also quite selective about which activities he eventually admitted to and he then proceeded to build a defense which he hoped would prove he had not engaged in the other, ostensibly more serious, judaizing activities. Part of the difficulty with such an approach is that while the defendant was being selective, the court was aware of the ongoing process and had every reason to assume that he had engaged in all of the described activities, whether or not he openly admitted to them.

At the beginning of the trial, in October 1518, the defendant "said that he was called Pedro de Villarreal, resident of Cogolludo, who is sixty years old and that he converted from Judaism in Murcia during the mass conversions, and that as a Jew, he was named Abraham, and that he has no brothers or sisters, and that his parents died as Jews." Thus Pedro né Abraham seems to have been an only (or the only surviving) child whose parents died as Jews prior to 1492. After providing details concerning his wife, a prisoner, and his four children, one of whom was also a prisoner, he received his first two warnings from the inquisitors. Upon each of these occasions in October, he claimed to have nothing to say or to admit.[59]

The third admonition, dated December 7, just one week after the unforgettable auto-de-fé in which Pedro lost his wife and daughter, was accompanied by the formal accusation. The defendant was accused of having joined others on Friday evenings in a cellar where a certain oil lamp was lit and left to burn out on its own. Jewish prayers and ceremonies appropriate for the Sabbath were enacted there behind closed doors. In addition, Pedro wore clean and festive clothes on Friday nights and Saturdays as did the Jews. Third, he removed all of the fat from meat, or had it removed, before it was cooked, cleaning it and washing it multiple times in order to remove the blood; this was done with other persons in observance of Jewish law. Next, Pedro was accused of having brought to his home and opened legs of meat lengthwise and removing or having removed the sciatic nerve and all the veins and fat together with others. The fifth charge involved cooking and eating stews and other Jewish dishes in the company of others. The sixth count referred to refraining from eating pork or anything cooked with it and likewise rabbit, hare, octopus, eel, spotted dogfish, or other fish without scales as prohibited by the Law of Moses. In addition, he had eaten meat on Fridays and other forbidden days, and lastly, he had aided and abetted heretics and participated in heresies; it had been a long time since he had confessed, and he had not revealed knowledge he had of his own and others' activities.[60]

The defendant provided a rather noncommittal response six days later; on January 22, 1519, he said he had done nothing except eat meat on prohibited days, including Lent, but on these occasions he had the permission of his priest and his doctor, both of whom could testify as to the veracity of his statement. In this as well as the following month, he claimed to have no response to the list of charges.

In March, Pedro was exposed to anonymous versions of six of the witness testimonies. His immediate response was that he needed some time to refresh his memory; he was allotted three days by the court.[61] On March 19, 1519, the defendant appeared before the audience and confessed. Pedro declared:

. . . he wanted to be brought out so that he could request mercy and in order to display his sins that have come to his notice that he has done and said. And he confessed that it was true that he had ordered the fat of the meat to be removed and for the leg to be opened and for the sciatic nerve to be removed and that one Sabbath day he wore a clean shirt when he went to a vigil of Mary before offering the Eucharist. Sometimes he had seen his wife prepare food and he ate what she had cooked. As for the said cellar, he was debating with his wife and they were beginning legal action in this matter that would be determined by Your Reverences, and for the time being he remembers no more than this, but if something will come to mind, he will come forth with it. And he requests penitence with me [*sic*] of your Reverences and then he turned to say that he remembered more. This confessant then said that sometimes he removed fat from meat after it was cooked.[62]

He was asked what were his intentions when he removed the fat and nerve from the meat and wore a clean shirt on the Sabbath. "He said that the removal of fat from meat and ordering the nerve to be removed were ceremonial and mandated by Jewish law as they removed them, but as for wearing a clean shirt, it was not a ceremony but only out of respect for the vigil of the mother of God until one [o'clock] because he was sick." When asked whom did he command to remove the nerve, Pedro said he did not recall. When asked how long it had been since he had done these acts and for how long he had done them, he said that he did them only once and could not remember when. He was then told to try again to refresh his memory and to rely on his conscience so that he could make a full confession. On the 28th of the month, another attempt was made to procure a full confession from the defendant, but to no avail.[63]

Four additional and rather brief witness testimonies were read to Pedro on July 8, 1519. The first and third shed no light on the issue, for the former referred to a business deal while the latter merely dated an obliquely referred to incident. In the second report, however, Pedro was said not to have eaten pork or thrown it in the pot. The witness did not see anything cooked with it or with lard; lastly, in the period of the year that was spent with this family, no one was seen fasting.

The last testimony presented referred to a closed door behind which Pedro and others sat. This was the wine cellar door through which one entered the cellar, which itself had no doors. On Friday evenings, oil lamps with new lit wicks were inserted in the cellar, but they were no longer lit when Pedro and the others exited. They were lit again and placed in Pedro's bedroom and were still lit late at night; some of them were still burning on Saturday morning. Lamps were not lit in this way on Sundays or other days of the week.[64]

On July 8, Pedro denied the validity of the business-related incident and insisted that he had eaten pork and that if he ever refrained, he did so only because of ill-ness. He affirmed having been in the location mentioned in the third account, but negated the fourth account regarding the cellar and lamps.[65]

One final response on Pedro's part is recorded in the trial, a response that was apparently presented in April 7 but was entered in the proceedings after July. In a lengthy prepared reply, he repeated his earlier claims. In other words, whatever had been admitted early was not being denied, and what had been denied was still to be viewed as false. For example, Pedro had eaten pork, and his claiming that he had not done so was "the greatest falsehood in the world."

> In addition, I say that it is also false and a lie to say that I was seen wearing clean shirts on the Sabbath and did not wear them on other days of the week because in reality, the truth is that this didn't happen and there was no such thing. And having said and declared that I ordered the fat to be removed from meat and to take out the nerve and other things that are done ceremo-nially through belief does not mean that I wore clean shirts on the Sabbath which also I stated and declared [it] and did not cover up; moreover even if I had worn a clean shirt on the Sabbath with some people, it was not done in compliance with any ceremony or law of the Jews.[66]

All these testimonies represented little more than perjury, he claimed. Conse-quently, fat had not been removed from meat, and anyone who claimed that rab-bits, eel, octopus, and the like had not been eaten in the household simply had never been present in his home! In addition, the defendant had never gone into his cellar to judaize or to hereticize. Besides, Jews do not dress up only on Friday after-noons or only on Saturday mornings, as one witness claimed, but, for the duration of the entire Sabbath day. Furthermore, he did no such thing in honor of the Law of Moses. Therefore, all of the testimonies were nothing more than infamy and per-jury fabricated by mortal enemies. The court must absolve the defendant and show its mercy.[67]

Unlike his wife and daughter, Pedro did not want to compile lists of indirectas, abonos, or tachas. His confession was partial, and rather unsatisfactory in the eyes of the court. Although he said that he was certain that the witnesses had perjured against him, he had a weak defense. His lawyer provided abonos and indirectas and informed the court that the same tachas that were compiled in the women's trials applied to him; they were not included in his proceedings.[68] While many of the tachas in María's and Isabel's trials were, as will be demonstrated, on the mark, the defense for Pedro as well as for the rest of the family was not destined to succeed.

6

The López Women's Tachas

THE EARLY STAGES

The noble attempt to invalidate witnesses for the prosecution by providing tachas was made by all three members of the López family. The men of the family helped the women compile their lists, and so Francisco de Murcia (Isabel's husband), Pedro de Villarreal (María's husband), and his son Pedro provided many of the names found in Isabel's and María's files. When María's husband was on trial, his lawyer suggested using the same list of tachas as did Maria (although they do not appear in the transcripts). While it would be logical to assume the rationale for this similarity is that the enemies of a married couple might be identical, by the time Pedro stood trial, he displayed no interest in compiling lists or defending himself as did his wife and daughter.

Isabel began to list her tachas first, on August 18, 1517, and eventually she specified fifty-five suspected individuals. The first was María, the daughter of Hernando Cavallero

> . . . who was and is an enemy of the said Isabel López and harbors hatred and enmity for her because she had been the mistress of the said Francisco de Murcia [Isabel's husband]; many quarrels and disagreements resulted from this. And the said María said that if the inquisitors should come to Cogolludo, that she would make sure they seize Isabel, and that she would do her as much harm as possible. She had boasted that even though he deeply feared her [Isabel], he [her lover] had given her many items and jewels from the store.[1]

Here María wanted to let Isabel know that she had even received gifts from the stock in her store! As can be seen, María had verbalized her vindictiveness in a way that left no doubt in Isabel's mind that her name should appear at the top of the list. A more likely candidate for a hostile witness would have been hard to find, although it turned out that María did not have the satisfaction of functioning as a witness for the prosecution.

Isabel assumed that María's mother would be a likely candidate as well, for the two women had unpleasant confrontations. Isabel, in her capacity as landlady, had evicted the wife of Hernando Cavallero from a house in which she resided that was in close proximity to Isabel's home. The affair had made Isabel's life miserable, and María and her mother were, in Isabel's eyes, persons of riotous living.[2]

The next tacha is not completely clear. Juana, the daughter of Martín the barber, was described as a filthy person who did not sweep the house. She and her mother, father, and sisters all hated Isabel because Isabel was the one to discover Juana's situation, and Martín had to be enlisted to administer to his daughter.[3]

The next tacha reveals that Juana de Jocar was suspected of enmity because when she was Isabel's servant, she stole certain things from the house and took them to her aunt's home. Isabel had apparently recovered some but not all of these items, and because of this incident, Juana resented Isabel.

Another former servant, Catalina de Congostrina, was suspected of enmity; "she was thrown out of her house because she was mean and wherever she went, she could be found saying she was going to do as much harm as she could to the said Isabel."[4] The next suspect was also a former servant, Catalina de Espinosa, who had been fired by Isabel; thus Isabel now feared revenge.

Yusta de Veguillas, the next candidate, was also a former servant who was hostile to Isabel and her husband. During an argument between mistress and servant, Francisco de Murcia interceded and hit Yusta with a jar, breaking her hand. Isabel had every reason to believe that this woman held a grudge and could have offered testimony to the inquisitors.

The next individual to be named was indeed a witness for the prosecution, namely the fourth. María de Aleas, a former servant of Isabel's, had stolen a great deal from her mistress's house and, as a result, the two women had quarreled and been furious with one another. Isabel assumed, this time correctly, that María was keen to present damaging information to the court.

Isabel named former servants of her own as well as of her mother. For example, she had cause to suspect Ana, who had worked for María. This servant and her father had said that they would cause as much harm as possible to both Isabel and her mother. Their hostility stemmed from altercations over two skirts, for which these two sued María. Although Isabel did not discuss the outcome of the suit, there was clearly no love lost.[5]

Isabel also feared repercussions by those who had tangled with her father. Because Pedro had evicted Pedro Callejo's wife from a house belonging to Don Alonso, quarrels ensued between the tenant and Isabel and her father. Also, a woman named Elvira was suspected, because she and Isabel had fought frequently; Isabel claimed that Elvira was a thief and an evil woman and had forbidden her to enter her home.

As can be seen, the scope of people listed in the tachas slowly broadened. Since these lists were made gradually, as Isabel attempted to reconstruct her life and uncover the unfortunate incidents that may have led to her imprisonment, there was no clear-cut internal order to the names that appeared. For example, former servants were not listed separately from family members. Consequently, the names of neighbors were interwoven with those of individuals with whom either of her parents or even other family members, had tangled. One is left with the impression that as Isabel recalled some altercation, the name of the prospective enemy and the justification for enmity were tossed off in a stream-of-consciousness style.

Thus the next tacha questions the reliability of a relative, Pedro de Murcia, Francisco's brother and Isabel's brother-in-law. Both Isabel and Francisco had a horrid fight with Pedro, after which Pedro promised to make their lives miserable. María de Arvancón, a servant of Isabel's, was not trusted because she was a thief, a foul-mouthed woman, and a bearer of falsehoods; she hated Isabel with venom as the result of fights concerning María's depravity and after Isabel said that she wanted to throw her out of her house.

Francisco had complained about the wife of Alonso Redondo, who was then incarcerated by the magistrate; this situation was sufficient cause for enmity with Isabel. Juana, a servant of María López, did not get along with her mistress and, as a result, both mother and daughter treated her poorly. Adeva, the daughter of Juan Carpintero, was her enemy because she had cut linen for her; apparently Adeva did not pay for the goods and was forced to replace the fabric.[6]

On November 16, 1517, Francisco de Murcia attempted to aid in the defense of his wife and presented his list of seventeen tachas, some of whom were already listed by Isabel. For example, the first candidate was none other than Pedro de Murcia, his own brother, mentioned above. He described his sibling as a thief, a poor drunkard, a man of ill reputation, and an enemy of himself and his wife because of things they had given him. Francisco also included his sister-in-law, Juana, the wife of Pedro. Juana was an enemy not only because of their relationship with her husband, but also because when she lived with María López, Isabel had collided with her and castigated her numerous times.[7]

Catalina, the wife of Hernando Cavallero, was the mother of María, the first of Isabel's suspects, because she had had an extramarital affair with Francisco. He referred to her first and foremost, as a woman of ill repute with whom he and Isabel had many hateful incidents. María, the wife of Martín de Hernán Péres, is similarly classified as a woman of ill fame and an enemy of Francisco and his wife.[8]

When Juana, the wife of Garrote, and a cleric's daughter, "was her servant, she stole some coral beads and ribbons and other items and carried them off to hide them in the home of the wife of Aparicio el Vivo. The said Isabel López became aware of the theft, discovered the stolen goods there, and evicted her from her home."[9] It follows suit that the woman who allowed Juana to hide stolen property in her home would also be an enemy of Isabel. After making her discovery, Isabel and this woman had terrible rows; in addition, according to Isabel, she was a woman of ill repute. Included in this group also is this woman's daughter Catalina, also a loose woman who got involved in this family feud.

The next tacha refers to the servant singled out by Isabel named María from Arvancón. Francisco referred to this daughter of Pero Martín as a dissembling thief who had a grudge against Francisco's wife. The two of them had argued a great deal because María had stolen wheat, barley, wine, money, and a silver cross, among other things. Another former servant named María, who lived with the wife of Rello of Humanes at the time of the trial, was also Isabel's enemy. This María had been castigated numerous times and beaten in the hope that she would become an honest woman; she had stolen a rolling pin, some ribbon, and other household belongings.[10]

The next tacha entry has a special notation alongside it, that this suspected person was indeed a witness for the prosecution. Francisco had justifiably suspected the wife of Pedro de Burgos, namely, Catalina de Cervantes, and included the wife of Fernando de Zamora in the same accusation. These women were neighbors of Isabel and her mother, and had fought frequently "because when Isabel was in her mother's home, she had refused to give or lend them various items that they had wanted to borrow; a few times she had called the wife of the said Pedro de Burgos a cripple."[11]

The wife of Pedro del Valle was listed by Francisco because her husband had an altercation with Isabel's father in which a part of a beam was thrown at del Valle. The same Yusta listed by Isabel was also listed by her husband; as Isabel had pointed out, Francisco beat this servant, breaking her hand, which apparently took quite a while to heal. Another ex-servant named was Madalena, who did not want to do her assigned housework and, as a result, was castigated and eventually beaten by Francisco.[12] Both Pedro (the father) and Isabel (his daughter) had attempted in vain to improve her behavior. "I castigated her and [so had] even my said daughter in order to make a good woman of her, so she should not be the wanton woman or thief that she is, and for this reason, at times, I gave her her share of beatings." This woman was indeed the fifth prosecution witness, the wife of Martín Simón; this was the third correct tacha in the list.[13]

The next suspect, also named Madalena, was also the third witness for the prosecution.[14] The wife of Martín, cabronero, of Corlo had worked for Isabel's mother and had been beaten and castigated frequently for not doing proper housework. Ana, the daughter of Pedro del Pozo, was already listed by Isabel and was listed twice by Francisco.[15] She had lived for a while with Isabel's mother and did not receive the skirt that she had requested and later demanded, presumably for services rendered or as a benefit. Juana, the daughter of Antón Peraylle of Membrilla, had also been a servant of María with whom the family had unpleasant dealings. Juana did not follow Isabel's instructions and, as a result, María castigated and beat the maid.[16] The next tacha seems to relate to the same Juana of Membrilla, who was an enemy because Isabel "fought with her frequently and had called her blubber-lipped and having fat lips like an ass and because she had castigated her for not doing what she supposed to do."[17]

Francisco the shopkeeper expanded his list. He included Juana, the wife of Porriño, who was also the daughter of Martín the local barber, Isabel's fifth tacha. Isabel referred to Juana's lack of hygiene, but Francisco pointed out that while she had been their servant, they argued frequently. "One day, while quarreling with her, my wife hit Juana over the head with a plate and injured her severely."[18]

Marcos de las Navas of Cogolludo, who had worked for the Villarreals, was a vile man who often became intoxicated. Isabel fought with him and affronted and dishonored him because he was inebriated so often. Pero González de Ganboa was an enemy of this couple because of a litigation he had with Isabel's father. The point of contention was access to certain water that passed between a dyer's shop and a mill; the men had numerous arguments and unpleasant incidents over the issue, and ultimately a decision was made in favor of Pedro de Villarreal by none other than his son-in-law Francisco.[19] Isabel mentioned Pero a second time in a group tacha that included men with whom her husband had quarreled over some houses; apparently these men had raised the bids on them.[20]

Francisco Yañes was also perceived to be an enemy of this couple, because de Murcia had, by public proclamation, dispossessed them from some houses belonging to Gonzalo de Rueda. Yañes contested the decision, entered into a lawsuit which lasted a whole year, and, needless to say, had many arguments with the defendant's husband.[21] This same name appears in the group mentioned above, with Pedro [*sic*] González de Ganboa, Juan Yañes, and Pedro's son, Gonzalo de la Fuente; all of these individuals had altercations with de Murcia because of real estate.

Apparently, these incidents were not minor, for all of the above residents of Cogolludo were listed first in a group and then as individuals; the unpleasant memories concerning their interactions were strong in Francisco's mind. Thus it comes as no surprise to discover that the next tacha concerned Gonzalo de la Fuente, who was the brother-in-law of Francisco Yañes and, as a result, influenced by him to the point where he and de Murcia exchanged words and enmity was created between them. The name of the fourth member of this group appears in the next tacha. Juan Yañes, the son of a *quemado* (one burned at the stake), was a ragman and dyer by trade who had denigrated Pedro de Villarreal. He broke a duct which carried water to the wheels of the mill, a duct that irrigated a portion of Pedro's land; Pedro and Francisco hampered this action and enmity resulted.

The last nominee in this list was María, the daughter of Alonso, the *escudero* (page); she was once a servant in Pedro de Villarreal's home. Bad feelings existed here because Isabel had beaten and castigated her for not doing her duties; Isabel's mother had also punished her and even hit her on her leg and wounded her seriously; the wound took a long time to heal, and afterwards the relations between the families were hostile.[22]

A list of witnesses to testify to the above hostilities appeared, followed by an additional two tachas provided by Isabel. Juana, the daughter of Juan Romo, had lived with María López where two of Isabel's children were also residing. The hired woman beat and mistreated them, and as a result, was dismissed from her position. Juana said that Isabel owed her money, but María managed to send her away and even threw a servant named Inés out of her house with her.

The final name on this list submitted in April 1518 concerned the wife of Juan Pastor and her sons and daughters; one of them was María, none other than the fourth witness for the prosecution. When she was employed by Isabel as a servant, she was thrown out of the defendant's home; it was said that she had been defamed as a thief.[23]

In May, various witnesses for the defense were asked to answer questions; these were witnesses who could verify the defendant's claims in the tachas. If the individual named in the tacha had not testified for the prosecution, there was no point summoning defense witnesses. Since, however, as has been seen, four of the five names offered had indeed testified against Isabel, the court confronted those who were named as able to prove the contentions claimed in the tachas. Some of these witnesses remembered none of the incidents mentioned. One recalled that the servant María had been fired for stealing;[24] another remembered that about six years before, Isabel had been castigating María de Aleas, and this witness was told that the woman had lost a pillow and a sheet. In addition, she recollected that Isabel had begged the brother of María to agree to his sister working for her for one year, but he refused because his sister had been defamed as a thief.[25]

María Gaytan, when asked to describe the relationship between the López women and the wife of Pedro de Burgos, recalled an altercation some seventeen years earlier when both María and Isabel fought with this woman and called her a cripple.[26]

At this point in the trial, there was a short hiatus followed by a new list of twenty-two tachas, provided at the end of September by Isabel's younger brother, Pedro, in the name of the entire family. As will be seen, many of these individuals had unfortunate encounters with Francisco when he was in public office. For example, Rodrigo de Yelves most likely held a grudge against the former clerk and tax collector. In the line of duty, Francisco had to recover certain sums of money from Rodrigo and forced him to pay what he owed. Everyone resents the tax collector, but it appears that this fellow worked with Francisco and, as a result, they had "professional" disagreements.[27]

Pedro de Romera and his wife also resented the public servant, who confiscated a blanket from them which he then sold in order to cover the sum of certain taxes that they owed. Likewise did Pero Magro the elder and his wife dislike Francisco for taking a female animal from their household. The story was identical to that of their neighbors above: the sale of the animal covered their tax debt. Pero Hortego was also unhappy about the role played by Isabel's husband, but for a somewhat different reason. He had been Francisco's predecessor as the clerk and tax collector and clearly was displeased about having to relinquish his position.

The next tacha is a repeat, but clearly worthwhile to list two or three times, for it was none other than Madalena of Corlo, the third witness for the prosecution. The first tacha had stressed the fact that one of the women, either María or Isabel, had beaten this servant because she was negligent in doing her work. In this round, the former servant of María was viewed as hostile

> . . . because while the said Madalena was living with the said Pedro de Vi-llarreal, resident of Cogolludo, she was castigated and beaten many times by María López, wife of the said Pedro de Villarreal, and because the said Isabel López castigated her and the said María López beat her frequently, and for this reason harbors enmity and malice towards me.

In the third mention, Isabel described Madalena as hating her and her mother because "she has swollen legs which were said to have been the result of venereal disease, and my mother and I quarreled with her and worked to have her thrown out of her mother's house, [and] over this they quarreled and there was vexation."[28]

Another former maidservant was listed because she had been punished many times by Isabel. María, the wife of Diego de la Questa from Jócar, was admonished not to steal or tell tales or lies and was clearly angry with Isabel. This was the fifth correct guess made by the family concerning potential enemies.

Juan Ropero, the second prosecution witness, was named in the seventh tacha in this section; his wife, son, and granddaughter are all perceived to have harbored ill-will toward Francisco. The Ropero family owed tax money, and the converso tax collector took pledges in place of the money due; needless to say, the debtors were not satisfied with this arrangement.

The next two tachas are almost identical; they refer to Pedro the weaver and his wife and Miguel de Bustares, all dissatisfied taxpayers from Cogolludo. Wrath was incurred when Francisco confiscated a blanket from each family and sold them to cover their tax debts; he had done the same with Pedro de Romera. García the red-head and his wife were also infuriated by the tax collector's behavior; he had, as in the case of the Ropero family, taken out a pledge to cover the taxes they owed.[29] Juan Pérez the trumpeter was suspected of enmity because of arguments he had with Francisco concerning a bill of exchange Juan was supposed to pay in regard to a minor difference the men had had.

Martín of Cogolludo was unhappy with this family for different reasons. Apparently, this fellow had requested the hand of one of Isabel's daughters, but the father did not agree to the match. Francisco feared the wrath of the jilted suitor.

The next tacha was a recurring one, and it was one of the five that were on the mark. Madalena, the wife of Martín Simón, had been punished by Isabel numerous times in the hope of making her a good and faithful woman rather than the evil thief that Isabel believed she was. Gonzalo de Rueda of Alcalá resented Francisco because the latter had bought some of Gonzalo's houses that were sold in an auction; it is not clear if the real estate was confiscated and sold publicly, but whatever the circumstances, the former owner of the property vented his anger on Francisco.

Ironically, the next person listed was not a witness for the prosecution in Isabel's trial, but was so in the trials of both her mother and her father. Francisco Yague, son of Juan Yague of Arvancón, had lived with Pedro de Villarreal and was beaten, presumably by Francisco, for having stolen walnuts from a neighbor's tree.[30] The next suspect was listed for identical reasons: Vicentico frequented the Villarreal homestead and was castigated for stealing walnuts from the tree of the same neighbor, Pedro González de Ganboa. Interestingly, this injured party was named in the previous list of tachas as someone who had a lawsuit with Pedro de Villarreal concerning water access rights by a mill. As becomes clear, in a small village there are endless occasions for friction and unpleasant dealings, which can easily occur and reoccur between the same parties.

Ana, the daughter of Pedro del Pozo, was mentioned for the third time by the defense. The two earlier incidents involved skirts that Ana claimed María owed her. In this case, Ana was perceived to hate Isabel "because the said Ana, while residing with Pedro of Villarreal, resident of Cogolludo, was castigated and reprimanded severely by María López, wife of Pedro de Villarreal, because she was lazy and had a sweet tooth, and for this reason, she despises me."[31]

This list also swings back and forth between different categories of suspected enemies, from ex-servants to neighbors to grieved taxpayers. Hernando del Olmo, a resident of Muriel, had owed taxes in Cogolludo and Francisco was forced to confiscate a beast in place of payment. Madalena, a maidservant from Carrascosa, had been castigated frequently by Francisco and therefore was thought to harbor animosity toward him. Pedro de la Casa del Val and his wife and daughter were not kindly disposed toward the former tax man because he had taken some hogs as pledges for certain sums of money which were owed.[32] The last two tachas in this list also refer to Isabel's husband's position as a tax representative. María, the wife of Antón de Estevan, was angered because some hogs had been taken out of the pen and a pledge had been taken from her house; apparently María owed taxes and was unwilling to pay in any form. A different María, the wife of Miguel Calleja, also owed taxes; again Francisco dealt with the situation by removing an item from her home, in this case a cloak, to cover the sum owed.[33]

The testimonies that followed generally failed to provide the names of individuals who could ascertain the claims made in the tachas. Only one of the witnesses who was supposed to corroborate the contentions of the defense was slightly helpful; the remainder could not recall the incidents mentioned or the people upon whom aspersions were cast. Pedro the tailor remembered having seen a servant named María suffer some blows of the fist in her face because she had stolen chickpeas from a field; he described the quantity as between what would fit in a small basket and half a peck's worth.[34] Needless to say, this testimony alone did not suffice to prove the claims of the defense.[35]

The file of María López reveals even more about the everyday life of a converso in Cogolludo. Isabel's tacha lists had included a fair amount of individuals who had worked for her parents or who had somehow encountered their daughter as well. The mother's list was by far the longest and most comprehensive. More than twenty of the names were listed by both mother and daughter, but at least sixty other persons on María's list were not on Isabel's. One again perceives how complex the relationships in a small village can be, even prior to the appearance of the Inquisition.

At first, María presented three group tachas to the court. The first mentioned Andres Moreno, Pedro de Burgos and his wife, Juan the tailor, Juan de la Ferrera, Juan Hismero, and others whose names she could not recall. This group had opposed Pedro de Villarreal's stewardship for Don Alonso,[36] which somehow entailed expenses for them. The wife of Pedro de Burgos was none other than Catalina de Cervantes, suspected by Isabel, and rightfully so, for she was the first witness in Isabel's trial.

The second tacha dealt with Pedro de Murcia, who had already been described negatively by his sister-in-law, Isabel. María confirmed that he had the reputation of being a thief and a drunkard who frequented taverns. Once he threatened the López women and was infuriated after being castigated for having such detestable vices. He later went to the home of Pedro the tailor and announced that he would do as much damage as he possibly could to the López women. The third tacha dealt with Mari, the niece of Juan de la Ferrera, described as a dishonest and evil woman who had stolen wine, money, and whatever she could from the home of her master, Gonzalo de la Rueda.[37]

On October 16, 1517, a formidable list of fifty-one tachas was presented by María; in December, her husband and her son Francisco added twenty-six more names. Additional shorter lists were also provided in 1518. The first tacha contained over thirty names, all of which then appear individually with explanatory passages.[38] For example, the first single tacha concerned Fernando Francés and Mari García, his wife, who had quarreled violently with the defendant. When Pedro was Don Alonso's steward, this couple was evicted from one of the don's houses, an incident that caused enmity. The next suspect was evicted from the very same house by María, and pursuant to a major argument, María, the wife of Miguel Calleja, became an enemy of the defendant. This house was apparently quite popular and had a turnover of residents from Cogolludo. The next tacha concerned a group of people who were evicted on the basis of a letter written by Don Alonso to a woman named Elvira, who was supposedly the mistress of a cleric from Sant Andrés. María had fought with this woman as well as with the cleric's sister, Juana, and with Juana's husband, Fernán de Moreno.

Pedro de Murcia, Francisco's brother, reappeared at this time, along with his wife and brothers. Again, he was cited as having been castigated for wasting his time in taverns; he was angry with María since she and her son would not give Pedro whatever he demanded of them. The next suspect is also familiar; the daughter of Pedro del Pozo had worked for María and had brought a suit to court in the matter of a skirt she thought was owed her. Ana, her mother, and her siblings all disliked María López as a result.[39]

A former servant named Catalina was singled out as having been reprimanded numerous times by her mistress, who tried to make her an honorable woman. Another former servant named Juana had been castigated and beaten frequently because she was suspected of stealing things from the family store. Madalena had been employed by María but was terminated because her service was unacceptable; needless to say, she had a major fight with her mistress concerning this matter. This Madalena was one of the prosecution witnesses, but it is not clear which of the two was intended, because here she was referred to as being married to a nephew of Antón de Colmo rather than to either Martín Simón or to Martín cabronero (goatherd); in all other instances, the specific name of the husband was cited. However there is no doubt that this woman was a witness for the prosecution, because the scribe made a clear notation alongside her name.

There were other former servants with whom María had unpleasant dealings. One Juana was beaten by her employers in the hope of making an honest woman of her and had been called a whore with a sweet tooth who cavorted with Don Alonso's male servants, asking them for "tidbits." María, the niece of a woman from Arvancón, had worked unsuccessfully for María and had also been disciplined because she had spread falsehoods and needed to be encouraged to behave decently. Juana de Membrillera was angry with María for identical reasons; this midwife's granddaughter had been beaten, as usual, to no avail. According to María, "Juana has hatred and enmity for her because she was wounded and castigated and beaten so that she would be an honorable woman and she was called a whore with a sweet tooth who cavorted with Don Alonso's male servants, asking them for 'tidbits.'" Similar complaints appeared repeatedly in various versions with regard to numerous maidservants; for example, Francisca, the daughter of Juan de Argete, was indolent and a drunk and had been castigated.[40]

The next tacha implicated three related individuals: Pedro de Burgos, Pedro's wife, and Juan Sastre, who was married to Pedro's niece. Apparently, while attending the wedding of a neighbor's daughter, María made a derogatory remark about the bride which provoked Pedro's wife;[41] the two women bickered, and they remained on hostile terms. In addition, the two Pedros argued often, because de Burgos was unwilling to take out pledges to cover what he owed to Don Alonso. Juan Sastre (the tailor) is mentioned later together with his wife as having been on bad terms with the defendant and her husband. As a result, María would not give them anything to sew and they would not buy cloth from María.[42] As will be seen, this type of tension between tailor and cloth store owner will repeat itself.

Catalina *la botera*[43] and her sons disliked María and her husband, because when Pedro was magistrate,[44] he would not let them sell their estate in the way that they wished, and they had an altercation. There were subsequent complaints and anger over the tremendous amount of work that resulted for María and her husband.

The names Pedro González de Ganboa and Gonzalo de la Fuente are familiar from Isabel's file; these men had legal problems with her father and her husband. In María's mind, the enmity of these men and their wives derived from a less formal encounter. There had been a major fight concerning some tapestries that these people claimed had been poorly folded;[45] it appears that Pedro and María had been accused of dishonest business dealings. Another angry neighbor was Antón Tamarillo, who, among other things, was angry that Pedro, as alderman, made him take out a pledge.[46]

Just as Isabel had tangled with her mother's servants, María had unpleasant encounters with some of her daughter's employees. The next tacha deals with Lucia, who had worked for Isabel and had been castigated as well as beaten by María; apparently she had entered the defendant's home a number of times and each time, according to María, had carried off as much as she possibly could, "without license." Also Juana, the daughter of Martín Barvero, had been described by Isabel as being an unclean person when she worked for Isabel. María added that she had been admonished and beaten in the hope of making her into a good woman.

Juan González, the smith, had fought with both María and her husband when Pedro was made the overseer of Don Alonso's estate. Juan objected to this arrangement and openly advocated removing Pedro from this position. A maidservant named Catalina created problems for María and was beaten and wounded by her; she later refused to leave the premises when she was relieved of her position. The mistress of the house also had problems with María de la Parra, an untrustworthy servant of wanton ways who had been reprimanded severely. The wife of Juan de Llolmo and his son hated María because she had them evicted from a house owned by Don Alonso. The tenants had treated María badly and had fought terribly with her, so they were all on extremely bad terms.[47]

There is no doubt that when an eviction takes place, the executor of this action does not endear himself to the evicted persons. Once again, in the line of duty, Pedro and his wife had to carry out their obligations and thus, for example, the de Las Navas family bore grudges against the couple on more than one count. In addition to the fact that they fought with Pedro and María and were evicted from one of Don Alonso's houses, Alonso de las Navas was the Don's miller and apparently was the cause of major financial losses. Lastly, his daughter had been one of María's servants who had been castigated, beaten, and suffered wounds.

Pedro Veguillas apparently worked for Don Alonso along with Pedro de Villarreal. The men had quarreled about the division of responsibilities in collecting monies, presumably from Don Alonso's tenants. María claimed that Veguillas was slack in his duties, and that at times he did not want to carry them out at all.

Two maidservants were mentioned in the next tacha; one was Ilana, the wife of

Aparicio, and the other was Madalena. Both had disagreements with their mistress and were severely punished; since there was a mark next to Madalena's name, she was indeed one of the prosecution witnesses, but, once again, there is no indication precisely which one (of the two Madalenas) was intended.

The next tacha lists a group of people related by marriage who all despised Pedro because of what he did when he was *alcalde*. Gil Fernándes had been condemned by Pedro, and for this action, Gil, his wife and children, and also his father-in-law could not forgive him.

Families seemed to stand together as hostile groups, and the next tacha refers to an even larger number of people. Fernando el Cavallero, his wife, their children, and his brothers and sisters held a grudge as the result of an eviction; this act was referred to twice by Isabel, who listed Fernando's wife, Catalina, after mentioning his daughter, with whom Pedro had had an affair. Pedro had also made them take out a pledge and negatively affected their means of making a living as bakers.

More servants appeared, such as María along with her parents; the former had been castigated, and the latter were angry at not having received the skirt they had requested of María López for their daughter.[48] Yusta, the maidservant, was twice listed in Isabel's tachas; this time her brother-in-law is named with her, for both had been beaten by their employer, María. Some confusion exists concerning the next tacha, which named a María of Aleas, because the name given for her father is not consistent. However, it appears that this woman was a witness for the prosecution in both Isabel's and María's trials[49] and was said to have been a thief. María confirmed this claim, adding that the woman had been beaten for stealing and, as a result, the servant's mother and brothers resented the defendant.

Property feuds led to long-lasting bitterness between María and her husband and Villanueva, his wife, and his children. These two families were interested in purchasing the same set of houses, but María and Pedro succeeded in making the purchase. Villanueva also began a lawsuit concerning water that passed through his yard; María apparently bought the yard, and the losing party was not gracious in defeat. Also, Francisco de Torres and his family were bitter about losing to Pedro in a competition to purchase some stores.

Juan the carpenter and his family were angry because the defendant and her husband did not employ him to work on either their or Don Alonso's house. In a separate tacha, the carpenter's wife was listed with her daughter and son-in-law and their children; the son-in-law was supposed to examine some cloth and instead of concluding the business, he fled. Juana, the daughter of Miguel de la Cueva, had an unsuccessful term in the employ of María; she had stolen from her mistress, was castigated, and was beaten, and the two women fought bitterly.[50]

García the redhead was named in Isabel's tachas because of tensions over a pledge, but according to María's list, he and his wife and children were enemies because of business hostilities.[51] This was a family of tailors who would know María since she sold fabric in her shop. Because of animosity between the two families,

María would not give them anything to sew, and the tailors did their utmost to prevent everyone from buying cloth from María. A member of Juan Yague's family served in María's house, but was accused of stealing and was subsequently fired. Juan himself had been punished; he had a bit placed on his tongue and he was paraded throughout the town, a source of endless humiliation for him.[52] His name reappeared later on this list along with Vicente and their families; apparently they had stolen walnuts from a walnut tree.[53]

María assumed that there were family vendettas galore to be reckoned with at this time. Toribio of Aleas and his wife and family were angry with her because her son-in-law, Francisco de Murcia, demanded a certain rent from them which they were obliged to pay to cover their own son-in-law's rent. In his role as alcalde, Pedro subjected Juan de Vella to public humiliation because the latter had denied Christ. The punishment was identical to that of Juan Yague; a bit was placed in his mouth.

Miguel Bravo and his wife and children were furious with Pedro and María because they lost an argument about quantities of wool. Miguel claimed he owed only two bundles, each weighing about 25 pounds, whereas Pedro claimed he was owed three. Pedro was able to prove that his claim was valid, but Miguel threatened both Pedro and his wife, and thus he appeared in her tacha. Fernando de Bejar and his family appeared in these lists because he was forced to pledge items numerous times by Pedro while the latter was tax-collecting clerk.[54]

Juan Estevan and his wife appeared on María's list because she and her husband had fought with them often. Juan was their miller but often left his post poorly guarded. Another servant, María de la Pena, had worked for the defendant, and a disagreeable situation arose when the maid asked for a blouse, which her mistress would not provide. A different María, from Carrascosa, had been frequently castigated and beaten while serving in the household; once she even fell from one of the corridors and was thrown out of the house. No love was lost here, as the defendant described her as a foolish woman of little intelligence. A servant named Antona had also been severely punished while working for María and was discharged because she was a scoundrel. The identical reason is presented as the cause of enmity between the defendant and a servant named María of Membrillera.[55] This is the final candidate in María's list of fifty-one tachas.

After naming prospective witnesses to the above statements on October 16, 1517, Pedro de Villarreal and Francisco de Murcia made a presentation of their own list of twenty-six tachas on December 17. The first name on this list was Francisco's brother Pedro de Murcia. Pedro had appeared three times on Isabel's various lists as well. Here he was described as a poor man whose brother did not want to support him. Consequently, Pedro swore to God that if the inquisitors should come to Cogolludo or to the general vicinity, even though he supposed that the result would be that his soul would burn in hell, he would make certain that María López was incarcerated. His brother added that Pedro was a drunkard and a blasphemer, had been detained by the alcalde Fernando de Zamora, and had been meted out excessive punishment. Pedro's wife, Juana, appeared in both women's lists; she had lived with María, had been beaten by her, and obviously held a grudge against her.

The name of Catalina, wife of Hernando Cavallero, had been the very first to appear on Isabel's list, for she had an extramarital affair with Pedro. However, in this list, she is cited as having committed adultery not with Pedro de Villarreal, but with Pedro de Brihuega!

> Catalina, the wife of Fernando [sic] de Cavallero was and is licentious with Pedro de Brihuega and has had and has hatred and enmity toward the said María López and her husband because when she was their neighbor, they would not lend her what she requested nor did they want to rent her a house which they had.[56]

Another woman of ill repute also had unpleasant dealings with the defendant. Both before and after her marriage, the wife of Martín de Fernán was not highly respected; there was also some nasty encounter between this María and one of María López's nephews which added to the family hostility.

The next name appeared in Isabel's lists twice; considering that she was a servant of Francisco de Murcia's, this is no surprise. She is cited here as well, as having stolen numerous items from the household and being beaten by Isabel upon María's instructions. The next tacha also concerns a former servant of María's daughter who had been named by Isabel as well. The reasons given in both tachas are identical; this cleric's daughter had stolen and stashed her booty at a neighbor's, where it was later found.

Juana de Membillera's name appears at the end of María's list above; she and her mistress had fought and insulted each other. Juana had been beaten because of her wine-drinking excesses and her irresponsibility. The next name is familiar as the María who testified against all of the members of this family. While at times she is identified as the daughter of Miguel of Aleas and at others as the daughter of the wife of Juan Pastor, she is one and the same witness.[57] She had an unsuccessful time in Isabel's employ because she stole from her, did not want to carry out her duties, and was beaten. In addition, she requested three and a half lengths of cloth for a skirt, and when she received only three, she was infuriated. The men of the family obviously felt that their additional information could disqualify this woman as a hostile witness.

The next name is also familiar; Ana, the daughter of Pedro del Pozo, was named three times in Isabel's trial and once before by María. No new details appeared in this particular list. María the wife of Miguel Calleja, appears for a second time and is characterized again as being embittered at being evicted by the defendant from a dwelling. Lucia, a former servant from Arvancón, also appeared on María's list because she had been beaten. Catalina la Nublera was a former servant of María who was singled out by María as being of ill repute; María had castigated her in the hope of curing her of her vices and making a decent woman of her.[58]

A servant named Elvira appeared because she had been reprimanded severely for her improper behavior and continued to be a loose woman. The next tacha referred to María, daughter of Alonso Escudero, who was already named by Isabel as a former servant and by the men here as María's former servant; perhaps she worked in both households. In Isabel's tacha, she explained that her mother had wounded this girl in the leg; here it is added that María injured her so severely that she remained crippled. The degree of physical violence that took place between employers and their help was clearly high; the fact that some of the beatings left permanent damage speaks for itself. While it was obviously an accepted norm for the servants to be harshly reprimanded, there was clearly a psychological residue that scarred those who had been beaten, whether or not the perpetrators had just cause. The very fact that so many tachas deal with servants who could have held or indeed did hold grudges on this basis is proof that even the employers were aware of inflicting potential damage that went far beyond the physical wounds.

The next tacha dealt with a new member of the Yague family, another daughter of Juan and sister of Francisco. Both siblings had been employed by these families. Juana "was and is the enemy of the said María López because she had wounded her and castigated her so that she would become a good woman and not dirty her bed and for this reason, she left the house."[59] Juana, the wife of Fernando Pablo, created problems for her mistress. She purportedly cavorted with Don Alonso's male servants and with other men who passed through the household. After retiring to her chamber at night, María often had to go down to the servants' quarters with a lamp in search of Juana, who was then subjected to beatings by her mistress.

The tacha to follow concerned Madalena of Corlo, who was a prosecution witness in all three trials. Here the fact that she did not want to wear shoes in María's house was perceived as creating tensions between employer and employee; she was chastised and beaten and thrown out of the house numerous times. Yusta was another maidservant named in most of the tacha lists of the various family members, for she had been wounded in the head by Isabel because she did not get a pitcher of water as instructed.[60] Another servant named María, the wife of Juan de la Cueva, was beaten, castigated, and fired for poor service.

Marcos de las Navas was listed by Isabel because he was a drunkard, but here he was said to be an enemy because he demanded certain *maravedis* (coins) that he owed her husband, Pedro. Francisco de Zamora was suspected of enmity because of an incident with Pedro de Villarreal when the latter was alcalde.[61] Certain monies were demanded of Francisco's son, who was forced to sell assets against his will.

The wife of Pedro de Burgos, namely Catalina de Cervantes, was named next. She was a witness for the prosecution in Isabel's trial, and it is no accident that her name followed the Zamoras, for Francisco's wife was her aunt. The men recalled that María had fought with Catalina, that the women were verbally abusive to one another, and that they remained antagonistic.

Juan de Vello appeared in this list for the identical reasons that he appeared in

María's; he had blasphemed and was punished by Pedro.[62] Likewise Pero González de Ganboa reappeared in this and in Isabel's trials because of litigation tensions with María and her husband. Pero's son Gonzalo de la Fuente followed, perceived as harboring anger for the injustice done to his father and then having his own grudges to bear as well. Lastly, Pedro and Francisco mentioned Juan Yanes for the same reasons articulated in Isabel's defense; there were property and border tensions between the two families concerning water and a mill.[63]

A long list of nominees of witnesses who could attest to the veracity of the second collection of tachas followed, but only six witnesses were actually brought to court and questioned. None was able to ascertain any of the claims. Nevertheless María remained undaunted and continued drafting lists of tachas. Thus on May 19, 1518, she appeared before the inquisitors with yet more names, some of which were already familiar. Alonso de San Pedro had been imprisoned by the alcalde upon the duke's orders; María did not specify who the alcalde was, but if he were not her husband at the time, the tacha would not make any sense. Apparently the fact that Alonso had a concubine and was not living with his wife had some significance as well.

Although Pedro had been the tax collector, he was not the only one in the family involved in finances. María not only was a shopkeeper but also had independent financial dealings. Martín de Fraguas had owed María money, which he reluctantly gave her before suing her for the sum paid. Needless to say, he lost the suit and resented the fact that he lost his claim. Likewise Juan Ropero owed María money and was annoyed that María asked for the debt to be paid; she said that "he owed me money and has ill-will towards me because he asked for it [the money] and went around saying that I asked him for what he did not owe me, and because we sold some houses in order [to cover] the debt, he harbors ill-will, he and his wife and his son Pedro." Juan Ropero's name appeared in all three trials as either the first or second witness for the prosecution. It is odd here that the notary did not make the appropriate sign next to his name to indicate that this tacha was on the mark. One might suspect that there were two individuals with the same name, but the fact that one of the witnesses named to verify this contention was indeed interrogated proves that Ropero was the man indicated.[64] One assumes that the notary simply erred; interestingly, the witness, Juan de Cañete, a scribe himself, recalled the incident, which was quite recent. He heard Ropero say that Villarreal and his wife were unjustly paid after the matter was settled; only after this affair did he perceive any differences between the two families. Unfortunately, the second witness, Pedro de Burgos, claimed not to have any knowledge of ill-will between the two; thus Ropero's testimony against María and Pedro de Villarreal was not invalidated.[65]

The last tacha in this short list referred to Rodrigo de Yelves and his wife, María; Rodrigo appeared in Isabel's lists because her husband had forced him to pay his taxes. Here María assumed that this couple was hostile because of a suit she had had with his uncle concerning water on a piece of cultivable land of hers that bordered on a dyer's shop owned by the uncle; he also owed her money and she had asked for it, and thus they were potential enemies.[66]

María and her defense councilor were indefatigable. On August 25, 1518, she began a new list with thirteen names appearing in eight tachas, and on September 23, the Villarreal men presented fourteen tachas to the court in yet another list. While in her cell, María's memory continued to recall incident after incident that might have induced someone to seek revenge upon her. The August list began with Andrés de Mojados and his wife together with their daughter, the wife of Pedro de Herrera, and Tercero and his wife and son. All of these people had used a farmyard that María and her husband purchased; this purchase angered them all. A neighbor named Gerónimo and his wife were evicted from a home that María and Pedro purchased; they went about town claiming that the defendant and her husband owed them money.

Three servants' names appeared; one was correctly named by Isabel twice and by María for a third time. María, a prosecution witness in all three trials, was unsuccessfully employed, first by the mother and then by the daughter. Her record as a thief was mentioned, and María López even called her crazy; in addition to being thrown out of both houses because of her thefts, she had been incarcerated and punished, and thus she held a serious grudge again the López women. In an earlier tacha, the maidservant's brother was angry because his sister had been defamed as a thief; the fact that she was imprisoned explains the alluded-to reputation. When the witnesses named to corroborate this animosity appeared before the court, three claimed to have no recollection of any incident; the fourth spoke at length of a dishonest servant named María, but the court determined that a different María was intended.[67]

Two other former maidservants were listed as having been beaten and thrown out of the household; they were Juana of Membrillera and María of Arvancón. Andre de Trilla was also a neighbor affected by the above-mentioned purchase of the farmyard. He thought that the family had taken advantage of him, and he had publicly stated that he would do this couple as much harm as he could. Last in this list was Antón Zamarillo, whose gripes could have been twofold. He considered himself to be an injured party in the farmyard deal; in addition, there had been an argument over an incident concerning his wife, the midwife, and service to be provided to María's daughter.[68]

On September 20, after the above-mentioned witnesses were called to corroborate the tacha against the servant María, Pedro Sr., his son Francisco, and Francisco de Murcia[69] empowered Pedro de Villarreal Jr. to present tachas on their behalf that very week. This family-compiled list contained the names of four of the six prosecution witnesses! The first was Juan Ropero, already named by both women; for the third time, the emphasis was upon his owing money to members of the family. Vicentico had been a family servant who stole walnuts from Pedro González de Ganboa's trees;[70] he was castigated and left his job as a result. In addition, he owed one of the Villarreal men a ducat and was furious when confronted about payment of his debt. This fellow was probably the son of Vicente, who was also accused of stealing walnuts in María's forty-first tacha and was mentioned for the same reason by Isabel.

Rodrigo de Yelves appeared once again, and here we learn that he had been employed to collect taxes together with Pedro. When Pedro asked him to pay a sum of maravedis that he was owed, Rodrigo sued him; as would be expected, Rodrigo was embittered after he lost the suit. The fourth tacha named Francisco Yague, the sixth prosecution witness in both María's and Pedro's trials, and their former servant. Isabel mentioned him as another employee who had stolen walnuts from a neighbor's tree; Pedro explained that the tree was next to his mill and that he had beaten Francisco numerous times in a vain attempt to dissuade him from engaging in dishonest activities. Complaints were registered in this regard and Francisco left without completing his service.[71]

The next individual was also the fifth witness for the prosecution in all three trials: Madalena, the wife of Martín Simón, who had served in María and Pedro's as well as Isabel's household, or so it seems.[72] Pedro was concerned about her wrath because he and his daughter had given Madalena her share of beatings in the hope of making her a decent and honest woman. In addition, her husband owed Pedro a quantity of wool for which he had been paid; Martín Simón had also stolen some sheep. On this basis, Pedro was certain that Madalena would have good cause to be a witness motivated by vindictiveness.

Madalena of Corlo, the third prosecution witness in all three trials, is the next person correctly suspected in this final tacha list. Pedro admitted to having beaten her numerous times; Isabel mentioned this fact in her list of tachas and elaborated upon her shortcomings at length. Pedro assumed there was animosity because she had been berated for not serving properly.

The rest of the names mentioned did not serve as prosecution witnesses. Martín de Salinas owed Pedro money and the men had argued about this debt and about a pair of pigeons exchanged between the two. The debtor wanted to equate the value of the pigeons to the sum of his debt and the two men did not see eye to eye on this issue.[73] The eighth tacha deals with a former maidservant, another María, the wife of Diego de la Questa, referred to as a liar and a thief. While employed by Pedro, she had been castigated both verbally and physically; Pedro had hoped she would desist in her unscrupulous ways. His daughter Isabel did likewise when María was in service there, and thus this name appeared in her final list of tachas as well.

Juana de Membrillera appeared twice on María's lists; Pedro added her since he had castigated her frequently, hoping she would not be so lazy and dishonest, but to no avail. Juan Pérez Tronpeta had quarreled with Pedro over revenue that was to be negotiated through payment of baked goods. The two men never agreed on the conditions. The wife of Pedro de la Casa del Val and her daughter María were angry with Pedro for not always lending them money upon request; she and her husband were listed in Isabel's tachas because of tax problems.[74]

The next two former maidservants were suspected by the family because each of these women thought she was owed a skirt by her mistress. Ana, the daughter of Pedro el Pozo, was mentioned three times by Isabel and twice by María in addition to the fact that Ana brought a suit before the alcalde. The other servant named María had also been castigated because of differences with her employer. The last name on this list also appeared before: María, the wife of Miguel Calleja, both because she owed taxes and because she harbored resentment after being evicted from a house by María.

In October, various witnesses were called in to corroborate the above allegations. Most stated that they did not know anything about the described circumstances; a few knew or had heard that there had been altercations or thefts or tensions, but they claimed not to know if any of these incidents had caused enmity. One went off on a tangent about how Francisco de Murcia had asked him if he had seen one of his wife's former servants, and if the Inquisition had summoned her.[75]

María made a final statement, accusing another four individuals of enmity. She pointed out that Juan Yañes, Pero Díaz, the wife of Miguel, and Vicente de Azconas were all related to one another. Pedro de Villarreal had physical fights with two of these men: a knife fight with Juan and a fist fight with Pero Díaz. Since none of the above were actual witnesses, this addition was not significant to the trial. The defense rested and, unknowingly, had failed in its attempt to invalidate the prosecution witnesses.

THE FINAL STAGES

By the time Pedro's trial opened in September 1518, María had presented most of her tachas; their son added the list compiled by the men while Pedro was in his first month of incarceration. In October, Pedro made his genealogical statement and was admonished to confess. When the court urged him to confess for the third time in December, Pedro already knew that his wife and daughter had been relaxed. As was previously noted, his confession was streamlined, mentioning kashering of meat, once wearing a clean shirt on the Sabbath, and seeing his wife prepare food in advance on that day, which he then ate.

When given the opportunity to present tachas, "the said Pedro de Villarreal said that he did not want to invalidate anyone but that he submitted himself to the inquisitors and requested clemency and that he did not want to list any tachas."[76] Pedro's advocate, de Bonillo, told him he must provide tachas, because the confession he offered was not complete; in other words, because he did not confess to all of the judaizing activities listed by the prosecution, he needed to prove that the sources of the prosecution's accusations were invalid. Pedro again insisted that he did not want to attempt to invalidate anyone and that he had said his piece. On May 2, 1519, de Bonillo announced that the tachas and proofs opposed by his condemned wife would be included in his file, but the defendant had no desire to add to this list. Two days later, the family defense lawyer presented a list of *indirectas*, hoping to prove Pedro's innocence.

These questions referred to the cave or cellar in the house and whether there had been doors there. They also dealt with Pedro's eating habits, and whether or not he had eaten pork and lard. In addition, witnesses were to be asked if he had dressed up on Friday afternoons. Then the defense presented substantive lists of as many as twenty names per question or issue at hand.[77]

The interrogation lists are worth examining, because of both the content of the answers and the identity of these witnesses. The first to be summoned was Juana, the daughter of Juan Romo, who had worked for Pedro and María for five years. Her name is familiar because she appeared in one of Isabel's *tachas* as having mistreated the *conversa's* children while at their grandparents' house. While his daughter suspected this woman, Pedro assumed that she might be able to testify on his behalf in regard to the questions posed. In fact, Juana testified "that during the said five years when she had lived in the said houses she had seen that in them there was a wine cellar that had doors and a key and that inside the said wine cellar was a cave without doors; and she had never seen any doors in it within these last said five years."[78] In response to the fourth question posed, Juana

. . . said that within the last said five years, this witness had seen the said Pedro de Villarreal eat pork and lard and other pork products and things cooked with them. However he ate very little and at other times he requested that it not be placed in the pot because it exacerbated his gout. And that this witness saw him suffering from the said gout, and yelling and complaining of discomfort.[79]

The second witness, Pero Val the elder, was probably the father of Pedro de la Casa de Val; the son's name appeared in María's *tachas*, while the father's and mother's names appeared in Isabel's. This Old Christian, who knew Pedro for twenty-five years, was familiar with the Villarreal house and knew that the wine cellar had a door, but he had never seen doors at the entrance to the cave. A second Old Christian, Bartolomé de la Vega, knew Pedro for eight or nine years and

. . . had often entered the wine cellar in order to fill a bottle with wine, in the cave referred to in the question. He never had seen a door in the said cave because there were some doors that opened and closed into the entrance of the wine cellar by which one entered the cave. With regard to the fourth question, he said that he did not know more than that on one day, perhaps six years ago, he saw him [Pedro] slaughter a pair of pigs in his home and, after his wife had been taken prisoner in Toledo, he observed him killing a pig.[80]

Another Old Christian, an hidalgo named Juan de Pañadilla, knew nothing of eating habits but basically reiterated the rest of Bartolomé's report; for ten years he entered the wine cellar and never saw separate doors to the cave.[81] Pedro the innkeeper, who knew Villarreal for twelve years or so, had been in the wine cellar and never saw doors to the cave either. Juan García of Congostrina knew which house was referred to and had carried wine to the house twice in the last ten years, but he did not recall more than that.

Another worker from the same village, Pedro Pastor, had been in the said cave in order to take wine out and ascertained that there was no separate door for the cave. Likewise another worker, Juan Gil Jr., had gone into the cave to remove wine and saw only doors to the wine cellar itself. The next witness, Juan Bajo, had also gone in to take wine out but recalled nothing of the structure of the cellar.[82] This family apparently employed many different hired workers to deliver and remove wine shipments from their cellar over the years. Juan Redondo, also a worker, could not remember seeing doors when he entered this area. Antón Galán had come to pick up wine and did not recall any doors to the cave either. A sixty-year-old local cleric named Pedro Sánchez recalled that some ten or eleven years before, "this witness had seen the said Pedro of Villarreal in the said holiday eat with many other persons, where they eat meat dishes and he believes that they had been cooked with pork."[83]

The next witness was the first New Christian in the group; Diego Fernándes was married to one of Pedro's nieces. He had taken wine from the cave a few times and noted that there were no doors, but he had never paid attention to Pedro's preferences for food. His wife, ostensibly Pedro's niece, gave her age as forty-four and, oddly enough, said she knew her uncle for twenty years; she had no replies to the queries.[84]

A local cleric named Antón Martínez, who knew Pedro for twenty years, recalled seeing the defendant eating mutton and hen that were cooked with pork. Bartolomé Carpintero, also of Cogolludo, had often entered the Villarreal cave, which, he contended, had no doors; the wine cellars had the entrance with doors.[85] Sancho de Horozco had testified as a character witness in María's trial, where he spoke of her habits and about the wine cellar. Since he was their son-in-law, he would be expected to know more intimate details of their lives. This thirty-year-old described a somewhat different construct: by his account, there were doors that opened and closed in the cave, but the main doors by which one entered the cave were in the wine cellar.[86]

> He said that for the said seventeen or eighteen years, this witness had seen the said Pedro of Villarreal, his father-in-law, eat bacon and lard and other pork products and things cooked with them. Sometimes this witness saw how the said Pedro de Villarreal had even argued with his doctors who advised him not to eat bacon and other things harmful because of his illness of the gout. After not being cured of it, he began to eat bacon which in turn caused him, as this witness saw, to fall ill.[87]

Pedro de Burgos had seen Villarreal eat meat cooked with pork but also knew that he usually did not eat pork products, since they affected his gout. This Pedro and his wife were listed in tachas by both of the López women; his wife, Catalina, was actually a prosecution witness in Isabel's trial, yet her husband Pedro was, more than once, listed as a defense witness. While his testimony here did not reflect the hostility described in the tachas, the fact that the same man suspected of enmity was trusted also to testify on behalf of the defense reflects both the state of confusion existing in such complicated trials and the defendant's desperation in attempting to prove his case by any means possible. Because the defendants never knew who testified against them, they also could not know how calculated a risk they were taking by appealing to the same person who was under suspicion.

An Old Christian named Juan del Corral had been in the wine cellar a few times and had seen doors only where one entered the main cellar.[88] The testimony of Alonso de Inglés was quite similar; he had frequently entered the cave and the only doors there belonged to the wine cellar. Pedro de la Casa del Val, whose father testified earlier, said basically the same thing as the two men who preceded him. A New Christian neighbor, Fernando de Córdova, reaffirmed the statements about the doors.

An Old Christian named Juan Carpintero testified that he had seen Pedro eat mutton, hen, and other foods cooked with pork. The name of another Old Christian, Fernando Moreno, can be found in María's tachas along with his wife's name, because María had fought with them and with his brother-in-law. Pedro had eaten breakfast at Fernando's home, where they definitely had served foods cooked with pork.[89] Juan Martínez Bravo, Old Christian and incumbent alcalde of Cogolludo, had seen the defendant on occasion eat pork, sausage, and dishes cooked with pork. A local worker named Miguel de la Magra had been in Pedro's cave and confirmed the description of the structure attested to by almost all the other witnesses including Fernando el Herrero, the witness that followed.[90]

Although some of the witnesses could not answer the questions, one can clearly see that the majority were able to verify the fact that the cellar where secret prayer sessions were supposedly held behind closed doors was simply not constructed in a manner that would permit these meetings; likewise the claim that Pedro did not eat pork or pork products was perceived as a fallacy. In July, Pedro made a statement asserting that these witnesses had clearly proven that the allegations were false, for he had eaten pork, lard, and foods cooked with them. In addition, the claims that there were doors in his cellar were nothing but falsehoods. Concerning lighting candles in honor of the Sabbath, the defendant included a convoluted and lengthy statement aimed at disproving the prosecutor's claim.[91] Pedro concluded his statement with a plea for absolution.

Two days later, on July 13, 1519, the tribunal of jurists met; it was composed of the licentiates and apostolic inquisitors, Sancho Vélez and Juan de Mendoza; the inquisitor Francisco de Herrera; the licentiate and senior alcalde of Toledo, Salvatierra; licentiate and canon of Toledo, Pedro de la Pena; the licentiate Diego Jiménez Pan y Agua; and Dr. Pedro Martínez. After a lengthy discussion, the vote was unanimous that the defendant should be turned over to the secular arm because he was a feigner and an incomplete penitent. His goods should be confiscated by the exchequer and royal treasury and he should be subjected to torture or examination of the second rank as a witness in order to name those accomplices who had been silent.[92]

This sentence was pronounced in the torture chamber in the presence of the defendant and the apostolic inquisitor. Pedro said he had nothing to negate concerning what he had remembered, since all he had stated was the truth and his confession was full and truthful. While it was recorded in the proceedings that he was to be given another day in order to refresh his memory,[93] the next entry in the trial was not made until September 16, two months later, again in the torture chamber.[94] Pedro insisted that his original confession was accurate and that he had nothing to add. Oddly enough, there is no record of actual torture taking place; perhaps the ambiance of the chamber was to serve as a stimulus for confession without use of the various instruments. He was again ordered to declare the truth of what he knew of others, or else he would be returned to torment; Pedro repeated that he had already affirmed the truth and could not recall anything at all of what he had been ordered to do.[95] Since other trials meticulously recorded torture sessions, one can assume that the tribunal concluded that Pedro could not or would not offer the names of collaborators and that his condemnation was inevitable with or without a fuller confession.

Thus the defendant was found guilty of the crimes of heresy and apostasy. He had not responded directly to the accusation or declared the truth until the witness testimonies were published, at which time he made a partial confession. His very existence as a Christian was an anathema to the Church, for he had committed many "crimes of heresy to Our Savior and Redeemer Jesus Christ." His blind belief in the Law of Moses led him

> . . . to join with other suspected individuals on Friday nights in a certain secret locale where there was a hidden oil lamp lit in observance and keeping of the Sabbath, wearing and dressing up in holiday clothes and clean shirts, removing and having removed the suet from the meat and all the fat before throwing it in to cook, cleansing and washing it many times by removing the blood and when a leg of meat was brought to the house, it was opened and made to open it lengthwise and remove the nerve and remove all the veins and fat and how he had eaten stews and other foods in the Jewish manner, not eating pork or anything that was cooked with it or rabbit or hare or octopus or eel or spotted dogfish or other fish without scales because of the prohibition in the Law of Moses. And that he had eaten many and numerous times meat on Fridays and other days forbidden by the Holy Mother Church,

being well and good and having been an abettor and concealer and participant in heresies.[96]

Pedro de Villarreal was declared to be a heretic and apostate of the Catholic faith
and Christian religion and to have incurred the sentence of anathema and loss of
all his goods dating to the time he began to commit these crimes. He was to be relinquished to the secular arm, and his descendants were to be excluded from public
office and honors, as was standard in such cases.[97] The inquisitor stood on one
scaffold while the condemned defendant stood on another, as was customary at an
auto-de-fé. In this manner, he was handed over to the magistrate Conde de Palma
and his senior official as his sentence was pronounced by Francisco de Herrera in
the plaza of Zocodover on October 4, 1519.

A final entry was noted on April 15, 1521. This was a declaration concerning the
period of time deemed appropriate for calculating confiscation of property. The
court decided that Pedro de Villarreal had been a heretic since 1512 and wanted this
decision to be duly noted. Thus ended the record of the proceedings of this trial.[98]

Although the outcomes of the trials of María and of Isabel are already known, it
should be noted that the penultimate stages of their trials were substantially different from Pedro's, despite the fact that all three were ultimately burned at the stake.
At the time of the *consulta-de-fé*, the members of the tribunal voted on the fate of
the defendant. Of the three, María's fate was determined first, on November 18, 1518,
by a relatively large group comprised of nine members, who unanimously agreed
that the defendant should be relaxed.[99] Immediately following this decision, the inquisitors decided that her possessions should be confiscated and that she should be
tortured because she had not named any accomplices. Essentially, this was a final
attempt to corroborate the prosecution's stance. In reality, however, she had not
confessed to anything, and as far as María was concerned, there were no accomplices as there were no heretical acts.

On November 24, the notary recorded the following:

> And then the said Lord Inquisitors ordered the said María López to be taken
> to the torture chamber and to be undressed and to be placed on the rack of
> torment and to be tied with some hemp ropes. She was undressed and placed
> on the said rack and tied with the said ropes and was required and admon-
> ished by the said Lord Inquisitors to tell the truth: who were those persons
> whom she had seen commit those heretical crimes of which she is accused?
> Because the intention of your Graces is none other than to know the entire
> truth, and if she dies during torture or receives an injury to any limb, it will
> be her fault and not that of your Graces. The aforesaid said, "Oh, Holy Mary
> of Monserrate [*sic*],[100] protect me, Lord Jesus Christ, for I have been a good
> Christian. Oh, look, Our Holy Lady Mary, why did you consent to such a
> thing? Your Lord Reverences, I entrust myself to you." The order was made to
> pour water with a pitcher [that contains up to four pints][101] and [to put]

something additional upon her face on top of the silk headdress that she had on her face.[102] It was ordered for the ropes to be tightened with a tourniquet and it was tightened with two tourniquets.

Unfortunately, the next page is blank and there is no record of the remainder of the session.[103] As was customarily done on the day of the auto-de-fé in which the defendant was to be relaxed, María's sentence was pronounced; it was November 30, 1518.

Isabel's consulta-de-fé transpired on November 19, just one day after her mother's. While all eight of the voting members present agreed unanimously[104] that the defendant should be relaxed and relinquished to the secular arm, when the fifth member of the board stated his position, he also advocated the use of torture in order to uncover as yet unnamed accomplices. This opinion was that of none other than the mayor of Toledo, de Salvatierra, a layperson who was anxious to send the defendant to the torture chambers. If nothing else, this tones down the popular image of the "cruel" inquisitor or fanatic churchman whose fervor presumably dominated these trials, for the source of the initiative here is clear. Needless to say, Salvatierra's colleagues readily agreed to the proposition, perhaps for fear of appearing lax in performing their duties in the eyes of a layperson.

Although her consulta took place the day after her mother's, the court decided to submit Isabel to torture first. The techniques used were no different for mother and daughter, and in this instance, the record is complete. As María appeared to have done, Isabel held her own and did not break down in the torture chamber, even after three successive rounds. Each round entailed pouring a half or a whole jar of water down her throat and tightening the hemp ropes an additional notch. In the long run, two and a half jars of water were used and three turns of the tourniquets were made. Like her mother, Isabel cried out for help; she invoked the name of the Señora of Guadalupe while crying aloud that she was being killed and had already told the truth. Her appeals for mercy and exclamations remained constant as each round of the torture continued.[105] Nonetheless, no confession was procured from this defendant.

On November 30, 1518, the day of the auto-de-fé in Zocodover Square, Isabel was sentenced to death in tandem with her mother.[106] No further notations appeared in Isabel's trial record, although in both parents' files, identical addenda were made on April 15, 1521, concerning the confiscation of their property as of 1512, calculated by the court to be the year when they began their unsavory activities.

The very same defense team, composed of the jurist Bartolomé de Bonillo, lawyer Pedro de Herrera, and attorney[107] Pedro Tello, failed three successive times to disprove the accusations of Alonso Ferrer, prosecutor for the Inquisition. In the two coterminous trials, there were numerous denials and rebuttals on the part of the López women, lengthy abonos and indirectas, and an overwhelming number of tachas. Isabel's lists included fifty-five names while her mother's contained at least eighty, and, has been seen, the men in the family took a very active role in comprising these lists. Needless to say, the women could not aid in the defense of Pedro, for they had already faced their demise.

Pedro's advocate, de Bonillo, the licenciado "who was present told the said Pedro de Villarreal that he must present tachas because his confession is incomplete. The said Pedro de Villarreal said that he did not want to attempt to disqualify anyone and that he has said what he had to say."[108] As is clear here, the defense lawyer argued with the defendant, who was less than enthusiastic about preparing his own defense. The inquisitors directed them to prepare abonos and tachas and indirectas, but the converso again contended that he did not want to list tachas. In the end, de Bonillo planned to use the tachas that had been prepared for María's trial; the inquisitors ordered the lists to be removed from his wife's proceedings and transferred to his.[109] Pedro refused to make any additions, apparently hoping that his confession would suffice despite the fact that his lawyer pressured him to present tachas. In stark contrast to Pedro's comportment is the glaring lack of confessions on the part of the two López women, both at the beginning and at the end of the trial, and the torture, while painful and disconcerting, procured no tangible results for the prosecution or for the tribunal. Pedro, on the other hand, having realized that this approach was not successful, chose a different alternative and confessed. Unfortunately, however, the court as well as his own defense lawyer were convinced that this confession was a partial one. Perhaps he naively hoped that admitting to a limited amount of judaizing would lead to a sentence of penance, fines, or imprisonment, but not death. The fact is that after reading only María's and Isabel's trial records, one might still justifiably wonder if they had been innocent of the accusations made. For despite the fact that the witnesses recounted numerous judaizing practices, both women gave convincing reasons to discount each witness as trustworthy. Unfortunately, as has been seen, they were not able to exonerate themselves, because their verification witnesses failed them.

Only after reviewing the evidence in Pedro's file does one realize that the Inquisition had not falsely accused them. Pedro himself provided this information in his confession, in which he referred to preparing kosher meat, wearing a clean shirt in honor of the Sabbath, and eating Sabbath meals prepared in advance. As did many a husband accused of judaizing, he pointed to his wife as the initiator of the third of the three "sins" which he chose to enumerate. The fact that he tried to downplay any active role on his part is reflected in the wording he chose for each item. For example, the confessant stated that he had ordered the removal of fat from meat and the nerve from the leg after it was opened lengthwise, but he did not specify who received and executed this order, that is, whether a servant, his wife, or someone else did the actual work. One cannot know if this omission was accidental or intentional, but the Inquisition still considered the giving of an order to be interpreted as a sign of judaizing. Pedro likewise neglected to specify if this was a habitual act or a one-time occurrence.

On the other hand, he claimed to have worn a clean shirt on the Sabbath only once, but for good Christian reasons, in order to attend a vigil. Presumably the clean shirt was laundered and prepared for him, most likely by a servant, but this part too was not mentioned. As far as Pedro was concerned, it was mere coincidence that the day on which he dressed up for the vigil of the Mother Mary also happened to be the Sabbath.

The confession began with Pedro admitting to giving an order, although he seemed not to be actively involved. According to his second statement, he only appeared to be honoring the Sabbath but was not actually doing so. The third item in the confession referred to a clear-cut act of judaizing and involved his deceased wife, who used to prepare food on Fridays in advance and in honor of the Sabbath. According to his own words, Pedro "saw" this heretical act taking place in his own home and then ate the prepared food. While he did not say so in so many words, María emerged as the active judaizer; he was the passive participant. After all, the implication here is that a husband's role is to eat the food prepared and served by his wife.

Lastly, Pedro included some unclear reference to the cave which seemed to be an attempt to dismiss its importance, although it is clear from the proceedings that it was of considerable importance concerning the alleged judaizing in his home. Behind the alleged closed doors of this cellar, two different judaizing activities were said to have taken place: lighting of the Sabbath candles and prayer sessions. Pedro made no allusion to either of these activities and presumably hoped his rather skimpy confession would suffice; clearly it did not. His defense lawyer immediately perceived this weakness and tried to cajole him into preparing tachas, and the court was convinced that he and his family had been active judaizers above and beyond the narrow confines of the meager confession provided.

Pedro was no more successful in saving his life than were his wife and daughter in their trials, but the women came much closer to having their trials dismissed. All that was lacking in the women's cases were more appropriate names of witnesses with better memories to corroborate their tachas. If they had provided the appropriate names, their trials would have been discontinued, because the prosecution witnesses would have been unacceptable to the court.

Ironically, whether consciously or not, Pedro did succeed in convincing the court that it had justly tried and sentenced the members of the López Villarreal family. By virtue of his partial and somewhat lame confession, he proved to the tribunal that all of them had indeed judaized and that the stoic behavior of the López women did not stem from bona fide innocence but rather from a desire to die as martyrs devoted to Judaism.

7

The Inquisition and the Midwife

Beatriz Rodríguez was a Castilian midwife, a resident of Santa Olalla, whom the inquisitors in the Archbishopric of Toledo were anxious to convict. During the course of fifty years the inquisition persistently collected information concerning this conversa. In the latter half of this period, from 1536 until 1563, Beatriz was summoned by an inquisitor numerous times to the central court in Toledo, as well as to interviews during local visitations to various towns and villages. Both the tactics employed and the accusations made by her adversaries seemed to vary on each occasion. While the court appeared to be preoccupied with the possibility that there might be a judaizer to expose, the fact that Beatriz was a midwife was by no means irrelevant.

By examining the trial proceedings, one discovers that the first time the suspicions of the Inquisitor Alonso de Mariana were aroused was while he was on *visita* in northwestern New Castile.[1] In a town not far from Santa Olalla, namely, Talavera de la Reina, two witnesses came forward to the inquisitor on February 26, 1514, to offer testimony concerning Beatriz.[2] Juan del Páramo, a cloth-weaver of Old Christian lineage, reported that in the winter of 1511, he made a trip to Santa Olalla to purchase a shirt for his servant. He and this servant lodged with Enrique Lencero and his wife, a New Christian couple. The midwife Beatriz Rodríguez, as fortune or, in this instance, misfortune would have it, was also present in this household, caring for Enrique's sick wife. Thus the *partera*[3] was busy preparing spices, presumably herbs, by grinding them before applying them to the abdomen of the afflicted conversa.

Juan decided to strike up a conversation with the "tall, round-faced woman." In the course of their conversation, the *comadre* inquired about the fate of an arrested New Christian woman from Juan's village, Maqueda, located north of Santa Olalla. The weaver, who would later pride himself on his guile, misled Beatriz by informing her that he, too, was a New Christian. The midwife, assuming that a fellow converso would be an empathetic listener, proceeded to malign Old Christians. For example, she said that she was certain that the woman from Maqueda was arrested because her Old Christian neighbors had informed upon her; this *cristiana nueva de judia*[4] had graciously given these neighbors leftover food, which they then claimed was none other than *adafinas* or the remains of the special Sabbath stew prepared by the Spanish Jews on Fridays before sunset. At first Beatriz obliquely referred to the misfortune of having bad neighbors by saying, "*Quien avia mal vezino avia mal maytino.*"[5] However, once Juan made his false declaration of solidarity, she became bolder: "The Old Christians want to harm us because we are prosperous, but we do not steal [from them]." She referred to God's love for "this law" and called the Jews the "apple of his eye." According to Juan, Enrique reentered the room at this time, and the conversation ceased.[6]

Similar but not identical testimony was provided by Juan's servant Alonso Sánchez, who explained that the "tall, heavy-set" *comadre* was called in to care for the mistress of the house, who was apparently suffering from menstrual cramps.[7] His own master flattered the ministering conversa, he said, complimenting her on her knowledge of her craft; the midwife was apparently grinding spices to place on the stomach of the suffering woman while Juan was eating.[8] Beatriz was not certain if she had met Juan previously; the latter assured her that indeed she had. When she asked if he knew the wife of Corcobado, who was a prisoner of the Inquisition, Juan replied that he did and then "naively" questioned Beatriz concerning the nature of the arrest. Alonso also reported that the midwife referred to the incriminating lies perpetrated by the imprisoned woman's Old Christian neighbors; then Beatriz affirmed God's love for the Jews. The servant recalled that his master told Beatriz that this particular Divine love was a well-known fact, for God had parted the Red Sea for them. Beatriz then added that whosoever offends a Jew offends the "apple of God's eye."[9] Alonso likewise noted that the conversation was interrupted when the master of the house, Enrique, summoned the midwife; his own master admonished him to remain silent, assuring him that "if this Jewess returns here, I'll take her to where they'll burn her!"[10]

While this inquisitor was by no means pleased to hear about Beatriz's unorthodox comments, these depositions could not justify initiating proceedings against her. Nevertheless, they were copiously recorded in a Book of Testimonies from Talavera de la Reina and stored for future reference.[11] The opportunity did not present itself until 1536, twenty-two years later, while the Inquisitor Gíron was on *visita*. In March, at Santa Olalla, he had collected new information concerning the midwife, but she was nowhere to be found. However, a month later, while the representative of the Holy Office was continuing his rounds in the village of Montalbán (west of Toledo and south of Santa Olalla), Beatriz was located and summoned to come to this neighboring village.

At the outset of her interview in April 1536, the inquisitor did not confront Beatriz with her rather unorthodox statements of 1514.[12] When these comments finally were brought to her attention, Beatriz first denied having made them; she later recognized the comments but was unable to recall any particular context. More than two decades had passed since the time of the unfortunate conversation. Very likely, she had made similar comments to various fellow New Christians during her more than forty years as a conversa. Since her memory did not serve her well, she wrongly attributed the conversation to a mere four years prior (1532) and as taking place either with another midwife or possibly with a neighbor named Cardeñas, the wife of Sándoval, with whom she frequently chatted.[13] In all honesty, how could she possibly have named Juan del Páramo or his servant, Alonso Sánchez, with whom she'd spoken so long ago and for such a short time? The actual names of these two witnesses may not even have emerged during that brief and fateful conversation.

The inquisitor, however, had amassed other evidence with which Beatriz was confronted on the previous day. It was precisely this evidence that was considered to be substantive and due cause for reopening her file. A number of depositions about her had been made in the presence of Girón while he was on *visita* in Santa Olalla between March 18 and March 21, 1536. Beatriz could not have appeared for questioning before the inquisitor prior to the session on April 3; during most of the month of March, she was not even in Castile, a fact that was by no means inconsequential to her trial or to the charges made against her.

The two accounts perceived by the court as providing incriminating evidence pertain to an odd incident in January of that same year. The following story was told by the parish priest, Diego de Casarrubios, and was corroborated by one of the local sextons, Diego de Tapia.[14] The baptism of the daughter of Gonzalo de Loarte of Santa Olalla was scheduled to take place in the Church of Sant Pedro after the vesper service on January 29, 1536. The priest performed the exorcisms and then asked the godparents, the midwife, Beatriz Rodríguez, and the others present if the child had been baptized in her father's home.[15] Beatriz replied that water had been poured on the child; however, the two sextons apparently wanted to confirm the fact that there was indeed water in the house of the infant's father, whereupon the midwife unhesitatingly affirmed her statement. The ceremony then proceeded on the basis of this affirmation; consequently the baby was anointed with oil and chrism and all that was deemed to be necessary for performing the rites of initiation was done, except for the pouring of water. After the baptism, the parents were accompanied home by one of the sextons. When the latter mentioned this detail of the ceremony to the father, perhaps fifteen to twenty minutes later, the father adamantly denied that any water had been poured on the infant in his house.[16] After the child's mother corroborated this assertion, the sexton and the father set forth for the home of the parish priest, who, once informed of the scandalous situation, ordered the family and the sextons to return to the Church, where he would properly baptize the infant.

The inquisitor learned of this incident only on March 18. Because the midwife was nowhere to be found in the village, four witnesses were summoned and questioned regarding her whereabouts. The first witness had heard from the *partera*'s son that his mother went to visit relatives in Portugal;[17] the witness himself raised suspicions regarding her true motives. Was it not fortuitous that she was absent at the very time the inquisitors appeared in Santa Olalla?

The others who were questioned were three of Beatriz's children. One of her daughters, Leonor, related that her mother had long wanted to visit a brother in Portugal; this plan finally materialized when she departed on March 6, accompanied by a son-in-law.[18] The inquisitor emphasized the fact that Beatriz did not say goodbye to her children, which was a detail that aroused suspicion. Leonor's brother, Juan Martín, thought their mother had set forth on March 4 for Evora, where she thought her brother was residing; on that day, she had indeed said goodbye to him.[19] Catalina, the daughter whose husband, Diego Díaz, had accompanied her mother, pointed out that this trip had been contemplated and discussed by her mother for over a year; as a matter of fact, Beatriz had frequently mentioned the prospective trip to her neighbors. Not only was there nothing surreptitious about her departure, but Beatriz told Catalina that she expected to return in about twenty days. When questioned about the possibility that her mother might have fled the kingdom, this daughter saw no reason whatsoever to entertain such a notion.[20]

This was the sum total of the evidence amassed by the Inquisition thus far and the basis of a potential case for the prosecution. When finally confronted with the problematic baptism, Beatriz claimed she had been covering up for the parents' negligence.

> When we got to the font, Diego de Tapia, the sexton, asked me if there was water in the house of the said infant. I said yes. When asked again by Diego Hernández, the sexton, if there was indeed water in the house, I said yes. And I said it because I thought that since ten days had passed since the birth of the infant and the father had not yet taken the child to be baptized, and no one takes his babies to be baptized seven or eight days early. And I did not say it because he was slipshod in baptizing nor intend by saying this that she [the mother?] was a malintentioned Christian but rather careless. For one must look at what had been in order to decide if she was Christian or not.[21]

The midwife apparently had feared for the soul of the child and was concerned that the maximum time period might transpire without baptism being performed. To avoid maligning the parents, she chose to pretend that the baptismal water had already been applied. She later admitted to her error in judgment.[22] It had been a simple woman's unintentional mistake, the consequences of which she had no knowledge until after her return from Portugal, where she had gone to find her brother, Francisco de Toledo. After an unsuccessful search in Evora, rather than wandering aimlessly about searching for her merchant brother, who traveled by land as well as by sea, Beatriz returned home, only to find the Inquisition waiting at her doorstep.[23]

The tribunal was definitely troubled by this woman's activities. Questioning at the first session on April 3, 1536, revealed that she was a woman in her fifties whose origins lay in Castile. When Castilian Jewry was faced with the Expulsion decree of 1492, Beatriz's widowed mother, Leonor Rodríguez, took her young daughter to Jerez de la Frontera in southwest Andalusia, where they both converted to Catholicism. The midwife's father and grandparents had all died as Jews; her conversa mother died in Santa Olalla.[24] After presenting this brief genealogy, Beatriz was told that there were certain things she had said as a Jewess, things she needed to contemplate before her next audience with the Inquisitor.

This was a reference to that unfortunate conversation with the weaver in 1514. When Beatriz returned in the afternoon of the same day, however, she simply repeated her version of the baptism episode. She was then released but was instructed not to leave town and to report daily to the court.[25] On the following day, she offered no additional information and was subsequently confronted with her reference to Old Christians as bad neighbors.[26] On the fifth of April, she appeared at the court in Montalbán and affirmed the explanations she had already presented. She suspected one or two individuals of bearing false witness against her but did not seem to understand that she could attempt to invalidate the testimony of unreliable witnesses by naming tachas.[27] Beatriz seemed anxious not to be troubled further with legal procedures and not have to come to court so frequently.[28]

The midwife's prayers were answered, for no formal accusation against her materialized that April. Indeed, what were the potential charges that could have been formulated by the prosecution? Had this conversa been judaizing? What were the reasons why she misinformed the parish priest concerning the baptismal waters? Did the priest and the sexton have any grudge to bear against this midwife? How incriminating were her comments against Old Christians? And, if she had fled to Portugal precisely at the time that the inquisitorial court established itself in Santa Olalla, why did she return while it was still in the vicinity? Had Beatriz actually done anything for which she could have been legally convicted? Would the Inquisition of Toledo opt to remain, so to speak, "on her case"?

Since the fact that these proceedings did not end in 1536 has already been mentioned, the last question is rhetorical. Yet, before proceeding with the remainder of the trial, it may prove useful to contemplate some of the relevant historical and legal circumstances concerning inquisitorial trials. The testimonies about her tactless comments were made in 1514, in the midst of an intensive drive by the Inquisition to extirpate judaizing heretics. At that time they did not have ample proof of judaizing on the part of Beatriz, however. While inappropriate and even blasphemous-sounding remarks often appeared in prosecutors' accusations, legal priority determined precedence, and charges of this nature were placed near the bottom of their lists. The top of the list contained more tangible deeds and actions of the converso judaizers, which were far more incriminating and therefore easier to prosecute effectively.

The testimonies received in 1536 did not necessarily point to a crypto-Jewish orientation. Why would a conversa midwife deliberately misinform the clergy concerning baptismal rites?[29] If the infant's parents had been fellow judaizers, then this would be a case of a perfectly constructed collaboration against the Church by three untrustworthy New Christians: the midwife and the parents.[30] A crypto-Jew hoping to "de-baptize" his or her child would rinse off the baptismal waters after the ceremony; as a matter of fact, he or she could avoid the entire sacrament by a clever collusion with a sympathetic conversa midwife.[31] This possibility would have been viable, had the parents not been the ones to object vehemently to the improper baptism. However, there was no such diabolical collaboration; the decision to lie about the baptismal waters was apparently made by Beatriz on her own.[32]

Certain conclusions may be drawn from the reactions of the clergymen. For example, it must have been acceptable for a midwife to pour water on a newborn prior to the church baptism; if not, why would the priest have asked if water was administered?[33] And obviously, it was acceptable for a midwife to do so in lieu of a priest. If Beatriz had not done as she had stated, why was there no immediate reaction to her lie on the part of the parents? Although the sextons apparently made certain to ascertain the *partera*'s contention, where were the others when Beatriz was being questioned and when she replied? And where would they have been when she was administering the water beforehand? Why did the parents not react until later, and only then deny the midwife's story?

The most likely explanation of the midwife's involvement with baptismal waters would be the fear that the child would not survive until the time of official baptism. Midwives were sanctioned to baptize a baby unlikely to survive; this pre-christening period was full of uncertainties, which often served to motivate as prompt a baptism as possible.[34] Beatriz clearly was perturbed because the parents had waited a full ten days before arranging for a proper baptism. Yet, in this particular case, no mention was made of any need for an emergency baptism, so this possibility must be ruled out.

There were also cases of rebaptisms in the sixteenth and seventeenth centuries when the regularity of the baptism was in question, or even when an endangered child had been baptized and, upon its survival, the parents hid this fact so as to celebrate properly the infant's birth at a "bona fide" baptism.[35] Had the latter been the case here, the parents would have reacted differently; essentially, the former option, a rebaptism, did not occur because the supposed pouring of water never transpired the first time around, resulting in a very questionable sacrament indeed.

The character and religious beliefs of a midwife were of utmost concern to the ecclesiastical authorities. The midwife was valued and trusted by the community; this situation presented a challenge to the Church, for "the acquisition of power by peasant women posed a threat to the Church."[36] How great was the resentment and how threatened were the men of the clergy? Only after assessing the activities of the midwives can one evaluate the fears of the midwives' activities on the part of the clergy and other males in power.

A midwife had varied duties, which included prenatal advice to the pregnant mother; psychological support of the woman in labor; possible easing of delivery by oiling the stomach; preparation of special drinks, herbal remedies, or food; and cutting of the umbilical cord. She would bring the infant to church for baptism or, in critical cases, perform emergency baptism and prepare the deceased infant's body for burial. She might remain to care for the postpartum mother as well as to attend to the newborn. In certain cities, a midwife would be called in to perform physical examinations of women in such cases as rape. Furthermore, "the midwife's close association with birth and death as well as her knowledge of abortifacients and other medicaments made her vulnerable to witchcraft accusations."[37]

During this period, there were attempts to impose legal limitations upon midwives in some Spanish cities; "many officials in the sixteenth and seventeenth centuries wanted a stricter rule for midwives, perhaps because birth remained in the hands of women. . . . Licensing was necessary not simply because midwives could be ignorant, but also because it was believed that they used sorcery and promoted immorality."[38]

Those who were not of Old Christian heritage were even more suspect. A regulation was passed in 1565 in Granada instructing New Christians to avoid using New Christian midwives; if possible, they were to employ only those of Old Christian lineage.[39] At the same time, the Inquisition used its own techniques, often denouncing and discrediting women healers, who had to take care not to disturb the clerical religious monopoly.[40]

Had Beatriz Rodríguez defied the Church? Was she playing an active role in this dialectic between herself and her accusors, or was she merely a passive victim of the Inquisition?[41] Were the inquisitors displaying a conscious or even subconscious fear of female power?[42] Was this conversa midwife a heretic, or was she a strong, independent woman whose actions and attitudes might have perturbed the inquisitor even had she not been a New Christian?[43] Was she merely a simple widow attempting to perform her role in the community as she understood it, thereby becoming more vulnerable to prosecution by the Inquisition because of her standing in the community?[44]

The very fact that Beatriz did not hesitate to lie to the clergymen attested to her spirit. Since she obviously was acting on her own, she might well have been attempting to protect the infant's parents, whom she thought had endangered the soul of their daughter. When confronted by the tribunal in 1536, she was steadfast in her version of the baptism story and was released. While the Inquisition was not comfortable with the various reports about this woman, it apparently was unable to justify going beyond the hearing stage at this time.

On July 10, 1550, the inquisitors at the central court of Toledo assessed the material amassed at the earlier *visitas* and hearings and decided that, if Beatriz was still alive, she was to be taken prisoner and have her goods sequestered.[45] Once the midwife had been summoned to Toledo, the prosecution took a more aggressive stand.

Beatriz, now over sixty-five years old, could not imagine why she had been called to court, for she was certain that she had been meticulous in reciting her catechism, in confessing, and in receiving communion. Although she was admonished to confess at what was effectively her first audience before the tribunal, on August 3, 1550, the conversa had nothing to add to the statements she had made in 1536 in Montalbán and Santa Olalla.[46]

The questioning became more intensive. When she referred to God's love for the Jews, why did she say *Dio* rather than *Dios?* Did she not know that the Jews say *Dio?* Beatriz admitted that the Jews say *Dio;* but the rationale for this usage was beyond her comprehension, since she herself was not literate and had been but a mere girl when she abandoned Judaism. The inquisitors, in pursuing this theological approach, also questioned her concerning her contention in 1514 that God loves "this" law.[47] After this session the inquisitors abided by their decision to imprison Beatriz.

After three weeks in prison (and no record of physical torture), the midwife was granted an audience and admonished to confess. On August 25, Beatriz repeated the story of her conversion in Andalusia, adding the fact that, soon after converting, she had married an Old Christian named Alonso Martín and later moved to Toledo with him.[48] The marriage lasted eight years, until her husband's death. Beatriz then moved to Santa Olalla, where, about six months later, she remarried. This marriage, to Jorge Díaz, a New Christian, lasted about five years, at which time she apparently reentered widowhood.[49]

At this point in the trial, Beatriz, most unexpectedly, confessed to judaizing.[50] During her marriage to the converso Díaz, she began to observe the Sabbath, abstaining from work, wearing clean blouses and her best clothes. When Beatriz attemped to reconstruct the chronology of her observance, her account became rather distorted. At first she claimed that she had observed the Sabbath by herself some seven or eight times while married to Jorge. Later she surmised that perhaps she had observed the Sabbath after his death as well but that she had ultimately returned to the fold of the Church.

The rationale provided by Beatriz to explain her judaizing was classic: she blamed external forces such as her marriage to a New Christian, the devil, madness, and even her own sheer stupidity. She even said that "the Devil and his cursed advice to a frail woman made me do it." She chose to present an image of herself as a weak, ignorant woman who had sinned through circumstances beyond her control. At first, she said that she "did not expect to achieve salvation through the said law of the Jews, but that her madness made her do it." The inquisitors informed her that this was not a likely story. Had not she thought she would be saved by observing the Jewish law? "Yes," conceded Beatriz, who was thereupon sent to her cell to think everything over; perhaps she had not made a full confession.[51]

At long last the prosecution could explain her actions; and subsequently it presented its formal charges against the defendant on August 19, 1550. Beatriz had fled to Portugal in 1536 for fear of imprisonment by the Inquisition; she was a believer in the Jewish law who had disappeared, hoping to be forgotten.[52] Concerning the baptismal ceremony in 1536, the midwife obviously had subverted this sacrament as a Jewess, misleading the priest because of her belief in the Law of Moses.[53] Next the prosecutor described her derogatory statements about Old Christians, made with the "intention" that she had toward the law of the Jews.[54] The rest of the charges were standard: Beatriz had observed the Jewish Sabbath, wearing good and clean clothes in its honor;[55] she had observed with other individuals and neglected to bring this information to the attention of the tribunal;[56] she had not admitted to the truth.[57]

On the following day, further questioning of the defendant did not prove fruitful. Beatriz did not attempt to defend herself, nor did her defense lawyer prove to be of any help.[58] Consequently, on September 10, 1550, the *consulta-de-fé* voted to reconcile her to the Church, sentencing her to life imprisonment and confiscation of all her goods.[59] The sentence was recapitulated on September 21;[60] the conversa midwife was summoned on the following day and admonished to provide additional testimony, but none was offered. The conditions of reconciliation were then pronounced; they included the requirements of consistent confession, communion, and attendance at mass and sermons on Sundays and holidays at the monastery of San Pedro along with other penitents in their *sanbenitos.*[61]

On April 13, 1552, Beatriz, who was already nearing seventy years of age, was permitted to go and live with her aunt, provided she remain within city limits.[62] On August 9, her request to return home to Santa Olalla was granted.[63] Eleven years later, on August 11, 1563, the final entry was made in this proceeding. Here the terms for confiscation of Beatriz's property were specified and were to be retroactive more or less as of the date of her marriage to her New Christian husband; the Court had determined that she had been a crypto-Jew for half a century.[64]

Beatriz Rodríguez confirmed the suspicions of the Tribunal of Toledo; she was, after all, a judaizer. She confessed to some observance of the Jewish Sabbath while married to a New Christian man, although she implicated no one else in these heretical activities. Beatriz never made any statement that could justify the court's conclusion that she had been judaizing for fifty years. Her anti-Old Christian comments of 1514 were made during or shortly after her judaizing phase. Yet it is evident that a New Christian did not have to be a judaizer to resent Old Christians in sixteenth-century Castilian society.

Certain details of this complex and fascinating trial remain elusive to the investigator. Why did the Inquisition release Beatriz in 1536 and then, fourteen years later, summon her to a formal audience in Toledo, despite the fact that no new information had been acquired? Why did she decide to confess to judaizing when no questions had been presented that dealt with specific rituals? At the same time, the inquisitors' persistence in their attempts to discredit this woman is quite significant. The first confrontation in 1536 was not fruitful; the suspicious statements she made in 1514 were not sufficiently incriminating; and her inappropriate behavior at the baptism in Santa Olalla remained extremely problematic. Having eluded an arrest in 1536, this conversa midwife would not be forgotten and would be hounded again, fourteen years later, although by that time, the court was not even certain if she was still alive.

Beatriz's profession as a midwife played a central role in these proceedings; a judaizing midwife would have been especially threatening to the men of the Church. The mere thought that a judaizer had participated in infant baptism was horrendous. The tribunal's struggle to indict the midwife ended in 1550, when Beatriz unexpectedly confessed to observing the Sabbath. The twice-widowed and aging conversa was, most likely, tired of confrontations and chose to reveal some ancient pecadillos in order to end the psychological torture. While her attempt to blame external forces for her deviation from the Church was unconvincing, she was nevertheless granted reconciliation to the Church.[65]

From what one can gather, Beatriz had long been an observant Catholic, although the most successful of crypto-Jews were those who perfected the façade of appearing faithful to the Church. And what she may have omitted in her confession will never be known. The Inquisitorial Court was, nonetheless, satisfied to have cornered the conversa midwife at long last. Despite its display of mercy by not relaxing her to the secular arm, it asserted its power by declaring that all possessions amassed during the fifty years prior to her arrest would be confiscated. When permission was granted to the near, if not already, octogenarian prisoner to return to her home in Santa Olalla, the Inquisition had effectively removed this erstwhile judaizing midwife from her practice.[66]

8

The Judaizers of Alcázar at the End of the Sixteenth Century

"Corks Floating on Water"

B<small>Y</small> 1550, THE FOCUS of inquisitorial activity in Spain had changed considerably.[1] While this institution was established because of the threat of the judaizing heresy, once the centers of judaizing had been dealt with, the courts did not cease their activities. New threats to the unity of the Catholic faith were perceived, and the inquisitors, and their massive bureaucracy managed to keep themselves busy with other heretics and apostates.[2]

The converso community received an infusion of new blood, most of it after the union of Spain and Portugal in 1580.[3] Although the Portuguese Inquisition was not established until 1536, it set about its task with impressive ferocity and quickly earned a fearsome reputation. As ironic as it might seem, the crypto-Jew in Portugal actually viewed the prospects of life in Spain as desirable, because the Spanish Inquisition was perceived to be less extreme. As a result, one finds a significant alteration in the onomasticons in the lists of accused judaizers in Spain toward the end of the sixteenth century.

The village of Alcázar stands out in sharp contrast to one's expectations of crypto-Jewish life in a Castilian village at the end of the sixteenth century.[4] Between 1588 and 1600, there was a series of interrelated trials of 100 converso residents from the eastern part of La Mancha,[5] belonging to the adjoining inquisitorial districts of Cuenca and Toledo. Not one suspected heretic was of Portuguese heritage. This phenomenon is not easy to explain. As a matter of fact, in a study of the Inquisition of Castile and La Mancha, Juan Blázquez Miguel claimed that the judaizing residents of precisely this area were essentially ignorant of Judaism by the end of the century.

With the passage of time, everything changed. After the second and third generations, there was a deterioration into a gradual religious ignorance, that only grew because it [crypto-Judaism] was based solely on oral transmission, realized by people who were not learned or cultured, until by the end of the century, where the judaizers of Quintanar de la Órden or Alcázar de San Juan, in the large majority, as we have seen, scarcely knew anything of the religion that they professed.[6]

As will become evident, the picture of crypto-Jewish life that emerges from the trials under consideration is by no means a reflection of the above statement. Perhaps this area was a sole last pocket of pure Castilian judaizers.[7] In the two trials to be analyzed here, reflecting the lives of those under jurisdiction of Toledo, the quantity of information about judaizing is strikingly abundant. In stark contrast, the defendants in the previously discussed trials of the López-Villarreal family either denied their participation in such activities or confessed to a meager level of complicity. As will be seen, although there were only one or two defendants actually on trial in the Alcázar case, the prosecution brought in an overwhelming amount of information concerning the defendants, their families, and their neighbors. Thus the encounter by the conversos of Alcázar with the Inquisition provides a fitting conclusion to the sixteenth-century Castilian conversa experience.

Alcázar is a village in the judicial district of Ciudad Real that was acquired by the Order of San Juan and then given the name of Alcázar de Consuegra.[8] There was a considerable amount of movement by various members of this community, mostly within short distances (30 to 40 kilometers), such as to other villages in this area or in the jurisdiction of the Inquisition of Cuenca to the east. Almost everyone involved in these depositions was referred to as a resident of either Alcázar de Consuegra, Quintanar de la Orden, or Argamasilla de Alba, and most of them were related either by blood or by marriage. In contrast to the Cogolludo trials, which were filled on the whole with tachas and defense tactics, the information here was obtained from confessions and witness testimonies. As a matter of fact, there are no tachas in either of the two files, an indication that the nature of these trials was quite different.

One of the most striking aspects of these two trials is the fact that there was a pair of incredibly long lists of names at the front of each of the proceedings. The first list in each trial consisted of names provided by the defendants, depositions given by Juan del Campo and Francisco de la Vega concerning other judaizers;[9] Juan named thirty-five individuals while Francisco named twenty-five.[10] The second list belonged to the prosecution; for each name provided, there subsequently appeared a confession taken or copied from the trial of that person, or a witness deposition. In many of these instances, he or she had made statements in which the name of the defendant on trial was mentioned, and the prosecutor was utilizing the relevant portions of these confessions to his advantage to muster up a powerful case. In Juan's trial, all twelve individuals listed on this page had been either reconciled or tried. In Francisco's, nine of the sixteen statements were taken from other trial records.[11]

Whereas in many other trials, suspected judaizers were often accused of withholding the names of those with whom they had committed heresy, in these trials, the contrary occurred. Many confessions made during other trials contained a great deal of "useful" information pertaining to fellow judaizers, and this information was transferred to these files. The irony here is that studying the names provided by the defendant as well as the prosecution reveals significant overlap in these two sets of lists.[12] The possibility exists that because the defendants knew that many of the people they named had already been or were on trial or had testified and confessed, they were not endangering these individuals by naming them in depositions. In addition, a percentage of those named were deceased and, while the tribunal never hesitated to prosecute a heretic posthumously, the risks involved were completely different. Nevertheless, the length of each list is still astounding; perhaps the defendant thought he might be exonerated if he named an overwhelming number of judaizers.

Be it as it may, the testimonies utilized by the prosecution are both revealing and intricately intertwined on many levels. For example, the very first witness testifying against Francisco de Vega was none other than Juan del Campo, the defendant in the other trial under discussion. Juan was the descendant of conversos from Quintanar and Alcázar; in his own trial, he provided a detailed genealogy in which he recounted the names of his grandfathers: Juan de Mora of Quintanar was the father of his mother, Isabel de Mora. She married his father, Diego del Campo, the son of Alonso del Campo of Alcázar.[13] Juan himself lived for at least six years in Alcázar before moving to Argamasilla. At the age of fifty, he was no longer a storekeeper but was living on his homestead in Argamasilla de Alba in La Mancha and married to his thirty-year-old wife of ten years, Isabel de Yepes.

Juan explained his connection to the defendant: Francisco was one of his many first cousins, the son of his deceased aunt Elvira de Mora of Alcázar. As a matter of fact, the de Mora family had a large contingency in Alcázar, and Juan named numerous members including aunts, uncles, first cousins, and first cousins once removed, all residents of this locale. The only observances he mentioned at this time pertained to the Sabbath and inconsistently refraining from eating pork, all done in the hope of achieving salvation.[14]

The second statement, also removed from another trial, belonged to the prisoner Alonso López de Armenia, a seventy-year-old store owner and the uncle of both Francisco and Juan. He was married to their aunt, known both as María de Mora and María López, and he lived in Alcázar with the rest of the family. He spoke of his deceased sister and brother-in-law, Alonso de la Vega and Elvira de Mora, and their four surviving children, Francisco, Lope, María, and Isabel, referring to them as of Jewish "caste."[15] He knew they all observed Jewish laws because his wife had told him so, but he had no additional information about this matter nor had he communicated with them about it.[16] Parts of his testimony appeared in Juan del Campo's trial, where he stated that when that defendant was a bachelor, Juan visited the home of his aunt and uncle, Elvira de Mora and Alonso de la Vega, where, according to his aunt, he judaized with them.[17] Alonso would be reconciled to the Church.

The third witness for the prosecution was Alonso's son, Juan, aged twenty-seven. His testimony seemed to have been made during a grace period, as is evident from the style, for he began with a statement requesting forgiveness for his sins; one later learns that he too was reconciled.[18] In del Campo's trial, where he was the second prosecution witness, he elaborated upon his transgressions, which included living according to the Law of Moses and observing the Sabbath, the New Months, the three annual festivals, and more. Juan emphasized the fact that his uncle, Diego de Mora of Quintanar, had taught him and his four sisters, and he claimed that the rest of their cousins judaized. It is not clear if the uncle began these lessons when his sister, the mother of these children, was still alive, or whether he simply made visits from Quintanar to Alcázar in order to edify and supervise his nieces and nephew. The confessant did comment, however, that he was not certain if the de la Vegas observed or not, since he thought he had seen them eat various pork products.[19]

The fourth testimony was from a third member of this family, María López, Alonso's wife and Juan's mother. In the audience with the inquisitors, this conversa, who was more than seventy years old, confessed to having lived according to the Law of Moses and named others, against whom she had testified. She mentioned four of her nieces and nephews from the de la Vega clan; the fifth was probably not named because he was already deceased. She knew that they observed the Sabbath and holidays for many years but that some of them had repented. Interestingly, an economic factor enters here. This aunt emphasized the fact that the de la Vega family was poor, and as a result they could not always afford not to work on the Sabbath and holidays.[20] This is not the first time such a consideration took place, but perhaps the fact that the eyewitnesses were family and neighbors rather than servants is relevant here. If this family was poor, it is possible that they could not even afford help in the house. Again, the contrast with the Cogolludo conversos is striking.

The testimony to follow belongs to the thirty-year-old daughter of Alonso and María named Catalina. She too had sought to be reconciled to the Church and confessed to observing the Sabbath from sundown to sundown, not working on this day, observing the New Months and the three annual festivals,[21] washing meat she was to roast or cook, and, although she sometimes ate pork, sometimes refraining as well. She also was taught to wash her hands, for reasons she thought were related to hygiene.[22]

Diego de Mora is singled out as having taught Catalina and her brother and sister, Juan and Isabel, to pursue such observances in order to save their souls and go to heaven. She dated this indoctrination to about 1578, when her uncle, on a visit from Quintanar, examined the three siblings about their heritage. He was shocked to discover that they were ignorant of Judaism, and he declared that their mother, his sister María, had been negligent. It is difficult to determine here if the uncle assumed that his sister would automatically carry on the family tradition, either in her role as mother or as a member of a judaizing family; it is also not clear if he knew about his brother-in-law's proclivities not to judaize. Yet on the basis of the above statements, the father, Alonso López de Armenia, did not confess to judaizing whereas their mother, María, did. However, she implicated nephews and nieces and not her own children, possibly because she had consciously decided not to teach them. If so, her brother had exposed them to Judaism behind their judaizing mother's back!

At any rate, Catalina said that the three of them had observed Jewish traditions until their relatives were taken to the inquisitorial court in Cuenca, at which point they decided that they had chosen the wrong path and that it was better to discontinue their erring ways. She claimed that she had planned to come to confess earlier but her mother had been ill and thus she could not undertake a journey. She had talked about these matters to four of her cousins from the de la Vega family—Francisco, Lope, Isabel, and María—but she never saw them judaize. Like her father, she had only heard from her mother about their activities.[23]

Isabel López, the twenty-eight-year-old sister of Catalina, more or less presented the same testimony, albeit streamlined. Uncle Diego had taught her; four of her cousins in Alcázar knew about the Law of Moses; her mother told her they were judaizers, and she herself requested mercy as she confessed her sins.[24]

The seventh prosecution witness was Francisco Ruíz de Armenia, who was related to the above López family; he was the son-in-law of María de Mora and Alonso López de Armenia and the brother-in-law of Juan, Isabel, and Catalina. He had married a sibling not mentioned by them, either because she was an older sister and quite possibly out of the house by the time their uncle came onto the scene, or because she was already deceased by the time of their confessions. At any rate, this sixty-five-year-old soap-maker began by admitting that he had observed some Sabbaths because his wife had taught him and persuaded him to do so. Francisco had been called in and incarcerated by the Inquisition in 1590.

Following this deposition was the statement from Francisco's first audience, when he provided interesting genealogical information. His paternal grandfather was said to have come from the mountains of Armenia and was an *hidalgo*. The other three grandparents were conversos,[25] and his paternal grandmother was even burned by the Holy Office! Despite the fact that his grandmother married an Old Christian, she continued to observe and was tried and convicted as a judaizer. As for his own involvement, he and his wife had observed the festivals, the New Months, and other Jewish observances. His wife had joined some of the offspring of Alonso de la Vega, such as Lope, Francisco, Isabel, and María, although he never saw them observe.[26] A portion of his testimony also appeared in del Campo's trial, although his name was not listed at the beginning of the proceeding. He did not offer particularly valuable information concerning this defendant; he stated that Juan communicated with Francisco's wife and that he supposedly washed and engaged in prayers.[27]

The testimony of Beatriz Ruíz, Francisco's daughter, appeared next. This twenty-eight-year-old conversa approached the Inquisition on her own volition. When asked what she wanted, she said she came to confess a sin that she had hidden. Her mother, María López, had taught her about the Law of Moses, to observe the Sabbath days by lighting lamps on Friday nights, to refrain from eating pork, and to observe certain holidays and other things commanded by the Law of Moses. When indoctrinating her, her mother had told her that her relatives in Alcázar observed the Law and that two households were involved. She was referring to her cousins, the children of Alonso de la Vega (and Elvira de Mora), and their parents, and to her other cousins, the children of María de Mora and Alonso López de Armenia, and their parents. Again, she had only her mother's word that these relatives were judaizing, for she had not seen them in action.[28]

This was the fifth time that a witness mentioned hearing of judaizing activities from a reliable source but was unable to provide eyewitness accounts. Perhaps this lack of eyewitness accounts explains why there were so many witnesses, for the Inquisition needed clear-cut proof, and hearsay could not effectively substantiate its claims. The majority of the evidence, thus far, is far from ideal.

Beatriz's younger sister, the twenty-three-year-old Elvira Ruíz, also came forth to confess that she had been taught by her mother to observe the Sabbath and other ceremonies. Her mother, María López, had also informed her that four of her cousins, namely the de la Vega clan, observed. Once again, this is a case of hearsay, for Elvira had never seen them observe nor had any contact with them on this level.[29]

The last member of this nuclear family included here was Ana Ruíz, the youngest sister, who was twenty-two years of age and unmarried. Ana confessed to having observed some rites and ceremonies of the Law of Moses. She claimed that her mother told her that her cousins, the de la Vegas, were judaizers, but she, too, had no firsthand proof.[30]

Lope de la Vega, the older brother of the defendant Francisco, was the eleventh witness for the prosecution, although his confession is to be found a bit later in the proceedings. This forty-one-year-old field laborer's testimony was also the third to appear in del Campo's trial.[31] While the López family had attributed its knowledge to their uncle Diego, Lope confessed that his mother Elvira, Diego's sister, indoctrinated him at the age of thirteen or fourteen without the knowledge of his father. There is no doubt that in Lope's opinion, his mother was totally responsible for all judaizing in this family. At first, Lope said that she did not explain why he should engage in such observances, but later he referred to her emphasizing that abiding by Jewish law would ensure one's salvation and access to heaven.

Elvira taught him to observe the Sabbath by preparing food in advance and wearing a clean shirt. She also taught him eight or nine prayers, the majority of which he recited to the inquisitors during the audiences;[32] most were psalms or variations of psalms, which were precisely recorded by the notaries as Lope recited them. In addition, his mother told him not to eat pork or the fat of meat and said that he should fast a full day on Yom Kippur; there may have been more to relate, but he did not recall anything else at this audience. Later he added having observed the New Month and the three festivals, one in September and one during the Holy Week. His family had eaten matsah around Easter time, and his father had quarreled with Elvira when he discovered this fact, but the rest of the family continued to observe Passover anyway. In addition, they had lit lamps on Friday nights after replacing their wicks. Then Lope explained that while residing in his mother's house, he had slaughtered birds according to Jewish law. He was certain that this task was incumbent upon him, because the Torah forbids women to behead fowl or animals. He then spoke of washing his hands when they were dirty and after attending to personal needs.[33] At the end of his testimony, he was asked about his father's role, which he described as nonexistent and even hostile. At this point, Lope recounted that he once took his father to meet with a man knowledgeable in Jewish law, and after this meeting, his father ceased objecting to the family's activities; on the other hand, in his son's opinion, Alonso de la Vega did not participate at all![34]

After Elvira de Mora passed away in 1570, her son maintained a sporadic observance until about 1585, although he began eating pork products almost immediately.[35] Lope presented himself to the tribunal as a penitent sinner who voluntarily returned to the fold; the last judaizing activity he could recall was fasting on Yom Kippur some five years earlier.[36]

The confessant mentioned that his mother had taught his brother Francisco and his sister María and that they observed all that he had described while they were living with their parents. On the other hand, he had not seen his siblings observe for years and could not ascertain whether or not they still were judaizing.[37] He later added another brother, Juan, to the core of crypto-Jews in the family, but Juan was already deceased. However, after Juan married a good Christian, Lope never saw him judaize, for he always seemed to be behaving as a proper Christian. When interrogated further about his own decision to discontinue judaizing, Lope said he had not discussed this with any siblings or cousins.

In the second file, one finds a few additional remarks Lope made concerning his cousin Juan del Campo. He had seen this cousin fast an entire day, ritually wash his hands, and observe the Sabbath.[38] Essentially, Lope provided a firsthand observation of each of the two defendants; his cousin and brother were clearly judaizers. In this testimony, the overwhelming role of the confessant's mother stands out. However, since this witness came forth voluntarily and had discontinued observing years beforehand, he would be reconciled to the Church.

Lope's and Francisco's sister, Isabel de la Vega, then provided an even more descriptive testimony. This voluntary confession of the forty-year-old wife of Francisco de Yepes, the saltpeter dealer who was away in the Indies, was utilized in both trials. Isabel referred to herself as a descendant of New Christians on both sides.[39] At first, she attributed her knowledge to her cousin, María López, the same mother of Beatriz, Ana, and Elvira who was credited with teaching these three daughters as well as with influencing her husband, Francisco Ruíz de Armenia. María had insisted that her cousin observe the Sabbath, prepare meals before sundown, and avoid work on that day. This conversa supposedly told the confessant that her own mother was to be condemned for neglecting her responsibilities and for not encouraging the daughter to return to the religion of her ancestors.

It appears that this was by no means the case, however. Isabel requested a second audience with the inquisitors, whereupon she revised her earlier statement. More than Sabbath observance was involved, for now she referred to Passover, some purity laws, and the New Month as additional Jewish activities in which she engaged. According to Isabel:

She said that it is true that she had requested an audience and she wanted it in order to tell and confess the whole truth that indeed she had not presented in the previous audience because she had been upset . . . the situation is that she was of tender age, more than forty-five or forty-six years [ago][40] and that she did not understand that she had a mother who was as evil as was hers who had taught her children things that were so offensive to Our Lord. And that her aforesaid mother and Luiza de Mora[41] knew all of the Law of Moses and she [the mother] taught it to her and she had done so and observed until thirteen or fourteen [years ago], following the law. But she did not discontinue [her observance] then, she did not come to this Holy Office to seek a remedy and she did not come to declare this; not out of evil intentions concerning these holy and honored men to whom with all her heart she declares and cries out, having put her mother in such a terrible state and living in fear these past twelve or thirteen years. Her mother told her to observe the Sabbath, dressing up on Friday evenings and preparing food on those same Fridays for the entire Sabbath. And in this way, they observed the Sabbath, preparing meals on Friday for the Sabbath and changing the sheets on the beds [to clean ones], and wearing clean blouses on the said Sabbath, and celebrating it as a holiday, and cleaning the oil-lamps on Friday afternoons and placing clean wicks into them and throwing out the oil, and lighting them until they died out by themselves. And her aforesaid mother said that one must observe the festivals of the Jews, and this [confessant] only remembers one festival that falls on the Holy Week, that lasts seven or eight days, and in this festival one eats unleavened bread and washes one's body after one has undressed, and her said mother did likewise. And the confessant and her mother used to cut their nails and when they grew, they threw them in the fire. They did the same for their hair that fell out while being combed, and she does not recall when the other festivals fell except that they were observed and celebrated and her said mother told her when they fell and that she also recalls observing the first day of the month as a holiday, and she does not remember anything else that was done, that only too well had [she] wanted to remember in order to tell him that she wants the salvation of her soul more than anything in this world, for one has but one soul which one does not want to lose.[42]

Isabel, in an addendum, also discussed the relationship between her mother and her siblings, reinforcing Lope's admission to having been influenced by his mother. She mentions that her brothers would join her and her mother and that they wore clean shirts on the Sabbath, as ascertained by Lope, and sometimes observed the holidays. Isabel also was under the impression that only men could properly slaughter and kasher meat, for she described how they removed the fat from it, soaked it in water and salt, cleaned it, and removed the blood from it.[43]

In del Campo's file, she added information about communication between the defendant and the members of her family, who all agreed that the Law of Moses was superior to the Christian law; now she realized that this was not so, and those who taught her had harmed her. In addition, she went into detail concerning the family of María López, and how this conversa had taught her daughters to observe the Sabbath, Yom Kippur, and the festivals. She then mentioned how her mother stressed washing one's body before the fast of Yom Kippur as well as after menstruation, and also washing one's hands after completing bodily functions. Her sister María had hidden her activities from her husband and discontinued her judaizing some two years ago. She did not know how much judaizing her other siblings did after they were married, but she was aware that sometimes her brothers were called in to slaughter birds for their sisters.[44]

In a subsequent audience, Isabel added rather surprising information about her father's judaizing. She said that she knew that her father observed Jewish law, especially the Sabbath, fast days, and the New Month; she was certain that he did so with her mother and siblings and that her mother had instilled in him a belief in the Law of Moses. Isabel testified that he had told his children these beliefs were good and would bring about salvation. She was convinced that he died believing in this law! This declaration stands in sharp contrast to the testimony of her brother Lope, who first described his father's role as nonexistent and hostile and then assumed that Alonso de la Vega eventually merely ceased objecting to the family's activities.[45] In this version, the mother successfully convinced the entire family of the merits of Jewish law.

Isabel's final addition to her confession concerned her sister-in-law Ana del Campo, the wife of the defendant Francisco de la Vega. She briefly described how Ana had approached her for lessons in Judaism three or four years earlier and how Isabel had refused her, but she knew that others did initiate this woman into Judaism. All of the people she mentioned who taught Ana were themselves prosecution witnesses in one or both of the trials: Juan López de Armenia taught her prayers, and María de Villaescusa and her daughter María de la O. were involved as well. De Villaescusa had asked Isabel if she helped out and also inquired whether her husband, Francisco de Yepes, judaized. When Isabel said that her husband did judaize, she was told to beware of her mother-in-law, who was a devout Christian; in addition, they were all to take special care, since the Inquisition had already come to Quintanar and such close proximity would jeopardize the lives of the judaizers of Alcázar as well.[46]

The thirteenth deposition was that of the thirty-four-year-old scribe Francisco de Vega, who voluntarily approached the inquisitor when he was visiting Alcázar in November 1590; he too was subsequently reconciled to the Church. This converso confessed that he had professed Judaism since the age of ten or eleven because his mother, Leonor Gómez, had taught him that he should do so in order to save his soul. Consequently, he prayed Jewish prayers, covering his eyes while praying and washing his hands beforehand.[47] He fasted entire days, and he observed the Sabbath by wearing a clean shirt and by changing the bed linens. On the other hand, because of the nature of his profession, he was unable to refrain from writing on the Sabbath, but he tried to observe the Sabbath in his heart.[48] Here is an example of another mother in Alcázar who taught her child, and, in this case, at a rather young age.[49]

All of the confessants were well aware of the precariousness of their lives and the lives of those around them. María, the sister of Francisco the scribe, was a prisoner of the Inquisition while her brother was presenting the confession above. Each of them had approached the local priest to confess and receive forgiveness, but the priest sent them to Toledo, because he knew that such transgressions were not within his jurisdiction. The conversa's testimony was used in both trials, for she mentioned both Francisco de Vega and Juan del Campo. María de la Vega, age thirty, said that her whole family was of converso caste and that she had believed in the Law of Moses and had observed it. She mentioned communicating with some of her first cousins, in this case, the children of Alonso de la Vega, including Francisco.[50] In Francisco's file, only brief parts of her confession were included, such as the fact that she began judaizing twenty years earlier but discontinued when her mother began to suffer from melancholy.[51]

In del Campo's file is María's statement that María López de Armenia and her sister Catalina Gómez came to indoctrinate her, her mother, and her brother. Since her brother, Francisco de Vega the scribe, did not live at home, he only observed when he visited the home of their mother, Leonor Gómez. Thus in the 1570s, these women began by teaching María, her mother, and her brother to abide by the Law of the Jews by observing the Sabbath. They were told to put clean wicks in their lamps on Friday nights and to let them burn out by themselves. In addition, they were not to eat pork, to eat only slaughtered birds, to wash and clean the blood from their meat, to cut their nails, and to fast on Thursdays.

Her mother, Leonor Gómez, was convinced by these women that this was the path to salvation and insisted that her children heed their words. The Law of the Jews and Moses would save their souls, and they would go to Heaven without passing through purgatory. When interrogated, her daughter recalled celebrating some festivals, in particular eight days of Passover, when they ate matsah supplied to them by these judaizing women. They also fasted on Yom Kippur and were taught some prayers, at which time they prayed with their feet together and occasionally covered their eyes with their hands.[52] The Sabbath prayer was the longest, and prior to praying they washed their hands and dried them with a clean cloth.

At this point, Juan del Campo entered the picture, for he too taught Leonor Gómez and talked to her at length when he visited Alcázar. María blamed him along with the other two women for influencing her mother; Juan would read to Leonor from a book, which he kept hidden in María López's home. During the three years that she and her mother (and occasionally her brother) judaized, Juan frequently read to her mother. Apparently, Leonor was convinced that Jewish observance was the true path, until she suffered from a breakdown, at which time she claimed to have been deceived by the Jews. Consequently, she refused to continue judaizing and her son seemed content enough to follow suit; María, however, continued for a while longer on her own.[53] Two of the three teachers involved with this family were women and while Juan del Campo, being literate, was obviously the most learned, the conversa sisters had introduced them to judaizing.

The last testimony used by the prosecution against Francisco was none other than that of his twenty-six-year-old wife, Ana del Campo,[54] also a prisoner whose name, albeit not consistently, appears with her husband's as a co-defendant in the trial. Ana's story is most interesting, for it seems that she had been unaware of her husband's judaizing when she married him. One day after attending mass in 1582, she complained bitterly to Ana Navarra about her husband's treatment of her and how they had argued upon her return from making confession. As a result, the eighteen-year-old bride was informed that her mother-in-law was "Jewish" and observed the Sabbath and other ceremonies. A few days later, she went to the home of this informant, who told her it was folly to believe that Christ was God, and that one must observe the Sabbath by wearing clean shirts and lighting lamps on Friday evenings without extinguishing them and also by fasting an entire day. Navarra emphasized that these actions guaranteed that one would go to Heaven.

Ana also learned that her sisters-in-law judaized and that one must recite certain prayers after having washed one's hands. She recalled that one prayer was called the *Shema*,[55] when one's feet were placed together and the eyes were covered by one's hands. She was told that many individuals in Alcázar and Quintanar judaized; Navarra provided her with a list of names, some of whom were people she knew. As a result, Ana del Campo decided to observe the Sabbath by wearing a clean blouse and lighting lamps on Friday evenings, by fasting one day in the fall, and by learning various prayers. She visited Navarra in order to receive instruction.

Francisco's reaction to her initiation was enlightening. When she confronted him, he denied that he was a judaizer. Ana then approached her sisters-in-law, who confirmed the fact that they observed but that her husband was evil and did not want to be saved. Eventually, Francisco admitted to his wife that he judaized, but he refused to pray with her; Ana had no idea what he actually did, since he isolated himself when she assumed he was praying. Since he was often out in the field working, she was also unaware of his activities at these times. Only when they were snowed in did he let her know he observed, when he and his brother Lope recited some psalms and declared that they observed the Sabbath in honor of the Law. She heard him teach one of his female cousins, María López, who was the daughter of his mother's sister, as well as María de Mora and her husband, Alonso López de Armenia.[56] This was the family that provided more than half of the testimonies for the prosecution in Francisco de Vega's trial, although this particular daughter was deceased by this time.

Portions of the testimony of Francisco de Vega were used in Juan del Campo's trial, just as del Campo's was the very first deposition used by the prosecution against de Vega. Francisco attested to having seen del Campo pray, wash his hands, fast an entire day, and observe the Sabbath. In another audience, he was asked from where his cousin del Campo as well as his father Alonso de la Vega derived their knowledge. Francisco replied, as did his sister Isabel in her addenda discussed above, that his mother, Elvira de Mora, had taught his father; although he knew Juan since he was a child, he had no idea from whom Juan had learned Jewish law.[57] Again, one sees how completely intertwined these two trials are by virtue of the familial and geographic affinities as well as the influential members of these families.

Five of the next seven testimonies appeared solely in del Campo's file; the other two, those of Francisco de Vega, the scribe, and his sister María, have already been described. All of the five are by women, four of them neighbors and the fifth his wife. The twenty-five-year-old Catalina de Moya of Alcázar did not provide significant information, for she herself had not seen the defendant in action, but rather she had information through her aunt, who claimed to be familiar with the de la Vega family, where del Campo had visited.[58]

The second woman, María de Villaescusa, was a widow also imprisoned by the Inquisition at this time. She began her statement by claiming to have a poor memory due to her age and exhausted physical state. Sixteen or seventeen years before, while she was tending to her linen and silk store, del Campo entered and invited her to the home of Francisco de Vega, the scribe. María accepted the invitation and watched the defendant take out a book from which he read passages that dealt with the patriarchs; then he discussed the meaning of fasting from sundown to sundown. The conversa was not sure what fast this was, but she believed that this was advocated by the Law of Moses and would facilitate going to Heaven. She recalled details about the Exodus from Egypt, but most of the information she offered was somewhat vague. She had been present at such gatherings twice, and when asked what else she learned there, she mentioned the Sabbath, which she herself did not observe. Del Campo had also taken her to the house of the scribe's mother, Leonor Gómez, where she learned about two festivals, one that took place in the spring and the other in September.

The inquisitors were loathe to believe that she had been with the defendant only these few times; María said he frequented her store, which was in her home, especially since he had amorous relations with her daughter! She also mentioned that his brother Alonso had visited her and told her he was a judaizer, and that she knew he had fasted. María said that she had not communicated with anyone else about these matters and that she remembered no more details.[59]

María de la O., wife of Antonio Falcón, was the previously mentioned daughter (who had an affair with del Campo) and who also confessed to the Holy Tribunal. This thirty-year-old-resident of Alcázar was able to date the interactions with del Campo and others to eighteen years prior, when she was twelve.[60] At this time, her mother initiated her into Judaism by telling her to fast according to the Law of Moses so that she would be saved. The mother had also received from del Campo a prayer written on a piece of paper which she was told to learn; while clutching it to her breast, the mother accidentally dropped it and lost it in the street, only to have it found by, of all people, a local cleric in the company of a deaf man.[61]

Undaunted, María de Villaescusa was first said to have sent her daughter to the scribe's house to talk to his mother about obtaining another copy of this prayer. Later María de la O. revised her statement, explaining that both mother and daughter went to see Leonor Gómez; del Campo was present and made them a new copy, which they were told to memorize.[62] While del Campo was a central figure because of his writing skills and knowledge of prayers, the house of Leonor Gómez was where the judaizers congregated, and the mother of María de la O. was influential in her daughter's decision to observe.

The fourth in this group of depositions belonged to none other than the thirty-year-old wife of the defendant; Isabel de Yepes had been married to del Campo for about ten years. During this period, she saw him engage in certain practices which she described to the court. Juan would wash his hands before he prayed and often before he ate as well. He would frequently sit and read from a book of Psalms written in Romance, and he instructed her, should he be taken to Toledo, to destroy this book, which Isabel did. At the tail end of her lengthy but not terribly enlightening deposition, Isabel was quoted as having witnessed Juan covering his eyes and sometimes even his face while engaged in prayer; she had no understanding of what he was doing.

His wife knew that quite a few of the women in his family were prisoners of the Inquisition in Cuenca, but she did not specify names other than one kinswoman, who had also served as his maid before he married Isabel. The slaughtering habits of her husband were described almost as idiosyncratic rather than as in conformity with Jewish law. Although he sometimes removed the blood from meat, Isabel insisted that these methods, which she herself employed, were nothing more than little concessions on her part to appease her husband. Once, when two of their guests, a second lieutenant and a surgeon, entered her kitchen, they seemed disturbed by her techniques of cleaning the meat, but their hostess was not in the least flustered. Isabel more than once asserted that this was not the way birds were slaughtered in her father's house, implying that her father was a judaizer and that she knew precisely what was involved in bona fide ritual slaughter.[63] The most unusual item found in her deposition is a copy of her own signature; perhaps Juan taught her to write, but the fact is that she chose to sign her own deposition, something that even most of the men in these files did not do![64]

The last name on the list of thirteen prosecution witnesses was Teresa Mexia. In actuality she was not the last to testify; three additional women were subsequently questioned. This twenty-eight-year-old resident of Argamasilla, who appeared voluntarily, claimed that the defendant's house was well adorned and contained no Christian image whatsoever. Other than that, she had little more than hearsay to offer: a(nother) María de la O.[65] told her how Juan del Campo's wife would hide her actions when she cooked herself a fritter of streaky bacon to eat. Later when she was called upon to ratify her statement, she too signed the verification on her own.[66]

The second María de la O. was summoned for questioning and explained that when Isabel de Yepes roasted pork for her breakfast, she tried to cover her tracks by throwing a piece of cloth or coarse wrapping paper in the fire; this ploy was necessary because her husband, del Campo, was a "low-down and treacherous" fellow who interfered with his wife's daily routine. She could not offer more details about what occurred in this household because she rarely entered it; the two families were not on the best of terms because of business competition between them, since they both owned stores.[67]

To delve further into this couple's culinary habits, the inquisitors questioned Ana, an eighteen-year-old who apparently lived with them for three or four months and helped out in the kitchen. She did not enlighten the tribunal, since she had seen none of the judaizing activities described to her or that she was asked about. On the contrary, she said she perceived no difference between the daily activities in del Campo's house and any other house; as a matter of fact, she knew that the defendant had prayed and done good deeds. Ana claimed that Isabel de Yepes hid her cooking of bacon because her husband was perturbed by the fact that there was food wasted in the house because more was prepared than could be eaten.[68]

Two sisters, Leonor and Isabel Gutiérrez, were called in as the last witnesses to provide information about the defendant. Leonor told a wild story about how the sisters were invited to the de la Vegas' house some thirty years before, when she was about ten years old. Juan was there with his cousins, and the boys seemed to have played a prank on the girls that involved letting loose a bull and resulted in the girls' rapid flight. Aside from this, no useful information was offered by either sister; Isabel, however, was the third woman to sign her own name to confirm her deposition.[69]

No further witnesses were summoned, but one final testimony did appear; it was given by the same converso whose confessional statement was the first one cited in the de la Vega file. Thus the depositions came full circle as they concluded with a more detailed testimony by the defendant, Juan del Campo. At that time, Juan dated his judaizing to thirty years prior, to 1560, when he was twenty years old. He had been initiated by his mother's brother, his uncle Diego de Mora of Quintanar, the same converso from Quintanar who had taught his nieces and nephews in the de Armenia household in Alcázar. Del Campo pointed out that this uncle behaved consistently, for he visited and taught all or most of his nieces and nephews in the Argamasilla branch of the clan as well.

The defendant did not discuss any of his own efforts to edify his relatives, although he listed more than twenty members of his extended family who were prisoners in various inquisitorial facilities and being charged with judaizing. As for his own observances, he kept the Jewish Sabbath, when one should not work at all; however, in order not to be suspected of judaizing, one had to pretend to be doing something! He occasionally ate pork although this was forbidden by Jewish law. He celebrated three festivals: the festival of the booths, of the lamb (Passover), and a third whose name he could not recall. All these actions were intended to save his soul, and he had communicated with many of his cousins and siblings about Jewish observance.

Nevertheless, according to del Campo, when he married Isabel de Yepes ten years prior, he knew he had to discontinue his ways, for they would be unacceptable to his bride. His wife was a pious Catholic, and he did not dare continue observing. Thus twenty years of living "like a cork [floating] on the water" came to an end; these are the very words that del Campo used to describe the quality of his life as a crypto-Jew.[70] By his abandoning this lifestyle, the defendant claimed, stability would prevail, for he would no longer be affected by every wave or gust of wind that crossed his path.

By del Campo's account, the moving force in initiating his judaizing was his uncle, whereas it was his wife's religiosity that precipitated his subsequent abandonment of the faith. According to her testimony, Isabel de Yepes appeared to be fairly ignorant of judaizing or of any inclinations on her husband's part. However, other women in this extended and unusual community were both judaizing and teaching fellow conversos; these included aunts and cousins of del Campo from the de la Vega branch, into which one aunt married, as well as the de Armenia clan, into which another aunt married. Both these aunts as well as his uncle Diego were from the de Mora line, which originated with del Campo's mother Isabel. Francisco de la Vega had been influenced by his mother and, like his cousin Juan, did not share his lifestyle with his wife.[71] When Ana del Campo learned of her husband's proclivities, rather than turning in the man with whom she quarreled incessantly, she asked the women of the community to teach her Jewish customs. She had her choice of quite a few conversas who were knowledgeable in this area.

The de Mora clan represented a tightly knit group of judaizers who managed to retain an incredibly high degree of Jewish observance. Numerous prayers were recited in the course of these proceedings, and the level of judaizing found here was certainly comparable to that of the previous century. There were, no doubt, some knowledgeable judaizing men with leadership traits in this community.

Alongside them, working in tandem or on parallel levels, were their sisters, nieces, mothers, and daughters; these conversos and conversas were committed to passing on their heritage to their sons and daughters. At the end of the sixteenth century, the Inquisition discovered a network of judaizers teaching and observing Judaism. It is hard to determine who was most successful or active, but the sheer numbers of confessions and depositions made at the two trials under discussion attests to the level of judaizing in Alcázar and the two neighboring villages, Argamasilla and Quintanar. The prominence of women in these proceedings cannot be ignored; they, along with the defendants, lived precarious lives, "like corks floating on water."

Conclusion

Heretics or Daughters of Israel?

Behind their silent submission, moriscas actually subverted Christian policies by preserving in their homes the language, rites and
customs of their people. Hidden in the subtext of most historical
documents, their subversion becomes apparent when the focus
centers on their experiences and their subcultures, not merely for
ascribed status and internalized gender definitions, but also for
their work, interactions, and consciousness. . . .

Not surprisingly, then, the most significant arena for the conflict
that grew between Muslims and Christians was not a battlefield nor
royal chambers, nor even the secret prisons of the Inquisition;
rather, it was the *morisco* home, a bastion of cultural resistance in
which women played leading roles in perceiving Muslim traditions
and resisting Christian hegemony.

Mary Elizabeth Perry, "Behind the Veil: Moriscas and
the Politics of Resistance and Survival"

THE EPIGRAPH SEEMS tailor-made not only for the moriscas of Spain,
but also for the conversas whose trials have been analyzed in this book. The
moriscas were women of Islamic descent who converted to Catholicism either voluntarily or by force, and while the number of moriscos or moriscas tried as heretics
by the Holy Tribunal does not compare with those of the conversos of Jewish heritage, there is clearly a parallel development that occurred in the two "New Christian" communities.[1] Moreover, the conclusions to be drawn about the role of these
women are uncannily similar. The converso home was, as was the morisco home, "a
bastion of cultural resistance in which women played leading roles" in preserving
their tradition and in "resisting Christian hegemony." These women used the
means at their disposal to subvert the attempts by the Church and the Inquisition
to eradicate their religious heritage. As has been demonstrated, these women
achieved such subversion[2] not only by means of their traditional role, but also

through their work, their sense of community, and a distinct awareness not only of what they were doing, but of why they were doing so.

The Inquisition was definitely interested in the deeds performed by the crypto-Jew, but the intention behind that deed was equally and perhaps sometimes even more important. Thus a crypto-Jewish woman who de-baptized her newborn baby might not qualify in rabbinic eyes as a daughter of Israel, but she was clearly a heretic in the eyes of the Church. By the same token, a conversa who chose to have a *hadas* celebration for her child was, once again, not following any legal obligation or rite, but rather engaging in a medieval custom adopted by the Sephardic Jews. Such a woman might not have been aware of the fact that the custom of making *hadas* was not halakhically binding, but for her, it was a Jewish custom that signified her identification with the Jewish people no less than did fasting on Yom Kippur. Both acts were carried out with the same intention, an identification with the people of Israel and the hope of achieving salvation through the Law of Moses.

Reviewing the experiences of the women whose trials have been examined here reveals great variety and heterogeneity; it is not always easy to discern who was or was not a heretic or a daughter of Israel. Most of the conversa women who were condemned or punished as judaizing heretics can indeed be defined as daughters of Israel as well.[3] Some cases are less clear-cut than others, but, as has been seen, even some of those consistently denying their affiliation to Judaism were essentially stoics rather than the sincere believers in Catholicism they strived to portray.

The group of crypto-Jewish women who had contact with the Jewish community before 1492 were outstanding in their observance. Some of them had even experienced life as bona fide Jews, having been born Jewish and then baptized, and their understanding of what it meant to observe was especially unnerving for the Inquisition. These women could easily be defined both as heretics by the Church and as daughters of Israel by their Jewish brethren. It has been shown that the Jews in Castile did not discriminate against their converso brethren; while they might not have encouraged them to judaize to the degree claimed by the Crown in the Expulsion Decree, they were willing to provide services and guidance to those with judaizing proclivities.

Thus it is not surprising to discover conversas engaging in numerous traditional and halakhic observances. The judaizers from this early period fasted and observed the Sabbath and other holidays; sometimes the Jews even supplied them with Sabbath stews or kosher wine. Examples were found of Sukkot and Passover observance; the crypto-Jewish women celebrated these days both passively, such as by lending clothes or rugs or jewelry to Jewish women, and actively, by attending a seder or receiving or buying or baking matsah. Also, they were knowledgeable in the dietary laws and often took care to eat only kosher birds and animals and meat that was properly slaughtered and prepared, by someone of either Jewish or converso heritage (or even Muslim). Conversas also made donations to the Jewish community or synagogue, such as for the purchase of oil for the synagogue. In ad-

dition, the Jews supplied the crypto-Jews with books and instructed them, sometimes even teaching them to read. The Crown also emphasized the fact that the
conversos were taught that Jewish law was the only law and contained the only
truth. These are heretical ideas if a baptized Catholic ascribes to them, but perfectly
acceptable for a Jew or a crypto-Jew in fifteenth-century Castile.

Once the Jewish community was expelled in 1492, the situation was destined to
change, but it did so not as drastically or as quickly as was expected. The major
change pertained to the focus of Jewish activities, for without the exiled community and its institutions, the private domain became the sole site tenable for continuing the tradition. In actuality, the focus of the women's lives did not change as
much as did the men's, because the latter were deprived of the public domain in
which they traditionally functioned as Jews. For the women, however, there was
now a greater responsibility and an awareness that they had become the central
bearers of the Jewish heritage.

During the post-Expulsion period, many of the trials still revealed activities that
occurred pre-1492. Some defendants were second-time offenders, in which case,
the inquisitors would bring in the first confession, usually from grace periods between 1483 and 1486, if they were available. In addition, there was a group of first-
time offenders, some of whom opted to convert rather than to abandon their
homeland.

Those who confessed are easier to categorize, for by means of their confessions,
they affirmed their status as the Church's heretics and the Jews' daughters of Israel.
In cases where the conversas were absolved, the question of determining each one's
status is a formidable task. Some were absolved because of lack of proof, which obviously does not mean they were not "heretics." Some of the accused second-time
offenders might have decided to become sincere penitents. For example, Constanza
Díaz was hounded in 1512 predominantly because of her attitude; ultimately, the
prosecutor did not provide a strong enough case to merit a conviction. Nevertheless, this woman claimed that the Inquisition burned not heretics but martyrs, that
the Holy Tribunal was interested only in sequestering their estates, and that the
souls of the condemned were destined for glory. Was this an attempt at subversion
by Constanza? While one cannot be certain, it most certainly was not submission.
But how can one determine if she was also a heretic or just an outspoken maverick
of New Christian heritage?

Francisca Alvarez, tried in 1514, was accused of not being a sincere Christian,
for she was never seen making the appropriate signs; in addition, this conversa was
perceived as and referred to by her family as a Jewess! If so, the question of her
identity is far less complex than in other cases, for despite her baptism, no one
seemed to have taken that sacred act seriously. All involved clearly considered her to
be a daughter of Israel, or a heretic, depending upon one's perspective.

Beatriz López and Isabel García of Hita had both converted in the 1490s. The
former, an octogenarian was, like Francisca, accused of making no outward acts of

a Christian and was even said to have belittled the saints. Beatriz was penanced rather than severely punished, most likely because of her advanced age, but the punishment was still intended for one who had engaged in heretical acts. Isabel, the younger defendant, faced a lengthy and detailed list of charges that described her as an active daughter of Israel. Fortunately for her, she and her defense lawyer were able to cast aspersions on the credibility of the prosecution witnesses; thus she was freed from being tainted as a heretic. There is still no proof that Isabel would not be considered as a daughter of Israel[4] even though the Church was unsuccessful in its attempt to prove heresy. As these post-1492 cases exemplify, it appears that while the Jews were no longer present in Iberia, the judaizing and the crypto-Jewish sub-culture was not as effectively exiled from Spanish soil.

At the start of the sixteenth century, the Inquisition faced a new phenomenon: messianic fervor that spread like wildfire among the conversos of Extremadura. The three prophetic figures involved succeeded in convincing many conversas that soon they would be going to the Promised Land; the ease with which these women were convinced only proved the reality of the threat of potential Judaism yet present in these descendants of Jews. The intensity of the tribunal's activity testifies to the power of the threat posed by this movement; heeding Elijah and anticipating salvation via the Jewish messiah and resettlement in the Holy Land was anathema to the Church!

While some of the women tried were not condemned, this was so mainly because of lack of information concerning their judaizing activities or because of weak witness testimonies; again, the status of these women remains undefined. In addition, the final chapters of the lives of the two female prophets, Inés of Herrera and Mari Gómez of Chillón, are not documented. While the latter probably fled to Portugal, the former was quickly tried and condemned to the stake between the spring and summer of 1500. Among their followers were both younger and older women. The older often included reconciled judaizers who were well versed in Jewish practice; the younger, some of them very young daughters of Israel, were often enticed into fasting and awaiting the Messiah without being fully indoctrinated into significant Jewish observance.

Subversion was clearly a central concern here, for although the Jews had been expelled, a Jewish spark seemed to linger deep within the converso community; Inés and the others quickly ignited this spark and thereby alarmed the Inquisition. The speed with which the inquisitorial campaign was organized in order to wipe out this movement attests to its fear of subversion. While the court continued to seek confessions and proof of judaizing in order to prove heresy, these conversas' identification with the fate of the Jewish people reveals that they still considered themselves daughters of Israel.

Although Juan Estevan preached that the conversos should not fear the Inquisition because it was God's will, neither the relapsed judaizers of the older generation nor the neophytes of the younger generation had planned to ascend the scaffold.

Although at least half of them ultimately were condemned to death as heretics, the messianic hopefuls were precisely that, fervently hoping that the coming of the Messiah was imminent and that they would be saved from the tentacles of the Inquisition. Unfortunately, their hopes did not materialize, but their statements had been made, and it was clear that these women and girls were identifying with the historical fate of the Jewish people.

As Perry clearly said, subversion was enacted via work and, needless to say, if this work was domestic work, then it played a part in turning the home into a "bastion of cultural resistance." As has been shown, the conversas of Castile in the fifteenth and sixteenth century engaged in many forms of work. Some were professional, working both inside and outside the home. Quite a few worked in the cloth industry; thus one finds seamstresses, sewing teachers, piecemeal workers, owners of fabric stores, and cloth weavers. Others were lye makers, wax makers or sellers, property owners and landladies, midwives, and professional keeners.

Only the last category, the keeners, is blatantly connected with religious observances, for these women would keen, wash and shroud the dead, and prepare meals for the mourners. The preparation of food, done in one's own kitchen, played a central role in the life of the crypto-Jewess, precisely as it did in the home of the Jewish woman. On a daily basis, the Jewess or crypto-Jewess had to deal with the dietary laws, and while only a few actually slaughtered birds on their own, a great many prepared and cleaned the meat according to Jewish law and took great care to cook only foods they perceived to be kosher.

Cooking and baking are central to Sabbath and holiday preparations. Jewish and crypto-Jewish women prepared special meals in honor of the Sabbath, Yom Kippur, and other holidays and festivals and baked hallah on Fridays and matsah for Passover. In addition, extra preparations were made in honor of these days and were carried out either by the conversas themselves or by the servants under their direction. Houses were cleaned and adorned, lamps or the wicks of the lamps were cleaned, and clean clothes or shirts were prepared for wear. All this entailed a great deal of domestic work and organization.

At the same time, these women often refrained from work in honor of the Sabbath and the holidays, avoiding their daily spinning, embroidery, sewing, and the like, or feigning light work. On Sundays, some of them even engaged in daily tasks, occasionally professional work as well, activities that were symbolic of clear defiance of the Church. While most of their professional work did not qualify these women either as heretics or as daughters of Israel, their domestic work did just that. Because the domestic domain became the center of judaizing, and the home was a bastion of cultural and, even more so, religious resistance, there is little doubt as to the nature of this work and the stance of the workers. While perpetuating their ancestral laws and traditions, the crypto-Jewish women were also engaged in subversion of the faith to which they openly adhered. These daughters of Israel worked hard to create a Jewish framework in their homes, and such work was perceived as acts of heresy by the Catholic Church.

The three members of the López-Villarreal family who were tried between 1516 and 1521 were all condemned as heretics by the Inquisition. All were charged with judaizing; the three accusations were not identical, but two clear emphases emerge. As far as the Inquisition was concerned, this family had been observing the Sabbath, in particular by praying, by wearing clean clothes, and by eating special stews, and had been observing the dietary laws by avoiding food that was not kosher and by taking care to process their meat according to Jewish law.

Both of the women in this family continually asserted their innocence and countered numerous charges by asserting that such activities were not heretical acts. On the contrary, they presented themselves as diligent and clean women; the numerous abonos and indirectas attested to their seriousness as Catholics and to the fact that all of the charges were inherently false. As they proceeded with their defense by means of tachas, one witnesses a desperate attempt to prove to the court that the prosecution had provided unreliable witnesses. Neither Isabel nor María succeeded in the tacha process, but even their doing so would not have proven that they were not judaizers.

Both women were burned at the stake at the auto-de-fé on November 30, 1518; Pedro subsequently provided a confession, albeit brief and undoubtedly partial. The court did not believe that the three acts of judaizing to which he confessed represented all of his actual observance, and its members were probably correct.

While there is no way of knowing precisely what Pedro had truly done, his attempt to appear passive in his observance and to portray the women, his deceased wife in particular, as responsible for actively judaizing, was unsuccessful. Pedro had admitted to engaging in some crypto-Jewish activities and had implicated his wife and daughter, about whose observances there were detailed descriptions. Consequently, it does not seem inappropriate to classify both Isabel and María López as two daughters of Israel who had died stoically in the hopes of avoiding a martyr's death. Ultimately, all three of the defendants were classified as heretics and, despite their reluctance to admit it, seemed to have been active judaizers.

The case of the midwife presents, in a certain sense, the mirror image of the López women. The latter denied judaizing yet appeared to have feigned sincerity as Catholics. Beatriz Rodríguez confessed to observing the Sabbath, but her testimony was neither convincing nor consistent. Essentially, her absurdly long encounter with the Inquisition reflected a two-pronged attack. The assumption was that anyone who could make comments such as she did or behave as she did was a crypto-Jew. The fact that she served the community as a midwife apparently pressured the tribunal into continuing to find fault with her lifestyle so that she could be neutralized in some way. The fact that it ultimately achieved its goal does not attest to the veracity of its claims or to the efficacy of its means.

The first report concerning this conversa, from 1514, assumed, as did the informer, that anyone making comments similar to those she made was a Jew. Thus the cloth weaver himself said that Beatriz was a Jewess because she referred to the Jews as the apple of God's eye; she also maligned Old Christians as wanting to steal from the New Christians. The possibility that these comments might have been indicative of a mentality rather than deep theological belief never occurred to the witness. The fact that New Christians suffered from blatant discrimination and from an ever-present fear of being hounded by the Inquisition was not deemed relevant. However, there is no doubt that Beatriz, who appears to have been a somewhat simple woman, was expressing popular New Christian beliefs that, while not cherished by the Church, still did not reflect the mindset of a heretic. The proof lies in the fact that no formal charge was made by the prosecutor even after Beatriz admitted to having made these comments.

The second inquisitorial attack came in 1536 when the peculiar baptism story came to the attention of the court. As soon as the discovery was made that Beatriz was not available, it was immediately assumed that she had fled to Portugal. Although this was clearly not the case, the midwife's timing would have been poor indeed, for in precisely this year, the Inquisition was being established in the other Iberian kingdom. Besides, if she had been such an active judaizer, why were her children not involved in any of these activities and why did she not convince them and their families to join her, either in observance or in her alleged flight to Portugal?

It is clear that the men of the Church coveted their religious monopoly; the power of the midwife, as limited as it was, threatened them. Because she could perform an emergency baptism, she already had too much power. Besides, as a New Christian, a midwife could ostensibly engage in collusion with other New Christians; if she put her mind to it, she could successfully subvert the policies of the Church. There was no end to the means by which a woman of Jewish heritage, in particular a midwife, might engage in heretical and subversive acts and abuse her power.

As we have seen, if the parents of the infant being baptized also had been New Christians or had remained silent regarding the midwife's unorthodox behavior, the accusations would be understandable. However, this was not the case, the evidence was not substantive or incriminating, and the dangerous, potentially subversive New Christian midwife was, once again, released without being charged.

The irony here is that when the Inquisition tried for a third time to deactivate the midwife, she herself provided them with the means of achieving their long-sought goal. After admitting that while married to her second husband, a New Christian, she had observed the Sabbath by not working and by wearing clean clothes, Beatriz added nothing of substance to her testimony. There were no witnesses to these alleged heretical acts, which, by the court's calculations began fifty years earlier! Beatriz tried to present herself as a victim of a temporary and short-lived error in her past. This presentation was in vain, for the inquisitors were convinced that at long last, they had unearthed the heretical midwife who had been judaizing for half a century.

The truth of the matter is that Beatriz might have been a Catholic who was influenced by her New Christian husband during their relatively short marriage—and she might not have been. She was clearly a New Christian harboring some identification with her Jewish past, for she was born Jewish. However, due to the fact that she was very young when her mother joined her in the act of baptism, the influence of the years she experienced as a daughter of Israel is questionable.

The life of this midwife remains an enigma. The Inquisition insisted that she was a classic judaizer and a heretic. Their first informer perceived her as a Jewess. While she clearly identified in her own New Christian way as a former Jew, her confession cannot be taken at face value. Ultimately, Beatriz might have seen herself as a daughter of Israel, but the tribunal had a hard time proving that she was a serious heretic and does not seem to have proven its case very effectively. On the other hand, her potential subversive powers as a midwife were surely an important factor in the inquisitors' steadfastness in pursuing this case. The bottom line was that the New Christian midwife no longer would provide any threat to the Church after 1550.

At the end of the sixteenth century, the conversos of Alcázar and its environs definitely presented a threat to the Church. The detailed sets of trials attest to the thoroughness with which the tribunal aimed to deal with this phenomenon as well as the pervasiveness of the judaizing in certain clans. Studying two related trials unearths a family network of crypto-Jewish observance that seems to be more comprehensive than that of the earlier half of the century. While a number of men were also active in this community, namely Juan del Campo and his uncle, Diego de Mora, many more women were involved on various levels.

There is no doubt that the Inquisition was alarmed to uncover such an active pocket of subversive activity. It successfully procured information from one judaizer about another, and these internal lists were unusually long. From them, one learns that Francisco Ruíz de Armenia, whose paternal grandmother was relaxed in an auto-de-fé, was taught by his wife, who also taught her own daughters to judaize. Lope de la Vega was taught by his mother, Elvira de Mora, as were his siblings. The impressive confession made by his sister Isabel describing the level of observance, including various prayers, attests to Elvira's knowledge and allegiance. There was no question that these conversas perceived themselves as daughters of Israel just as the court classified them as heretics.

These women openly said that the Law of Moses was superior and that it would save one's soul and guarantee one's ascent to Heaven. Some tried to recant at the time of their statements, claiming that now, or in some cases years earlier, they realized the error of their ways. For the Inquisition, however, their affiliation had been clear enough. The scribe Francisco de Vega's mother, Leonor Gómez, was certain that Jewish observance was the only path, and her daughter, María de la Vega, had been taught well, since she too fervently believed in the Law of Moses.

When Ana del Campo attempted to ameliorate the relationship with her husband, Francisco, she was simply informed that her mother-in-law was Jewish! The Jews had been expelled almost an entire century before, but her mother-in-law was still considered "a daughter of Israel" by converso society. The tribunal must have been dismayed to hear such terms being used, for it had been striving to extirpate the heresy in this community, only to discover that the judaizers continued to defy both the institution and the odds. All of these women, the mothers, aunts, sisters, and wives, who had judaized and had taught or been taught, were identifying with their Jewish heritage. All of them were taught to consider themselves as daughters of Israel, knowing fully well that they were taking the risk of their lives. All were willing to silently subvert the teaching of the Catholic Church and to ignore the threat of a fate in the inquisitorial prisons or on the scaffold. All had a clear consciousness of what they were doing.

The heresy that seemed so awful to the men of the Church did not seem to faze these conversas. Their homes provided them with the means to attempt to observe Judaism clandestinely and provide for continuity in their nuclear and extended families. These daughters of Israel, whether from Alcázar or Cogolludo, Herrera or Ciudad Real, were well aware of the risks. Yet their primary identification had been decided; a crypto-Jewess left no doubt in the minds of her fellow judaizers or of the Inquisition itself. Her so-called heretical acts were a necessary and inseparable part of her heritage and her seemingly indestructible links to the Jewish people.

Appendix 1

Witnesses for the Prosecution in the López-Villarreal Trials

María	Isabel	Pedro
1. Juan Ropero, blacksmith, of Cogolludo	1. Catalina de Cervantes wife of Pedro de Burgos of Cogolludo	1. Juan Ropero, blacksmith of Cogolludo
2. Mayor, wife of Pablo (farmer) of Sant Andrés	2. Juan Ropero blacksmith, of Cogolludo	2. Mayor, wife of Pablo (farmer) Sant Andrés
3. Madalena, wife of Martín, goatherd of Corlo	3. Madalena, wife of Martín, goatherd of Corlo	3. Madalena,wife of Martín, goatherd of Corlo
4. María, daughter of Miguel of Aleas, shepherd	4. María, daughter of Miguel of Aleas, shepherd	4. María, daughter of Miguel of Aleas, shepherd
5. Madalena, wife of Martín Simón of Sant Andrés	5. Madalena, wife of Martín Simón of Sant Andrés	5. Madalena, wife of Martín Simón of Sant Andrés
6. Francisco Yague, son of Juan of Arvancón		6. Francisco Yague, son of Juan Yague of Arvancón
		7. Juan Rodeznero, farmer of Cogolludo
		8. Juana, wife of Francisco de Pablo of Membrillera

Alphabetical List of Witnesses Nominated by
the Defense in Abonos and Indirectas

* Represents each time a witness was summoned by the tribunal; if no asterisk
  appears, the court decided not to summon that witness.
+ Nominated as a witness again.
# Resident of Cogolludo
† Identified self as Old Christian

Trial of María López

* Adeva, daughter of Antón Martínez, cleric
** Señor Don Alonso de la Cerda of Guadalajara
* Ana, wife of Juan Díaz of Cogolludo
* Antón Martínez, cleric and chaplain #
* Wife of Antón Nieto and her servants # †

  Maidservants of Doña Barrio
* Beatriz, wife of Pedro the tailor #

  Canpos, handmaiden of wife of Don Alonso
* Catalina, wife of Pedro de Casalvar ++ #

* Diego de Zamora #

* Elvira, wife of Juan de Rueda #

*** Felipe de Angulo, servant of Señor Don Alonso, of Guadalajara

** H(F)ernando Herrero # †

** Inés, relative of Obregón, wife of Juan de Medina of Cogolludo

** Juan, servant and page of Don Alonso +
** Juan Crespo, accountant of Don Alonso
* Juan Díaz #
  His (Juan Francés's) other daughter (unclear to court which one)
* Juan Herrero
** Juan Martínez, cleric of Casalvar
* Juan Ropero #
  Juan Toquerón
  Wife of Juan Toquerón
  Juana, María and Madalena and Francisca (deceased), maidservants
* Juana, daughter of Juan Romo of Membrillera
* Juana, wife of Pero Martínez, sexton

* Lucia, wife of Juan Francés #

Luis de Balbuena

** Marcos de las Navas + # †
 * María Gaytan, wife of Luis de Balbuena #
 * María, wife of Juan de Llolmo
 * María, daughter of Pedro Gómez #
 * Marina, La Lanzara (slang nickname) #
** Miguel de la Magra # †

The parish registrars for each year
** Pedro the tailor #
Pedro, son of Luis de Balbuena
Wife of Pedro Núñez, sexton of Espinosa
 * Pedro Sánchez, priest of Santa María
Pero Martínez, cleric of Casalvar

** Sancho Horozco, servant of Señor Don Alonso ++

The Trial of Isabel López

** Señor Don Alonso of Guadalajara ++
 * Antón Martínez, chaplain of San Pedro †

** Beatriz López, wife of Pedro de Medina, the tailor + # [rejected]

Campos, maidservant +

** Felipe de Angulo, Don Alonso's curator of Guadalajara +
 * Fernando de Paredes, trumpeter #

 * Hernando the blacksmith

 * Inés de Valverde, maidservant
 * Isabel, wife of Francisco, furrier # †

 * Juan de Ortega # †

** Lucia, wife of Juan Francés + # †

 * Mari Díaz, wife of Gonzalo de Rueda, of Alcalá
** Doña María Arias, wife of Don Alonso +
María de Jotar
María, wife of Peña
 * Martín de Alcaraz, judge #

 * Pedro de Burgos, constable
 * Pedro Martínez de Casalvar, cleric # †
** Pedro de Medina, the tailor + # [rejected]

* Sancho de Horozco, Don Alonso's curator + #

* Tomas de la Peña, barber, hijodalgo (of noble descent) # †

The Trial of Pedro de Villarreal

* Alonso de Inglés # †
  Alonso de las Navas
* Antón Galán, farmer of Palmazes †
* Antón Martínez, chaplain # †
* Antón Tavonero, farmer of Palmazes †
* Aparicio Bravo, registrar # †

* Bartolomé, the carpenter #
* Bartolomé de la Vega, farmer †

* Diego Fernández, the horseman , New Christian + #

  Escobar, the notary #

** Fernando, the blacksmith + # †
 * Fernando de Córdova, New Christian #
 * Fernando Moreno # †
 * Francisco de Almagro, registrar # †

* Gil Fernández, judge + # †

* Helena, wife of Juan de Rueda #

* Isabel, wife of Diego Fernández, New Christian #

* Juan Bajón of Palmazes †
* Juan the carpenter # †
* Juan de Corral # †
* Juan García of Congostrina †
* Juan Gil, the younger (junior), farmer of Palmazes †
* Juan Martínez Bravo, judge # †
* Juan de Pañadilla, hijodalgo (of noble descent) †
* Juan Redondo, farmer of Palmazes †
* Juan de Rueda # †
* Juana, servant, daughter of Juan Romo of Membrillera
* Juana, wife of Fernando Moreno #

  Lucia, wife of Marco de las Navas

  Marcos de las Navas #
* Miguel de la Magra, farmer #

* Pedro, tavernkeeper of Congostrina †
* Pedro de Burgos # †
* Pedro Bustares # †
* Pero Val of Congostrina †
* Pedro de la Casa del Val #
* Pedro Pastor, farmer of Congostrina
* Pero Sánchez, cleric #
  Pero Val, the elder

* Sancho de Horozco + + #
  Wife of Sancho de Horozco

TACHAS

These lists will be in alphabetical order by first name of individual or of immediate family member rather than in the order named by the defendants and their family. Many were named more than once, either by different family members or because more than one unpleasant incident was recalled.

+ Named by defendant or her family again
# Resident of Cogolludo
† Identified self as Old Christian
¥ Noted by Notarial Scribe as a Witness for the Prosecution
   (Actual notation looks like + inside a square.)

Trial of María López

Agosto de la Fuenta and wife and children
Alonso de la Navas and wife of Arvancón
Alonso de San Pedro
Andres de Mojados and wife #
Andres Moreno
Andres de Trilla #
Anita, daughter of Pedro del Pozo of Penilla, maidservant
Antón Zamarillo + #
Antona, daughter of Lanzarro

Catalina, la botera and sons
Catalina, wife of Nublero + #
Catalina, wife of Fernando Cavallero
Catalina, daughter of Pedro Gómez of Arvancón

Elvira, concubine of cleric from Sant Andres
Elvira, maidservant

Fernando de Bejar and family #
Fernando Francés #
Wife of Fernando Moreno
Fernando Moreno
Fernando el Cavallero (horseman) and family #
Francisca, daughter of Juan de Argente of Muriel
Francisco de Torres and family
¥ Francisco Yague, servant of Arvancón
Francisco Yañes and wife and children
Francisco de Zamora #

García bermejo (redhead) and family #
Gerónimo and wife #
Gil Ferrández and wife and sons and father-in-law Alonso #
Gonzalo de la Fuente #

Illana, wife of Aparicio, farmer

Juan de la Ferrera
Juan, spicedealer
Wife of Juan Carpintero
Juan Estevan and wife
Juan González, blacksmith #
Juan Hismero de Arvancón
Wife of Juan de Llolmo and son #
Juan Perez Tronpeta
¥ Juan Ropero
Wife and son and grandson of Juan Ropero
Juan Sastre #
Juan de Vello
Juan de Villa and family #
Juan Yague and daughter Juana and Vicente and families
Juan Yañes +
Juana de Arvancón, maidservant of Membrillera
Juana, wife of Fernando Pablo of Membrillera
Juana, wife of Garrote of Alcalá
Juana, daughter of Juan de Algezilla de Espinosa
Juana, niece of la de Mateo of Membrillera
Juana, daughter of Martín the barber #
Juana of Membrillera, maidservant +

Juana, daughter of Miguel de la Cueva of Jocar
Juana, wife of Pedro de Murcia and brothers #

Lucia, maidservant of Arvancón

Madalena, wife of nephew of Antón de Llolmo #
¥ Madalena, wife of Martín Simón of Sant Andres, maidservant +
¥ Madalena of Corlo, maidservant +
Marcos de las Navas #
María, daughter of Alonso Escudero
María, maidservant of Arvancón
María of Carrascosa
María, wife of Diego de la Questa of Jocar, maidservant
María García, wife of Fernando Francés #
¥ María, daughter of Juan Pastor of Aleas, maidservant +
María, daughter of Martín Fernán
María, niece of Matiz's wife of Arvancón +
María, wife of Miguel Calleja + #
María of Membrillera, maidservant
María de la Parra
María de la Pena, maidservant #
María, daughter of Pelingres of Fuencenyllan, maidservant
Martín de Fraguas
Martín de Salinas
Miguel Bravo and family

Pedro the tailor and wife #
Pedro de Burgos #
Wife of Pedro de Burgos #
Pedro González de Ganboa and wife and sons and servants
Wife of Pedro de Herrera, daughter of Andres de Mojados #
Pedro de la Casa
Pedro de Murcia #
Pedro de Veguillas #
Pero Díaz

Rodrigo de Yelves and wife, María + #

Terrero and wife and son #
Toribio of Aleas and family

Vicente de Azconas
Vicentico, servant, son of Vicente of Montarron

Wife of Villanueva and sons #

Yusta, maidservant
Yusta, wife of Estevan, of Sant Andres

Witnesses Nominated by the Family to Verify Tachas

Often the same individual was suggested to verify more than one
   tacha.

   * Summoned to testify
   ~ Summoned by court, but not on defendant's list!
   + Named again
   # Resident of Cogolludo
   † Old Christian

   Adeva #
   Alcalde Mayor, chief judicial officer in the city government + #
   Señor Don Alonso
   Alonso de los Fuentes of Xadraque
   Alonso Herrero #
~* Alonso de los Fuentes of Xadraque †
   Alonso Machuca #
   Wife of Alonso de Medina
   Wife of Alonso las Navas #
   Angulo, servant of Don Alonso of Guadalajara +
   Antón, potter #
   Antón Gordo #
 * Antón Martínez, cleric + #
   Aparicio de Llamón
   Aparicio Bravo #
   Wife of Aparicio Bravo #

   Bachiller Contreras and household
* Beatriz López, wife of Pedro the tailor, New Christian +++++++++ #

   Catalina, daughter of Aparicio el Bravo #
   Catalina, sister of Fernando, laceseller #

   Diego Bravo #
   Diego de Zamora, former judge #

   Estevan de Aleas #

Wife of Fernando, the furrier #
Fernando Escubo
Fernán Martínez, cleric of Sant Andres
F(H)ernando Moreno and wife + #
~* Francisca Díaz, wife of Pedro Bustares of Alcalá
Francisco de Muriel of Jocar
Wife of Francisco Yagues #

Gaspar de Uzeda
Gil Fernández, judge
Wife of Gonzalo de Rueda

 * H(F)ernando Herrero + # †
Wife of Hinojosa + #
Hernando de Córdoba + #

Inés la obregona #
Inés, wife of Juan de Medina # †
~* Isabel, wife of Francisco the furrier, New Christian #

Wife of Juan Blanco #
Juan Bravo of Rincón +
Juan de Brihuega #
** Juan de Cañete, scribe +++++ #
Juan Carpintero + #
 * Juan de Corral, farmer + †
 * Juan de la Daga of Fuencenyllan
Juan Díaz (treasurer or boxmaker)
Juan de Diego
 * Juan de los Fuentes of Xadraque †
Juan Martín de Casa del Val #
Juan Martínez Bravo +
 * Juan de Medina + #
Juan de Palencia #
Wife of Juan de Palencia + #
Wife of Juan Rodrigo of Arvancón +
~* Juan Ropero of Humanes †
Wife of Juan Redondo
Juan de Rueda and wife #
Juan Sardina #
Wife of Juan Sazedo #
Wife of Juan de la Torre
Juan de Veguillas the younger #
Juan Verde of Fuencenyllan +

Wife of Luis de Valbuena +

~* Mari Díaz, wife of Pedro Butares of Alcalá †
Señor Martín de Alcaraz, judge
Martín the barber
  * Wife of Martín Blanco # †
Martín Bravo #
Martín de Casalvar #
  * Martín Moreno of Sant Andres
Martín de Negredo and son Juan + #
  * Wife of Martín de Negredo ++ # †
Wife of Martín Ruíz #
Wife of Martínez de Arvancon
Miguel Gordo #
Miguel Magro
Wife of Miguel de la Puebla
Miguel Sánchez Taheno, cleric #

La obregona

Pedro de Brihuega #
  * Pedro de Burgos ++ #
Pedro of Monesterio
  * Pedro the tailor, New Christian +++++++++ #
Pedro de Alonso Sánchez #
Wife of Pedro Blanco #
  * Pedro de Burgos, constable + # †
Pedro Bustares #
Pedro Cabeza, brother of wife of Palencia
Wife of Pedro Pascual #
  * Pedro Veguillas # †
Wife of Pedro Veguillas
Pero Bravo #

Rodrigo de Yelves #

Sancho de Horozco +
Sayavedra el bachiller #

Vallacuela, servant of Don Alonso
Vicente Carpintero #
Villanueva's wife #

Mother of Yusta of Veguillas

TACHAS

Trial of Isabel López

Wife of Alonso Redondo
Ana del Pozo, daughter of Pedro of Ponilla, mother's maidservant +++
Wife of Aparicio el Bivo

Catalina, daughter of Aparicio el Bivo
Catalina de Congostrina, maidservant +
Catalina de Espinosa, maidservant +
Catalina, wife of Hernando Cavallero ++

Elvira, wife of Juan Nuevo

Wife of Ferrando de Zamora

Francisco Yague, son of Juan Yague of Arvancón
Francisco Yañes +

García bermejo (redhead) and wife #
Gonzalo de la Fuente +
Gonzalo de Rueda of Alcalá

Hernando del Olmo of Muriel

Wife and children of Juan Pastor
Juan Pérez, trumpeter #
¥ Juan Ropero
Wife, children and grandchildren of Juan Ropero
Juan Yañes # +
Juana, sister of Antón, woolcomber's wife, maidservant
Juana, wife of Garrote of Alcalá
Juana, daughter of Martín barber +
Juana of Membrillera, mother's maidservant +
Juana de Jocar, maidservant +
Juana, daughter of Juan Romo
Juana, wife of Pedro de Murcia, sister-in-law
Juana, wife of Porriño

¥ Madalena, wife of Cabronero of Corlo, maidservant ++
Madalena, wife of Miguel Larios of Carrascosa, maidservant
¥ Madalena, wife of Martín Símon of Sant Andre, maidservant +
Marco de las Navas
¥ María de Aleas, maidservant

María, daughter of Alonso, mother's maidservant
María, wife of Antón de Estevan #
María, wife of Diego de la Questa of Jocar, maidservant
María, daughter of Hernando Cavallero +
María of Humanes, maidservant
María, wife of Martín de Hernán Peres
María, wife of Miguel Calleja #
María, daughter of Pero Martínez de Alvarcón +++
Martín #
Martín, barber, and wife and children +
Miguel de Bustares #

¥ Wife of Pedro de Burgos (Catalina) #
Wife of Pedro Calleja +
Pedro de la Casa del Val and wife and daughter María #
Pedro, weaver and wife #
Wife of Pedro del Valle
Pedro de Murcia, brother-in-law ++
Pedro de Romera and wife #
Pero González de Ganboa +
Pero Magro the elder and wife #
Pero Hortega #

Vicentico, son of Vicente of Montaron

Yusta de Veguillas, daughter of Miguel Estevan, maidservant +

Witnesses Nominated to Verify Tachas

Alcalde Mayor, chief judicial officer of the city government
Señor Don Alonso and wife
Alonso, blacksmith ++ #
Alonso de Ingeles, swineherd + #
Alonso Machuca
* Alonso de los Puentes of Xadraque
Andres de Bustanes
* Antón Martínez, cleric +
All the sisters of Antón Martínez, cleric
* Antonia, wife of Martín de Negredo + # †
Aparicio de Llamon

** Beatriz López, wife of Pedro, tailor, New Christian +++++++ + #

Canizares

Catalina, daughter of wife of Aparicio el Bivo
* Catalina, bootmaker, New Christian ++ #
Catalina, wife of Casalvar (e Casa)

Diego Bravo + #
Diego Hernández
Wife of Diego Hernández #

Sister of Elvira de Costas

Fernando de Paredes, trumpeter #
Francisco, furrier, New Christian + #

García
Gil de Almirnete
Gil Hernández + #
Wife of Gonzalo de Rueda

Wife of Hernando de Córdova
Hernando Francés

* Inés la obregona, wife of Juan de Medina
Isabel, wife of Francisco, furrier, New Christian + #
Isabel López, wife of Juan Romo

Juan Bravo del Rincón
Juan de Cañete, scribe ++ #
Wife of Juan Francés +
Juan de Medina #
Juan de Palacio
Wife of Juan de Palencia
* Juan de los Puentes of Xadraque †
Juan de Rueda + and wife
Wife of Juan Sazedo
Juan Símon, scribe #
* Juana, daughter of Pedro Blanco # †
Juana Sánchez, wife of Pedro Blanco + # †
Juana, daughter of Juan Romo, maidservant

Luis, woolcomber
* Luis Fernández, court messenger +++++++ # †

* María Gaytan, wife of Luis de Valbuena +
Martín de Alcaraz, judge
Martín Bravo #
Martín de Negredo, son and daughter-in-law
Miguel Sánchez Taheño, cleric

Wife of Pedro, sexton
* Pedro, tailor, New Christian ++++++ #
Pedro de Alonso Hernándes
Pedro de Brihuega
Pedro de Burgos, constable +
Pedro de la Fuente #
Pedro López, cobbler #
Wife of Pedro Pasable
Pedro de Veguillas, the elder, court messenger ++ #
Wife of Pedro de Veguillas
Penebroso
Pero Bravo #
Pero González de Ganboa #

Rodrigo de Yelves #

Bachiller Sayavedra
Sancho de Horozco

Wife of Villanueva

Mother and siblings of Yusta

Appendix 2

Appendix to Alcázar Trials

Witnesses Testifying Against Francisco de (la) Vega in Leg. 187, n° 8

    *   Reconciled to the Church
    =   Testimony also used in trial of Juan del Campo

        1. Juan del Campo
* =   2. Alonso López de Armenia
* =   3. Juan, son of Alonso López de Armenia
        4. María de Mora, wife of Alonso López de Armenia
        5. Catalina, daughter of Alonso López de Armenia and María de Mora
        6. Isabel López, daughter of Alonso López de Armenia and María de Mora
  =   7. Francisco Ruíz de Armenia
        8. Beatriz Ruíz, daughter of Francisco Ruíz and María López, wife of Cristoval Ruíz
        9. Elvira Ruíz, daughter of Francisco Ruíz and María López
    10. Ana Ruíz, daughter of Francisco Ruíz and María López
* = 11. Lope de la Vega, son of Alonso de la Vega and Elvira de Mora
  = 12. Isabel de la Vega, daughter of Alonso de la Vega and Elvira de Mora, wife of Francisco de Yepes
* = 13. Francisco de Vega, scribe, son of Alonso de la Vega and Leonor Gómez
* = 14. Maria, daughter of Alonso de la Vega and Leonor Gómez
    15. Ana del Campo, wife of Francisco de Vega
   (16. Francisco de Mora: never testified)

Witnesses Testifying Against Juan del Campo in Leg. 138, n° 8

    *   Reconciled to the Church
    =   Testimony also used in trial of Francisco de (la) Vega

* =   1. Alonso López de Armenia
* =   2. Juan, son of Alonso López de Armenia

 * =   3. Lope de Vega, son of Alonso de la Vega and Elvira de Mora

  *   4. Francisco de Vega

  =   5. Francisco Ruíz de Armenia

  =   6. Isabel de Vega, daughter of Alonso de la Vega and Elvira de Mora, wife of Francisco de Yepes

      7. Catalina de Moya

      8. María de Villaescusa, widow

      9. María de la O., wife of Antonio Falcón, daughter of María de Villaescusa

 * = 10. Francisco de Vega, scribe, son of Alonso de la Vega and Leonor Gómez

 * = 11. María, daughter of Alonso de la Vega and Leonor Gómez

  *   12. Isabel de Yepes, wife of Juan del Campo

  *   13. Teresa Mexia of Argamasilla, wife of Andrés Falcón

     14. María de la O., wife of Pedro Barrera

     15. Ana, daughter of Pedro de Lope

     16. Leonor Gutiérrez, wife of Alonso Marín

     17. Isabel Gutiérrez, widow

Appendix 3

Legajo 165, número 2 (1530-1532)
Trial of Juana Martínez, wife of Alvar García, cobbler, resident of Alcázar de
    Consuegra
Confessions presented in April, 1486

(Fol. 2r) *Constanza Núñez* April 10, 1486 {mother}

I, Constanza Núñez, wife of Juan Núñez, deceased, God help him, resident of the
    village of Alcázar de Consuegra, appear before Your Reverences to state and
    manifest my guilt and sins that I have committed and done in offense of our
    master and redeemer Jesus Christ . . .
I state my guilt that some Friday nights I lit candles.
I sinned in that I observed some Sabbaths and wore clean clothes on those days.
I state my guilt, Reverend Fathers, in that I prepared cooked food on Friday for the
    Sabbath and I ate from it.
I sinned in that sometimes I ate meat slaughtered by the hand of Jews and I ate
    their foods.
I state my guilt in that I removed the fat from meat.
I sinned in that I fasted some fasts, especially the Jewish fast of Yom Kippur and on
    that day I asked forgiveness of others and they asked it of me.
I sinned in that I ate unleavened bread and observed the Jewish festivals, especially
    the Festival of Unleavened Bread.
I sinned in that I gave alms to Jews and others and oil for the synagogue.
I sinned in that sometimes when I kneaded bread, I took a piece of the dough and
    tossed it into the fire.
I state my guilt in that when I gave birth, on the seventh night, I had *fadas* [*hadas*]
    and on days forbidden by the Holy Mother Church I ate meat; although it was
    not to be eaten, I ate it.
I sinned in that some festivals and days of the Holy Mother Church that were sup-
    posed (Fol. 2v) to be observed, I did not do so and did work on those days.
I sinned in that when my children and grandchildren kissed my hand, I put my
    hand on their head and did not bless them by crossing them.
I sinned in that sometimes I believed what I was told concerning the future and I
    poured drops on my children and grandchildren and other persons [in places]
    where I found myself . . .

I sinned in that when someone in my household died, I prepared a table with a
clean tablecloth and I lit a candle and put a glass of water on the table.

I sinned in that whoever passed away in my house, I bathed him and had him
bathed and aided to bathe him; I and one whose name is Francisca, we washed a
baby.

The said things and each one of them I did in recognition of the Law of Moses,
thinking that doing them would help me to be saved.

. . . these things were taught to me by my husband, these things were done for
thirty-five years . . .

(Fol. 9v) *Benito González* April 10, 1486 {brother-in-law}
Much revered and devoted Fathers:

I, Benito González, cobbler, resident of the town of Alcázar of the Order of San
Juan, appear before you, Our Reverend Ones, to state and declare my faults and
sins which I have done and committed in offense of our holy Catholic faith, of
those and of all those in my memory . . .

I sinned in allowing my wife to light candles on Friday nights sometimes.

Reverend Sirs, I sinned in observing some Sabbaths and on that day wearing clean
clothes.

I state my guilt in that I sinned by eating cooked food made on Friday for the
Sabbath and in consenting to let my wife do this; I request penance.

I state my guilt that I sinned by sometimes fasting the Jews' fasts, especially Yom
Kippur and I asked for forgiveness on that day and others asked me for forgiveness for everything.

I state my guilt in that I read and heard read from a book of the Law of Moses a
few times; I beg forgiveness for this.

I sinned in that I allowed the fat to be removed from meat and I removed it and
ate meat slaughtered by the hand of Jews sometimes; I demand penance for it
all.

I state my guilt in that on Lent and days that the Holy Mother Church forbids the
eating of meat and other things, I ate them; I request penitence.

(Fol. 10r) I state my guilt in that when a daughter I have was ill, I said she had the
evil eye and I allowed drops of oil to be poured on her; I request penance.

I state my guilt in that sometimes I gave charity to Jews, especially that I gave for
oil for their synagogues; I demand penitence for this.

I state my guilt in that sometimes I was in the presence of a deceased [person] and
he was being bathed and I helped to bathe him; I request penitence for this.

I state my guilt in that when my father died I set a clean table in the evenings and a
glass of water; I demand penitence for this; I lit a candle.

I state my guilt in that sometimes I ate fish and eggs where there were post-burial
meals on low tables; I demand penitence for this; they say this is a *coguerzo*.

I state my guilt that when my wife gave birth, on the seventh night male and
female relatives came to my house and ate fruit and dinner afterwards; they
say these are *fadas*; I demand penitence.

I state my guilt that I said hateful words against Our Lord Jesus Christ and against
our holy Catholic faith; I demand penance for this.

I state my guilt in that I sinned by not observing some holy days established by the
Holy Mother Church; I request penance.

I state my guilt in that I ceased eating things forbidden by the Law of Moses; I
demand penitence.

I sinned in that in all of the above I was the consenter to my wife, who is now
deceased.

I sinned in that all these things I did according to the ceremony of the Law of
Moses.

(Fol. 10v) Addendum:

Benito González, cobbler, resident of Alcázar, said in his confession that he saw his
wife, who is deceased, enact many ceremonies of the Law of Moses, especially
preparing food on Fridays for the Sabbath, lighting candles, observing the Sabbaths, listening to Jewish prayers, removing the fat from meat, fasting on Yom
Kippur and other things contained in his confession that is onerous. He said
that he heard readings sometimes and didn't say whom he heard [read]. In his
ratification, he said that on Yom Kippur, he saw fast and pray prayers of the
Law of Moses on that night, [the following]: Fernando de Mora and Juan de
Carrascosa and Juan de Bartolomé, brothers, and Fernando de Soria of
Madridejos, and likewise he said that he saw Alonso de Campo, the butcher,
resident of the said village, in the house of Juan García, cobbler, praying prayers
of the Law of Moses.

In addition he said that he saw his wife go to request forgiveness of her mother
and her sisters on Yom Kippur and of Pero Núñez, the cobbler, and Diego
Núñez, her brothers and of the wife of García de Alcalá, the cobbler, and of
Juana Martínez, the wife of Alvar García, the cobbler, residents of Alcázar.

(Fol. 8v) *García de Alcalá* April 10, 1486 {brother-in-law}

Reverend Fathers, I state that sometimes I consented to my wife's lighting candles
on Friday nights.

I say, Reverend Fathers, that sometimes I allowed my wife to fast the fasts of the
Jews and sometimes I forbade her, and so as not to have a bad home life, I consented to it; likewise one day on Yom Kippur I bought a pair of young doves and
killed them for supper.

I allowed my wife to remove the fat from the meat and so as not to make life bad, I
consented to it.

How I covered up desecrating Sundays and holidays established by the Holy
Mother Church.

I sinned in that some Lents and forbidden days by the Holy Mother Church, I ate
meat and other things.

I sinned in that sometimes when my wife gave birth, [people] came to my house
on the seventh night and I gave them fruit; now they say that these are *fadas*.

I sinned in that once a niece of my wife passed away and we went there and ate fish
and eggs on low tables.

I sinned in that I helped bathe some deceased and the way of this land is (that)
the custom [is] to sit vigil over the dead who pass away at night [and] because the watchmen found me when it was night; I helped to bathe some
deceased.

(Fol. 7r) *Mari Núñez* April 11, 1486 {sister}

I, Mari Núñez, wife of García de Alcalá, resident of Alcázar de Consuegra of the
Order of San Juan, appear before Your Reverends to state and manifest my guilt
(Fol. 7v) and sins that I have done and committed by act as well as by thought,
in offense of our Master and Redeemer Jesus Christ and against our holy
Catholic faith; of these and of all those that my memory at present omits, and
I recall them with great shame and [with] contrition in my heart. I protest
in satisfaction of those to fulfill the penitences that Your Reverences will
give me.

I sinned in that some Fridays I lit candles earlier than on other nights.

I sinned in that sometimes I prepared food on Fridays for the Sabbath and I ate it.

I sinned in that I observed some Sabbaths more by intent than by deed, and I wore
clean clothes and gave charity to Jews.

I sinned in that sometimes I ate meat beheaded by Jewish hand and I took the fat
off the meat.

I sinned in that I fasted some fasts of the Jews, especially Yom Kippur and on that
day I asked forgiveness and others asked forgiveness of me.

Reverend Sirs, I state my guilt in observing some festivals of the Jews, especially the
Festival of the Unleavened Bread, and I ate [it].

I state my guilt that when I gave birth, on the seventh night I had *fadas*.

I sinned in that on days forbidden by the Holy Mother Church ordering one
not to eat meat, I ate it and I abrogated some holidays of those that the Holy
Mother Church commands us to observe, doing laundry on those very
days.

I state my guilt, Reverend Sirs, in that I ate at post-burial meals at low tables, fish
and eggs and I was told that this is the *cohuerzo*.

I state my guilt that when my mother had me [visiting] in her house, she showed
me how one takes the babies, (that one) puts one's hand on their heads without
making the sign of the cross.

I sinned in that when my children were sick, I poured drops on them
(Fol. 8r) and on other people who put me in charge, and once they were poured
on me, although this pained me.

I sinned in that when I kneaded dough, I threw a piece of dough in the fire and I
helped to bathe and to enshroud some dead; these things were done according
to the Law of Moses, thinking that by doing them I would be saved.

(Fol. 11v) *Fernando Núñez* April 14, 1486 {Half-Brother}

Fernando, son of Juan Núñez, the younger, and son of Constanza Núñez, resident
of Alcázar de Consuegra of the Order of San Juan, appears and presents himself
before Your Reverends to state and manifest my guilt and sins that I have done
in offense of our Lord Jesus Christ and against our holy Catholic faith, of those
and of all those that occur in my memory at present and that I recall them with
shame and contrition in my heart I protest [so as] to complete the penance that
will be put upon me by Your Reverends for the satisfaction of those.

I state, Reverend Sirs, that as a young boy and of a young age in the house of my
said mother, I was ordered to observe those things in the Law of Moses and
through this I would be saved, for that reason I sinned and erred in the following things.

I state my guilt that I observed some Sabbaths as best as I could and wore clean
clothes on them and ate food prepared on Fridays for the Sabbath and fasted
some days, especially Yom Kippur and on that day, I asked for forgiveness and
sometimes I didn't observe Easter and Sundays and holidays mandated by the
Holy Mother Church to observe, and sometimes I ate meat and cheese, milk and
eggs during Lent and on other forbidden days by the Holy Church Mother and I
ate meat of the Jews.

(Fol. 11v)

Addendum June 20, 1530

In the town of Alcázar of Consuegra, on the twentieth of the month of June, 1530
years, before the Lord Inquisitor the bachelor Juan Yañes spoke the said (Fol.
12r) Fernando of Villarreal that had done those said things of the Law of Moses
that he had confessed since the beginning that his said mother had gotten him
accustomed to them in the house of his said mother who was then living in a
store of Rodrigo de Villarreal, her husband, that is in this town in the plaza next
to the baker's shop.

And likewise he did them in the house of Pedro Núñez, his brother, and in the aforesaid houses he did all the things contained in his confession for all of the time until he came to be reconciled.

Also he said on the twenty-first day of the month of June in the said year in the said village before the said Lord Inquisitor, being advised by him in the last audience to declare those things and places and times that he did the aforesaid things and that he should unburden his conscience and state with which persons he had acted in the house of his said mother and step-father and in the house of Pedro Núñez, his brother, also on the part of his maternal relatives and his paternal relatives as well as the relatives of his step-father, Rodrigo of Villarreal as with any other persons, residents of the said village who congregated in the said houses.

He said that in the house of the mother of this confessant, that they did the said things to which he had confessed of the Law of Moses together, this confessant and his said mother and Rodrigo of Villarreal, the step-father of this confessant, and all his sisters Mari Núñez and Elvira Núñez and Juana Núñez.

Also in the house of the said Pedro Núñez, his brother, he did the said ceremonies and things of the Law of Moses with certain persons that he declared in his said statement.

(Fol. 3r) *Juana Martínez* April 24, 1486 {the defendant}

Juana, the younger daughter of Rodrigo of Villarreal, deceased, resident of the village of Alcázar de Consuegra, appears before Your Reverences with pain in my soul and showing the way to repentance, to state and confess my guilt and sins that I have done and committed in offense of our redeemer Jesus Christ and our Holy Catholic Faith. I say, Reverend Sirs, that since I was a girl in the house of my said mother where I now am, my mother taught me and had me understand that one observes the Law of Moses, having me understand that that was the truth and through it I would be saved and I, thinking in this way, erred and sinned. I state my guilt.

I sinned in that I observed some Sabbaths and wore clean clothes on some of them and I lit clean candles on Friday nights and I prepared cooked food on Friday for the Sabbath and ate it.

I sinned in that I observed some Jewish festivals, especially that of the Festival of Unleavened Bread, and I ate it. And I fasted some Jewish fasts, especially Yom Kippur and I asked forgiveness of others; and I removed the fat from meat and the pellet from the ball of dough and threw it in the fire; and I ate meat slaughtered by Jewish hand; and I stopped eating bacon and meat and fish forbidden by the Law of Moses; sometimes I didn't observe Sundays and holidays mandated by the Holy Mother Church, and sometimes on Lent and on other forbidden days (Fol. 3v) by the Church to eat meat and cheese and milk and eggs.

. . . These very things I did six years on my part, more or less until the edict was read in Alcázar, and all for the Law of Moses, not believing in the law of Jesus Christ . . .

I saw my mother do all those things that I did.

(Fol. 12v) *Genealogy*

In the said village of Alcázar de Consuegra, seventeen days of the said month of March [1530], before the said Señor Inquisitor Hernand Juan Yañes:

Juana Martínez, wife of Alvar García, cobbler, resident of the said village of Alcázar, appeared before the said Señor Inquisitor by his order, who was received, sworn in the form of the true right by duty, of which being asked, declared the following:

She said she was of an age that she did not know how much time [since her birth].

She was asked how many years had it been since she married her said husband. She said that thus God forgive her, she doesn't correctly know because she knows very little math. Asked if she had been reconciled, she said that as a young girl, her mother took her to Toledo [to stand] before the inquisitors and that they were presented with a charter. And that she didn't know how to give an account of what was in the charter and that then she was already engaged to her said husband, it could have been a year or two; and that she was engaged to her said husband three years before the veiling ceremony, and that she would have been fourteen years, this testifier, when she was engaged, according to what her mother told her then.

Asked if she remembers being reconciled with the others who went to be reconciled, she said that at the time that she presented that written [testimony], God forgive her thusly, that she didn't know what was in it. She didn't know anything else and that she had not done any penitence.

Parents of this Testifier

Rodrigo of Villarreal, farmer, and Constanza Núñez, residents who were in this town, and (that) her father was a native of Ciudad Real and her mother was of this town; both (Fol. 13r) are deceased and (that) the Inquisition did not touch her father and (that) her mother was reconciled; and (that) it's been twenty years or more since her mother died, and her father died before this testifier was engaged.

Grandparents on her father's side:

She said that she did not know nor could she recall their names and Juana
Martínez [sic] and that the Inquisition did not deal with them and that they
passed away before the Inquisition came and that they were *conversos.*

Grandparents on her mother's side:

She said that she did not know them nor know their names and that they were
conversos and the Inquisition did not touch them.

Brothers and Sisters of Her Father: She said that she did not know any.

Brothers and Sisters of Her Mother: She said that she did not know any brothers
or sisters of her mother.

Brothers and Sisters of this Testifier:

Fernando of Villarreal, cobbler, resident of Belmonte, who is older than this testifier, she doesn't know how much, and that the Inquisition had not touched him.

Mari Núñez, wife of García Alcalá, cobbler, former resident of this town, who are
deceased, and (that) the said Mari Núñez was reconciled and she was older than
the said Fernando of Villarreal, and that her husband was not touched by the
Inquisition and that he was a native of Alcalá.

Elvira Núñez, former wife of Benito de García Díaz (Fol. 13v), cobbler, who were
residents of this town, already deceased, and that the Inquisition did not touch
them and that she was the eldest of all her siblings.

Asked if she heard the charters of the edict that were read in the churches of this
town, she said yes but that she doesn't know anything of what was contained in
them.

Asked where this testifier grew up from the time she was born until she married
her said husband, she said that she was raised in this town by her mother and
that all her siblings, that those she mentioned she had, were raised together with
this testifier in the house of her said parents until they married and that they
were already married when her father died except for this testifier.

She was asked if she remembers for which things she was reconciled. She said that
she didn't know how to account for this. Thus she remembers that the Inquisitors commanded her mother and this testifier that they should give account in
writing of all their possessions and landed property that her said father had left
and thus they went to give it and that they did not confiscate the said property.

And then His Reverence said that he would wait because he wanted to read that
document that was said to be presented to the Inquisitors in the time of the
grace [period] since she said that she did not remember what was written there
because by reading it to her, it might be able to be brought back to her memory;
and asked if this is the document that was presented before the inquisitors and
having it read, a confession that was in the Second Book of Confessions of Al-

cázar on Fol. 25r, word for word. She was asked if this was the written document
that was presented to the lord inquisitors in the grace period. She said that yes,
it is that over there and sat down, that it well appeared that that was it and that
it was that. (Fol. 14r)

She was instructed to [be] read the first segment of her confession and said that it
is true, that this testifier stated and confessed what was contained in the said
segment and that in this way this testifier did so because of her mother's confessing as is contained in the said segment.

She was read the second chapter of her said confession in which are contained all
the things that she confessed to have done of that which her said mother taught
her and thus having [been] read it all word by word, she said that it was true,
that this testifier did all those things contained in the said segment that were put
there then.

She was asked specifically about each one of them and about the first of them that
spoke of the observance of the Sabbath. She was asked in what manner did she
observe the said Sabbaths, and which clean clothes were those that she said she
wore on the said Sabbaths. She said that it is true that she kept the said Sabbaths, observing them and that the clothes she wore were clean blouses. Asked if
she observed the said Sabbaths as a holiday, she said yes. Asked with which persons she did observe and keep the said Sabbaths, she said that with her said
mother, and that she doesn't remember observing them with any other persons
and that they were observed in the home of her said mother.

Asked concerning the lighting of candles and the preparing of food on Fridays for
the Sabbath, with whom did she eat the said dishes thus prepared together, she
said that she ate with her mother and doesn't recall any other persons, and that
she ate the said prepared meals the following Sabbath and that this testifier lit
the said candles by order of her said mother (Fol. 14v) and that she also saw
them lit by her said mother.

Asked if they adorned and swept the house on those said Friday afternoons, she
said that she did not remember it.

She was asked at what hour did she light the said candles and in what way. She said
that they lit them in the evening, and that the rest, she did not know how to account for.

She was told that thus it says in this segment that she observed some Jewish festivals, especially the Festival of Unleavened Bread; she should reveal with which
persons she observed the said festivals and in what way. She said that with her
mother and with her sisters she observed them in the home of her said mother
and that her said sisters came there to celebrate and being asked, she said that
she doesn't remember if the husbands of her sisters came there as well to celebrate and that she didn't know know to explain how they kept and observed the
said festivals.

She was asked together with which persons did she eat the said matsah. She said that with her said mother and with her sisters and being asked, she said that she didn't recall if her brother ate the said matsah and that she doesn't remember who made the said matsah.

Asked in what way did she fast the Jewish fasts that were confessed to in this segment, especially Yom Kippur that was mentioned. She said that thus God would help, that she did not know how to explain it because she was very much a [young] girl when she did it.

Asked at what hour did they eat on the said day of the Great Fast, she said that she didn't remember it nor could she explain it.

(Fol. 15r) Asked when the said Yom Kippur fell, she said that she did not know.

Asked with which persons did she make the Great Fasts, she said that with her said sisters Mari Núñez and Elvira Núñez and with her said mother, and that her said sisters came on that day of the said fast to the home of her said mother and they were there all that day and ate together.

Asked what it is that they ate on that day, she said that it is true that she doesn't remember.

Asked if the house was adorned on the day of Yom Kippur and if they dressed up on that day and if they celebrated it like a holiday, she said that then they began to do the thing that would be [considered] to adorn it and they celebrated and that she was sorry for not knowing how to explain it.

Asked if the husbands of her said sisters, if on that day they ate together with their said wives and with this testifier and with her mother, she said that they didn't eat.

Asked what is the reason for the said husbands not eating together with their wives, she said that she did not know.

Asked if on those days of the Great Fast of the Jews which the said persons did together with this testifier, if, on this day, they prayed any prayers and went barefoot. She said that she did not recall.

Asked which prayers did this testifier and her (Fol. 15v) said sisters and mother pray on the said days of Yom Kippur, she said that she did not know how to account for this.

Asked if everyone fasted together all of that day of Yom Kippur without eating anything until a star appeared or if they fasted only half a day, she said that she did not know, may God help her thusly.

Asked from which persons did she ask forgiveness on the day of Yom Kippur, [which] this testifier said then in the said segment of her confession that she asked forgiveness from others when she fasted the said fasts. She said that she did not remember any more of it, that it had never crossed her mind.

Asked what she said to those people when she requested forgiveness, she said that she did not know.

Asked which persons had she seen remove the fat from meat and the pellet from the dough and throw it in the fire then [as] said in her confessions that she re-

moved the fat from meat and the pellet from dough and threw it in the fire. She
said that she does not remember this.

Asked who were the Jews who slaughtered the meat that this testifier ate, [as] said
then in her confession that she ate meat beheaded by the hand of Jews, she said
that she did not know.

Asked with which persons did she eat the meat slaughtered by Jewish hand, she
said that with her sisters and with her mother she ate it and that they ate it in
the house of her said mother and that she did not know how to account for
which days they ate it.

(Fol. 16r) Asked which other persons did she see observing the Sabbath at that
time that this testifier observed them with her said mother and sisters, she said
that her mother and her sisters that came to her mother's house all observed together and she didn't see any other persons celebrating, and at the time that the
Señor Inquisitor began to ask this question, before having just made my declaration of that which was asked of the said Juana Martínez, she answered that she
did not know.

Asked if this testifier had seen that her said sisters Mari Núñez and Elvira Núñez lit
candles with new wicks on Friday evening earlier than other evenings both in
the house of their husbands as well as in the house of the parents of this testifier,
she said that she saw them light the said candles in the way in which she'd been
asked on the said Friday evenings both in their homes as well as in the home of
her mother.

Asked if she saw in the home of her said sisters and in each one of them decorating
of the house on Friday evenings like the eve of a holy day and observing those
Fridays in the evening in honor of the Sabbath in their homes or in the house of
her said mother, she said that they did observe both in their own homes as well
as in the house of her said mother and adorned their home on those said nights,
and the same was done in the home of her said mother on those said Friday
nights.

Asked if her said sisters Mari Núñez and Elvira Núñez indeed did those things
that were said due to the belief in the Law of Moses, not believing in the law
(Fol. 16v) of Jesus Christ, and if she knew that her mother had taught them
these as she had instructed this testifier, she said yes. Asked how did she know,
she said because everyone talked about how they did it on account of the Law
of Moses.

(Fol. 17v) From the Trial of *Rodrigo de Villarreal*, deceased, for the trial of *Alvar
García*

November 23, 1530

She [Juana Martínez] said that it is true, everything that is in her confession and
all the rest that she has said in front of the said Señor Inquisitor Mexia except

that she never saw her husband Alvar García do anything against our Holy Catholic faith.

She was told to look well at that which she said pertaining to her said husband because it appears in the last segment of that which she said before the said Señor Inquisitor Mexia, that her said husband and the other persons that she spoke of there that had gone together to reconcile themselves of all those things that together they had committed according to the said final segment. The aforesaid was read again and thus having the final segment read to her, she said that she never saw her said husband do or say anything (Fol. 18r) against the faith and that there never was anything that he did together with this testifier and with her parents and sisters and that everything that she knows in the said last segment is true, that the said persons together did what was contained in the final segment with this testifier, but not with her said husband; that she marvels how it was written thusly, although she said that her said husband was [not] together with this testifier and with the other persons contained in the said segment.

(Fol. 18v) July 1, 1530

. . . She was asked if she knows why she was a prisoner. She said that she did not know until His Reverence told her.

She was asked if she knew the prayers of the Church. She said, yes, she knows, she said, the Pater Nostre and the Ave Maria, the Creed. She did not know it all or the Salve nor did she know how to sign [cross] herself.

She was told that she is a prisoner because she had hidden [the names of] some people whom she saw commit crimes of heresy, and she knew other things besides that which she had confessed at the time of grace; therefore she is admonished and advised on the part of God our Lord and of our Mistress the virgin Mary to say and confess the truth entirely of that which she feels guilty, and if she knows of other people who were against our Holy Catholic Faith, and that doing this thusly would do that which is advantageous to her soul and person . . .

The said Juana Martínez said that this testifier did those things contained in her confession that she gave at the time of grace with her father and with her mother and with her sisters and brothers.

She was asked who were her said father and mother and brothers and sisters. She said that her father was named Rodrigo de Villarreal and her mother, Constanza Núñez, and her brothers were Fernando de Villarreal who is a prisoner and the sisters, Mari Núñez, wife of García de Alcalá, and Elvira Núñez, wife of Benito, son of García Díaz, who were deceased. She returned to say that she doesn't remember anything of her father as it seems to her that he was deceased when this testifier was reconciled . . .

(Fol. 19r) And after the aforesaid, on the following day, the second of the said
month of July in the said year, being in the room of the audience of the Holy
Office of the said Señor Inquisitor Alonso Mexia, he ordered to bring out before
him the said Juana Martínez who was warned again as the second warning in
the form according to which she was above warned that she should say and
confess the whole truth as to what is her guilt and what she knows others have
done besides what she said and declared in her reconciliation. She said that the
truth is that she remembers that Rodrigo de Villarreal, her father, and the said
Fernando de Villarreal, her brother, did all the things that she had declared
in her confession together with her said mother and sisters and with this
confessant.

She was asked if her brothers-in-law, Benito and García Díaz, if they likewise did
the said ceremonies together with those that she had said and with this testifier.
She said that they did.

She was asked if she did the said ceremonies with her said husband Alvar García,
or if she knew that the said Alvar García was of the belief in the Law of Moses
before she reconciled herself. She said that she did not know [any] information.

She was asked how long she was married to the said Alvar García.
She said that it was two or three years.

She was asked how long had she been married to him when she came to reconcile
herself. She said that she did not know.

She was asked if they had come together to this city, the said Alvar García, her husband, and this testifier. She said that the mother of this testifier and her sisters
and the said Alvar García and this testifier had come together, and together they
had been reconciled and that among them all they talked about their coming together to be reconciled because together they had committed the crimes for
which they were reconciled, in this way her said husband, like her said mother
and father and sisters and brothers and brothers-in-law.

(Fol. 19v) Asked if she had seen the said crimes done by other persons, some of her
relatives or neighbors, in addition to those that she has said, she said no.

Asked if her said husband had said to her and ordered her that if the inquisitors
call her and ask her anything, that she should say and respond that she doesn't
remember anything and if he referred to the reconciliation, she said that he did
say to this testifier and to her brother, Fernando de Villarreal, telling them that
he was referring to their confessions and that they should say that they don't
remember anything and that when he told them this, they were alone.

Asked if this testifier advised her said husband and sent him word not to return
from Herenda because they want to capture him. She said that she had not
warned him.

July 9, 1530: Third warning to the defendant, who added nothing.

(Fol. 21r) After the aforesaid, on the 15th of the month of September, 1530, the

Señor Inquisitor, the licenciate Alonso Mexia, being in his audience, accustomed to sending to have brought out before him the said Juana Martínez, prisoner, and [once] brought out, he ordered the confession that she had made on the second day of the month of July of this said year [which was] against her father to be read . . . And asked if this was indeed the truth as she had then stated. She said that she never saw her said father do anything that was against the Holy Catholic Faith, and that if this is written and assented to, that she doesn't remember any such thing.

Asked what was her intention when she said that she and her father and mother and her sisters did the ceremonies to which she confessed, she said they must have been confused or it was a defense.

She was told that there is information that this testifier and her father and mother and brothers and sisters did the ceremonies contained in her reconciliation; she may say what she likes because she is not in danger.

She said that she never saw her said father do anything against our Holy Faith.

September 17, 1530

And after the aforesaid, on seventeen days of the said month of September of the said year, before the said Señor Inquisitor, being in his audience as was his custom, the said Juana Martínez came out and said that she had thought about what had been asked of her concerning her father Rodrigo de Villarreal, and that she had remembered that it is true that which she had first said, how her father and her brother Fernando de Villarreal together with her said mother and sisters and with this testifier did the things that had been confessed in her reconciliation and that this is the truth and that thusly she affirms [herself].

Synopsis of Final Stage of Trial

(Fol. 21v) January 4, 1531: Vote of *Consulta de fé*
Decision: Reconciliation to the Church requiring punishment - a year's imprisonment (total confinement to the prison) and confiscation of goods.

(Fol. 23r) April 19, 1532
Request: Because she was old [apparently in her sixties] and sick, permission was requested to grant freedom from incarceration after the year.

(Fol. 24v) Decision: Her year had passed; she did her time.
July 18, 1532, in the court of Toledo
Order:
Remove the *sanbenito* from the reconciled; Juana Martínez was free to go home.

Notes

Introduction

1. See Yitzhak Baer, *A History of the Jews in Christian Spain* 2 (Philadelphia: Jewish Publication Society, 1966), pp. 95–169; the chapter is entitled "Destruction and Conversions (1391–1412)."

2. General studies of these developments by Haim Beinart include "The Converso Community in 15th Century Spain," in *The Sephardi Heritage* 1, ed. R. D. Barnett (London: Vallentine, 1971), pp. 425–456, and the more recent "The Great Conversion and the Converso Problem," in *The Sephardi Legacy* 1, ed. Haim Beinart (Jerusalem: Magnes Press, 1992), pp. 346–382.

3. Ecija is located about 50 miles east of Seville.

4. See Baer, *History*, pp. 95–96.

5. Baer, *History*, pp. 96–110.

6. For example, Stephen Haliczer maintains that "the popular masses who rose to attack the Jewish ghettos in 1391 hoped that by shattering the Jewish community they would deprive the social elite of a powerful tool of oppression, since the Jews had played a major role in tax and revenue collection for the crown, church and nobility." "The First Holocaust: The Inquisition and the Converted Jews of Spain and Portugal," in *Inquisition and Society in Early Modern Europe,* ed. Stephen Haliczer (Totowa, N.J.: Barnes & Noble Books, 1987), p. 8. Jane S. Gerber refers to the various sources of instigation and asserts that "the mobs, in particular, were also motivated by economic envy of the size, wealth, and prominence of the medieval Jewish community." *The Jews of Spain* (New York: Free Press, 1992), p. 113.

7. This term appears in Baer, *History*, p. 97.

8. One cannot turn to Baer for an assessment of the aftermath of 1391. He himself wrote that "regarding the Jews of Castile, the data at hand are too scanty to enable us to describe their situation thereafter. The absence of any literary sources for that period is in itself an indication of spiritual aridity. The large and leading communities, like those of Seville, Toledo, and Burgos, were destroyed not only by the violence of their enemies, but chiefly by their own moral deterioration." Baer, *History*, p. 117.

Other historians, however, ventured to assess the damage more concretely. Beinart explained that some communities were destroyed while others were left with very small numbers. "An evaluation of the scope of the damage wrought by the riots would seem to indicate that about one third of the Jewish population was martyred; one third accepted baptism under duress; and the remaining third, which remained faithful to the Jewish people and its religion, survived." "The Great Conversion," p. 347. Gerber, *Jews of Spain*, p. 113, made a similar assessment, estimating 100,000 for each of the three groups.

9. Foremost among these leaders was Rabbi Hasdai Crescas of Saragossa; see Baer, *History*, pp. 110–130.

10. Some took this opportunity to go to the Holy Land. See Baer, *History*, p. 159; and Beinart, "The Jews in Castile," in *The Sephardi Legacy* 1: 31.

11. Baer creates the impression that Ferrer traveled about, seeking to implement these laws in different locales. Once again, this activity did not reflect a royal policy or a unilateral decision of any sort. See *History*, pp. 166–169. Beinart cites these restrictions as taking effect in 1476 and 1480, in "The Converso Community," p. 442.

12. Baer was the first to address this psychological devastation; see *History*, pp. 131–134, for some heartbreaking examples.

13. These are rabbinic issues and they were numerous indeed. For information on the early North African school of rabbis and their dealings with these exiles, see B. Netanyahu, *The Marranos of Spain from the Late Fourteenth to the Early Sixteenth Century According to the Hebrew Sources* (New York: American Academy for Jewish Research, 1966). The analysis of these texts is, however, rather biased. For a poignant review of the book and its flaws, see Gershon D. Cohen, "Review of B. Netanyahu's *The Marranos of Spain*," *Jewish Social Studies* 29 (1967): 178–184. A deeper look into the difficulties posed by conversos returning to Judaism appears in Simha Asaf, "The Marranos of Spain and Portugal in Responsa Literature" [Hebrew], *Me'assef Zion* 5 (1932–33): 19–60.

14. For a detailed study of these purity of blood statutes, see Albert A. Sicroff, *Les controverses des statuts de pureté de sang en Espagne du XVe au XVIIe siècle* (Paris: Didier, 1960). These laws were not fully implemented for almost a century; a later version, of 1547, was approved by Pope Paul IV in 1555 and by King Philip II in 1556.

15. There were varying opinions as to whether or not the conversos should be incorporated into Christian society in the middle of the fifteenth century; see Beinart, "The Converso Community," pp. 429–438.

16. Edward Peters discussed the background of the papal inquisitions, citing the period from 1231 to 1252 as the time when the heretic was viewed as a danger that necessitated severe action. The first manual for inquisitors was compiled in 1248; see his *Inquisition* (Berkeley: University of California, 1989), p. 55.

17. King James II organized the court in 1254; see Peters, *Inquisition*, p. 76.

18. Baer refers to inquisitorial activity in Valencia in *History*, pp. 291–292, 299; he said that it seemed lenient compared to the later Castilian institution. More details are offered by Ricardo García Cárcel, *Orígenes de la Inquisición Española: El tribunal de Valencia 1478–1530* (Barcelona: Ediciones Peninsula, 1976), p. 48; the names of the defendants are listed. Thirteen of them were penanced, one was absolved, and one woman was condemned to death.

19. There was intense opposition to the notion of a Castilian inquisition in Aragon; the political elite were particularly antagonistic. See William Monter, *Frontiers of Heresy* (Cambridge: Cambridge University Press, 1990), p. 321. Bartolomé Bennassar wrote that this establishment was an "instrument of royal policy" and an "agent of centralization" which was countering the local laws of Aragon. See *L'Inquisition espagnole: xve–xixe siècle* (Paris: Hachette, 1979), pp. 50–51.

20. See Haim Beinart, "Jewish Witnesses and the Prosecution of the Spanish Inquisition," in *Essays in Honour of Ben Beinart* (Cape Town: Juta, 1978), pp. 37–46.

21. Its jurisdiction included the entire Spanish Empire; not only did the local inquisitors

send reports, but tribunals were inspected and closely scrutinized. The collection of these reports, or *relaciones de causas*, has provided scholars with rich data banks for the period after 1540. While the first reports were similar to the earlier *auto-de-fé* lists, they eventually became more detailed and regularized. See, for example, Jaime Contreras and Gustav Henningsen, "Forty-Four Thousand Cases of the Spanish Inquisition (1540–1700): Analysis of a Historical Data Bank," in *The Inquisition in Early Modern Europe*, ed. G. Henningsen, J. Tedeschi, and C. Amiel (De Kalb, Ill.: Northern Illinois University Press, 1986), pp. 100–129. It is interesting to note that only six of the twenty-one tribunals' archives have survived; these provide the richer source of information on individual trial records, but the central storehouse of the Suprema provides data, albeit less detailed, for the remainder of the lost archives and enables many of the recent Inquisition historians to engage in statistical studies.

22. Jean-Pierre Dedieu is best known for his periodization in which the first antijudaizing phase dated from 1483 to 1525. See "Les quatre temps de l'inquisition," in *L'inquisition espagnole*, ed. B. Bennassar et al. (Paris: Hachette, 1979), pp. 13–40. This division is being challenged on the basis of more recent scholarship; see, for example, the discussion in chapter 8 here.

23. See Monter, *Frontiers*, p. 54.

24. Anti-Jewish campaigns were high on the agenda of the Dominican preacher Vicente Ferrer and of the anti-pope Benedict XIII. The apostate Jerónimo de Santa Fé (Joshua Halorki) initiated a disputation with twelve Aragonian rabbis who were summoned to the papal court in Tortosa (Catalonia). The length of the proceedings (1413–1414) left these communities without leaders, and vulnerable to unrelenting pressure upon them to convert, which many indeed did. For details, see Baer, *History*, pp. 170–243.

25. See Peters, *Inquisition*, pp. 131–134, for a discussion of this legend.

26. See Leg. 164, nº 4 (1531–39), the trial of Magdalena de Morales. The statement of the witness, Juan García, is on folio 3v.

27. Many examples of less than pure motives for testifying will be forthcoming; one of the most famous incidents of ulterior motives involved Diogo Mendes, the brother-in-law of Doña Gracia Nasi, who was arrested in 1532 in Antwerp. The informers were jealous of the family monopoly of the spice trade; see Cecil Roth, *Doña Gracia of the House of Nasi* (Philadelphia: Jewish Publication Society: 1977).

28. Usually the denunciation appeared first, followed by the decision by the tribunal to pursue the case. Available information would appear as testimonies presented before a notary, and the tribunal would decide whether or not to continue. The defendant was then present at one or more hearings (*audiencias*), often with admonitions and questioning. At this time, the defense could present its case, which was followed by the tribunal's vote of sentence and then the final sentence. For more details, see Jean-Pierre Dedieu, "The Archives of the Holy Office of Toledo as a Source for Historical Anthropology," in Henningsen et al., *The Inquisition in Early Modern Europe*, pp. 178–180.

29. For example, almost half of those 778 individuals burned as heretics cited in Gustav Henningsen's study were in effigy, as they either were deceased or had disappeared. "The Eloquence of Figures: Statistics of the Spanish and Portuguese Inquisitions and Prospects for Social History," in *The Spanish Inquisition and the Inquisitorial Mind*, ed. Ángel Alcalá (New York: Columbia University Press, 1987), p. 230.

30. Contreras and Henningsen wrote that most of the fortunes confiscated belonged to judaizers. "The Spanish Inquisition always maintained its anti-Semitic stance, even though with markedly different nuances and varying degrees of intensity." See "Forty-Four Thousand Cases," p. 124.

31. In Valencia, for example, there are records of the tensions between the king and the pope concerning the proper way to conduct an inquisition. This conflict is documented in García Cárcel, *Orígenes,* pp. 57–63. The Valencians cited their *fueros* or ancient customary laws, and the king ultimately determined that they could not be applied to the Inquisition. García Cárcel, *Orígenes,* pp. 66–69.

32. See Peters, *Inquisition,* p. 66, regarding the option that was the precursor to *tachas.* See appendix 1 for lists of abonos, indirectas, and tacha witnesses.

33. Unfortunately, this did not mean that abuse did not occur; cases of false confessions made under stress exist. Jaime Contreras discovered trials in Murcia in which false statements were made about entire converso communities. See "Alderman and Judaizers: Crypto-judaism, Counter-Reformation and Local Power," in *Culture and Control in Counter-Reformation Spain,* ed. Anne J. Cruz and Mary Elizabeth Perry (Minneapolis: University of Minnesota Press, 1992), pp. 93–123. See the expanded version in his book *Sotos contra Riquelmes: Regidores, inquisidores y criptojudíos* (Madrid: Anaya, 1992).

34. Henningsen, in his study of 44,000 individuals accused by the Inquisition between 1540 and 1700, asserts that 90 percent of them were not tortured. "Eloquence of Figures," p. 230. Peters claims that torture "appears to have been extremely conservative and infrequently used." *Inquisition,* p. 92.

35. The tribunal of Navarre condemned seventeen Jews to service in the galleys between 1560 and 1640; Saragossa, another Aragonese court during this period, sent only one. See the chart by Monter in *Frontiers,* appendix 2, 328.

34. Monter, *Frontiers,* p. xiii.

35. See I. S. Révah, "Les marranes," *Revue des études juives* 118 (1959–60): 46, regarding this realization.

1. Jews and Conversas

1. These include Castile, Leon, Aragon, Sicily, Granada, Toledo, Valencia, Galicia, Mallorca, Sevilla, Sardinia, Cordova, Corçega, Murcia, Jaén, the Algarve, Algeciras, Gibraltar, and the Canary Islands.

2. This translation appears in *The Expulsion 1492 Chronicles,* ed. David Raphael (North Hollywood, Calif.: Carmi House Press, 1992), pp. 189–193; the original appeared in Luis Suarez Fernández, *Documentos acerca de la Expulsión de los Judíos* (Valladolid: Consejo Superior de Investigaciones Científicas, 1964) pp. 391–395. Another translation can be found in H. Beinart, *Atlas of Medieval Jewish History* (New York: Simon & Schuster, 1992), p. 83, based on the Spanish text that appears in Pilar León Tello, *Judíos de Avila* (Diputación Provincial de Avila: Instituto Gran Duque de Alba, 1963), pp. 91–95.

3. The Jewish community of Andalusia (especially Seville and Córdoba) was expelled beforehand, in 1483. See H. Beinart, "La Inquisición española y la Expulsión de los Judíos de Andalucía," in *Jews and Conversos: Studies in Society and the Inquisition,* ed. Yosef Kaplan (Jerusalem: Magnes Press, 1985), pp. 103–123.

4. See Mark D. Meyerson, "Aragonese and Catalan Jewish Converts at the Time of the Expulsion," *Jewish History* 6:1–2 (1992): 131–149. Not only is there mention here of Jewish–converso interactions, particularly of an economic nature (p. 136), but the contention is made that hatred of conversos was essentially Castilian based (pp. 141–142).

5. It must be noted that various attempts, some of them successful, were made to separate the Jews from the Christians. As early as 1393, the Dominican friar Vicente Ferrer was

calling for such action. Immediately after the forced conversions, conversos were commanded to change their places of residence in Valencia and some other cities. For an example of a royal decree, see King Juan's statement sent to Tortosa in August 1393; see Fritz Baer, *Die Juden Im Christlichen Spanien* 1 (Berlin: Schocken, 1929), pp. 716–718. In the 1470s, there was a more concerted attempt to separate the two groups. For a detailed discussion which traces the residence problems posed by the riots of 1391 up until the Expulsion and which documents the Crown's attempts to deal with these issues, see Haim Beinart, "The Separation of Living Quarters in 15th Century Spain" [Hebrew], *Zion* 51 (1986): 61–85. Beinart concludes that despite all of these restrictions, contact between the two groups persisted; the Crown, the Church, and the Inquisition perceived the obvious failure of their policy of separation.

6. Meyerson points to the interesting attempt of the *aljama* (religious community) of Teruel to tax those who converted in 1492 more than double the contribution of the wealthy Jews. *Aragonese*, p. 134.

7. See Leg. 133, n° 5 (1484–85); the original is recorded in Haim Beinart, *Records of the Trials of the Spanish Inquisition in Ciudad Real* 1 (Jerusalem: Israel Academy of Sciences and Humanities, 1974), p. 229.

8. Beinart, *Records* 1: 231–232.

9. See Leg. 164, n° 15 (1484–85) in Beinart, *Records* 1: 539.

10. Beinart, *Records* 1: 546.

11. This and much more information is provided in her confession of 1496 in Leg. 132, n° 8 (1500–1501).

12. See Leg. 131, n° 5 (1493–94). Teresa used the term "Romance" concerning the language of instruction. Romance languages are those of Latin origin; most likely she meant Castellaño, the Spanish developing at the time.

13. Ibid.

14. Cases of circumcision were not common even among the men; it would be hard to deny this act as proof of judaizing. One outstanding example is Juan Calvillo of Ciudad Real, who consented to be circumcised along with his children. See Beinart, *Records* 1: 248 (accusation) and 256 (witness testimony).

15. The knowledgeable conversa here was none other than the aforementioned María Alonso of Ciudad Real; see Beinart, *Records* 1: 229.

16. See Leg. 160, n° 15 (1510–11); this confession was made in 1485.

17. See Leg. 154, n° 33 (1500). This Jew, Frayme Husyllo, testified in the trial.

18. Ibid.

19. See Leg. 183, n° 11 (1502–3).

20. See Leg. 177, n° 6 (1493).

21. See Leg. 153, n° 10 (1487–94).

22. See Leg. 158, n° 12 (1506–7).

23. This interrogation, which occurred in 1530, centered on the confessions provided by Francisco Toledo and his family in 1485; see Leg. 157, n° 2 (1530–31), fol. 7v.

24. See Leg. 160, n° 14 (1492–94).

25. See her second confession in Leg. 131, n° 5 (1493–94); this woman lived in Toledo, a city in which the Jewish community had been ordered to move away from the Christians in 1480. See Beinart, "Separation," p. 70.

26. See Leg. 164, n° 15 in Beinart, *Records* 1: 545; this testimony was provided in 1484 by Mari López, who lived with this family for eleven years during the 1450s.

27. Within the Jewish community, fowl might be taken to the ritual slaughterer by the

owner, but it was less cumbersome to have him slaughter larger animals at one's home. The conversos frequently slaughtered their own fowl; presumably the Jewish slaughterer came to deal with steer, lamb, sheep, and the like. One can assume that these were wealthier converso households under discussion, since only they would have such livestock in their possession.

28. See Leg. 154, n° 22 (1484–92) in Beinart, *Records* 1: 323. The prosecution witness heard this from a family servant in 1475; the two women lived side by side.

29. This was Alonso de Cazeres, who also testified in 1484; see ibid., p. 324.

30. See Leg. 137, n° 12 (1484) in Beinart, *Records* 1: 340.

31. See the confession in Leg. 164, n° 21 (1509–12); also see Leg. 160, n° 14 (1492–94) or Francisco Cantera Burgos and Carlos Carrete Parrondo, "Las juderías medievales en la provincia de Guadalajara," *Sefarad* 34 (1974): 350.

32. The servant, Pascuala, was the first to testify against this conversa. See Leg. 154, n° 36 (1511–12) in Beinart, *Records* 2: 214.

33. The entire family presented confessions in 1486; the testimonies are recorded in the trial of Juana Martínez of Alcázar de Consuegra, Leg. 165, n° 2 (1530–32), and appear in the order presented above.

34. See Leg. 157, n° 2 (1530–31), fol. 14r.

35. See Leg. 154, n° 33 (1500) or Haim Beinart, "Judíos y conversos en Casarrubios del Monte," in *Homenaje a Juan Prado,* ed. L. A. Verdes (Madrid: Consejo Superior de Investigaciones Científicas, 1975), pp. 652–653. Her husband, Juan González, had confessed in 1486 as well and was also tried in 1500; see Leg. 154, n° 19. Juan was condemned to life imprisonment, but María's fate is unknown. Neither trial is complete, although the information available in each corroborates the other.

36. Ibid.

37. Ibid., p. 653.

38. Leg. 132, n° 8 (1500–1501).

39. Beinart, "Judíos y conversos," pp. 647 and 653.

40. Beinart, "Judíos y conversos," p. 654. There is evidence that María occasionally offered support to the Jewish community. She apparently donated money as well as material to Jews to be used in making shrouds.

41. This was Elvira Martínez of Toledo, who made this point during an interrogation in 1509; she happened to be in this Jewish home during Passover and ate matsah and fruit with the family. See Leg. 164, n° 21 (1509–12).

42. See Leg. 152, n° 14 (1484) in Beinart, *Records* 1: 310.

43. On a weekday, there would be the question of her proper observance of the dietary laws. The Sabbath added the complication of her having cooked the food prior to sundown.

44. The non-Jew can carry out various tasks on the Sabbath that are forbidden to the Jew, as long as there is an arrangement made in advance. See Leg. 160, n° 14 (1492–94).

45. See Leg. 177, n° 6 (1493).

46. See the testimony of Clara in Leg. 144, n° 3 (1491–92). For more descriptions of *hadas* and birth ceremonies, see Encarnación Marín Padilla, "Relación judeoconversa durante la segunda mitad del siglo XV en Aragon: Nacimientos, hadas, circuncisiones," *Sefarad* 41:1 (1981): 273–300 and 42:1 (1982): 59–77. See also Renée Levine Melammed, "Noticias sobre los ritos de los nacimientos y de la pureza de las judeo-conversas castellanas del siglo XVI," *El Olivo* 13:29–30 (1989): 235–243.

47. This witness added that Alonso said, "Tomorrow I have to baptize and you must celebrate with me tonight." Levine Melammed, "Noticias," p. 238.

48. This was a ceremony instituted by the Catholic Church in order to add solemnity to the act of matrimony; it consisted of covering the couple with a veil at the nuptial mass, which usually took place immediately after the marriage ceremony.

49. See Leg. 143, n° 11 (1483–84) in Beinart, *Records* 1: 53. The Jew referred to was the "rabbi of the conversos," who tended to the communities of Palma and Ecija. Ironically, he himself converted prior to giving testimony to the Inquisition. As rabbi, he had privy to a tremendous amount of information and provided a detailed account of María's judaizing activities while she lived in Palma. He specified, among other things, that she would not eat meat that had not been slaughtered either by himself or by another Jew who was knowledge-able in these matters. See *Records,* 1: 58.

There is a description of a converso wedding ceremony in which, before going to church, two Jews came to a house where the Jewish marriage was performed, including the appropri-ate blessings. This incident appears in a book of responsa dealing with halakhic (legal) prob-lems in the pre-Expulsion converso community. See Zemah b. Shlomo Duran, *Yakhin u-Boaz* 2 (Livorno, 1782), p. 19.

50. See the interrogation of the defendant in Leg. 164, n° 21 (1509–12).

51. See Leg. 153, n° 10 (1487–94). Sukkot is one of the three pilgrimage festivals. A booth is built to commemorate the fleeting nature of the Israelites' accommodations in the desert af-ter leaving Egypt. All meals are eaten there during the seven (or, in the Diaspora, eight) days of the holiday; some even sleep in the sukkah.

52. See Leg. 151, n° 6 (1515–16).

53. See Leg. 131, n° 5 (1493–94).

54. See Leg. 160, n° 15 (1510–11).

55. See Leg. 180, n° 10 (1498–99).

56. See Leg. 154, n° 33 (1500).

57. This confession is found in the trial of Aldonza de Herrera, Leg. 157, n° 2 (1530–31).

58. See Leg. 154, n° 22 (1484–92) in Beinart, *Records* 1: 323.

59. See Leg. 181, n° 3 (1492–93), the trial of Mencia Rodríguez de Medina; also noted in Cantera Burgos and Carrete Parrondo, "Juderías medievales," 34: 2(1974): 363–364.

60. See Leg. 165, n° 2 (1530–32), the trial of Constanza's daughter Juana Martínez. She does not explain who these "others" were.

61. Ibid.

62. See Yom Tov Assis, "Welfare and Mutual Aid in the Spanish Jewish Communities," in *The Sephardi Legacy* 1, ed. Haim Beinart (Jerusalem: Magnes Press, 1992), p. 339. Here Assis mentions a responsa in which a reservation is "expressed by some members of the commu-nity about their participation in the cost of lighting the synagogue, since they themselves did not benefit from it. This opposition provides a clear explanation for the individual initiative taken to establish a *Ma'or* society."

63. See Leg. 157, n° 2 (1530–31), the trial of Aldonza de Herrera.

64. See Leg. 181, n° 5 (1497).

65. This conversa, Mencia Rodríguez de Medina, did not consider this a sin. See Leg. 181, n° 3 (1492–93).

66. See Leg. 183, n° 11 (1502–3); Catalina was a resident of Madrid.

67. The wording here is unusual; she gave charity for the *bolsa* of the *aljama. Bolsa de Dios* is charity given for the love of God, and perhaps her intention was to give alms for the love of the Jewish community. See Leg. 177, n° 6 (1493).

68. See Leg. 134, n° 4 (1492–93).

69. In this case, the Holy Tribunal had not only her statement of intent, but her admission to having given alms at other times. She herself was not sure how many times she had done so, but she distinctly recalled giving a *blanca* (a silver coin) to a Jew or Jewess who had come to her house.

70. See Leg. 133, n° 20 (1495–96) in Beinart, *Records* 2: 47 and 51.

71. See Leg. 181, n° 12 (1498–99).

72. See Leg. 132, n° 8 (1500–1501).

73. See the accusation in Leg. 181, n° 14 (1492-94).

74. See the accusation in Leg. 153, n° 10 (1487–94).

75. See Leg. 181, n° 3 (1492–93); also mentioned in Cantera Burgos and Carrete Parrondo, "Juderías medievales" 34: 363–364.

76. See the confession in Leg. 160, n° 14 (1492–94). The Kol Nidre service is short but extremely significant, for one is released from vows that were made in the past year and thus can begin the new year with a clean slate.

77. See the lengthy confession made in 1486 in Leg. 132, n° 8 (1500–1501).

78. See Leg. 178, n° 13 (1498–99).

79. H. Beinart discovered the trials of two of the sisters, although four of the siblings were incarcerated and tried simultaneously. Isabel's confession is recorded in her trial, Leg. 167, n° 4 (1521), as well as in her sister's trial, Leg. 157, n° 3 (1521). This quote appears in the original Spanish in Beinart, *Records* 3: 636–637.

80. Ibid., p. 637.

81. See Leg. 157, n° 3 (1521) in Beinart, *Records* 3: 604.

82. Beinart, *Records* 3: 606.

83. Beinart, *Records* 3: 597.

84. Beinart, *Records* 3: 597.

85. Beinart, *Records* 3: 606.

2. The Lives of Judaizing Women after 1492

See chapter 4, "Castilian Conversas at Work," for details of many judaizing activities.

1. I use the word "apparently" intentionally. There is often a discrepancy between the laws on the books and the reality of everyday life. The Crown instructed numerous localities to separate the Jews (and Muslims) from the Christians by forcing the minority groups to sell their homes and businesses, and often their synagogues and cemeteries as well. Haim Beinart, in "The Separation of Living Quarters in 15th Century Spain," *Zion* 51 (1986): 61–85, traces the development of this separation throughout the fifteenth century and shows how it led to the logical expulsion of the same community. It will become obvious, however, that while the separations might have been successfully implemented in some locales, they were neither universally applied nor always executed in the desired manner.

2. It is hard to determine a literacy rate for women in medieval Spain. While some clearly knew how to read and even to write, they seem to be the exception rather than the rule. For example, among *moriscas* (female Christianized Moors), there are few examples of literacy. Mary Elizabeth Perry, "Behind the Veil: Moriscas and the Politics of Resistance and Survival," *Spanish Woman in the Golden Age: Images and Realities,* ed. Magdalena S. Sánchez and Alain Saint-Saëns (Westport, Conn.: Greenwood Press, 1996), p. 37. One cannot draw conclusions on the basis of sporadic evidence, such as of one woman trying to teach another to read, or a conversa here or there who actually signed her own statement during a trial (see chapter 8).

Regarding Sephardi women and literacy, see Joel L. Kraemer, "Spanish Ladies from the Cairo Geniza," *Mediterranean Historical Review* 6 (1991): 237–267. Kraemer has examples of letters, mostly from the sixteenth century, that were written in Hebrew and Judeo–Spanish by exiled women of Spain. Eliezer Gutwirth refers to Judeo–Spanish letters involving women in "The Family in Judeo–Spanish Genizah Letters of Cairo," *Vierteljahrschrift für Sozial-und Wirtschaftgeschichte* 73 (1986): 210–215.

3. The most striking exception here is the disappearance of the ritual bath or *miqveh;* there were some hidden *miqvaot* at first, but eventually the best that could be done was to bathe at home instead.

4. This woman, the wife of Diego Rodríguez, remains anonymous; the records are in Leg. 134, n° 14 (1492–93).

5. See Leg. 134, n° 5 (1492–93). This resident of Guadalajara is also discussed in Francisco Cantera Burgos and Carlos Carrete Parrondo, "Las juderías medievales en la provincia de Guadalajara," *Sefarad* 34:2 (1974): 315–316.

6. See Leg. 134, n° 4 (1492–93), the trial of María Alvarez, wife of Fernando de Cuellar, *platero* (silversmith). There is a synopsis of the accusation and confession in Cantera Burgos and Carrete Parrondo, "Juderías medievales," 34:2 (1974): 316–317.

7. The situation in which families were torn apart as the result of the conversion of only some of their members has been alluded to in the discussion of the damage done in 1391. While in this case the mother converted, this was by no means the only possibility. Any conceivable combination of family members was feasible. For example, see Asunción Blasco Martínez, "Mujeres Judías zaragozanas ante la muerte," *Aragon en La Edad Media* 9 (1991): 77–120. The fifteenth-century wills of four Jewish women from Aragon deal with a similar dilemma. In 1401, Jamila provided for her three Jewish sons as well as for her converted son, Salvador né Salomón. Another Jewish mother in Saragossa had a daughter who in 1415 abandoned her Jewish husband, her two sons, and her daughter. The mother in her will left some money to her converted daughter and a provision for the granddaughter to receive her inheritance if she was still Jewish in five years. A third Jewess, Tolosana de la Caballería, had seven children, of whom only two daughters remained Jewish. From the tone of her will of 1418, she seems to have had good relationships with all of them. Lastly, Fermosa's testament dated the same year reveals that this widow had two brothers, one who converted and one who did not, and two children; her son converted and her daughter died Jewish, leaving a Jewish granddaughter.

8. See Leg. 160, n° 14 (1492–94). Reference is also made to this trial in Cantera Burgos and Carrete Parrondo, "Juderías medievales," 34:2 (1974): 350. These foods were among the standard fare for postburial meals; the round-shaped foods symbolized the continuity of the life cycle. For further reading regarding death and burial rites, see Encarnación Marín Padilla, "Relación judeoconversa durante la segunda mitad del siglo XV en Aragon: enfermedades y muertes," *Sefarad* 43:2 (1983): 251–344; and Renée Levine Melammed, "Some Death and Mourning Customs of Castilian Conversas," in *Exile and Diaspora,* ed. A. Mirsky, A. Grossman, and Y. Kaplan (Jerusalem: Ben Zvi Institute, 1991), pp. 157–167.

9. See Leg. 177, n° 6 (1493); this was the wife of Juan Lorenzo, who was relaxed and burned at the stake. Her file is incomplete.

10. See Leg. 181, n° 4 (1493–94). In Cantera Burgos and Carrete Parrondo, "Juderías medievales," 34:2 (1974): 362, the trial of this resident of Guadalajara is briefly discussed. Also mentioned is the fact that her daughter participated with her and that her grandson knew Hebrew (p. 353).

11. Both trials contain the same wording, which described the classic image of crypto-Judaism. The women were said to have lit candles or lamps in hidden built-in cabinets. The word used here is *alhania,* an archaic word for *alacena,* or a hollow made in the wall that has doors and shelves to protect the contents.

12. The term used is *sabadear,* or to pray in the Jewish manner; the non-Jews assumed that the swaying motion or raising and lowering of the head that they had observed while Jews prayed the silent devotion was a Sabbath prayer stance.

13. See Leg. 164, n° 11 (1493–94) for the trial of the deceased wife of Alvaro Gil; see Leg. 164, n° 12 (1493–94) concerning the wife of Juan Alvarez de Alcolea.

14. See Leg. 155, n° 4 (1494); the confession appears in Haim Beinart, *Records of the Trials of the Spanish Inquisition in Ciudad Real* 2 (Jerusalem: Israel Academy of Sciences and Humanities, 1977), pp. 10–11. Beinart explains that the confession was used as a basis for trying her but that she had worn a red skirt, garb that was prohibited to the reconciled. She was also suspect because she had been educated in Córdoba, "a city whose Conversos were known for their loyalty to Judaism" (p. 8). Note that a judaizer faced a clear conflict regarding choice of menu for the Sabbath. Traditionally, Jews eat meat or fowl in honor of the Sabbath (and festivals); however, the Church forbade the consumption of meat on Fridays and during the entire period of Lent, which would usually coincide with the holiday of Passover.

15. Beinart, *Records* 2: 12.

16. Beinart, *Records* 2: 21–22; Pedro de Teva was a friend of Francisco de Toledo.

17. See Leg. 153, n° 11 (1497); she was the wife of Juan Barzano.

18. See Leg. 181, n° 5 (1497); Mencía was condemned to life imprisonment. She was also accused of saying that the Old Christian women had no notion of what it meant to observe the Law.

19. This is a very short file; since Isabel confessed, there was an interrogation whose aim was to elaborate upon her confession, and then she was sentenced. See Leg. 133, n° 18 (1497–99); she was the wife of Alfonso de Pulgar. The prayer recited was *Ashrei,* an acrostic poem read daily that is relatively easy to remember; she had recited it in Spanish.

20. See Leg. 178, n° 13 (1498–99); this resident of Illescas had either attended the evening Kol Nidre service or perhaps listened to the prayers during the day of Yom Kippur. The mistreatment of icons was clearly viewed in a negative light but could be used only to strengthen a case, not as sufficient evidence of judaizing.

21. If she had gone to confess in the 1480s, she would have been automatically damned. Her particular case is interesting, because she was absolved. Her defense succeeded on the basis of tachas, a means of attempting to disqualify the prosecution witnesses. If she correctly guessed the names of the witnesses and could provide two of her own witnesses to testify to the fact that the testifier had reason to wish her harm, that testimony was not valid. Apparently, Inés and her lawyer succeeded in this way. See chapter 6 for a detailed discussion of tachas.

22. See Leg. 183, n° 11 (1502–3); the trial of the wife of Fernando Tondidor is incomplete.

23. See Leg. 134, n° 15 (1507); the trial of this anonymous conversa is incomplete and suspended.

24. The fat portions attached to the stomach and intestines (*heilev*) cannot be eaten.

25. See the confession in Leg. 164, n° 21 (1509–12). Christian women were forbidden to serve Jews as wet nurses (and servants); this prohibition can be found in canon law—for example, Innocent III's *Patrilogia Latina* 215, col. 694. In general, interactions of this sort, no matter who served whom, were frowned upon. While employing a Jewish wet nurse was not

viewed as negatively as being employed by a Jew as a wet nurse, Elvira knew that such contact would not be viewed kindly by the Church. Nevertheless, this was by no means an act of judaizing.

26. Leg. 164, n° 21 (1509–12).

27. See the accusation in ibid.

28. This very substantial confession appears in Leg. 141, n° 14 (1511–12). This resident of Ciudad Real was married to Alfonso de Villarreal. The burial rites to which she referred included placing a bowl of water and a lit candle in the room in which her father died. Taking a piece of dough refers to the biblical command to remove a portion of the dough for the priest of the Temple. After the destruction of the Temple, the woman, after kneading the Shabbat bread dough, takes the equivalent portion from the bread and throws it into the oven to burn before baking the hallah. This is considered to be one of three essential obligations of the Jewish woman in the Talmud.

29. See the accusation in ibid.

30. This is the Jewish manner of blessing children and was stressed often by crypto-Jews. The blessing of the children traditionally occurs on Friday evening.

31. Here is another example of folk beliefs that were not signs of judaizing but were perceived to be counter to the teachings of the Church. Many conversos used folk medicine such as *echar de gotas* or *gotillas,* applying oil to the ill, in their confessions. The prosecutors never included this act in their charges. See Marín Padilla, "Relación," pp. 254–255.

32. The last statement, the twenty-eighth in the list of transgressions, directly relates to the Jewish purity laws. During menstruation, the woman is unclean and refrains from sexual intercourse. Although María was already a widow by 1509, in 1486 her husband Diego Rodríguez was alive; he had confessed on the same day as did his wife. His statement from 1486 was procured from a book of confessions, and a copy was included in his widow's trial. See Leg. 163, n° 7 (1512–22) for all of the above details.

33. See the accusation in ibid.

34. Leg. 143, n° 18 (1498–99), of the wife of Alonso Pérez Plazuela, is incomplete.

35. See Leg. 149, n° 7 (1511–12); María and her lawyer presented many tachas in this very lengthy file. Her mother's file was Leg. 155, n° 7 (1513–20) and is transcribed in Beinart, *Records* 3, 378–533; her father, Pero Núñez Franco, whose file is not extant, was condemned as a judaizer in 1516. According to her mother's testimony, María was born in 1497 and thus was a mere fourteen-year-old at the outset of her trial.

36. See Leg. 133, n° 13 (1514–15); she was the wife of Diego Herrador.

37. See Leg. 165, n° 7 (1520–21) of the wife of Pedro Meléndez, resident of Guadalajara. This accusation is also alluded to in Cantera Burgos and Carrete Parrondo, "Juderías medievales," *Sefarad* 34:2 (1974): 356–357.

38. Cantera Burgos and Carrete Parrondo used these two trials as pivotal in their reconstruction of the Jewish and converso community of Hita. See "La Judería de Hita," *Sefarad* 32 (1972): 249–305. The original proceedings are available at the Archivo Histórico Nacional in Madrid.

39. This detailed accusation appears in Leg. 159, n° 15 (1520–21); the defendant was the wife of a Jew named Batix, who died in 1490. Her son, Antonio Pérez, helped her prepare a formidable defense; Beatriz was the mother of four.

40. The confession follows the accusation in Leg. 159, n° 15 (1520–21).

41. Isabel was examining the sharpness of the knife by passing it along her nail; the knife must be regularly examined before and after use so as to ensure that it is perfectly

smooth, without a notch that might tear the flesh. *Shulhan Arukh,* Yoreh Deah, Hilkhot Shehitah 6:1.

42. Rodrigo García passed away in 1508, twelve years before the trial. Isabel also buried a baby girl, María, in 1506; her son claimed she could not have engaged in the activities attributed to her, since she was very ill and bedridden after childbirth. The "closed door" image refers to Jewish mourning or sitting shiva. The witness offered an inaccurate count of the seven days and extended it to nine; the prosecutor, knowing no better, repeated the mistake. Reference is made here to the bandage or *barbillera,* in the accusation called a *barba* or beard. This bandage is placed under the chin of the dead person in order to keep the mouth closed, but in this context the word refers to covering the chin of the mourner. The Jews of Spain followed the practice, dating back to the talmudic period, whereby the mourner would cover his head with a scarf in a way that it concealed his mouth. Biblical precedents for covering the head can be found in Samuel II 15:30 and Jeremiah 14:3–4. See also Targum to Leviticus 13:45; Babylonian Talmud, Moed Katan 15a; Maimonides, *Mishneh Torah,* Hilkhot Avelut 5:19. In the thirteenth century, Rabbi Moses b. Yaakov of Coucy mentioned that the Jews of Spain were still following this practice, in *Sefer Mitsvot Gadol* (Mukachevo [Hungary]: Druck von Káhn & Fried, 1905), p. 181b. The lamenting is called *guayas,* which means sorrows or afflictions; it was characterized by *endechas* or dirges. Women who comforted those in mourning would join them in rather vocal mourning rituals. While the crypto-Jewish women could not mourn in this way at the graveside, they sang the traditional lamentations and dirges within the confines of the home. In this manner, they were following the medieval tradition of the professional Jewish female mourners who sang and clapped their hands in grief.

43. See Leg. 158, n° 9 (1520–23) for the original accusation.

3. *Messianic Turmoil circa 1500*

For details on additional observances, see chapter 4, "Castilian Women at Work."

1. There was a prophetess of Old Christian heritage as well during this period.

2. A number of articles deal with this movement. See Haim Beinart, "A Prophesying Movement in Cordova in 1499–1502" [Hebrew], *Zion* 44 (1980): 190–200; Beinart, "The Spanish Inquisition and a 'Converso Community' in Extremadura," *Medieval Studies* 43 (1981): 445–471; Beinart, "Herrera: Its Conversos and Jews" [Hebrew], *Proceedings of the Seventh World Congress of Jewish Studies* B (1981): 53–85; Beinart, "The Prophetess Inés and Her Movement in Pueblo de Alcocer and Talarrubias" [Hebrew], *Tarbiz* 51 (1982): 633–658; Beinart, "Conversos of Chillón and the Prophecies of Mari Gómez and Inés, the Daughter of Juan Esteban" [Hebrew], *Zion* 48 (1983): 241–272; and Beinart, "The Prophetess Inés and Her Movement in Her Hometown, Herrera" [Hebrew], *Studies in Jewish Mysticism, Philosophy and Ethical Literature,* ed. Y. Dan and Y. Hacker (Jerusalem: Magnes Press, 1986), pp. 459–506. Many of the women discussed in this chapter appear in some of these articles, especially the last, which is an in-depth analysis of Inés and her influence in Herrera. Included in the messianic fervor of the times are the conversos of Córdoba, where a father and his daughters together with a Muslim girl they converted, led a very large group of conversos. Two of the daughters functioned as the chief prophetesses, but, unfortunately, little is known about them or their fate. See Beinart, "A Prophesying Movement," p. 190 ff.

3. Inés is referred to as a twelve-year-old girl; no age is available for Mari.

4. See chapter 1 for mention of this conversa; she had a good deal of contact with Jews.

María was the widow of Ruy García; both of her confessions appear in Leg. 132, n° 8 (1500–1501).

5. María noted that the Inquisition had departed Herrera at the time.

6. Mayor was the wife of Diego de Córdova, the cobbler. Her confessions are to be found in Leg. 155, n° 6 (1500–1501).

7. There was definitely a period when these prophets overlapped; Beinart raises the possibility that Alonso was influenced by Mari of Chillón and points out that it is difficult to know when each prophet influenced whom. See "The Prophetess Inés and Her Movement in Her Hometown," p. 477.

8. The original states that when she fasted, she said "Cadoz, cadoz" and she said those words in this way. This is a clear reference to a portion of the repetition of the *Amidah,* when the words *Kadosh, Kadosh, Kadosh* (Holy, Holy, Holy) are recited.

9. Both confessions appear in Leg. 153, n° 13 (1500–1501), the trial of the wife of Fernando Sánchez de la Barrera.

10. She does not mention Juana Gómez by name, but this is a clear reference to this conversa maiden.

11. Both confessions appear in Leg. 150, n° 11 (1500–1501); María was the wife of Fernando, the (iron)smith.

12. My only conjecture here is that this standing is a distortion that can be traced to the closing service of Yom Kippur, *Neilah;* this portion, perhaps an hour long, is conducted with the entire congregation standing. Because this occurs so late in the day, when one is tired and hungry, the impression is that one stands for a much longer period of time.

13. This is not a halakhic tradition but might well be Kabbalistic. Hands, and particularly nails, were supposed to retain impurities and needed special cleanliness. The required washing of hands, other than before eating bread, is after awakening rather than prior to retiring.

14. Isabel Alonso of Chillón was tried from 1502 to 1503; since this discussion follows a chronological order, her case will be discussed presently.

15. All of this information is contained in Leg. 134, n° 12 (1500–1501).

16. She was the wife of Pedro González or García, the potter. The file is Leg. 178, n° 15 (1501).

17. This is the Spanish pronunciation of *tevila,* or ritual purity bathing necessary following menstruation and childbirth; blessings are also recited at this time.

18. Parts of the trial of the wife of Ruy Sánchez are preserved in Leg. 169, n° 6 (1501); there were six witness accounts and then three more followed by three additional anti-Inquisition statements.

19. See Leg. 153, n° 17 (1502), dealing with the wife of Alonso Gutiérrez.

20. This explains the earlier reference to the making of a new blouse for the journey by Isabel Rodríguez of Agudo.

21. It is likely that she was the aunt of María Gómez of Chillón. At any rate, the trial of the wife of Gonzalo Díaz appears in Leg. 132, n° 7 (1502–3).

22. These are the *quemados,* a reference to those heretics who had been burned at the stake.

23. María was married to Mendo Gutiérrez of Bonillo; her trial can be found in Leg. 154, n° 35 (1502–3).

24. In Paul's theological system, the belief that the Law has redemptive value stands in the way of recognition of the impaired will of man and acceptance of Christ. Hence the Law would be considered blind or deadly.

25. The oath was probably taken at her reconciliation in the 1480s, for she had promised to be a good Catholic. There were tachas in this trial, but they were obviously not effective.

26. The file of the former wife of Gonzalo Vargas is in Leg. 133, n° 2 (1504–6).

27. This claim is identical to that of Elvira Núñez of Toledo, discussed above.

28. This practice appears frequently; the conversos were clearly under the impression that this was a Jewish practice.

29. The conversos were not the only messianic hopefuls to espouse this belief. For a description that is uncannily similar, see Gluckel of Hameln's reference to the state of readiness of her in-laws as part of the Sabbatian movement in 1666. See *The Memoirs of Gluckel of Hameln,* trans. M. Lowenthal (New York: Schocken Books, 1977), p. 46.

30. All of this information is available in Leg. 176, n° 1 (1500–1501), trial of the wife of Juan Estevan, cobbler, resident of Herrera.

31. According to Beinart, Juan Esteban fled to Portugal. See "The Prophetess Inés and Her Movement in Her Hometown," p. 467.

32. As is noted above, Leg. 154, n° 34 (1500) is incomplete. The discrepancies between the description presented by the prosecutor and that by María probably imply that there were additional witness testimonies during the trial which contained such details.

33. As one can see, direct quotes of conversations with Inés are contained in this confession. See Leg. 137, n° 7 (1500–1501).

34. Witnesses had apparently provided this information to the prosecution. Some of the details are rather unusual, such as the notion of marrying the king of Judea. See Leg. 134, n° 7 (1500–1501).

35. See Babylonian Talmud, Baba Batra 74–75. The rest of the fish was to be distributed and sold in the markets of Jerusalem. There it is stated that "in time to come," a tabernacle for the righteous will be made from the skin of the leviathan. Either way, this fish has a role in the end of days, and it was accurate that the conversos referred to a dead fish, for then he could be eaten or the skin could be utilized. Beinart pointed out that during this period, a whale had appeared on the Portuguese shores and was captured. See "The Prophetess Inés and Her Movement in Her Hometown," p. 466.

36. The transcript appears to claim that she was baptized twice!

37. See Leg. 143, n° 14 (1500–1501) for the above details.

38. While most conversas refer to preparing meat in honor of the Sabbath, some did not do so. One had to ponder whether the absence of meat on Friday is a direct result of living a Catholic life or whether it reflects the desire not to stand out by preparing and eating forbidden foods on Fridays.

39. The wife of Juan Díaz was tried from 1500 to 1501. Her file, Leg. 153, n° 12, is incomplete but contains this confession and accusation.

40. See Leg. 137, n° 8 (1500–1501); the file is incomplete.

41. See Leg. 158, n° 2 (1500–1501); the defendant was the daughter of Marcos González, *herrador* (ironworker or blacksmith) and Leonor Jiménez.

42. Presumably she did this two or three times rather than fasting two or three consecutive days.

43. See Leg. 158, n° 7 (1501).

44. Beatriz said that because of her father's position, people were in their home until midnight. Presumably this shoemaker did not hold an official position but was an accommodating craftsman.

45. See Leg. 137, n° 9 (1500–1502). Included in this file are the names of six other conver-

sos, all absent from the trial. They were Catalina, daughter of Lope González; Fernando, son of Juan Alfonso, *zapatero* (cobbler); Inés, daughter of Rodrigo de Villanueva (sister of Beatriz, Leg. 137, nº 8, the twelve-year-old discussed above); Martín, son of Ruy González; Fernando de la Peña, son of Alvar González; and Martín Sánchez, *carnicero* (butcher), resident of Pueblo de Alcocer. Since the first five are listed as the son or daughter of someone, they were also young unmarried conversos. The only confession in this file belongs to Beatriz, the only one to appear in court.

46. See Leg. 178, nº 2 (1500–1502); Elvira was the wife of Diego.

47. This reference should be to the star that rises from Jacob, as appears in Numbers 24:17. This passage is traditionally explained as having messianic implications; see, for example, the commentaries of Nahmanides and *Or Ha-Hayim* (Hayyim Ibn-Attar).

48. See Leg. 181, nº 13 (1500–1517) for details of the tachas, or attempt to disqualify prosecution witnesses. Here the defense was successful.

49. It is extremely likely that this Juan Alonso is identical to the Juan Alfonso, *zapatero*, referred to above in the case of Beatriz Alfonso. The trial of Beatriz included the names of six absent conversos including Fernando, the son of Juan Alfonso, probably the cousin of Isabel.

50. See Leg. 158, nº 6 (1501).

51. See Leg. 158, nº 3 (1501–2). The cover page of the proceedings has the age of fifteen noted, but her confession leads one to believe that she was younger.

52. See Leg. 163, nº 11 (1501–2).

53. See Leg. 158, nº 19 (1501–3).

54. See this incomplete file, Leg. 148, nº 10 (1502). Since the sentence is recorded as condemned but not relaxed, it is possible that her fate was imprisonment or another of the less than fatal options.

55. See Leg. 143, nº 9 (1502–3).

56. See Leg. 153, nº 18 (1502–3); Elvira was the wife of Gonzalo Palomino.

57. It is interesting that in her confession, the term *quemados*, or those burned at the stake, is not used. The reference is to "our deceased," which the prosecutor transposed to burned heretics.

58. Leg. 158, nº 8 (1502–3) contains this confession as well as this accusation. The additional information appearing in the accusation might have come from witness accounts, since the charges are not identical to the list in the confession.

59. See Leg. 183, nº 17 (1502–4).

60. In Leg. 132, nº 7, the prosecutor makes this claim regarding Mari, the wife of Juan López, the woolcomber. See Beinart, "Conversos of Chillón," p. 242.

61. See Beinart, "The Prophetess Inés and Her Movement in Her Hometown," p. 461.

62. Knowledge of the fates of these four would obviously affect the numbers under discussion.

63. Because of the four that are incomplete, the statistics are problematic; however, if they are subtracted, then fifteen of twenty-eight trials with known results resulted in condemnations.

4. Castilian Conversas at Work

1. See Simha Asaf, "The Marranos of Spain and Portugal in Responsa Literature" [Hebrew], *Me'assef Zion* 5 (1932–33): 21, n. 4. He claims that this "ancient custom" (in accusations made by Portuguese inquisitors), developed out of respect for the *mezuzah* on the doorpost.

2. This woman was anonymous; her file is Leg. 134, n° 14 (1492–93). For López, see Haim Beinart, *Records of the Trials of the Spanish Inquisition in Ciudad Real* 2 (Jerusalem: Israel Academy of Sciences and Humanities, 1977), p. 65.

The third conversa's file is Leg. 134, n° 5 (1492–93).

3. See Leg. 154, n° 36 (1511–12), the trial of the wife of Pedro Díaz of Villarrubia as transcribed in Beinart, *Records* 2: 195.

4. See Leg. 158, n° 9 (1520–23).

5. See Leg. 133, n° 21 (1511–13), in Beinart, *Records* 2: 324.

6. See Leg. 172, n° 2 (1512–14), Beinart, *Records* 2: 472.

7. This was María González, wife of Rodrigo of Chillón, also a resident of Ciudad Real. See Leg. 155, n° 2 (1512–13), in Beinart, *Records* 2: 380.

8. Leg. 153, n° 14 (1511–13), in Beinart, *Records* 2: 163.

9. See Leg. 159, n° 15 (1520–21).

10. See Leg. 154, n° 37 (1511–13), the trial of María González, in Beinart, *Records* 2: 251.

11. See Beinart, *Records* 2: 374. This is one of the three charges in the accusation; this is an unusually short list, considering the fact that she was burned at the stake.

12. See Leg. 154, n° 33, or H. Beinart, "Judíos y Conversos en Casarrubios del Monte," in *Homenaje a Juan Prado: Miscelánea de estudios bíblicos y hebraicos,* ed. L. Alvarez Verdes (Madrid: Consejo Superior de Investigaciones Científicas, 1975), p. 654.

13. The wife of Antón Ramírez was considered to be a relapsed heretic in 1503; see Leg. 173, n° 6 (1503–4) in Beinart, *Records* 2: 151.

14. The accusation is quite long; see Leg. 158, n° 9 (1520–23).

15. See Leg. 155, n° 2 (1512–13), in Beinart, *Records* 2: 380.

16. Leg. 154, n° 36 (1511–12) in Beinart, *Records* 2: 196.

17. See Leg. 154, n° 37 (1511–13) in Beinart, *Records* 2: 250.

18. There is an interesting comment by a conversa who confessed to observing the Sabbath with a cohort but never wearing clean blouses or *tocas* or festive clothes on that day for fear of their husbands. This informant, Beatriz Alonso, was burned at the stake in 1513 and has no extant file except this confession, where she implicates herself and the wife of Alonso de Merlo. See Leg. 155, n° 1 (1512–13) in Beinart, *Records* 2: 439.

19. See Leg. 172, n° 2 (1512–14) in Beinart, *Records* 2: 472.

20. See Leg. 153, n° 14 (1511–13) in Beinart, *Records* 2: 163.

21. Ibid., p. 167.

22. See Leg. 164, n° 4 (1531–39), the trial of Magdalena de Morales of la Mota; this testimony appears on fols. 2r–4r.

23. This was María González, the wife of Pedro de Villarreal, and the same servant she had sweeping the house on Fridays who is mentioned above; see Leg. 154, n° 37 (1511–13) in Beinart, *Records* 2: 250.

24. See Leg. 153, n° 14 (1511–13) in Beinart *Records* 2: 164.

25. See Leg. 133, n° 21 (1512–14) in Beinart *Records* 2: 324.

26. See Leg. 153, n° 14 (1511–13) in Beinart, *Records* 2: 163.

27. See Leg. 173, n° 6 (1503–4) in Beinart, *Records* 2: 151.

28. See Leg. 154, n° 36 (1511–12) in Beinart, *Records* 2: 195 for the charge and 213 for the testimony of a maidservant named María.

29. The verb used here for smoothing out is *desmotar,* which is the process of removing the nodules that form in the cloth, either by scissors or with tweezers. See Leg. 154, n° 37 (1511–13) in Beinart, *Records* 2: 267.

30. Ibid., p. 279; this testimony is a bit problematic, because after being tortured, she claimed that she had lied about the activites of Mayor as a matter of spite; ibid., p. 304.

31. This confession appears in the trial of Inés de Mérida, Leg. 167, n° 4 (1513, 1522) in Beinart, *Records* 3: 360–361.

32. This testimony appears in the trial of María González, wife of Rodrigo de Chillón, Leg. 155, n° 2 (1512–13) in Beinart, *Records* 2: 385. Juana's husband, Juan de Teva, had a rag business, and the wife usually sewed or embroidered. This testimony, from Luzia Fernández, wife of Francisco de Lillo, appears in Juana's file as well, Leg. 133, n° 1 (1512–14) in Beinart, *Records* 2: 490.

33. Loc. cit. Luzia said that she would usually recover by the afternoon and then go to visit her neighbors.

34. This was María González, the wife of Pedro de Villarreal, whose trial is Leg. 154, n° 37 (1511–13) in Beinart, *Records* 2: 250.

35. See Leg. 133, n° 21 (1511–13) as transcribed in Beinart, *Records* 2: 326.

36. See Leg. 154, n° 36 in Beinart, *Records* 2: 214; this is the same conversa accused above of elaborate Sabbath preparations.

37. See Leg. 155, n° 4 (1494) in Beinart, *Records* 2: 22.

38. See Leg. 157, n° 5 (1503–4) in Beinart, *Records* 2: 142.

39. This is part of the very elaborate and sometimes contradictory confession of María González, wife of Pedro de Villarreal in Leg. 154, n° 37 (1511–13) in Beinart, *Records* 2: 257. Juana was tried and condemned in 1513, although her record is not extant. María later added that another conversa's maid had told her that her masters would not work on the Sabbath and sometimes sent the servants out to the vineyards so that they would not see what was or was not done on the Jewish day of rest; ibid., p. 260.

40. This was the wife of Juan González Pintado; see Leg. 154, n° 29 in Beinart, *Records* 1: 483.

41. See Leg. 148, n° 6 (1483–84) in Beinart, *Records* 1: 184.

42. See Leg. 133, n° 21 (1512–14) in Beinart, *Records* 2: 334–335.

43. See Leg. 176, n° 4 (1512–24) in Beinart, *Records* 2: 24. Francisco included Juana in his list of tachas, claiming that the women had a bad relationship.

44. See Leg. 158, n° 12 (1506–7); the fact that this charge was listed first meant that it was the most serious of the defendant's transgressions.

45. This is found in Leg. 155, n° 6 (1500–1501); the second confession, given in 1500, describes how she fasted the entire day and wore a clean blouse. Both confessions are in the same file; the earlier one was used simply to show that she was a relapsed heretic. Her trial took place during the local messianic movement referred to in the previous chapter.

46. See Leg. 132, n° 8 (1500–1501).

47. See Leg. 133, n° 20 (1495–96) in Beinart, *Records* 2: 49.

48. See Leg. 162, n° 21 (1509–12); presumably this meal was prepared the day before Yom Kippur despite the fact that the prosecutor's wording implies that work was done on this holy day. There is always the possibility that these conversas did not realize that they were forbidden to cook on this day, but this does not seem likely.

49. See Leg. 160, n° 5 (1503–4).

50. See Leg. 172, n° 4 (1513–15).

51. See Leg. 150, n° 11 (1500–1501).

52. This was Mayor, the wife of Diego of Córdova; in Leg. 155, n° 6 (1500–1501), she reported that she and the wife of Gonzalo Sánchez would sometimes bake in the home of the wife of García Fernández.

53. See Leg. 132, n° 8 (1500–1501).

54. For Marina's confession, see Leg. 155, n° 4 (1494) in Beinart, *Records* 2: 10. For Constanza's statement, see Leg. 141, n° 14 (1511–12).

55. See Leg. 153, n° 13 (1500–1501).

56. See Leg. 178, n° 15 (1501).

57. See Leg. 158, n° 9 (1520–23).

58. See Leg. 154, n° 35 (1502–3).

59. See Leg. 163, n° 7 (1512–22).

60. See Leg. 149, n° 7 (1511–12).

61. See Leviticus 7:26–27 and 17:10–14.

62. See Genesis 32:33 and for *heilev,* Leviticus 3:15–17 and 7:23–25.

63. Deuteronomy 14:21; Exodus 22:30.

64. Anyone may slaughter with his slaughter being considered kosher except for the deaf, the insane, and minors. Babylonian Talmud, Hullin 1a.

65. See Leg. 154, n° 36 in Beinart, *Records* 2: 215.

66. See Leg. 159, n° 15 (1520–21).

67. See Leg. 158, n° 9 (1520–23).

68. Yosef Caro *Shulhan Arukh,* Yoreh Deah, Hilkhot Shehitah 6:1.

69. See Leg. 173, n° 6 (1503–4) in Beinart, *Records* 2: 152.

70. Beinart wrote that "the porging of the animal's hind quarters was a task performed by both men and women" and that all the trials of women in his possession from Ciudad Real contain mention of separating the fat as well as salting and rinsing the meat ("porging" refers to making a slaughtered animal ceremonially clean by removing the forbidden fat, veins, and sinews according to Jewish ritual). See Haim Beinart, *Conversos on Trial* (Jerusalem: Magnes Press, 1981), p. 264.

71. See n. 69 above.

72. See Leg. 155, n° 4 (1491) in Beinart, *Records* 2: 12.

73. See Leg. 158, n° 20 (1503–4) in Beinart, *Records* 2: 129 and Leg. 172, n° 2 (1512–14) in *Records* 2: 473.

74. See Leg. 134, n° 4 (1492–93) as well as Francisco Cantera Burgos and Carlos Carrete Parrondo, "Las juderías medievales en la provincia de Guadalajara," *Sefarad* 34 (1974): 316.

75. The former's accusation is in Leg. 165, n° 7 (1520–21) and Cantera Burgos and Carrete Parrondo, "Juderías medievales," p. 356. The latter's confessions appear in Leg. 162, n° 3 (1495–96, 1511–12) in Beinart, *Records* 2: 63 and 68.

76. See Beinart, "Judíos y Conversos," p. 652, and Leg. 154, n° 33 (1500).

77. See Leg. 159, n° 15 (1520–21).

78. See Leg. 158, n° 9 (1520–23).

79. See Leg. 153, n° 14 (1511–13) in Beinart, *Records* 2: 163; the servant was Catalina Martín.

80. See Leg. 154, n° 37 (1511–13) in Beinart, *Records* 2: 267–268.

81. This was the wife of Pedro de Villarreal, whose trial was Leg. 155, n° 1 (1512–13) in Beinart, *Records* 2: 252–253.

82. See Leg. 155, n° 4 (1494) in Beinart, *Records* 2: 24.

83. See Leg. 133, n° 21 (1511–13) in Beinart, *Records* 2: 343.

84. Her confession appears in her sister's trial, Leg. 133, n° 21 (1511–13) in Beinart, *Records* 2: 344.

85. See Leg. 173, n° 5 (1512–13) in Beinart, *Records* 2: 543 and 548.

86. See Leg. 153, n° 14 (1503–4) in Beinart, *Records* 2: 166.

87. See Leg. 155, n° 4 (1494) in Beinart, *Records* 2: 24.

88. See Leg. 181, n° 3 (1492–93) and also Cantera Burgos and Carrete Parrondo, "Juderías medievales," p. 364.

89. Beinart, *Conversos on Trial*, p. 281.

90. See Leg. 132, n° 8 (1500–1501).

91. She was the wife of Diego González, *mayordomo* (steward); the confession is found in Leg. 153, n° 10 (1487–94).

92. Dov Zlotnick, trans. and ed., *The Tractate "Mourning"* (New Haven, Conn.: Yale University Press, 1966), p. 82.

93. See Leg. 160, n° 15 (1510–11).

94. The charge stated that "likewise she remained silent as to how she bathed some of the dead and helped to bathe them and put a cup of water in the spot where they had died and some towels and a saddler's needle with lit candles, believing as a Jewess that the souls of those very deceased would come there to bathe their souls." Leg. 162, n° 3 (1495–96). Here is a fine example of some of the Sephardi rituals in the home of the deceased.

95. See Leg. 158, n° 9 (1520–23). The witness account was given by a woman named Beatriz Lorenzo.

96. See Leg. 150, n° 6 (1484–85) in Beinart, *Records* 1: 531 and 534. The quantity was thirty *varas* of linen; each *vara* is two feet, nine inches in length.

97. See Leg. 141, n° 14 (1511–12).

98. See Leg. 158, n° 9 (1520–23).

99. This lengthy description is contained in Leg. 158, n° 9 (1520–23). The witness even quoted a few lines from one of the dirges she heard chanted.

100. See Leg. 188, n° 12 (1484) in Beinart, *Records* 1: 389, 390, and 393. It was also said, according to Beinart, that María González, wife of Juan González Pintado, publicly served as a keener at the death of Alvaro de Madrid; however, her file, Leg. 154, n° 29 (1484–85), does not mention this.

101. See Leg. 158, n° 9 (1520–23).

102. This is recorded in Leg. 134, n° 8 (1516–18). The novenas are days of prayer to the Creator, the Virgin, or the saints who suffered; the prayers are offered on the part of the deceased. In theory, these devotions last nine days, although they are usually completed in one or two days.

103. In the arraignment, the prosecutor said that Catalina Gómez was a seamstress (*costurera*) and would sew on Sundays until mealtime. Leg. 148, n° 6 (1483–84) in Beinart, *Records* 1: 184. She refers to her profession as well, ibid., p. 186, and confessed in 1483, during a grace period, that sometimes she had sewn on Sundays.

104. This is part of the recollection of Leonor Alvarez, who went to this teacher's home as a child. See Leg. 133, n° 2 (1495–96) in Beinart, *Records* 2: 49.

105. The proceedings of her trial appear in Leg. 177, n° 4 (1536–63); an analysis of this trial can be found in chapter 7.

106. This was Elvira López of San Gil, who actually rented the houses to Jews prior to 1492; the tenants sent her and her husband matsah as a gift at Passover. See Leg. 160, n° 14 (1492–94).

107. See Leg. 155, n° 7 (1513–20) in Beinart, *Records* 3: 420.

108. Haim Beinart, *The Sephardi Legacy* 2 (Jerusalem: Magnes Press, 1992), p. 57.

109. See Leg. 163, n° 8 (1516–21); this information can be gleaned from two tachas (XXXIX and XL), both of which are located on fol. 37v.

110. The first witness was Catalina Martínez and the second was María Sánchez; they testified for the prosecution in Leg. 133, n° 5 (1484–85) in Beinart, *Records* 1: 228 and 232.

111. This is a small portion of the list presented by a different Mari Sánchez, who might have been a conversa herself. See Leg. 152, n° 14 (1484) in Beinart, *Records* 1: 309–310.

112. See the title page of her trial, Leg. 143, n° 11 (1493–84) in Beinart, *Records* 1: 41.

113. Marina explained that she and Mari Godias fought over this matter; see Leg. 155, n° 4 (1494) in Beinart, *Records* 2: 30.

114. This information appears in a tacha against Luzia de Cuenca; this was the reason for enmity between the two women. See Leg. 133, n° 21 in Beinart, *Records* 2: 355.

115. This information appears in a tacha in the trial of María González. It was said that Luzia de Cuenca was a whore, a drunkard, a thief, and a liar and had sold the wool she was given in order to buy herself wine. See Leg. 155, n° 2 (1512–13) in Beinart, *Records* 2: 413. Nonetheless, Luzia's testimony was not invalidated.

116. A witness explained that she extracted distilled water all week except for Saturdays, but she did work on Sundays. See Leg. 137, n° 3 (1484–85) in Beinart, *Records* 1: 470.

117. See Leg. 155, n° 7 (1513–20) in Beinart, *Records* 3: 399.

118. An Old Christian tacha witness mentioned this while attempting to discredit María González as a witness. See Leg. 133, n° 21 (1512–14) in Beinart, *Records* 2: 357.

5. The López-Villarreal Family

1. During the period these trials occurred, the tribunal in Toledo seems to have concentrated its efforts on this movement, since almost all of the conversos tried at that time were those affected by the prophetic messianism.

2. Francisco Cantera Burgos and Carlos Carrete Parrondo, "Las juderías medievales en la provincia de Guadalajara," *Sefarad* 33 (1973): 35–38.

3. See appendix 1 for complete lists of prosecution witnesses, defense witnesses nominated and summoned by the court, tachas, and tacha witnesses. All but the first list are alphabetically arranged in order to enable the reader to find any given individual easily. The women's trials contain lists of tachas, but Pedro declined to supply names.

4. María's trial was Leg. 163, n° 8 (originally 420), and transpired from 1516 to 1521. Isabel's trial was Leg. 162, n° 6 (originally 400), dating from 1516 to 1518; Pedro's trial was Leg. 188, n° 9 (originally 840), from 1518 to 1521.

5. The accusation appears in Leg. 163, n° 8, fols. 2r–2v.

6. Ibid., fol. 6v.

7. Ibid., fol. 7r.

8. Ibid., fol. 6v.

9. Ibid., fol. 7r.

10. Ibid., fol. 8r. It is interesting that various other children of María are mentioned more than once in these testimonies, yet the prosecution chose to focus on her oldest daughter, Isabel.

11. Ibid., fol. 10r. The term used here is *criadas* rather than *mozas,* implying a lower class of servants.

12. Ibid., fol. 6r. In the discussion of Isabel's counts, this description would be most damning for her.

13. Ibid., fol. 7r.

14. Ibid., fol. 10r.

15. Ibid., fol. 10r.

16. Ibid., fol. 7r.

17. Ibid., fol. 8r.

18. Aberrations in conforming with restrictions were often attributed to health problems; the prosecutor was making the point clear that this was not an issue here.

19. Leg. 163, n° 8, fol. 7r.

20. Both the fifth and sixth testimonies were presented much later, in 1518. Madalena, the wife of Martín Simón, discussed many Sabbath activities which will be referred to presently, ibid., fol. 9r. The testimony of Yague, the sixth witness, followed that of Madalena yet was used by the prosecutor; see the above discussion of the second, third, and fourth charges.

21. Leg. 162, n° 6, fol. 8r.

22. Ibid., fol. 11r. Madalena suggested that the clothes were worn until the time that the lamp that was lit on Friday burned out on Saturday morning; she stated that she never saw them dressed up in this way on Sundays or on Saturday afternoons. This is a bit confusing, as one would expect them to have remained in Sabbath attire until sundown, or the appearance of three stars on Saturday evening. Perhaps once their prayer session, which will be discussed in the context of Pedro's accusation, was concluded, they preferred to wear everyday clothing so as not to be too conspicuous. Elsewhere in her testimony Madalena explained that the lamp that was lit on Friday afternoons remained lit until the next day (the Sabbath) until nine or ten o'clock, when she suspected that it had burned out on its own. Ibid., fol. 11r.

23. The term used was *sabadeando,* or praying in a Jewish way.

24. Leg. 162, n° 6, fol. 8r.

25. Ibid., fols. 11r–v.

26. The "fat" might have been the sciatic nerve. Ibid., fols. 8r–v.

27. Ibid., fol. 9v.

28. Ibid., fol. 9r.

29. Ibid., fol. 9v.

30. Ibid., fol. 9v.

31. It is a bit difficult to date the time of this first response; there are a number of torn pages in the beginning of the record. The accusation seems to have been presented on January 29, 1517. Although María's response is recorded by a different notary, it does follow directly and gives the impression that she responded immediately, most likely on the same day.

32. Leg. 163, n° 8, fols. 3r–3v.

33. Leg. 162, n° 6, fol. 5r.

34. Ibid., fol. 3r.

35. Here María is trying to prove the absurdity of the charge by insisting that women did not engage in such activities. However the Inquisition knew that in times of stress, when it was difficult to continue traditional roles, significant changes often transpired and conventions were often ignored.

36. Leg. 163, n° 8, fols. 4v–5r.

37. Ibid., fols. 12r–12v and 13v. The first four testimonies were read to her and she responded, and then the last two were added and she responded again. Needless to say, the identity of all of the witnesses was withheld from the defense.

38. Ibid., fols. 14r–15r.

39. Isabel was trying to prove that the prosecution had not done its homework; like her mother, she claimed that their description of judaizing was incorrect. In this case, the limited amount of swaying that occurs in the process of a portion of the prayer service is not an act

of judaizing but rather a series of motions prescribed by rabbinic law. As for the continuous swaying that became habitual in Ashkenazi services, if it was present in Sephardi services as well, it was most definitely not a rite or ceremony. See Leg. 162, n° 6, fol. 6v.

40. Her response appears in ibid., fols. 6r–7r.

41. Ibid., fols. 13r–13v.

42. Ibid., fol. 15v.

43. Ibid., fols. 16r–16v.

44. This statement begins in ibid., fols. 14v, and concludes on fol. 17r.

45. Leg. 163, n° 8, fols. 16r–16v.

46. Don Alonso de la Cerda appears to have been a wealthy landowner who is listed as residing in Guadalajara but had many ties to the Cogolludo community (despite the fact that there was a distance of 33 kilometers between them). It is possible that he had a homestead in Cogolludo because the amount of interaction between him and residents of this village was so great.

He and his wife are cited as character witnesses and nominated to verify tacha claims; they were in their early thirties at the time, and Alonso states that he has known them for eighteen years. In addition, many of his employees including servants, pages, accountants, and curators are named to support the defense claims. None of these individuals appear as suspected informers in the tacha lists. See appendix 1 for details regarding the defense lists.

The fact that none of the above appeared on tacha lists only confirms the sense that the López-Villarreal family had positive experiences with Don Alonso and the fact that María cared for him when he was ill only confirms this impression. Unfortunately there is not a great deal of information to elaborate upon the nature of their relationship. Pedro had been granted the position of his steward by Don Alonso and this seemed to have given him a fair amount of power in the community. Don Alonso had been in the Villarreal home as well as in their cellar, and seems to have protected Pedro when there were frictions.

47. Ibid., fols. 18r–19r.

48. The witnesses who were rejected and not allowed to testify were all New Christians. One must not forget that the names of the prosecution witnesses were withheld from the defense; otherwise, Ropero never would have been considered a trustworthy witness for the defense.

49. These testimonies appear in ibid., fols. 21r–23r.

50. The questions and the list appear in ibid., fols. 24r–24v.

51. See ibid., fol. 27v.

52. See ibid., fols. 27r–27v.

53. Ibid., fols. 30v–33v.

54. Leg. 162, n° 6, fols. 18v–19r.

55. Ibid., fols. 20r–23r.

56. Ibid., fols. 23r–23v.

57. Ibid., fols. 25r–25v.

58. Ibid., fols. 27r–28r.

59. Leg. 188, n° 9 (previous number 840). The genealogy appears on fol. 2v; the warnings are on fols. 2v–3r.

60. Ibid., fols. 3v–5r.

61. Ibid., fols. 6v; 15r–16r.

62. Ibid., fols. 16v–17r.

63. Ibid., fols. 16v–17v.

64. Ibid., fols. 18r–18v. It is possible that when the oil was prepared on Friday evenings, an ample supply was not inserted that would last through the night. Consequently, the servants had to relight the lamps after the gatherings in the cellar. If enough oil was available to burn throughout the night, that is what occurred; if not, the lamps extinguished by themselves.

65. Ibid., fol. 18v.

66. This appears in ibid., fol. 20v. Pedro's run-on sentences make it rather hard to translate while retaining the logic of his statement. In his original confession, he said he had worn a clean shirt on the Sabbath, but for no Jewish-related reason.

67. Leg. 188, n° 9, fols. 20r–21r.

68. See appendix 1 for his lists.

6. *The López Women's* Tachas

See appendix 1 for alphabetical list of tachas and tacha witnesses.

1. Leg. 162, n° 6, fol. 29r.

2. Loc. cit.

3. Loc. cit. Isabel did not provide enough information to make this incident fully comprehensible. Perhaps Juana had fallen ill as the result of living in foul quarters and because Isabel was the one who found her, she was blamed for having created an embarrassing situation for the barber and his family.

4. Leg. 162, n° 6, fol. 30r.

5. All of the above tachas appear in loc. cit. Ana will reappear in Francisco's list.

6. See ibid., fol. 30v.

7. The term used is *herir,* which can mean to wound, to harm, to irritate, or to collide; it is clearly used as "wound" in other tacha descriptions.

8. The above appear in Leg. 162, n° 6, fol. 32r.

9. Ibid., fol. 32v.

10. Loc. cit.

11. Ibid., fols. 32v–33r.

12. Ibid., fol. 33r.

13. Leg. 163, n° 8, fol. 51v.

14. The defense had now correctly named four of the five witnesses for the prosecution.

15. This is the twelfth tacha; see Leg. 162, n°6, fol. 30r. Francisco's references appear in Leg. 162, n° 6, fols. 33r and 40v; the latter appears in a separate list.

16. The above tachas appear in ibid., fol. 33r.

17. Ibid., fol. 33v.

18. Ibid., fol. 35r.

19. This suit hardly seems fair, with the decision being made by one of the claimants' son-in-law.

20. The first tacha appears in ibid., fol. 35r; the second on fol. 44r.

21. All of the above tachas appear in ibid., fol. 35r.

22. See ibid., fol. 35v.

23. These tachas appear in ibid., fol. 37r.

24. This was Inés *la obregona,* who could not remember when this incident occurred. See ibid., fol. 38r. An *obregon* is a member of a hospital order established in the sixteenth century; presumably Inés was affiliated with a member of this order as once she is called the wife and at another time the sister of *obregon.*

25. This incident implies that Isabel was desperate for household help, begging to rehire a servant who had not proved herself trustworthy. This witness was Beatriz López, a forty-year-old New Christian woman who had converted in 1498; she was a neighbor of Isabel for six years and was suggested as a witness to verify many tachas but did not remember most of the incidents that were mentioned.

26. This María was a thirty-six-year-old woman who had known Isabel for almost twenty years; she also mentioned that Francisco de Murcia approached her three days prior to her hearing and begged her to tell what she knew to the court. See ibid., fol. 38v.

27. The positions held were *recebtor,* or clerk assigned to collect monies, and *cogedor,* or collector. At the end of María's trial, there is a reference to a period of time when Francisco was *recebtor* and Rodrigo was *cogedor.* See Leg. 163, n° 8, fol. 51r. Ironically, Rodrigo was nominated elsewhere as a witness for the defense. This shows not only the precariousness of the entire defense, but the incredible vulnerability of the defendant as the tachas were prepared.

28. The first tacha appears in ibid., fol. 33r; the quotation from the second tacha is in ibid., fol. 39r. The third mention was in October; see ibid., fol. 44r. The term used to describe Madalena's legs are *las buas,* or scabs or growths which result from the venereal disease yams, an endemic disease prevalent at that time.

29. These tachas appear in ibid., fol. 39v.

30. See ibid., fol. 40r. Walnuts must have been valued in this society.

31. There is no elaboration here; perhaps she overindulged and freely helped herself in the López-Villarreal pantry, and perhaps this reference meant that instead of working, she sat and ate sweets. See ibid., fol. 40v.

32. The above tachas appear in ibid., fol. 40v.

33. See ibid., fol. 41r.

34. Ibid., fol. 43r.

35. I have written elsewhere about the judicial aspects of this trial. It was highly unusual for the defense to have successfully named every single witness for the prosecution only to fail to find appropriate witnesses to corroborate their claims. See Renée Levine Melammed, "Sixteenth Century Justice in Action: The Case of Isabel López," *Revue des études juives* 145:1–2 (1986): 51–73.

36. This is the same Don Alonso de la Cerda of Guadalajara who is referred to toward the end of the previous chapter. He, his wife, and his employees appear in the defendants' lists.

37. These appear in Leg. 163, n° 8, fol. 28v.

38. See ibid., fol. 34r.

39. Ibid., fol. 34v.

40. These appear in ibid., fol. 35r.

41. Pedro de Burgos's wife was Catalina de Cervantes, the first prosecution witness in Isabel's trial. The notary made a notation alongside this tacha, but since Catalina did not testify in María's trial, it appears to be an error. Ibid., fol. 35v.

42. The later tacha appears on fol. 37v, tacha 40.

43. A *botero* is a maker or vendor of leather bags and bottles for wine.

44. This is the third official position that Pedro held; here he is referred to as *regidor.*

45. The term used here is *mal doblados;* a *doblado* was also the measure of the fold in cloth.

46. These tachas appear in Leg. 163, n° 8, fol. 35v.

47. Ibid., fol. 36r.

48. Ibid., fol. 36v.

49. The notary marked the sign for correct tacha alongside her name; perhaps Isabel or María erred as to whether her father was named Pedro Pastor or Miguel.

50. See ibid., fol. 37r.

51. This does not mean that there is not a connection between the two realms.

52. It is not clear if he was doing penance for theft by a female member of his family, or if María neglected to explain the deed for which he had to face public humiliation.

53. See ibid., fol. 38r.

54. Ibid., fol. 37v.

55. Ibid., fol. 38r.

56. Ibid., fol. 39r.

57. Perhaps her mother remarried Juan Pastor and the identification through the different parents accounts for the confusion.

58. She is referred to as the wife of Nablero in the fifth tacha and as la Nublera here; this is one and the same person. Ibid., fol. 41r.

59. There is no mention here of her age or of whether she had other problems; see ibid., fol. 41v.

60. Francisco had broken her hand, according to the tacha in Isabel's list.

61. *Alcalde* is the mayor or chief magistrate of the village.

62. Ibid., fol. 42r.

63. Ibid., fol. 42v.

64. These two tachas appear in ibid., fol. 45r. Another tacha referring to Ropero appears on fol. 51r.

65. The two witness testimonies appear in ibid., fol. 46r; fol. 45v was blank.

66. Loc. cit.

67. Juan de Medina, his wife, Inéz, and the wives of Martín Blanco and Martín de Negredo all appeared to testify. The latter, an Old Christian, had employed a dishonest servant named María, whom she had heard was imprisoned, but whose husband she thought was a carpenter and who she thought was from Lozón. On this basis, the court assumed that this was not the María under discussion. Ibid., fol. 49r.

68. See ibid., fol. 47v.

69. Here he referred to himself as Francisco Hernández, the husband of Isabel López, although he was usually called Francisco de Murcia. See ibid., fol. 50r.

70. The wife of González de Ganboa, María González, faced trial from 1528 to 1530; see Leg. 155, n° 3.

71. Leg. 163, n° 8, fol. 51r.

72. At different times, she is referred to as having been in each one's employ. There is good reason to assume that she had worked for both families at one time or another.

73. Ibid., fol. 51v.

74. Ibid., fol. 52r.

75. This was a resident of Humanes named Juan Ropero; he referred to María of Humanes. See ibid., fols. 54r–v.

76. See Leg. 188, n° 9, fol. 21v.

77. The questions appear in ibid., fols. 23r–v; the lists are on fols. 24r–25v.

78. She testified on June 5, 1519; see ibid., fol. 26r.

79. Loc. cit.

80. Ibid., fol. 27r.

81. These testimonies appear in ibid., fols. 26v–27r.

82. These statements appear in ibid., fols. 27v–28v.

83. See ibid., fols. 29v–30r.

84. Perhaps his sibling lived elsewhere and Isabel did not become acquainted with her uncle until she was twenty-four.

85. See ibid., fols. 30v–31r.

86. This description complements the testimony of Bartolomé de la Vega above.

87. Ibid., fols. 31r.

88. Loc. cit.

89. Ibid., fols. 32r–33v.

90. Ibid., fol. 34r.

91. Pedro said that "[if] to light candles on Friday nights and to do forbidden household tasks were in the law of the Jews, then it follows that if they are lit, that the Sabbath is not being observed because if it were being observed, they wouldn't have to light them as on Friday nights, and if on those Friday nights they did indeed light the said candles as on the obvious Sabbaths, this was not done as a rite or a Judaic ceremony." Perhaps Pedro was distinguishing between Friday evening (*tarde*) and Friday night (*noche*), aware that lamps would not be lit on the latter. See ibid., fol. 35r.

92. Ibid., fol. 36v.

93. Ibid., fol. 37r.

94. Ibid., fol. 37v.

95. Ibid., fols. 37r–37v.

96. Ibid., fol. 38r.

97. Male descendants until the second order and females of the first were prohibited from receiving benefits, honors, or offices; from wearing clothes with gold or silk or camlet (a medieval Asian fabric made of camel hair or angora wool), coral, pearls, or precious stones; from riding horses; from bearing arms; from being advocates, surgeons, apothecaries, or landlords, or from using any of the other offices arbitrarily. Ibid., fols. 38v–39r.

98. Ibid., fol. 39v.

99. Leg. 163, n° 8, fol. 58r. It is interesting to compare the makeup of the consulta for each family member. The two main inquisitors were identical for all three; they were Sancho Vélez, a judge as of 1515, Juan de Mendoza, a judge as of 1516, and Don Francisco de Herrera, who was also a representative of the Archbishop of Toledo. Haim Beinart claims he was highly revered and began his career in this court in 1511; see Beinart, *Records of the Trials of the Spanish Inquisition in Ciudad Real* 4 (Jerusalem: Israel Academy of Sciences and Humanities, 1985), p. 70. The *licenciado* de Salvatierra was mayor of Toledo at the time and also a member of the court as of 1517. Additional judges were Pedro de la Peña, an abbot from a monastery who appeared in trial records from 1512 to 1535; Diego Jiménez Pan y Agua, who sat in many consultas from 1512 to 1521, as did Dr. Pedro Martínez from 1515 to 1521. All seven of these men were present in all three consultas. A Dominican monk from the order of Señor Santo Domingo sat in María's and Isabel's, and a minister from the monastery of the Holy Trinity of Toledo was the ninth member of María's group, while the first eight composed Isabel's consulta.

100. This is a reference to the Black Madonna of Montserrat, a medieval statue of the virgin kept in a shrine on the mountain of Montserrat, near Barcelona; it was considered to be a seat of divine wisdom. Pilgrimages, often accompanied by rituals of pain, offerings, and

vigil, were made to the site. The Black Madonna was considered to be a protectress with special powers, and the call here, akin to a call for a miracle, is ever so appropriate. See Mary Elizabeth Perry, "The Black Madonna of Montserrat," *Views of Women's Lives in Western Tradition*, ed. F. R. Keller (Lewiston, N.Y.: Edwin Mellen Press, 1990), pp. 110–128.

101. The quantities of liquid here are measured in *azumbres*, which are the equivalent of four pints.

102. This water torture consisted of tying the defendant down on a scaffold with the head lower than the body and covering the face with a headpiece. The victim experienced a sense of suffocation when the water was poured; pressure was simultaneously applied as the various ropes were tightened.

103. Leg. 163, n° 8, fol. 59r contains the partial information on the torture; fol. 59v is blank.

104. A unanimous decision by the consulta was required.

105. See Leg. 162, n° 6, fols. 46r–46v for the torture session.

106. Ibid., fol. 47v.

107. Each man was accorded a different title, namely *letrado* (university graduate in law, qualified to be part of senior Inquisition staff), *licenciado* (possessing advanced university degree, thus of higher status), and *procurador* (attorney or solicitor).

108. Leg. 188, n° 9, fol. 21v.

109. Ibid., fols. 21v–22r. In this case, there is no additional copy of the tachas in Pedro's file. Perhaps the tachas were used for the duration of the trial and then returned to the original file. The fact that the lists were so long might have discouraged the court from requesting that a notary make an additional copy for Pedro's file.

7. The Inquisition and the Midwife

1. A district inquisitor would travel about with a small staff, making inspections or *visitas*. This practice began in 1500. See William Monter, *Frontiers of Heresy* (Cambridge: Cambridge University Press, 1990), pp. 66–68; for a more detailed account, see Jean-Pierre Dedieu, *L'Administration de la Foi* (Madrid: Casa de Velazquez, 1989), pp. 183–190; and Dedieu, "Les inquisiteurs de Tolede et la visite du district," *Mélanges de la Casa de Velázquez* 13 (1977): 234–256. The proceedings appear in Leg. 177, n° 4 (696); the records cover the years 1536 to 1563.

2. This testimony appears on fols. 7v–7r. It will reappear much later, in 1550, in the form of witness testimony (number 3) for the prosecution.

3. *Partera* and *comadre* are Spanish terms for midwife.

4. She is referred to as being a New Christian of Jewish (ancestry).

5. Literally, he who has a bad neighbor has a bad morning or bad early morning prayers. See fol. 7v for these details as recounted by Juan.

6. See fol. 8r.

7. This description appears on fols. 8v–9r. Jacques Gélis points out that the midwife was expected to have a strong and sturdy physical build. See *The History of Childbirth* (Boston: Northeastern University Press, 1991), p. 105.

8. See fol. 8v.

9. The expression used was: *"Quien enojare a judio enoja ojo mio."* Fol. 9r.

10. Fol. 9r.

11. They were indeed copied from the Book of Testimonies twenty-two years later in an attempt to build a case for the prosecution and would emerge again in 1550; see above.

12. See fol. 6v. She was first presented with other information, and only at the end of the interrogation was she asked about this incident.

13. Fol. 6v.

14. The deposition of de Casarrubios appears on fols. 3r–3v and will later be used by the prosecution. Diego de Tapia's deposition will also appear later as testimony for the prosecution; see fols. 4r–4v.

15. The question of the role of the midwife in baptism arises here. In 1277, the Trier Synod stipulated that priests should give instruction to laywomen, usually midwives, in case of emergency baptism. "Because baptism was a necessary prerequisite to the salvation of the soul, midwives were under an obligation to ensure that the ultimate destiny of a baby unlikely to survive was the Kingdom of God and not the Kingdom of the Devil." Jean Towler and Joan Brumall, *Midwives in History and Society* (London: Croom Helm, 1986), p. 53. Sometimes, however, a priest was present at the time of delivery in case the newborn's life was at risk. *Midwives*, p. 30. Yet in Spain, the art of midwifery was exclusively female because of the "necessity of protecting women's modesty." See Teresa Ortiz, "From Hegemony to Subordination: Midwives in Early Modern Spain," *The Art of Midwifery: Early Modern Midwives in Europe*, ed. Hilary Marland (London and New York: Routledge, 1993), p. 96. I would like to thank the editor for sending me a prepublication manuscript as well as the author for allowing me to read it.

In various countries, including Spain in the sixteenth century, there were books available in the vernacular which could guide midwives and which often contained oaths for them to say at the time of baptism. Unfortunately, most of the midwives in Europe were illiterate. For an example of such an oath as sworn by an English midwife in 1567, see Towler and Brumall, *Midwives*, pp. 56–57. Here the oath included "that in such time of necessity, in baptising any infant born, and pouring water upon the head of the same infant, I will use pure and clean water, and not any rose or damask water, or water made of any confection or mixture; and that I will certify the curate of the parish church of every such baptising."

In Spain, Damián Carbón, a Castilian doctor, published the first book on childbirth in Spain (and the second in Europe), *Libro del arte de las comadres y del regimiento de las preñadas y paridas y de los niños* (Mallorca, 1541), which was presumably intended for midwives. See Ortiz, *Art of Midwifery*, p. 97, for a discussion of these first Spanish medical books for midwives. Rosa Ballester points out that these guidebooks ostensibly emphasized the importance of the midwife due to their social and cultural access to their patients and how they could work in tandem with the doctors. In addition to their technical skills, the midwife had to be moral, devoted to the Virgin Mary and all the saints, and above all, not engage in superstitious practices. See "Ethical Perspectives in the Care of Infants in Sixteenth to Eighteenth Century Spain," *Medicine and Medical Ethics in Medieval and Early Modern Spain: An Intercultural Approach*, ed. Samuel S. Kottek and Luís García-Ballester (Jerusalem: Magnes Press, 1996), pp. 205–206. This book has an interesting collection of essays dealing with Jews, conversos, and medical practices.

16. This incident is odd indeed, since the parents appear to have been present during the entire church baptism; how had they been so oblivious to Beatriz's declaration and affirmation?

17. This was Francisco Pérez, whose deposition appears on fol. 1v.

18. On March 18, 1536, Leonor Rodríguez, wife of Bernaldo Díaz, testified that her mother had gone to Portugal twelve days before. See fol. 2r.

19. Only Juan gives his age (about thirty years old), so the sibling order is unknown in

this family. The son testified, "It is fourteen days today since his said mother told him that she wanted to go to Portugal to Evora, the city where the brother she had is [located]; this witness did not say anything. And he saw her go one day before dawn and she said goodbye to this witness. And the same [man] that guided Diego Díaz, the drover, husband of Catalina Méndez, the sister of this witness, went with her." See fols. 2r–2v. Juan's father was clearly the first (old Christian) husband of Beatriz, for both men's names were Martín. Leonor retained her mother's name of Rodríguez, while her sister Catalina was called Méndez. Since Beatriz had been married for a longer period of time to her first husband, perhaps she had all three children with him during those eight years.

20. This testimony appears on fol. 2v; Beatriz appears to have had three children, since Catalina mentions two siblings, the same two who were also questioned.

21. See fol. 5r.

22. This midwife had lied, and the Church could not tolerate untrustworthiness on the part of such an important layperson. "The midwife's character and religious beliefs were of vital concern to the ecclesiastical authorities who were anxious that she should not shield from discovery and punishment those falling short of the standards of chastity laid down by the Church." While this is not a case of a concealed birth, a destroyed child, or a bastard birth, the lack of honesty was equally disconcerting. See Jean Donnison, *Midwives and Medical Men* (London: Heinemann, 1977), pp. 3–4.

23. See fol. 5r.

24. See fol. 5v.

25. See fol. 6r.

26. See fols. 6r–6v.

27. The fact that Beatriz did not seem to know about the tacha process is surprising; by 1536, the converso community had sufficient experience with inquisitorial procedure and was aware of the fact that, with luck, one might even manage to have the trial dismissed on the basis of effective tachas.

28. See fol. 7r.

29. In the list of transgressions of conversos against Christianity published in 1460 by Alonso de Espina in *Fortalitium Fidei*, book 2, the claim is made that they pretended "that at birth the lives of their children were in danger, so that their baptism had to be held at home without church ceremony." See Haim Beinart, *Conversos on Trial* (Jerusalem: Magnes Press, 1981), p. 13.

30. At no point in the trial was there mention of the background of the parents; one assumes they were Old Christians, but no classification was made.

31. This instance does not appear to be a case of dechristianization; see Beinart, *Conversos on Trial*, p. 290, for references to this practice in Ciudad Real.

32. If this couple were New Christian, one might speculate that Beatriz was trying to protect the infant and that her act was one of defiance. However, it appears that she feared for the soul of the baby; knowing she was allowed to apply the water, she hoped to avoid rebuke of the parents by the clergymen.

33. The appropriate source to consult concerning local church law in Toledo during this period would be *Constituciones Sinodales del Arzobispado de Toledo*, published in 1536 by Archbishop Juan Tavera. Unfortunately it is nowhere to be found in the United States. Thus the only source pertaining to the Archbishopric of Toledo that I have been able to obtain is *Concilios provinciales y Sínodos toledanos de los siglos XIV y XV* (La Laguna: Universidad de la Laguna, 1976) by José Sánchez Herrero. In the discussion of baptism on page 126, one finds:

"La materia de este sacramento es el agua verdadera y natural, no pudiéndose bautizar con vino, aceite, agua rosada o algún otro licor, . . ." (The material for this sacrament is true and natural water, baptizing with wine, oil, rosewater, or any other liquid not being permitted . . .). Concerning emergency baptisms, *"El ministro es el sacerdote, pero en caso de necesidad puede administrarlo la comadrona o cualquier otro hombre o mujer, hasta el padre o la madre utilizando la materia y forma debida, imponiéndole el nimbre y diciendo: Ego te Petrum vel Martinum baptizo. . . ."* (The ministerer is the priest, but in case of emergency, the midwife or any other man or woman may administer it, even the father or mother, using the material and form required, imposing the name and saying: I baptize you, Petrus or Martinus, . . .) No other mention is made of midwives or partial baptisms; however, the site of baptism is also discussed on the same page: *"El bautismo, a no ser en caso de necesidad, debería administrarse en la iglesia, pues allí es donde hay pilas especialmente preparadas para ello."* (Baptism, except in case of emergency, must be administered in church, because that is where there are fonts specially prepared for it.)

34. See Gélis, *History of Childbirth,* p. 194.

35. Examples of such cases can be found in sixteenth-century pre-Reformation Germany. "This conditional baptism assured parents that their child had been baptized correctly and was not considered an actual rebaptism." See Merry E. Wiesner, *Working Women in Renaissance Germany* (New Brunswick, N.J.: Rutgers University Press, 1986), pp. 72–73, for a discussion of this phenomenon. This book has marvelous material on midwives in sixteenth-century Nuremberg; I would like to thank the author for helping me to familiarize myself with material on European midwives and for her encouragement as well.

36. See Towler and Brumall, *Midwives in History,* p. 39. The authors, contend (p. 38) that "wise women-midwives were valued by the community because they were known and trusted, and therein lay their challenge to the *Church which hated both women themselves and their power of healing"* (my emphasis). Women healers were considered to represent an unacceptable part of peasant subculture. See Barbara Ehrenreich and Deirdre English, *Witches, Midwives, and Nurses: A History of Women Healers* (London: Compendium, 1974), p. 13.

37. This quotation as well as the above information was obtained from the entry, "Midwifery," in the *Women's Studies Encyclopedia* 1 (New York: Greenwood Press, 1989), pp. 236–240, by Alison Klairmont Lingo. I would like to thank the author for sending me this piece along with other material. Concerning superstition, Jean Donnison writes: "Indeed the whole process of childbirth was the focus of a mass of ancient superstitious beliefs which still played an important part in Christian thinking. The act of giving birth was believed to defile the mother, who could be re-admitted to the church only after a service of purification or 'churching.' Moreover, the fact that the umbilical cord, caul, afterbirth and still-born foetus played an important part in the rites of witchcraft provided additional justification for the Church's attempts to control midwives and to punish those who in any way departed from the prescribed code." *Midwives and Medical Men,* p. 4. An example of fear of midwives appears in the 1575 *Tractatus de fascinatione* by Frommann: "The Devil arranges through the midwives not only the abortive death of the fetuses lest they be brought to the holy font of baptism, but also by their [the midwives] aid he causes newborn babies secretly to be consecrated to himself." See Thomas Rogers Forbes, *The Midwife and the Witch* (New Haven, Conn.: Yale University Press, 1966), p. 127.

38. Mary Elizabeth Perry, *Gender and Disorder in Early Modern Seville* (Princeton, N.J.: Princeton University Press, 1990), p. 27. In Seville in 1538 and in 1558, requests were made to examine midwives in the presence of two doctors, who would notify the government offi-

cials if they were competent. See Luis S. Granjel, *La medicina española renacentista* (Salamanca: Ediciones Universidad de Salamanca, 1980), p. 136. Forbes (*Midwife and Witch*, p. 112) wrote that "the midwife, particularly in rural areas, was often ignorant and superstitious. The dubious skill which she brought to the delivery was a blend of hearsay, empiricism, and superstition." Concerning charges of immorality, see Perry, *Gender and Disorder*, p. 27.

39. See Luis García Ballester, *Los Moriscos y la medicina* (Barcelona: Labor Universitaria, 1984), p. 116.

40. In "Male Discourse and Female Deviance in the Spanish Inquisition," Mary Elizabeth Perry writes (p. 2 of unpublished manuscript): "A critical rereading of these documents reveals a gendered language and gender stereotypes, but it also uncovers significant silences, male fears and bewilderment, covert female subversion, and clues to female experience." The same historian discusses midwives and women healers in her article, "Las mujeres y su trabajo curativo en Sevilla, siglos XVI y XVII," *El trabajo de la mujeres: Siglos XVI–XX,* ed. María Jesús Matilla and Margarita Ortega (Madrid: Universidad Autonoma de Madrid, 1987), pp. 40–50; in English, a similar discussion appears in Perry, *Gender and Disorder*, pp. 20–32. I would like to thank the author for sending me papers, both unpublished and published, and especially for enthusiastically supporting my research.

41. "Inquisition records show that women played active roles as well as the passive roles of victimization. Indeed, women participated in the inquisitors' discourse, giving testimony as both witnesses and the accused. They tried to obey in saying what they believed inquisitors wanted them to say, but they also sought influence and ways to express criticism through denouncing themselves and others, making confessions, and answering questions." Perry, "Male Discourse," p. 3.

42. Again, Perry contends that the "Inquisitors used language to reimpose gender limitations on women who had defied them." "Male Discourse," p. 2. María Helena Sánchez Ortega writes: "In Spain, the view of women as the supreme embodiment of carnality, promulgated by the Church fathers compelled to wage a war against women, was inherited by the Hapsburg Regime. The Inquisition trials contain many examples of this juxtaposition of classical and Christian ideas, which transforms many women into objects of suspicion because of their evil powers, especially since society believed them to be endowed with sexual energies capable of weakening, effacing, or corrupting men's wills." See "Woman as Source of 'Evil' in Counter-Reformation Spain," *Culture and Control in Counter-Reformation Spain,* ed. Anne J. Cruz and Mary Elizabeth Perry (Minneapolis: University of Minnesota Press, 1992), p. 197.

43. This possibility was suggested by Mary Elizabeth Perry in her comments on my paper presented at the session entitled "Women, Gender, and Jewish Identity" at the conference, "The Expulsion of the Jews 1492 and After," at the University of California, Davis on April 2, 1992.

44. Perry comments.

45. Fol. 7v.

46. Fols. 10r–10v.

47. Fols. 11v–12r.

48. Fol. 14r.

49. Fol. 14v.

50. There is no doubt that the Inquisition had a psychological edge on its prisoners; it has been termed the "pedagogy of fear" by Bartolomé Bennassar in "L'Inquisition ou la pédagogie de la peur," *L'Inquisition espagnole: XVe–XIXe siècle,* ed. Bartolomé Bennassar et al. (Paris: Hachette, 1979), pp. 105–141.

51. This interrogation appears on fol. 15r.

52. Fol. 16r. This is not terribly convincing, since the Inquisition had no depositions concerning any judaizing activities on her part.

53. Fol. 16v. This explanation is likewise dubious, since the child was not of New Christian stock. Why should she have acted in this manner—merely for spite?

54. This is the third count; see fol. 16v. Her comments did not prove any judaizing involvement on her part; any New Christian would have just cause to resent Old Christians in sixteenth-century Castile.

55. This is part of the fourth charge listed on fol. 16v.

56. The fifth marks the beginning of standard closing charges presented to judaizers; see fol. 17r.

57. The sixth and seventh counts are almost formulae; loc. cit.

58. Lawyers could help if tacha lists were being drawn up, but in this case, Beatriz did not seek to invalidate witnesses. On the contrary, she confessed to actions which were never even mentioned in any of the witness testimonies. For his part, her lawyer simply admonished his "client" to tell the truth. See fol. 18v.

59. See fols. 22r–22v.

60. Fol. 27v.

61. This was the "sacred cloth" or penitential scapular worn by reconciled penitents as well as by convicted heretics. See fol. 28r.

62. Loc. cit.

63. Fol. 28v.

64. This pronouncement was made in August 1550; see fol. 25v.

65. On one hand, this tribunal seems relentless in choosing to seek out and imprison Beatriz without having new evidence against her. On the other hand, it must have taken into account her age, the fact that she probably had been a "good Catholic" since her encounter with the inquisitor in 1536, and the fact that her observance of Judaism was minimal.

66. At this advanced age, it is doubtful if Beatriz returned to her practice; in addition, now that she was an affirmed judaizer, both Old and New Christians would be reluctant to employ her even if she were able to function in her profession. Perry commented: "Wasn't hers really a death sentence? How could she survive in her eighties, with no position to support herself and her goods confiscated . . . how effectively the Inquisition silenced this woman—once strong, outspoken, independent and respected—now in her old age, penniless, positionless, powerless." Expulsion Conference, University of California, Davis.

8. The Judaizers of the Alcázar at the End of the Sixteenth Century

1. William Monter notes the end of this first phase for Aragon in 1530: "by 1530 there were signs that the great hunt for conversos was finally ebbing in the Crown of Aragon." *Frontiers of Heresy* (Cambridge: Cambridge University Press, 1990), p. 26. He points out that the record of the various tribunals in this kingdom "during the first half-century of activity was relatively impressive both in quality and quantity. Over 500 conversos (and a few dozen offenders of other sorts) had been executed in public, while thousands more had been publicly penanced and heavily fined." Loc. cit. At the same time, new research is challenging the assumption that the Inquisition did not deal with native Spanish judaizers after this period. See, for example, Rafael Carrasco, "Preludio al 'Siglo de los Portugueses': La Inquisición de Cuenca y los judaizantes lusitanos en el siglo XVI," *Hispania* 47:166 (1987): 503–559; and

Charles Amiel, "El criptojudaísmo castellano en La Mancha a fines del siglo XVI," in *Judíos. Sefarditas. Conversos. La expulsión de 1492 y sus consecuencias*, ed. Ángel Alcalá, (Valladolid: Ámbito Ediciones, 1995), pp. 503–512. I thank Claude Stuczynski for bringing these two articles to my attention.

2. "Because these tribunals, conveniently grouped in a separate Secretariat after 1518, had begun to branch out beyond converso Judaizers in their constant search for heretical delinquents, they were able to prosper anew in the latter part of Charles' reign, after heretical conversos became scarce." Monter, *Frontiers*, pp. 26–27. Charles I ruled Spain from 1516 to 1555; this was Charles V, the Holy Roman emperor.

3. Carrasco claims that Portuguese immigration began beforehand as the result of commercial interests; "Preludio," p. 540. As a matter of fact, he refers to various waves of immigration in the sixteenth century (p. 548).

4. This phenomenon was noted, albeit erroneously, by the eminent historian of the Inquisition, Henry Charles Lea, who thought these judaizers were Portuguese conversos from Quintanar del Rey. See *A History of the Inquisition of Spain* 3 (New York: Macmillan, 1907), p. 267. Charles Amiel points out this error and assumed that Lea (mis)read the 1598 publication by the Sicilian Inquisitor Luis de Páramo entitled, *De origine et progressu Officii Sanctae Inquisitionis* 3, p. 304. Even in this contemporary report, an error was made, this time numerical, for only thirty (rather than one hundred) judaizers were mentioned. See Amiel, "El criptojudaísmo," pp. 503 and 511, n.1.

5. This area is called Mancha de Aragón or de Montearagón and includes the communities of Quintanar de la Órden, Argamasilla de Alba, and Alcázar de Consuegra, today known as Alcázar de San Juan.

6. Juan Blázquez Miguel, *La Inquisición en Castilla–La Mancha* (Madrid: Libreria Anticuaria Jerez, 1986), p. 74 (translation mine). French scholar Charles Amiel is also dealing with the phenomenon under discussion in this chapter; he notes that he is currently engaged in writing a book about the five generations of pure Castilian converso crypto-Jews, their observances, and their "sophisticated perceptions" of Judaism. "El criptojudaísmo," p. 505. He agrees wholeheartedly that this was not a revitalization of observance as the result of a Portuguese presence (p. 509). At the same time, Carrasco refers to this community and writes that the discovery of these native judaizers led to a revived and somewhat aggressive interest in judaizers on the part of the Inquisition at the end of the century; this revival included an interest in the Portuguese newcomers. "Preludio," p. 523. He also points out that when the Portuguese arrived, they had no contact with the locals and that in Castile, the native conversos and judaizers in La Mancha intentionally avoided còntact with the Portuguese (which was not the case, for example, in Andalusia). See "Preludio," pp. 516, 532–533.

7. Nevertheless, there are precedents for active judaizers in this community, and the Inquisition dealt with them. Juana Martínez, the wife of Alvar García, the cobbler, resided in Alcázar de Consuegra but was tried sixty years prior to the conversos whose trials will be analyzed here. Her trial record, Leg. 165, nº 2, is very rich and offers a great deal of insight into crypto-Jewish life in this village in the earlier part of the century. Juana first confessed in 1486, when she specified that her mother had been the source of her knowledge. Her sister's confession, also from 1486, as well those of two of her brothers-in-law and a half-brother, are included in the files. There was a distinct style in the confession of the men: they attributed initiating activities to the women and referred to "allowing" or "consenting" as opposed to actively observing. Juana was questioned about her confession forty-four years later, and she pointed out that she had never observed with her husband. The tribunal ultimately decided

to imprison her and confiscate her goods, but she was eventually absolved and, being old and not in the best of health, was freed after a year of prison. For descriptions of this trial, see my article, "Les femmes crypto-juives face à l'Inquisition espagnole: Leur rôle dans la transmission du marranisme," *Transmission et passages en monde juif,* ed. Esther Benbassa (Paris: Publisud, 1997), pp. 229–245. The English version is "Crypto-Jewish Women Facing the Spanish Inquisition: Transmitting Religious Practices, Beliefs, and Attitudes," *Christians, Muslims and Jews of Medieval and Early Modern Spain,* ed. Mark D. Meyerson (Notre Dame, Ind.: University of Notre Dame, 1999). For details of this trial, see appendix 3 for translations of relevant excerpts from the trial, and a synopsis of its outcome.

8. It seems that Alcázar was more or less in ruins when acquired by this order, but it was then repopulated.

9. The former's trial is Leg. 138, nº 8 (1590–94); the latter's, which essentially includes his wife, Ana del Campo, is Leg. 187, nº 8 (1590–91).

10. These lists appear on fols. 1v in each trial.

11. These lists appear on fol. 2v in each trial. There is an additional witness who testified in del Campo's trial, Francisco Ruíz de Armenia, whose testimony was included in de la Vega's trial as well. Four women, also not listed on fol. 2v, were interrogated by the inquisitors in del Campo's proceedings in the framework of the prosecution depositions. Concerning the list in de la Vega's trial, one of the thirteen witnesses never testified, namely, the sixteenth, Francisco de Mora. See appendix 2 for complete lists from both trials.

12. Seven of them appeared in both lists in Juan's trial; in de la Vega's trial, thirteen of the witnesses for the prosecution appeared in the defendant's deposition as well.

13. See Leg. 138, nº 8, fol. 43v. for these details regarding his family.

14. Leg. 187, nº 8, fols. 3r–3v.

15. It is interesting that this term, *"de la casta de judíos,"* of Jewish caste, seems to have entered the vocabulary of the conversos themselves by the end of the sixteenth century. The term *"casta y generación"* is cited by Angela S. Selke as being used in seventeenth-century Mayorca; see *The Conversos of Majorca* (Jerusalem: Magnes Press, 1986), p. 89.

16. Leg. 187, nº 8, fol. 4r.

17. See Leg. 138, nº 8, fols. 3r–3v.

18. See ibid., fol. 2v; seven of the prosecution witnesses are common to both trials, and in Juan's file are notations as to who was reconciled, such as Juan López de Armenia and his father and six others.

19. Ibid., fols. 4r–4v and Leg. 187, nº 8, fols. 5r–5v.

20. Leg. 187, nº 8, fol. 6r.

21. She specified that one was at the time of Easter, one was in May, and the third was in September at the time of the annual fair in Alcázar. Ibid., fol. 7r.

22. There are other mentions in these trials of washing one's hands prior to engaging in prayer.

23. Catalina's testimony appears in Leg. 187, nº 8, fols. 7r–v.

24. Ibid., fol. 8r.

25. His precise words were that the three of them were *"de casta y generación de confesos."* See ibid., fol. 8v.

26. This statement appears in ibid., fols. 8v–8r.

27. Leg. 138, nº 8, fol. 7v. One washes one's hands before the morning prayers; at this time, a blessing is recited as well.

28. Leg. 187, nº 8, fols. 9r–9v.

29. Ibid., fols. 9v–10r.

30. Ibid., fols. 10r–10v.

31. It should be kept in mind that the members of this family were termed poor, and a laborer would not be able to afford household help. The short version appears in Leg. 138, n° 8, fols. 4v–5v; the information to follow is from Leg. 187, n° 8, fols. 14r–23r.

32. For an attempt to analyze some of the prayers found in these two files, see Renée Levine Melammed, "Judaizers and Prayer in Sixteenth Century Alcázar," *In Iberia and Beyond,* ed. Bernard Cooperman (Newark, Del.: University of Delaware Press, 1998), pp. 273–295

33. These additions appear in Leg. 187, n° 8, fols. 21r–22v. Here he presented two misconceptions, that women were forbidden to slaughter, and about when one is required by Jewish law to wash one's hands.

34. See ibid., fol. 23r.

35. See ibid., fols. 14r–15v.

36. This detail emerged during an interrogation recorded in ibid., fol. 17v.

37. An interesting comment appears here: Francisco supposedly told Lope not to observe in the presence of his children, for he had not taught them. Ibid., fol. 16r.

38. See Leg. 138, n° 8, fols. 4v–5r. Note that the testimonies included in each trial differed, depending upon which information was relevant to the case.

39. She said she was *"de parte de padre y madre de casta y generación de christianos [sic] nuevos."* Ibid., fol. 8v.

40. There is clearly an inconsistency here regarding her age, for she originally claimed to be forty. One must assume that she was considerably older.

41. This was probably an aunt, although her name does not appear elsewhere in these files.

42. Leg. 138, n° 8, fols. 9v–10r.

43. Ibid., fols. 10r–10v.

44. See Leg. 187, n° 8, fols. 25r–26r. Perhaps the brothers married first and came to their mother's house to help out; if the sisters married first, then they would have to slaughter when their brothers-in-law were not home.

45. Ibid., fol. 26r.

46. Ibid., fol. 26v.

47. As was already mentioned, the washing was accompanied by a blessing before morning prayers, but there is no mention of time of day and whether a blessing was indeed made.

48. Leg. 187, n° 8, fols. 10v–11r. In the file of del Campo, Leg. 138, n° 8, the scribe also appeared. Here he referred to communications between various cousins, del Campo, and his mother. For example, he referred to a letter from del Campo auguring the grape harvest, which he understood to be an allusion to an upcoming Jewish holiday. See fols. 16v–17v.

49. See Renée Levine Melammed, "The Ultimate Challenge: Safeguarding the Crypto-Judaic Heritage," *Proceedings of the American Academy for Jewish Research* 53 (1986): 91–109, regarding the age at which children were initiated into judaizing.

50. It is rather difficult to determine the family ties here, for the father of the defendant Francisco was named Alonso de la Vega, as was the father of both María and Francisco the scribe. Because the mothers' names differ, it is quite possible that Alonso married twice, one wife being Elvira de Mora and the other being Leonor Gómez. If that was indeed the case, it is odd that María referred to her half-brothers and sisters as cousins; perhaps this was a euphemism.

51. See Leg. 187, n° 8, fol. 11v.

52. One's feet are placed together during the silent *Amidah* portion of morning, afternoon, and evening prayers, said daily as well as on the Sabbath. During recitation of the *Shema* (Hear O Israel), the eyes are covered with one's hand.

53. See Leg. 138, n° 8, fols. 18r–22v. María said that her mother had literally gone crazy, but she did not blame her mother for convincing her to observe. She was clear about three influential figures: the defendant, Juan del Campo, who was preceded by María López de Armenia, and her sister Catalina Gómez.

54. Ana did not seem to be related to Juan del Campo.

55. This is the beginning of "Hear O Israel."

56. Leg. 187, n° 8, fols. 12r–13v.

57. Leg. 138, n° 8, fol. 6v.

58. Ibid., fols. 11r–11v.

59. Her age is not stated, so it is hard to know if her vagaries were intentional or could be attributed to advanced age. Ibid., fols. 12r–14v.

60. María de la O. made no mention of a romantic tie to the defendant, Juan del Campo.

61. The daughter claimed that she snatched it out of their hands, but since she mentioned wanting a new copy, one assumes she was not successful in reclaiming it. At the same time, this clergyman, deceased by 1590, must not have reported the incident, since no trials were begun at that time in Alcázar. Leg. 138, n° 8, fol. 15v.

62. Ibid., fols. 15r–16r. Interestingly, Francisco the scribe referred to this piece of paper, explaining that it was retrieved from María de la O. when the men realized that neither she nor her mother could read it! Ibid., fol. 16v.

63. There is also the possibility that her father was a devout Catholic and that Juan was judaizing, but Isabel's defense of her husband was either accurate or naive. See ibid., fols. 23r–28r.

64. Ibid., fol. 28r.

65. It is difficult to discern if this was the same woman mentioned above, although one would tend to assume so if only because of the uncommon name. However, the thirty-year-old María de la O. said that she was a resident and native of Alcázar and that Antonio Falcón was her husband, whereas Pedro Barrera was cited as the spouse of this twenty-two-year-old woman from Argamasilla.

66. Leg. 138, n° 8, fols. 28v–29v, for original testimony; ratification and signature appear on fols. 31v–32r.

67. Ibid., fols. 29r–29v.

68. Ibid., fols. 30r–31v.

69. Ibid., fols. 33v–36r.

70. Ibid., fol. 36v.

71. It is possible that they were of Old Christian stock, although not likely. When an Old Christian appeared before the tribunal, he or she usually made an effort to emphasize the untainted ancestry.

Conclusion

1. The similarities are striking and numerous enough to merit a separate comparative study. For example, Perry points to birth and death rituals as well as food and bathing rites such as "changing into clean clothing on Fridays and eating meat cooked in oil rather than lard" (p. 44). See "Behind the Veil," *Spanish Women in the Golden Age: Images and Realities,*

ed. Magdalena S. Sánchez and Alain Saint-Saëns (Westport, Conn.: Greenwood Press, 1996), pp. 37–53.

2. At first, the Crown accused the Jews of subversion because they were communicating with and instructing the conversos. Once they were expelled, the conversos became guilty of subversion.

3. The encounter between Spanish and Portuguese émigrés of New Christian past and Jewish communities outside of Iberia is the proof of the pudding. The majority of these men and women miraculously managed to adapt to normative Judaism and were accepted into (or created their own) Jewish communities without a conversion ceremony. This aspect of adaptation by New Christians joining their brethren in the Diaspora is itself fascinating. See, for example, the articles in Haim Beinart, *The Sephardi Legacy* 2 (Jerusalem: Magnes Press, 1992).

4. A successful defense did not prove or disprove the guilt or innocence of the defendant, but indicated only that he or she had managed to disqualify the witnesses for the prosecution. As has been pointed out, once the testimonies were disqualified, the question of judaizing remained a possibility that could yet be entertained in another trial, albeit with different and more dependable witnesses.

Bibliography

Primary Sources

Archivo Histórico Nacional, Madrid. Inquisition Files, Judaizantes, Archibishopric of Toledo

Leg. 131, n⁰ 5 (1493–94).

Leg. 132, n⁰ 7 (1502–3).

Leg. 133, n⁰ 2 (1504–6).

Leg. 132, n⁰ 8 (1500–1501).

Leg. 133, n⁰ 13 (1514–15).

Leg. 133, n⁰ 18 (1497–99).

Leg. 133, n⁰ 20 (1495–96).

Leg. 134, n⁰ 4 (1492–93).

Leg. 134, n⁰ 5 (1492–93).

Leg. 134, n⁰ 7 (1500–1501).

Leg. 134, n⁰ 8 (1516–18).

Leg. 134, n⁰ 12 (1500–1501).

Leg. 134, n⁰ 14 (1492–93).

Leg. 134, n⁰ 15 (1507).

Leg. 137, n⁰ 7 (1500–1501).

Leg. 137, n⁰ 8 (1500–1501).

Leg. 137, n⁰ 9 (1500–1502).

Leg. 138, n⁰ 8 (1590–94).

Leg. 141, n⁰ 14 (1511–12).

Leg. 143, n⁰ 9 (1502–3).

Leg. 143, n⁰ 14 (1500–1501).

Leg. 143, n⁰ 18 (1498–99).

Leg. 144, n⁰ 3 (1491–92).

Leg. 148, n⁰ 10 (1502).

Leg. 149, n⁰ 7 (1511–12).

Leg. 150, n⁰ 11 (1500–1501).

Leg. 151, n⁰ 6 (1515–16).

Leg. 153, n⁰ 10 (1487–94).

Leg. 153, n⁰ 11 (1497).

Leg. 153, n⁰ 12 (1500–1501).

Leg. 153, n⁰ 13 (1500–1501).

Leg. 153, n⁰ 17 (1502).

Leg. 153, n⁰ 18 (1502–3).

Leg. 154, n⁰ 33 (1500).

Leg. 154, n⁰ 34 (1500).

Leg. 154, n⁰ 35 (1502–3).

Leg. 155, n⁰ 6 (1500–1501).

Leg. 155, n⁰ 7 (1513–20).

Leg. 157, n⁰ 2 (1530–31).

Leg. 158, n⁰ 2 (1500–1501).

Leg. 158, n⁰ 3 (1501–2).

Leg. 158, n⁰ 6 (1501).

Leg. 158, n⁰ 7 (1501).

Leg. 158, n⁰ 8 (1502–3).

Leg. 158, n⁰ 9 ((1520–23).

Leg. 158, n⁰ 12 (1506–7).

Leg. 158, n⁰ 19 (1501–3).

Leg. 159, n⁰ 15 (1520–21).

Leg. 160, n⁰ 5 (1503–4).

Leg. 160, n⁰ 14 (1492–94).

Leg. 160, n⁰ 15 (1510–11).

Leg. 162, n⁰ 3 (1495–96).

Leg. 162, n⁰ 6 (1516–1518).

Leg. 162, n⁰ 21 (1509–12).

Leg. 163, n° 7 (1512–22).

Leg. 163, n° 8 (1516–21).

Leg. 163, n° 11 (1501–2).

Leg. 164, n° 4 (1531–39).

Leg. 164, n° 11 (1493–94).

Leg. 164, n° 12 (1493–94).

Leg. 164, n° 21 (1509–12).

Leg. 165, n° 2 (1530–32).

Leg. 165, n° 7 (1520–21).

Leg. 169, n° 6 (1501).

Leg. 172, n° 4 (1513–15).

Leg. 176, n° 1 (1500–1501).

Leg. 177, n° 4 (1536–63).

Leg. 177, n° 6 (1493).

Leg. 178, n° 2 (1500–1502).

Leg. 178, n° 13 (1498–99).

Leg. 178, n° 15 (1501).

Leg. 180, n° 10 (1498–99).

Leg. 181, n° 3 (1492–93)

Leg. 181, n° 4 (1493–94).

Leg. 181, n° 5 (1497).

Leg. 181, n° 12 (1498–99).

Leg. 181, n° 13 (1500–1517).

Leg. 183, n° 11 (1502–3).

Leg. 183, n° 17 (1502–4).

Leg. 187, n° 8 (1590–91).

Leg. 188, n° 9 (1518–21).

Books

Baer, Fritz. *Die Juden Im Christlichen Spanien* 1. Berlin: Schocken, 1929.

Baer, Yitzhak. *A History of the Jews in Christian Spain*, 2 vols. Philadelphia: Jewish Publication Society, 1966 and 1992.

Beinart, Haim. *Records of the Trials of the Spanish Inquisition in Ciudad Real*, 4 vols. Jerusalem: Israel Academy of Sciences and Humanities, 1974–85.

———. *Conversos on Trial*. Jerusalem: Magnes Press, 1981.

———. *Atlas of Medieval Jewish History*. New York: Simon & Schuster, 1992.

———. *The Sephardi Legacy*, 2 vols. Jerusalem: Magnes Press, 1992.

Bennassar, Bartolomé et al., ed. *L'Inquisition espagnole: XV–XIX siècle*. Paris: Marabout, 1979.

Blázquez Miguel, Juan. *La Inquisición en Castilla–La Mancha*. Madrid: Librería Anticuaria Jerez, 1986.

Carbón, Damián. *Libro del arte de las comadres y del regimiento de las preñadas y paridas y de los niños*. Mallorca, 1541.

Contreras, Jaime. *Sotos contra Riquelmes: Regidores, inquisidores y criptojudíos*. Madrid: Anaya, 1992.

Dedieu, Jean–Pierre. *L'Administration de la Foi*. Madrid: Casa de Velazquez, 1989.

Donnison, Jean. *Midwives and Medical Men*. London: Heinemann, 1977.

Ehrenreich, Barbara, and Deirdre English. *Witches, Midwives, and Nurses: A History of Women Healers*. London: Compendium, 1974.

Forbes, Thomas Rogers. *The Midwife and the Witch*. New Haven, Conn.: Yale University Press, 1966.

García Ballester, Luis. *Los Moriscos y la medicina*. Barcelona: Labor Universitaria, 1984.

García Cárcel, Ricardo. *Orígenes de la Inquisición Española: El tribunal de Valencia 1478–1530*. Barcelona: Ediciones Peninsula, 1976.

Gélis, Jacques. *The History of Childbirth*. Boston: Northeastern University Press, 1991.

Gitlitz, David M. *Secrecy and Deceit: The Religion of the Crypto-Jews*. Philadelphia: Jewish Publication Society, 1996.

Gerber, Jane S. *The Jews of Spain*. New York: Free Press, 1992.

Granjel, Luis S. *La medicina española renacentista*. Salamanca: Ediciones Universidad de Salamanca, 1980.

Lea, Henry Charles. *A History of The Inquisition of Spain*. New York: Macmillan, 1907.

León Tello, Pilar. *Judíos de Avila*. Diputación Provincial de Avila: Instituto Gran Duque de Alba, 1963.

The Memoirs of Gluckel of Hameln, trans. M. Lowenthal. New York: Schocken Books, 1977.

Monter, William. *Frontiers of Heresy*. Cambridge: Cambridge University Press, 1990.

Netanyahu, B. *The Marranos of Spain from the Late Fourteenth to the Early Sixteenth Century According to the Hebrew Sources*. New York: American Academy for Jewish Research, 1966.

Perry, Mary Elizabeth. *Gender and Disorder in Early Modern Seville*. Princeton, N.J.: Princeton University Press, 1990.

Peters, Edward. *Inquisition*. Berkeley: University of California, 1989.

Raphael, David, ed. *The Expulsion 1492 Chronicles*. North Hollywood, Calif.: Carmi House Press, 1992.

Roth, Cecil. *Doña Gracia of the House of Nasi*. Philadelphia: Jewish Publication Society, 1977.

Sánchez Herrero, José. *Concilios provinciales y Sínodos toledanos de los siglos XIV y XV*. La Laguna: Universidad de la Laguna, 1976.

Selke, Angela S. *The Conversos of Majorca*. Jerusalem: Magnes Press, 1986.

Sicroff, Albert A. *Les controverses des statuts de pureté de sang en Espagne du XVe au XVIIe siècle*. Paris: M. Didier, 1960.

Suarez Fernández, Luis. *Documentos acerca de la expulsión de los Judíos*. Valladolid: Consejo Superior de Investigaciones Científicas, 1964.

Towler, Jean, and Joan Brumall. *Midwives in History and Society*. London: Croom Helm, 1986.

Wiesner, Merry E. *Working Women in Renaissance Germany*. New Brunswick, N.J.: Rutgers University Press, 1986.

Zlotnick, Dov, trans. and ed. *The Tractate "Mourning."* New Haven, Conn.: Yale University Press, 1966.

Hebrew Books

Babylonian Talmud. Baba Batra, Hullin, Moed Katan.

Maimonides. *Mishneh Torah*, Hilkhot Avelut.

Moses b. Yaakov of Coucy. *Sefer Mitsvot Gadol*. Mukachevo (Hungary): Druck von Káhn & Fried, 1905.

Yosef Caro. *Shulhan Arukh*. Yoreh Deah, Hilkhot Shehitah.

Zemah b. Shlomo Duran. *Yakhin u-Boaz*. Livorno, 1782.

Articles and Essays

Amiel, Charles. "El criptojudaísmo castellano en La Mancha a fines del siglo XVI." In *Judíos. Sefarditas. Conversos. La expulsión de 1492 y sus consecuencias*, ed. Ángel Alcalá, pp. 503–512. Valladolid: Ámbito Ediciones, 1995.

Asaf, Simha. "The Marranos of Spain and Portugal in Responsa Literature" [Hebrew], *Me'assef Zion* 5 (1932–33): 19–60.

Assis, Yom Tov. "Welfare and Mutual Aid in the Spanish Jewish Communities." In *The Sephardi Legacy* 1, ed. Haim Beinart, pp. 318–345. Jerusalem: Magnes Press, 1992.

Ballester, Rosa. "Ethical Perspectives in the Care of Infants in Sixteenth to Eighteenth Century Spain." In *Medicine and Medical Ethics in Medieval and Early Modern Spain: An Intercultural Approach*, ed. Samuel S. Kottek and Luís García-Ballester, pp. 188–214. Jerusalem: Magnes Press, 1996.

Beinart, Haim. "The Converso Community in 15th Century Spain." In *The Sephardi Heritage*, ed. R. D. Barnett, pp. 425–456. London: Vallentine 1971.

———. "Judíos y conversos en Casarrubios del Monte." In *Homenaje a Juan Prado: Miscelánea de estudios bíblicos y hebraicos*, ed. L. Alvarez Verdes, pp. 645–657. Madrid: Consejo Superior de Investigaciones Cientificas, 1975.

———. "Jewish Witnesses and the Prosecution of the Spanish Inquisition." In *Essays in Honour of Ben Beinart*, pp. 37–46. Cape Town: Juta, 1978.

———. "A Prophesying Movement in Cordova in 1499–1502" [Hebrew], *Zion* 44 (1980): 190–200.

———. "The Spanish Inquisition and a 'Converso Community' in Extremadura," *Medieval Studies* 43 (1981): 445–471.

———. "Herrera: Its Conversos and Jews" [Hebrew], *Proceedings of the Seventh World Congress of Jewish Studies* B (1981): 53–85.

———. "The Prophetess Inés and Her Movement in Pueblo de Alcocer and Talarrubias" [Hebrew], *Tarbiz* 51 (1982): 633–658.

———. "Conversos of Chillón and the Prophecies of Mari Gómez and Inés, the Daughter of Juan Esteban" [Hebrew], *Zion* 48 (1983): 241–272.

———. "La Inquisición española y la Expulsión de los Judíos de Andalucía." In *Jews and Conversos: Studies in Society and the Inquisition*, ed. Yosef Kaplan, pp. 103–123. Jerusalem: Magnes Press, 1985.

———. "The Prophetess Inés and Her Movement in Her Hometown, Herrera" [Hebrew]. In *Studies in Jewish Mysticism, Philosophy and Ethical Literature*, ed. Y. Dan and Y. Hacker, pp. 459–506. Jerusalem: Magnes Press, 1986.

———. "The Separation of Living Quarters in 15th Century Spain" [Hebrew], *Zion* 51 (1986): 61–85.

———. "The Prophetess of Extremadura: Inés of Herrera del Duque." In *Women in the Inquisition: Spain and the New World*, ed. Mary Giles, pp. 42-52. Baltimore: Johns Hopkins University Press, 1999.

Bennassar, Bartolomé. "L'Inquisition ou la pédagogie de la peur." In *L'Inquisition espagnole: XVe-XIXe siècles*, ed. Bartolomé Bennassar et al., pp. 101–137. Paris: Marabout, 1979.

Blasco Martínez, Asunción. "Mujeres Judías Zaragozanas ante la muerte," *Aragon en La Edad Media* 9 (1991): 77–120.

Cantera Burgos, Francisco, and Carlos Carrete Parrondo. "La judería de Hita," *Sefarad* 32 (1972): 249–305.

———. "Las juderias medievales en la provincia de Guadalajara," *Sefarad* 33 (1973): 3–44; 259–323; and 34 (1974): 43–78, 313–386.

Carrasco, Rafael. "Preludio al 'Siglo de los Portugueses': La Inquisición de Cuenca y los judaizantes lusitanos en el siglo XVI," *Hispania* 47:166 (1987): 503–559.

Cohen, Gershon D. "Review of B. Netanyahu's *The Marranos of Spain*," *Jewish Social Studies* 29 (1967): 178–184.

Contreras, Jaime. "Alderman and Judaizers: Cryptojudaism, Counter–Reformation and Local Power." In *Culture and Control in Counter–Reformation Spain*, ed. Anne J. Cruz and Mary Elizabeth Perry, pp. 93–123. Minneapolis: University of Minnesota Press, 1992.

Contreras, Jaime, and Gustav Henningsen. "Forty-Four Thousand Cases of the Spanish Inquisition (1540–1700): Analysis of a Historical Data Bank." In *The Inquisition in Early Modern Europe*, ed. G. Henningsen, J. Tedeschi, and C. Amiel, pp. 100–129. De Kalb, Ill.: Northern Illinois University Press, 1986.

Dedieu, Jean-Pierre. "Les inquisiteurs de Tolede et la visite du district," *Mélanges de la Casa de Velázquez* 13 (1977): 234–256.

———. "Les quatre temps de l'Inquisition." In *L'Inquisition espagnole*, ed. Bartolomé Bennassar et al., pp. 13–40. Paris: Marabout, 1979.

———. "The Archives of the Holy Office of Toledo as a Source for Historical Anthropology." In *The Inquisition in Early Modern Europe*, ed. G. Henningsen, J. Tedeschí and G. Amiel, pp. 158–189. De Kalb, Ill.: Northern Illinois University Press.

Gutwirth, Eliezer. "The Family in Judeo-Spanish Genizah Letters of Cairo," *Vierteljahrschrift für Sozial- und Wirtschaftgeschichte* 73 (1986): 210–215.

Haliczer, Stephen. "The First Holocaust: The Inquisition and the Converted Jews of Spain and Portugal." In *Inquisition and Society in Early Modern Europe*, ed. Stephen Haliczer, pp. 7–18. London: Croom Helm, 1987.

Henningsen, Gustav. "The Eloquence of Figures: Statistics of the Spanish and Portuguese Inquisitions and Prospects for Social History." In *The Spanish Inquisition and the Inquisitorial Mind*, ed. Ángel Alcalá, pp. 217–235. New York: Columbia University Press, 1987.

Klairmont Lingo, Alison. "Midwifery," *Women's Studies Encyclopedia* 1: 236–240. New York: Greenwood Press, 1989.

Kraemer, Joel L. "Spanish Ladies from the Cairo Geniza," *Mediterranean Historical Review* 6 (1991): 237–267.

Levine Melammed, Renée. "Sixteenth Century Justice in Action: The Case of Isabel López," *Revue des études juives* 145:1–2 (1986): 51–73.

———. "The Ultimate Challenge: Safeguarding the Crypto-Judaic Heritage, "*Proceedings of the American Academy for Jewish Research* 53 (1986):91–109.

———. "Noticias sobre los ritos de los nacimientos y de la pureza de las judeo-conversas castellanas del siglo XVI," *El Olivo* 13:29–30 (1989): 235–243.

———. "Some Death and Mourning Customs of Castilian Conversas." In *Exile and Diaspora*, ed. A. Mirsky, A. Grossman, and Y. Kaplan, pp. 157–167. Jerusalem: Ben Zvi Institute, 1991.

———. "Les femmes crypto-juives face a l'Inquisition espagnole: Leur role dans la transmission du marranisme." In *Transmission et passages en monde juif*, ed. Esther Benbassa, pp. 229–245. Paris: Publisud, 1997.

———. "Crypto-Jewish Women Facing the Spanish Inquisition: Transmitting Religious Practices, Beliefs, and Attitudes." In *Christians, Muslims and Jews in Medieval and Early Modern Spain: Interaction and Cultural Change*, ed. Mark D. Meyerson and Edward D. English. Notre Dame, Ind.: University of Notre Dame Press, 1999.

———. "Judaizers and Prayer in Sixteenth Century Alcázar." In *In Iberia and Beyond*, ed. Bernard Cooperman, pp. 273–295. Newark, Del.: University of Delaware Press, 1998.

Marín Padilla, Encarnación. "Relación judeoconversa durante la segunda mitad del siglo XV en Aragon: nacimientos, hadas, circuncisiones," *Sefarad* 41:1 (1981): 273–300 and 42:1 (1982): 59–77.

————. "Relación judeoconversa durante la segunda mitad del siglo XV en Aragon: enfermedades y muertes," *Sefarad* 43:2 (1983): 251–344.

Meyerson, Mark D. "Aragonese and Catalan Jewish Converts at the Time of the Expulsion," *Jewish History* 6:1–2 (1992):131–149.

Ortiz, Teresa. "From Hegemony to Subordination: Midwives in Early Modern Spain." In *The Art of Midwifery: Early Modern Midwives in Europe*, ed. Hilary Marland, pp. 95–114. London and New York: Routledge, 1993.

Perry, Mary Elizabeth. "Las mujeres y su trabajo curativo en Sevilla, siglos XVI y XVII." In *El trabajo de las mujeres: siglos XVI–XX*, ed. María Jesús Matilla and Margarita Ortega, pp. 40–50. Madrid: Universidad Autonoma de Madrid, 1987.

————. "The Black Madonna of Montserrat." In *Views of Women's Lives in Western Tradition*, ed. F. R. Keller, pp. 110–128. Lewiston, N.Y.: Edwin Mellen Press, 1990.

————. "Male Discourse and Female Deviance in the Spanish Inquisition" (unpublished manuscript), 1992.

————. "Behind the Veil: Moriscas and the Politics of Resistance and Survival." *Spanish Women in the Golden Age: Images and Realities*, ed. Magdalena S. Sánchez and Alain Saint-Saëns, pp. 37–53. Westport, Conn.: Greenwood Press, 1996.

Révah, I. S. "Les marranes," *Revue des études juives* 118 (1959–60): 29–77.

Sánchez Ortega, María Helena. "Woman as Source of 'Evil' in Counter-Reformation Spain." In *Culture and Control in Counter-Reformation Spain*, ed. Anne J. Cruz and Mary Elizabeth Perry, pp. 196–215. Minneapolis: University of Minnesota Press, 1992.

Index